THE
ENCYCLOPEDIA
of
THIRD PARTIES
IN AMERICA

Volume Two

Edited by

IMMANUEL NESS AND JAMES CIMENT

Foreword by

FRANCES FOX PIVEN

SHARPE REFERENCE
an imprint of M.E. Sharpe, Inc.

SHARPE REFERENCE

Sharpe Reference is an imprint of ℳ.*E. Sharpe* INC.

ℳ.*E. Sharpe* INC.
80 Business Park Drive
Armonk, NY 10504

© 2000 by ℳ.*E. Sharpe* INC.

All rights reserved.

Library of Congress Cataloging-in-Publication Data

Ness, Immanuel.
Encyclopedia of third parties in America / Immanuel Ness, James Ciment.
p. cm.
Includes bibliographical references and index.
ISBN 0–7656–8020–3 (set : alk. paper)
1. Third parties (United States politics)—Encyclopedias.
I. Ciment, James. II. Title.
JK2261.N46 2000
324.273′003—dc21
99–25375
CIP

Printed and bound in the United States of America

The paper used in this publication meets the minimum requirements of
American National Standard for Information Sciences—Permanence of
Paper for Printed Library Materials,
ANSI Z 39.48.1984.

BM (c) 10 9 8 7 6 5 4 3 2 1

Vice President and Publisher: Evelyn M. Fazio
Vice President and Production Director: Carmen P. Chetti
Reference Production Manager: Wendy E. Muto
Editorial Coordinator: Aud Thiessen
Editorial Assistant: Esther Clark
Copyeditor: Arden L. Kuhlman
Fact Checker: Jeff Jensen
In-house Typesetter: Wilford Bryan Lammers
Cartographer: Jon Kalb

CONTENTS

☆☆☆☆☆☆☆☆☆☆☆☆☆☆☆☆☆☆☆☆☆☆

FREE SOIL PARTY

1848–1850s

The Free Soil party formed in 1848 to try to block the extension of slavery into territories recently acquired from Mexico. Its members believed that while constitutionally the federal government could not abolish slavery where it already existed, it could prevent it from expanding into newly acquired regions. Free-Soilers argued that these territories belonged to the central government rather than to the states, and in turn, the Constitution granted to Congress the authority to prevent the expansion of slavery. In contrast, the two-party system of Democrats and Whigs, sensitive to southern beliefs that slaveholders had the right to bring their slave property into any territory, rejected the Free-Soilers' contention and in effect forced them to seek a new political home. The result was a third party that existed for six years until the new Republican organization adopted its principle that Congress should contain slavery within its existing boundaries.

OPPOSITION TO SLAVERY

The immediate catalyst for the formation of the Free Soil party was the explosive issue of slavery in territories seized from Mexico in 1848. During the previous decade, as Democrats and Whigs consistently evaded slave-related issues, antislavery factions of both major parties had become increasingly frustrated. The issue became especially explosive as the Republic of Texas sought annexation in 1844 and as the United States acquired California and southwestern areas at the conclusion of the war

against Mexico in 1848. Following Texas annexation and statehood in 1845 opponents of slave expansion found a vehicle on which to focus their efforts to contain slavery within its existing boundaries. The Wilmot Proviso was their proposal through which Congress would ban slavery in all territories acquired from Mexico. Introduced by David Wilmot, Democrat from Pennsylvania, the concept won approval in the House of Representatives with the support of northern Democrats and Whigs but could not find a majority in the Senate where southern influence was greater.

Advocates of the containment of slavery were further thwarted when the 1848 nominating conventions of Democrats and Whigs refused to consider the Proviso and nominated southern-leaning candidates. Realizing the need for a broader-based appeal than that of the existing Liberty party, which advocated total abolition, they agreed to form a new third party that could bring together all antislavery groups, abolitionist as well as the more moderate who sought only to prevent the spread of slavery.

The process was ignited when, after Liberty delegates had nominated John P. Hale of New Hampshire in late 1847, factions of both Democrats and Whigs walked out of their respective conventions in the spring of 1848. New York Democratic antislavery leaders, called the "Barnburners," already angered by their party's rejection of their leader, former president Martin Van Buren in 1844, now bolted when the party rejected the Proviso. To make matters worse Democrats chose a conservative candidate, Lewis Cass, senator from Michigan and advocate of popular sovereignty—the proposal that each territorial legislature would decide whether or not to legalize slavery. In the same manner, Massachusetts antislavery advocates (the Conscience Whigs), angered with their state party's commitment to textile manufacturers allied with cotton planters, walked out of the national Whig nominating convention. This followed the convention's refusal to take any stance on slave-related issues and its choice of Louisiana slaveholder and Mexican War general Zachary Taylor as its nominee.

FORMATION OF THE PARTY

The stage was thus set for the creation of a new party. Thousands of excited spectators poured into Buffalo, New York, in August 1848, to witness its birth. The new party formed under the leadership of antislavery advocates who included Salmon P. Chase and Joshua Giddings of Ohio and Charles Sumner of Massachusetts. The movement was endorsed by numerous newspapers, led by the Washington-based *National Era* (edited by former Liberty leader Gamaliel Bailey of Cincinnati). The party nominated Van Buren for president and Charles Francis Adams (son of the recently deceased Whig leader and former president John Quincy Adams) for vice president. It had successfully brought together the formerly diverse elements of Barnburners, Conscience Whigs, and Liberty party advocates. Campaigning with vigor following the emotional Buffalo meeting, the party won only a disappointing 10 percent of the popular vote. The results revealed that the North was not yet sufficiently aroused to give the antislavery movement significant support and that the new party faced problems common to all third parties in raising money, finding press support, and countering major-party arguments that a vote for Free Soil was a wasted vote and one that would advance the cause of extremism. A grassroots movement organized on the local and state level, it faced difficulties creating the party machinery to wage a nationwide contest

for the presidency. Yet following the election, the small Free Soil congressional delegation fought valiantly against efforts of major-party leaders to compromise North-South differences and, in Free-Soilers' opinions, sacrifice antislavery principles. Third-party members' efforts temporarily foundered in the atmosphere that produced the Compromise of 1850, a settlement which Democrats and Whigs claimed resolved the outstanding sectional differences.

Yet the Free-Soilers labored on with reduced numbers as many defectors returned to the safer haven of one of the two major parties. In 1852, the party, now renamed the Free Democrats, maintained its principles in support of the containment of slavery and nominated Hale as its presidential candidate. Despite the party's poor showing, the members were rewarded two years later when the Kansas-Nebraska Act's repeal of the ban on slavery north of 36°30' in the Louisiana Territory created a political maelstrom. The resulting furor climaxed with the formation of the Republican party, which combined the Free Soil party with antislavery Whigs and Democrats. As the Whigs declined, the new party soon assumed its place in the two-party system, a position never attained by the Free-Soilers. The Republicans, however, adopted the position that the third party had advocated throughout its six-year history—the containment of slavery within its existing boundaries.

PREVENTING THE EXTENSION OF SLAVERY

Although Free-Soilers put most of their emphasis on preventing the spread of slavery, they were by no means a one-idea organization and their national platforms in 1848 and 1852 recognized that voters were interested in other issues. Of major concern to residents of the Great Lakes states was the need for federal funds for internal improvements to rivers and harbors. Since southerners typically opposed such expenditures and Democrats reflected this bias in their silence on the issue, Free-Soilers opportunistically seized on it and made it a key campaign pledge. In a similar effort to win middle- and lower-class northerners away from their Democratic loyalties, the third party endorsed the homestead concept and called for the "free grant to actual settlers" of public lands, again recognizing that such a proposal was an anathema in the South and thus one that Democrats could not endorse.

Ironically, in both national campaigns Free-Soilers concluded their platform with the stirring slogan, "Free Soil, Free Speech, Free Labor, and Free Men." Certainly they hoped to appeal for the support of northern workingmen and small farmers. They thus emphasized the fear of slave labor in the territories and the degrading influence slavery had upon free labor. This approach made little effort to hide the racist appeal of the Free-Soilers, and orators on numerous occasions spoke of the Proviso as an assurance that western lands would be preserved for free white labor. David Wilmot himself never apologized for his appeal "to the cause and the rights of white freemen." The platforms omitted all mention of ending racial discrimination in the North, knowing that laboring men, especially immigrant groups, as well as farmers were either indifferent or outwardly hostile to free blacks and feared those few who lived or might live among them. The platform suggested that a vote for Van Buren would "elevate and dignify labor," but few denied that Wilmot's proposal was the "white man's proviso." It was clear to all that when the 1848 platform urged that the territories "be kept free for the hardy pioneers of our own land and the oppressed and banished of other lands," that blacks, free or slave, were not among those groups being welcomed.

Not surprisingly, the largely disfranchised northern free black community looked on the Free Soil party with mixed emotions. On the one hand, it was the only party in 1848 and 1852 that took a stand against slavery, albeit one that opposed only the extension of slavery, not the peculiar institution per se. Thus, many blacks looked on it as the lesser of two evils. But the party's lack of any commitment to racial justice and equality and its none-too-subtle appeal to white fears of African Americans was even worse. Free-Soilers knew that since more than 90 percent of the northern black population lived in states that legally or de facto excluded them from voting, the third party had no practical incentive to make an appeal on their behalf. Several black leaders including Frederick Douglass, Samuel Ward, Henry Garnet, and Charles Remond attended the Buffalo convention, with Douglass speaking briefly to the convention. But it was clear that most delegates were embarrassed by their presence.

The situation left northern black leaders in a quandary, and their indecision reflected their dilemma. Douglass referred to the party as "a noble step in the right direction," but he vacillated throughout the 1848 campaign between urging support or withholding it. Samuel Ward was especially critical of the Barnburner faction, for he saw nothing in it to merit optimism. Most agreed with the view of a small gathering of free blacks who met in Cleveland in September 1848, concluding "that while we heartily engage in recommending to our people the Free Soil movement and the support of the Buffalo convention, nevertheless, we claim and are determined to maintain the higher standard and more liberal views which have heretofore characterized us abolitionists." In 1852, even with the more racist Barnburner element largely back in the Democratic party, the remaining third-party leaders made no appeal to free blacks. Nor did they include any attack on northern racial discrimination. Free blacks, as a result, remained divided as they had four years earlier between this reality and their idealism.

ELECTORAL EFFORT

Measured solely by election returns, the Free Soil movement could not be characterized a success. With an appeal limited to the northern free states and a few areas of the upper South, in 1848, it won only 10 percent of the national vote, slightly less than 300,000 of the almost 3 million votes cast. In no state did it gain even 30 percent of the vote. Even in New York,

Free Soil presidential candidate Martin Van Buren's inability to bridge the gap between the Conscience, or antislavery, Whigs and his former Democratic colleagues is seen as destroying his party's chances in the 1848 election. *(Courtesy of the Library of Congress)*

where the Van Buren Barnburners' appeal was strongest and where it gained 40 percent of its total national vote, it received only 26 percent of the state vote. Combining Liberty with Barnburner and Conscience Whig factions, it drew supporters in roughly equal numbers from Whig and Democratic parties. In 1852, its total vote fell to slightly more than 150,000 out of more than 3 million cast or approximately 5 percent of the total. With much of the Barnburner element back in the Democratic party, the third party's greatest appeal was among former Liberty and Whig voters. The Barnburner defection and the willingness of the voters to accept the Compromise of 1850 as a solution to divisive sectional questions meant that the future of the movement appeared bleak.

LEGACY OF THE PARTY

Yet third-party successes are rarely measured solely in the number of votes cast and elections won. Surely the Free-Soilers were no exception, for when the Whig party suffered its devastating defeat in 1852, carrying only four states in Democrat Franklin Pierce's landslide victory, it already appeared to many that Whig days were numbered. Its great national leaders, Henry Clay and Daniel Webster, both died shortly before Pierce's victory, and there appeared to be no one of national stature who could hold its shaky coalition of northern and southern Whigs together. Thus when Stephen A. Douglas's Kansas-Nebraska bill destroyed the sectional truce in 1854, northern Whigs knew that their party had ceased to be an effective organization with which to oppose the southern domination of federal government. So too were numerous northern Democrats angered with the Douglas "sell-out" to the South and were in a mood to bolt if a more effective organization could be created. With Free-Soilers seeking a way to revitalize their movement, the way opened for a new organization that could reassert the principles of the Wilmot Proviso and apply them to Kansas.

It was not an easy or automatic transition to the new Republican party for the Free-Soilers. Rather it was fraught with many pitfalls and roadblocks—most especially the appeal of the new American party, which threatened for a time to use its anti-Catholic and anti-immigrant appeal to assume the Whigs' place in the two-party system. Antislavery leaders like Salmon P. Chase were forced to form temporary coalitions with the Know-Nothings while others for a time deserted their antislavery convictions when nativism appeared a more attractive philosophy. Most Free-Soilers rejected this appeal, however. Chase, Sumner, Giddings, Wilmot, Hale, and Adams led the most radical wing of the Republican party in insisting on the centrality of the containment principle in its platform of 1856, even as more conservative Whig and Democratic factions sought to elevate other issues.

Thus, the Free-Soilers' six-year history came to an end with the formation of the Republican party in the mid-1850s. Clearly they had an important impact on the major parties and on the American political system. They had played a central role in the decline of the Whigs and emergence of the Republicans. It would be their principle of containment, which had been too advanced for voters in 1848 and 1852, that would be the focus of the Republican appeal in 1856 and place Abraham Lincoln in the White House in 1861.

FREDERICK BLUE

See also: Charles Francis Adams; Salmon P. Chase; Joshua Giddings; Zachary Taylor; Whig Party.

Bibliography

Bell, Howard H. "The National Negro Convention, 1848." *Ohio Historical Quarterly* 67 (1958): 357–368.

Blue, Frederick J. *The Free-Soilers: Third-Party Politics, 1848–54.* Urbana: University of Illinois Press, 1973.

Congressional Globe. 29th Cong., 2d Sess., Appendix, pp. 317–318.

Foner, Eric. *Free Soil, Free Labor, Free Men: The Ideology of the Republican Party Before the Civil War.* New York: Oxford University Press, 1970.

Gienapp, William E. *The Origins of the Republican Party, 1852–1856.* New York: Oxford University Press, 1987.

Mayfield, John. *Rehearsal for Republicanism: Free Soil and the Politics of Anti-Slavery.* Port Washington, NY: Kennikat Press, 1980.

Morrison, Chaplain W. *Democratic Politics and Sectionalism: The Wilmot Proviso Controversy.* Chapel Hill: University of North Carolina Press, 1967.

Morrison, Michael A. *Slavery and the American West: The Eclipse of Manifest Destiny and the Coming of the Civil War.* Chapel Hill: University of North Carolina Press, 1997.

North Star (Rochester), August 11, 25, September 10, 22, 1848.

Porter, Kirk, and Donald Johnson, comps. *National Party Platforms, 1840–1960.* Urbana: University of Illinois Press, 1961, pp. 13–14.

Rayback, Joseph G. *Free Soil: The Election of 1848.* Lexington: University Press of Kentucky, 1970.

Sewell, Richard H. *Ballots for Freedom: Antislavery Politics in the United States, 1837–1860.* New York: Oxford University Press, 1976.

Smith, Theodore C. *The Liberty and Free Soil Parties in the Northwest.* Cambridge: Harvard University Press, 1897.

Volpe, Vernon. *Forlorn Hope of Freedom: The Liberty Party in the Old Northwest, 1838–1848.* Kent: Kent State University Press, 1990.

☆☆☆☆☆☆☆☆☆☆☆☆☆☆☆☆☆☆☆☆☆☆☆☆☆☆☆☆

FREEDOM NOW PARTY

1963–1965

ORIGINS OF THE PARTY

The Freedom Now party was an all-black political party that launched its political program at the civil rights march on Washington in 1963. Formed by veteran foreign correspondent for the *Baltimore Afro-American*, William Worthy, the party literature argued that African Americans had no choice but to fight as a cohesive bloc since the two main parties gave blacks a "choice between a Democratic Lucifer cuddled up with the Dixiecrats and Republican Satan." The party sought to organize blacks in areas of heaviest concentration and distributed leaflets in Washington, Detroit, Chicago, Cleveland, San Francisco, Los Angeles, Seattle, and particularly targeted the Ford Motor Company.

The party was established against the backdrop of the civil rights movement and before passage of the Civil Rights Act of 1964 and the Voting Rights Act of 1965 to push for immediate passage of expanded civil rights legislation. Nineteen sixty-three represented a period of flux in the party system as the Democrats and Republicans both expressed mixed and unclear messages about their positions on and willingness to push civil rights issues. While northern liberal Democrats were generally sympathetic to civil rights, southern Democrats led the charge in support of segregation. The Freedom Now party's national chairman, Conrad Lynn, argued that the major parties offered African Americans (and all Americans) little "genuine alternatives" and that an all-black political party could elect tens of congressmen and be the balance of power in Washington. While its main thrust was all-black political action, and

all its candidates for office were black, the party maintained that it did not bar whites from support and it would work with other groups whose goals were congruent with the Freedom Now party; however, it argued that all-black political action was important since it would provide blacks with a sense of "belonging" and an opportunity to develop their own political leadership free from white control. From its inception, the party found it necessary to "fend off" white liberals, such as the *New York Times* editors who lambasted the party, and black separationists. A principal internal disagreement that was shakily resolved at a five-hour meeting at the Park Sheraton Hotel prior to the 1963 march in Washington was between integrationists, who argued in favor of openness to whites as candidates and members, and separationists, who wanted no participation of whites in the organization. The compromise reached was that all candidates would be black but that individuals of whatever color were free to join (an especially appropriate resolution since William Worthy's wife was of Chinese descent).

PARTY PLATFORM

The Freedom Now party was disenchanted with the Democratic party due to its association with southern segregationists. The party literature argued it was nonsense for blacks to support the party of Bull Connor (the commissioner of public safety for Birmingham, Alabama, who ordered police dogs and water hoses to be used to control crowds) and asked why blacks should "register to vote at the risk of death when the only choice is a James Eastland or a George Wallace." Thus, the party sought to "repudiate and break with the established two-party system which serve[d] only to sustain the enslavement of Afro-Americans" and which was inadequate in providing appropriate and timely civil rights legislation.

There were three principal figures in the party. Worthy originated the idea of forming the Freedom Now party early in 1963 and was the chief party intellectual. The national chairman was Conrad Lynn, a veteran civil rights attorney who was involved in cases such as the famous "Kissing Case" in Monroe, North Carolina, which involved two black children who were charged with raping a young white girl after they kissed her during playtime. Lynn also defended Puerto Rican nationalists who were charged with firing shots from the Capitol gallery and tried a case involving black participation in a segregated army during World War II. The party's chief political figure was the Reverend Albert Cleage, Jr., who was the party leader in Michigan, the party's area of greatest strength.

The party's general platform maintained that blacks needed, after 188 years of subservience, to establish an "independent political movement dedicated to the unity and liberation of all black people." Their scope was international, making specific reference to liberation movements in Africa and Cuba. Its platform, while not strong on specifics, committed the Freedom Now party to three important planks. First, the party was committed to "take" African American freedom. Second, the party emphasized the need for economic changes and employment guarantees. Third, it emphasized the necessity for an "end to racism in Africa, Asia, Latin America, and in the United States north and south." Additionally, Cleage argued that an essential function was to educate blacks that all-black political action was the only course blacks could follow to "demonstrate to the Republican and Democratic parties the political importance of the Negro" and to show Democrats that they took blacks for granted even though blacks were responsible for winning the Democrats

key seats (and the presidency in 1960). The party recognized its potential to hurt the Democrats and liberals, a point that a critical *Detroit Daily Press* editorial emphasized in saying that the "inevitable result will be the defeat of progressive candidates." When asked about the potential for the Freedom Now party to harm liberals and the Democratic party by siphoning votes from their candidates, the party's simple response was "So what?"

PARTY'S ELECTORAL EFFORTS

From its inception, the party evoked controversy. Its launch in August 1963 was met with opposition from the *New York Times* (which labeled the party "racist"), and from civil rights organizations (which quickly formed the National Civil Rights party to respond to the formation of the FNP). In early 1964, the party considered running a national slate but concentrated its effort on lone seats in various states such as New York (where Paul Boutelle, the chair of the metropolitan committee for the Freedom Now party, contested the twenty-first district state senate seat and was arrested twice while trying to give speeches), Connecticut, and California. The party's main effort was concentrated in Michigan where it was hoped the state's 750,000 African-Americans would provide the party with a firm base of support. In 1964, the party ran thirty-nine candidates for major and minor offices in Michigan, such as governor and lieutenant governor, and secretary of state. Cleage, the party's candidate for governor, garnered 4,767 votes (0.2 percent), the highest aggregate vote total of any of the party's thirty-nine candidates in Michigan in 1964. All of the candidates fared poorly in the balloting; the party's best showing was in the first congressional district where Milton Henry captured 0.9 percent (1,504 votes) against Congressman Conyers.

While the party concentrated its efforts on Michigan, it received considerable national attention including some unwanted attention from national civil rights leader Martin Luther King, Jr. The *Illustrated News*, a publication edited by Cleage, showed a picture of Cleage with King with the caption that King supported the idea of an all-black political party. After being alerted to the article, Dr. King blasted the Freedom Now party, noting that he never supported all-black political action but that blacks should participate "not in isolation but along with the labor movement, the churches, and liberals to make firm alliance" in order to achieve passage of a civil rights bill.

While performing dismally in 1964, the party attempted to continue, focusing its attention on elections for the Detroit Common Council in 1965. While not running candidates under a party label, Freedom Now emphasized the need to "vote black" and initiated a slogan of "Four No More." The slogan was meant to encourage blacks to vote only for African-American candidates for the Detroit Common Council to enhance their chances of winning. This approach encouraged blacks to vote only for the African Americans on the ballot and led to an angry debate between the coordinator of the campaign and its black opponents who argued that the Freedom Now party and its supporters were using a "racist argument as an escape mechanism and taking the cheap route to racial harmony." The party disbanded after the 1965 elections, and the passage of the Civil Rights Act of 1964 and the Voting Rights Act of 1965, which encouraged blacks to participate in the Democratic party.

MICHAEL LEVY

See also: Albert Cleage, Jr.

Bibliography

Deatrick, Owen. "All Negro Ticket Puzzles Veteran State Politicians." *Detroit Daily Press,* September 24, 1964.

Freedom Now Party. *The Black Advocate: Official Organ of the Freedom Now Party.* Detroit: Freedom Now Party, 1965.

Freedom Now Party. *Why We Need a Freedom Now Party.* Detroit: Michigan Committee for a Freedom Now Party, 1963.

"Freedom Now (?) Party." *Detroit Daily Press,* September 26, 1964.

Jones, David. "Negro Party Puts Strength to Test." *New York Times,* October 4, 1964.

Lynn, Conrad. "No Racism in Negro Party." *New York Times,* October 23, 1963.

Mueller, John. " 'Freedom Now' Repudiated: King Rips Negro Party." *Detroit Daily Press,* October 31, 1964.

"Racism in Politics." *New York Times,* August 26, 1963, editorial.

Strickland, Joseph. " 'Vote Black' Issue Stirs Up Heated Debate by Negroes." *Detroit News,* October 28, 1965.

GREENBACK PARTY
1873–1886

THE MONEY QUESTION

The Greenback party was one of the most important third parties during the late nineteenth century. Its origins lay in the interaction of the fiscal legislation of the Civil War and Reconstruction years and the massive economic and social changes of the post-war years; its legacy influenced both national politics and policy debates and subsequent third parties.

To help meet its fiscal needs during the Civil War, the federal government issued Treasury notes totaling more than $400 million. These greenback dollars, as they were called, were acceptable as legal tender, but were not backed by gold and had no fixed date for redemption by the Treasury. Indeed, the entire financial system temporarily abandoned the gold standard. At the end of the war, most authorities favored the rapid resumption of specie payments, preceded by the contraction of the volume of greenbacks, for they had depreciated in terms of gold. In 1866, the Treasury began retiring greenbacks from circulation and reducing the nation's money supply. Congress furthered deflationary financial policies by adopting new limitations on the use of silver as currency in 1873 and by passing the Specie Resumption Act of 1875, withdrawing more greenbacks from circulation, and requiring that the remainder be convertible into gold after 1878, effectively placing the nation on the gold standard.

Several groups fought against these deflationary policies and came to see in the retention and even expansion of a greenback system not merely a way to resolve short-term economic issues, such as declining prices, but a means to promote economic opportunity and democratic control. Such "greenbackers" believed that currency value was based on public authority rather than intrinsic worth and that the government should expand the money supply to match the nation's growing population and economy. They expected this inflationary policy to stimulate the economy, reduce debt burdens, and increase opportunities. Simultaneously, they objected to the National Banking System, another part of the nation's Civil War fiscal legislation. This system authorized nationally chartered private banks to issue their own currency, and the same Specie Resumption Act that threatened the larger role of greenbacks also removed all limitations on the issuance of such bank currency. Rather than have private interests manipulate the currency system for private profit, Greenbackers demanded a currency system operated by the national government to promote the general welfare. They proposed the "interconvertible bond"—a managed currency whereby the volume of money grew with economic expansion.

Such ideas first emerged among several eastern economic theorists including Edward Kellogg and Henry C. Carey. These ideas were then seized upon by labor reformers in eastern cities, who in 1868 organized the National Labor Union on a program of financial and social reform. Currency inflation under public control might offer workers the capital necessary to undertake cooperative production and avoid wage slavery under corporate capitalism. At the same time, some industrialists also saw currency expansion as a means of financing their own entrepreneurial activities and became leading advocates of greenbackism. Agricultural groups became another source of support, especially once a lengthy depression began in 1873, and mortgage indebtedness and falling farm prices provided further reasons to support currency inflation, not contraction.

Monetary policy was a major focus of postwar public debate, but it divided both major parties, which accordingly attempted to obscure it as an issue of electoral politics. Greenbackers thus eventually moved toward the creation of a third party. In 1873, a group of Indiana farm leaders and reformers denounced the major parties and began organizing as independents. In June 1874, they nominated a state ticket on the interconvertible bond platform. Two months later, they issued a call for all "greenback men" to convene in Indianapolis in November to form a new national party. The Indianapolis convention did not formally organize a new party but signaled its intentions by adopting a platform endorsing "a new political organization of the people, by the people, and for the people, to restrain the aggressions of combined capital upon the rights and interests of the masses." It also appointed an executive committee to call a national convention.

This committee summoned greenbackers together in Cleveland on March 11, 1875, and launched the National Independent (or Greenback) party. Still largely controlled by the Indiana Independents, together with midwestern (especially Chicago) labor reformers, the Cleveland convention authorized the executive committee to make plans for a national nominating convention, continuing the series of meetings that were designed to build support for the new party movement.

Eastern labor reformers were holding parallel meetings of their own and took the lead in calling a national conference of greenbackers for September in Cincinnati. This was a tumultuous gathering, as groups and individuals vied for influence. "The most kindly expressions were used by each to the other," reported one Wisconsin Granger, "damn liars, infernal thieves, and sons of bitches . . . among the most polite." But by bringing together substantial numbers of farm and labor leaders and eventually coordi-

nating their plans, the Cincinnati meeting was an important turning point for political greenbackism. "For the first time," declared one New York delegate, "that old dream [of producer unity] of the earnest mechanics and laborers of the East and farmers of the West has been realized." The Cincinnati meeting established an executive committee that soon merged with the committee of the Cleveland convention and chose May 17, 1876, and Indianapolis for the party's national nominating convention. S.M. Smith, secretary of the Illinois Farmers' Association, became chair of the joint executive committee and led in organizing Greenback Clubs throughout the West in an effort to expand the constituent appeal of the new organization.

THE GREENBACKS ORGANIZE

Nevertheless, the Indianapolis convention had but 230 delegates representing only eighteen states. The party was still less a mass organization than one built from the top down by ideologues. It nominated for president Peter Cooper, the elderly New York ironmaster-philanthropist who had established and endowed the Cooper Institute (later Cooper Union), and adopted a platform promising "financial reform and industrial emancipation." But the campaign was disappointing, plagued by problems of mismanagement and lack of campaign funds (the feeble Cooper gave the party little money or commitment). Most importantly, traditional party allegiances held most voters, and in Ohio, Indiana, and Illinois, Democrats aped the Greenbackers' platform to keep their own adherents loyal. The Greenbackers' national ticket polled only 75,973 votes (0.9 percent of the total) and did not carry a single state, peaking in Kansas with but 6.2 percent of the vote; the party did not even nominate presidential electors in a third of the states.

The great and widespread labor disturbances of 1877, however, soon brought increased support for the new party among the nation's workers. In the 1877 state elections, Greenbackers, often fusing with the Labor Reform party, scored impressive gains. To consolidate their forces, the Greenbackers held a national convention in Toledo on February 22, 1878. Though still controlled by the earlier activists, the Toledo convention had delegates from twenty-eight states and a much stronger labor representation than the 1876 Indianapolis convention. Attempting to broaden their appeal among workers, the Greenbackers added to their usual platform attacking unresponsive major parties and demanding currency reform a series of pro-labor planks, including reduced working hours, an end to contract labor, and regulation of working conditions. The convention also adopted a new name for the party, the National party, but it was henceforth commonly referred to as the Greenback Labor party. State conventions of the invigorated party similarly adopted platforms with a strong labor emphasis and also added demands for still more social, economic, and political reforms, including suffrage for women, direct election of the president and U.S. senators, railroad regulation, a graduated income tax, and anti-monopoly legislation. Still, the major focus remained on what the Ohio state platform called "the infamous financial system which takes all from the many to enrich the few. We demand cheap capital and well-paid labor in the place of dear capital and cheap labor."

Thus strengthened, Greenbackers nominated candidates in every state and polled more than a million votes in 1878, an achievement the party's executive committee proudly described as "unprecedented in the history of political parties." They elected fifteen congressmen, nearly enough to gain the balance of power in the divided House, as well as many state legislators. They were most successful in the Midwest, where they often fused with Democrats, as in Iowa where they polled 48 percent of the vote and elected James B. Weaver and E.H. Gillette to Congress. Even in the South, where they were weakest, they polled more than a fifth of the vote in Texas and Mississippi, thanks to Republican support. But the party made its greatest gains in the East, earning a respectable

showing in nearly every state and peaking with 34.4 percent without fusion in Maine (electing two congressmen and as many state legislators as did the long-dominant Republicans) and drawing 42.7 percent in fusion with the Democrats in Massachusetts. Thus, while retaining its rural supporters, the party in 1878 generally attracted even greater strength from urban and industrial areas.

Unfortunately, this was an uneasy alliance between western agrarians, who dominated party leadership, and eastern labor reformers, who wanted more influence. Moreover, while both favored currency expansion, other issues affected their particular constituencies in differing ways. One hostile Iowa newspaper caught these contradictions by declaring that Greenbackers promised "an era of high wages, lots of employment, high prices for wheat for farmers, cheap flour for the mechanic, high prices for cattle for the stock raiser, cheap beef for the workingman, lots of money, low interest, and good times for everybody but contractors, manufacturers, railroads, and bankers, who are to be very poor and have no money to pay their hands."

FUSION POLITICS

The issue of fusion with other parties also disrupted the Greenback coalition. Fusionists such as Weaver favored it as a pragmatic policy that increased the likelihood of election; anti-fusionists, many of whom were eastern labor leaders, objected to cooperating with any party held responsible for the very evils that they now denounced.

These differences shaped the party's 1880 campaign. The national convention in Chicago even temporarily split into two factions meeting in separate halls as delegates debated possible fusion with Democrats on a compromise platform. Eventually, the party adopted its usual statement of principles, but it also nominated Weaver for president, confirming the influence of western leadership and irritating some eastern labor leaders. Convinced that "the great av-

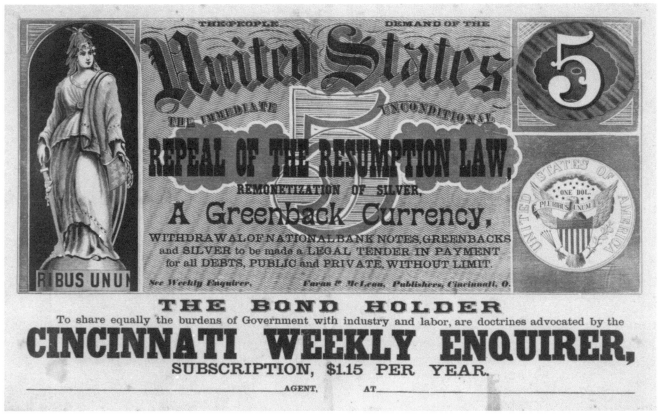

Midwestern and southern supporters of the Greenback party opposed the Resumption Act of 1875 because it limited the amount of money in circulation in their regions, as this notice from a Cincinnati paper of 1878 makes clear. *(Courtesy of the Library of Congress)*

enues to public opinion—the press, the bar and pulpit—[were] under the control of the enemies of [the] movement,'' Weaver conducted a vigorous national canvass, the first presidential candidate to do so. He also pursued divisive tactics. His effort to force Greenbackers to form a coalition with Democrats in Maine alienated some eastern labor groups. One Pennsylvania Greenbacker warned Weaver, ''National Greenback-Labor men are such by principle, and, therefore, not marketable by leaders.'' Some prominent Greenbackers, including several from the Knights of Labor, dropped out of the party's ranks.

Besides internal dissension, other influences also undermined Greenback prospects. The successful resumption of specie payments in 1879, coinciding with the gradual return of prosperity, weakened the practical appeal of the party.

And the major parties' stress on traditional partisan loyalties proved more effective in a presidential campaign; third parties nearly invariably did better in off-year elections.

Weaver received but 305,997 votes, only 3.3 percent of the national poll, and everywhere the Greenback party fell behind its 1878 voting levels. The sharpest drop-off came in the urban industrial areas of the East, where labor organizations had withdrawn active support from the party. The basic Greenback constituency, as before in 1876, lay in the relatively undeveloped agricultural counties of the Midwest.

After 1880, the Greenback party declined swiftly. Fusion with Democrats produced a few more midwestern victories, especially in Michigan, where a joint ticket carried the state offices as late as 1886, and in Iowa, where Weaver was elected to Congress as a fusionist in both 1884 and 1886. Elsewhere, the party quickly sank into insignificance in all states except Maine and Massachusetts, where an alliance with the Democrats elected the mercurial Benjamin F. Butler governor in 1882. Discouraged, B.J. Chambers of Texas, the 1880 Greenback vice-presidential candidate, soon described the party as "disorganized and disintegrated beyond the hope of a successful rally."

Indeed, in 1884, the Greenback national convention supinely accepted Butler as its presidential candidate following his nomination by a small new third party, the Anti-Monopoly party. Butler did not bother to accept the Greenback nomination for three months and then conducted a controversial campaign, advocating coalition with both major parties, depending upon the locale, and accepting Republican campaign funds. Demoralized and nearly irrelevant, the Greenbackers drew but 175,096 votes (1.7 percent of the electorate). Several midwestern state organizations would cling to the party name for a few more years, but the national Greenback party was dead.

As often with third parties, the Greenbackers had important effects on the political system and the major parties despite failing to achieve their own original objectives. Indeed, even their victories in national politics availed them little. Their representatives in Congress were rarely able even to introduce or discuss measures they deemed crucial to the economic and political survival of the republic because of partisan and procedural opposition by both Republicans and Democrats. On the other hand, the major parties did have to accommodate the Greenbackers in some ways, making nominations and shaping campaign tactics to blunt the third-party challenge and eventually adopting many of the Greenback platform demands, particularly on labor issues. In some states, the Democratic party, either to retain its own supporters or to facilitate a coalition, even accepted the Greenbackers' chief tenet of currency inflation. The Greenbackers also provided some of the themes, rhetoric, and leadership of subsequent third parties, such as the Union Labor party and, especially, the People's party. Perhaps, too, their verbal assault on the major parties weakened partisan loyalties enough that later third parties, in still more critical times, came closer to developing the mass base that the Greenbackers never did.

PETER H. ARGERSINGER

See also: Benjamin Franklin Butler; **Map 6:** Greenback Party (1880); **Map 7:** Greenback Party (1884); James Baird Weaver.

Bibliography

Argersinger, Peter H. "No Rights on This Floor: Third Parties and the Institutionalization of Congress." *Journal of Interdisciplinary History* 22 (Spring 1992): 655–690.

Colbert, Thomas B. "Political Fusion in Iowa: The Election of James B. Weaver to Congress in 1878." *Arizona and the West* 20 (Spring 1978): 25–40.

Haynes, Fred E. *Third Party Movements Since the Civil War, with Special Reference to Iowa.* Iowa City: State Historical Society of Iowa, 1916.

Kleppner, Paul. "The Greenback and Prohibition Parties." In *History of U.S. Political Parties*, ed. Arthur M. Schlesinger, Jr., Vol. 2. New York: R.R. Bowker, 1973.

Nugent, Walter T.K. *Money and American Society, 1865–1880.* New York: Free Press, 1968.

Ritter, Gretchen. *Goldbugs and Greenbacks: The Antimonopoly Tradition and the Politics of Finance in America, 1865–1896.* New York: Cambridge University Press, 1997.

Unger, Irwin. *The Greenback Era: A Social and Political History of American Finance, 1865–1879.* Princeton: Princeton University Press, 1964.

☆☆☆☆☆☆☆☆☆☆☆☆☆☆☆☆

THE GREENS

1980s–

With fledgling local Green party groups under way by the second half of the 1980s, the Greens are the oldest of the current new national progressive third-party efforts. The Greens are not simply a U.S. phenomenon but part of an international Green movement. The flagship of this movement, the German Green party, made world headlines when it broke into that country's party system in 1983. As of 1997, Green parties have parliamentary delegations in at least eighteen European countries. Green mayors govern in cities such as Dublin and Rome.

GREEN MOVEMENT PRINCIPLES AND ORIGINS

While the term "Green" is associated with ecological ideals, the Green movement is not simply another term for the environmental movement. Not all environmentalists identify with the Greens, and, more importantly, Green activists come from movement currents of which environmentalism is only one part. Both in Europe and the United States, the Greens can more accurately be described as the electoral expression of the New Left of the 1960s. Three major social movement strands came together to form the Greens: the environmental movement, the women's movement, and the peace movement. In Germany, for example, individual Green activists fought against nuclear power and the deployment of *U.S. Pershing II* and Cruise short-range nuclear missiles. They worked for laws protecting the environment and establishing pay equity for women and paid parental leave. They set up alternative papers, food and housing cooperatives, women's shelters, and coffee houses. Some also tried unsuccessfully to transform the Social Democratic party in a New Left image.

These "post-material" movements all traced their origins to the 1960s revolt by middle-class students, and later professionals, against the post-war boom society. Each in their own way, these New Left movements saw the existing society as repressive, destructive, and spiritually dead. Within the Greens, ecological principles provided the glue for joining these currents together. With its emphasis on holistic thinking and interconnectedness, its critique of modern bureaucratic structures, its call for social responsibility, and its vision of a cooperative, life-affirming society, ecology provided a common ideological reference point within which New Left activists could find a common home.

While a central characteristic of the Green movement has been its considerable internal diversity, we can identify several general principles that help define the movement. One of the German Greens' early federal programs begins with a representative statement of these principles:

The Establishment parties in Bonn behave as if an infinite increase in industrial production were possible on the finite planet Earth. . . . The worldwide ecological crisis worsens from day to day: natural resources become more scarce; chemical waste dumps are subjects of scandal after scandal; whole species of animal are exterminated; entire varieties of plants become extinct; rivers and oceans change slowly into sewers; and humans verge on spiritual and intellectual decay in the midst of a mature, industrial, consumer society.

Our policies are guided by long-term visions for the future and are founded on four basic principles: ecology, social responsibility, grassroots democracy, and nonviolence.

This statement makes clear the central role of ecology. The Greens see our societies heading toward complete environmental and societal disaster. Simply cleaning up the worst ravages of our industrial system is not enough. The Greens reject basic assumptions of Western thought, including its tendency to break down reality into hierarchically arranged separate and discrete components as well as its uncritical faith in unbounded industrial growth. They point toward a society built around the truth that all life is interconnected. In terms of immediate policy, the German Greens, for example, have proposed dismantling the chemical industry's most dangerous production and convert the remaining industry toward more ecological and human-friendly chemicals.

The Greens use their ecological understanding not simply to spotlight and counter environmental destruction, but to offer a comprehensive vision covering all aspects of life and politics. Social responsibility is best understood as a call for social justice. For Greens, the same hierarchical institutions that destroy the environment also prey off the poor, working classes, women, immigrants, and so on. The Greens seek a new kind of social contract informed by ecological wisdom. The German Greens, for example, have called for a universal, guaranteed income that provides minimum basic needs to all people not currently working in the market regardless of their individual circumstances or reasons. If willing to live quite modestly, the system would free people to pursue the kinds of socially beneficial activities, such as child care, personal development, and community work, that the market fails to assign a monetary value. They have also called for a major reduction in the work week (to as low as thirty hours) and a vastly expanded paid family leave (up to three years).

To build a new society the Greens seek to move power away from depersonalized, bureaucratic authority toward participatory democracy. Green thought has a heavy anarchist streak that rejects centralized authority in favor of people's direct participation in decisions that affect them. Greens question capitalism, the modern technocratic state, the traditional patriarchal family, and, for some, union and social democratic bureaucracies. The German Greens have advanced ways to decentralize the nation's public health care system and to transform the one-dimensional logic of Western medicine toward more holistic and preventive conceptions of health. The Greens have also favored worker participation and control within the workplace as well as outright community and worker-owned businesses.

With heavy influence from the peace movement, Green politics promote the practice of non-violence. The German Greens have pledged to withdraw from NATO and gradually disarm the country. For the Greens, non-violence not only applies to affairs between states, but also provides a critique of economic violence, violence against women, and environmental destruction.

GREEN ROOTS IN THE UNITED STATES

The roots of the current U.S. Green movement date back to a 1984 meeting of sixty-two activists in St. Paul, Minnesota. This gathering produced a basic statement of Green thought called the "Ten Key Values" which expanded upon the German Greens' four basic principles. The values are ecological wisdom, grassroots democracy, nonviolence, social justice, decentralization, community-based economics, feminism, respect for diversity, personal and global responsibility, and future focus. The participants established a fledgling organization called the Committees of Correspondence—later renamed the Green Committees of Correspondence. The Committees of Correspondence was not a political party but a loose regional-based network intended to tie together new and existing local and state groups.

During the second half of the 1980s, local Green groups did achieve some notable success. For example, in New Haven, Connecticut, the Greens won as much as 23 percent of the vote when they ran candidates for mayor, town/city clerk, and alder seats. The Maine Green party played a major role in a successful referendum campaign to require a statewide vote to approve any radioactive waste disposal plan. In Chapel Hill, North Carolina, the Greens ran a campaign for mayor that gained significant publicity. In California, the Central Coast Greens and East Bay Green Alliance succeeded in blocking the release into the environment of Frostban, a genetically engineered microorganism manufactured by a firm in Oakland.

CONTROVERSY OVER THE NEW PARTY STRUCTURE

At their first fully delegated congress in 1991, the Greens established a national party structure. Delegates approved the first National Green Program and formally launched the Green/Green Party USA (G/GPUSA). As the name suggests, the new organization sought to unite the movement (the Greens) with a political party (the Green Party USA) into a structure more formalized and national in scope, yet controlled by the movement at the grassroots level. This founding, however, highlighted controversy and division among the Greens. Activists debated questions of the relative weight and independence assigned to electoral and non-electoral work, whether the Green Party USA should have a dues-paying membership, the role of state parties organizations in the overall structure, how binding national decisions should be on local groups, and other organi-

zational questions. One group, who chose not to join the new national organization, formed the Green Politics Network. In turn, this group produced the Association of State Green Parties. At the same time, several state Green parties, including California and Hawaii, chose not to affiliate with the new organization.

Despite internal conflicts, the Green movement continued to expand. Indeed, several fledgling state and local efforts came into their own in the first half of the 1990s. While in 1989 no organized Green parties formally existed, by 1994, eighteen states had electorally active Green parties: Alaska, Arkansas, California, Colorado, Florida, Hawaii, Maine, Missouri, New Mexico, New York, North Carolina, Ohio, Oregon, Pennsylvania, Rhode Island, Virginia, West Virginia, and Wisconsin. By 1995, the Greens had established state parties with official ballot status in five states: New Mexico, California, Maine, Alaska, and Rhode Island. (Two other states, Arizona and Hawaii, had gained ballot status in 1992 only to lose it in 1994.)

In 1994 in New Mexico, Roberto Mondragon, a former Democratic lieutenant governor turned Green, ran for governor. Not only did he win 11 percent of the vote, but other statewide candidates' totals ran as high as 33 percent in a two-way race. These returns qualified the New Mexico Greens as the first third party in the state history to achieve "major party" status. It also gave the Greens the potential power to draw enough votes to prevent Democrats from winning. In Santa Fe County that same year, two Green candidates for state assembly won 32 percent and 43 percent of the vote, respectively. Earlier that year, Green candidate Chris Moore was elected to the Santa Fe City Council. In 1996, the Greens elected a municipal judge in Santa Fe as well.

GREENS IN CALIFORNIA

In California, the Greens qualified for the ballot by registering more than the legally mandated 80,000 voters as Greens. In 1996, the Greens won a majority on the Arcata City Council and elected representatives in Berkeley, Santa Monica, Humbolt City, and Davis. Two years later, Arcata voters passed a referendum on corporate power. The new measure establishes two town meetings around the theme "Can we have democracy when large corporations wield so much power and wealth under the law?" and mandates that the city council pursue a mechanism for increasing public control over corporate activity within the city. In 1998, California Greens were elected in Santa Cruz, Yucaipa, Santa Monica, Berkeley, Menlo Park, and San Diego.

The Maine Green party won ballot status in 1994 when its candidate for governor, Jonathan Carter, won 6.5 percent of the vote in a four-way race. Rhode Island Greens gained 6.1 percent of the vote that same year when they ran Jeff Johnson for lieutenant governor. The Alaska Greens were the first state Green party to achieve ballot status when, in 1990, Jim Sykes, their candidate for governor, received 4 percent of the vote. In 1992, their candidate for the U.S. Senate, Mary Jordan, won 8 percent of the vote. Candidates for the Alaska state legislature have achieved as much as one-quarter of the vote.

Hawaiian Greens made history in 1992 by electing the first third-party candidate since the islands became a state. Keiko Bonk-Abrahamson not only won election to the big island of Hawaii's governing council, but won re-election in 1994 despite a strong $50,000 effort to unseat her. When, in 1994, the Greens ran several ultimately unsuccessful candidates for the Hawaii state assembly, they garnered 41 percent and 38 percent of the vote in two-way races and 17 percent and 10 percent in multi-challenger contests.

CHALLENGES OF THE GREEN MOVEMENT

Because of their relatively long history and internal diversity, the Greens offer a kind of lab-oratory for examining the strategic issues facing third-party organizing today. Indeed, the Greens have had to confront four major questions that face all progressive third-party activists: internal organization; electoral political participation; candidates; and balancing ideological purity and broad electoral appeal.

The first question revolves around internal organization. The U.S. Greens, like their European counterparts, have witnessed high levels of internal division and conflict. The Greens have tried to build their values of democracy, decentralization, and respect for diversity into the very structures of their organizations. As a brief introductory flyer of the national Green Party USA states, the party is structured as an association of locally based activist groups, local, state, and national organizations attempting to coordinate their tactics and strategies democratically.

The Green Party USA's national structure is weak. The Greens have a clearinghouse staffed by a single individual, rather than a national office with centralized resources suitable for allocation to local groups. The base of Green politics lies in the hundreds of largely independent local chapters, which are run almost exclusively on volunteer energy. Within these local experiences, Greens place considerable emphasis upon broad participation, consensus decision-making, and respect for diversity.

The challenge facing the Greens is how to combine these core values into effective and coherent strategies. The autonomy of local groups has produced a rich diversity of activities and strategies within the Greens. At its best, such diversity can allow the movement to develop quite sophisticated strategies that combine local activity into an effective synthesis. However, local diversity can also paralyze higher-level decision-making by pitting differing local perspectives against each other. Instead of producing a creative synthesis, national meetings, for example, can become battlegrounds between firmly entrenched localized perspectives. Some Green congresses, for example, have witnessed sharp and heated debates between different Greens.

The rich debates and strategies that originate

at the grassroots level need to be transformed so that people can adequately deal with the issues particular to building a national movement. Otherwise, the movement will remain a loose federation of local activism rather than a strong grassroots-driven national project. In addition to developing coherent national strategies, the Greens also need to raise the level of resources needed for national and regional organizing. Thus far, the Greens have proven weak fundraisers. As a result, the party has no staff of field organizers to complement volunteer activity and help move it to higher levels.

WINNING ELECTIONS VS. CHANGING SOCIETY

A second issue animating Green debates has centered around the relative balance between electoral and non-electoral work. The Green Party USA was founded upon the principle that the party grows out of and is responsible to a broader movement. Some Greens, however, have expressed a deeply held distrust of the entire electoral process. Diana Balto Frank of the Lehigh Valley Greens (in Pennsylvania) expressed an explicit version of this hostility: "For North American activists, participating in electoral games serves one purpose: to divert us from working to make real, fundamental change." As she went on to note, electoral politics takes time and money away from "building grassroots movements, which can become the basis for a new social system."

Indeed, many local Green chapters have done almost no electoral work, but have focused entirely on issue activism. A fall 1994 issue of the Green party's newsletter listed Green activity in Upstate New York, including the following: The Buffalo Greens had fought against a nuclear waste facility and established a Solidarity Buying Club to support family and organic farming; Syracuse activists had helped develop a Green Cities Youth project; Ithaca Greens had pioneered an alternative money system, the "Ithaca Hours," where coupons for

work and goods are exchanged locally in place of money; and elsewhere in the state, Green groups had worked to stop a hydroelectric project, block a toxic-chemical-releasing cardboard recycling plant, and prevent timber harvesting in the Allegheny State Park. Even the most electorally active Green groups also support an array of non-electoral activities. The Santa Fe Greens, for example, established their own "Ithaca Hours" and set up a Tenants' Council at the same time that Chris Moore ran for city council.

While sharing an orientation that sees grassroots activism as the core of their politics, other Greens place a greater emphasis on electoral work as something valuable in its own right. For example, David Spero of the Green party of California offers a view at the opposite end of the issue organizing versus elections debate.

> Those who claim an opposition between electoral work and "movement" work chose to ignore the tremendous power and resources of the state. Ignoring it will not make it go away. You have to engage the state and do the tremendously difficult work of transforming it and dragging it closer to the people.
>
> That is why the main business of the Greens should be electoral. Not because we want to "administer an oppressive system" as Left Greens put it. And not to get the message out. The message is already out. We run to win, and we win to use government resources to help organize and empower communities.

WHEN SHOULD CANDIDATES RUN FOR OFFICE?

Further complicating this debate is a third question of when to run and when not to run candidates for office. Green electoral activity has displayed the full range of possible practices. Many Greens have been willing to run for offices that were quite out of reach—only to win a few percentage points. Green bids for governor, the U.S. Senate, and Green support for

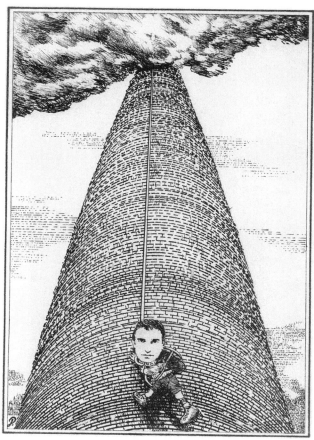

Ralph Nader (1996 Green party presidential candidate) won a reputation as a fighter of corporate America, as depicted in this 1972 illustration where he climbs a smokestack to protest industrial air pollution. (New York Times, *March 30, 1972, Courtesy of the Library of Congress)*

Ralph Nader's 1996 presidential campaign are all reflective of this tendency. Other Green groups have been much more selective—often confining themselves to local races in which fledgling political groups often have the greatest prospects for either strong showings or outright victories.

At issue is a fundamental question of how electoral efforts can best build a movement. Should activists use elections as an educational tool in which Green candidates enter high-profile contests primarily to gain publicity for the cause? In this case, Green-issue activism grows because more people have exposure to Green ideas. Or alternatively, should local

groups focus on seriously contesting for local power? Green elected officials then partner with grassroots issue activism to further build the movement by achieving actual power and actual changes in policies.

This debate affects not only the question of individual candidacies, but also the timing of efforts to seek official ballot status. Because of the restrictive and undemocratic nature of many state qualification laws, achieving a formal line on many state ballots involves considerable time and energy. The political logic favors seeking access early so that many Green candidates can be placed in high-profile contests without needing to collect petition signatures for each candidacy. By contrast, strategies that carefully select among winnable local opportunities have much less use for statewide ballot status—the petition signatures required for local contests can be collected as needed.

The track record of local Green activism, as well as other third-party projects such as the New party, suggest that those groups that have pursued the latter strategy have witnessed the greatest overall growth and staying power. Winning office and participating in actual policy has proven effective in not only attracting a growing membership, but also securing endorsements and support from local progressive unions and community groups. By contrast, running for offices that are well beyond a group's reach runs the danger of becoming a substitute for the steady and painstaking task of locally based organizing. The mild gains in new recruits attracted by Ralph Nader's 1996 presidential bid, in which his best return was 3 percent in California, has to be compared, for example, to the steady growth of local New party chapters coming from their continued victories in targeted local elections.

Finally, the Greens face the question of balancing their origins in distinct social movement currents with the electoral need to build majorities. While New Left and Green activism is not exclusively tied to people with a white, middle-class, and professionally trained background, today many Greens do share these characteristics. In Europe, the Greens have established a very clear base constituency that produces electoral results roughly running around 10 percent of the vote. In electoral systems organized by proportional representation, such Green vote returns produce seats in legislatures and prospects for participating in governing coalitions. The U.S. winner-take-all system, however, rewards only those who win majorities.

ADVANTAGES OF U.S. GREENS

The U.S. Greens do have the advantage of not having to compete with an already well established Social Democratic–style party with organic connections to working-class voters. This situation does present possibilities for Greens to offer their ballot line or candidacies as a collective asset for all progressive groups seeking alternatives to the Democrats. The challenge is to organize this potential at the ground level. Indeed, successful local Green groups have often been the ones who have succeeded in translating the holistic nature of Green thinking into concrete coalition-building. In Santa Fe, for example, the Greens have worked with other community groups around such projects as a living-wage campaign, preserving a neighborhood grocery store, reforming property taxes, opposing NAFTA, raising awareness around the five-hundredth anniversary of the European conquest of America, and starting a Tenant-Landlord Association. All of this non-electoral work established the contacts and mutual trust that allowed Chris Moore's candidacy as a Green to receive the support of a wide range of groups, including the city's growing Latino activism.

As with other third-party groups, the Greens continue to struggle with these questions. However, one point is clear. Almost two decades of Green activism both in the United States and worldwide demonstrate that the Green movement is not only here to stay, but a key part of the future. Any survey of the news suggests that issues driving Green activism will become even more salient as we move into the next century. The Green challenge is to translate their twenty-first-century values into ever more effective movement-building.

DAVID REYNOLDS

See also: **Map 5:** Green Party (1996); Ralph Nader.

Selected References

The Green Party USA publishes *Green Politics,* which provides good overviews of Green activity and debate. Their Web site (http://www.greens.org) has information on the national organization as well as links to various local and state groups.

Synthesis/Regeneration is a magazine of Green thought, which routinely covers debates and Green activities both in the United States and internationally.

Bibliography

Coleman, Dan. *Eco Politics.* New York: Routledge, 1995.

Gaard, Greta. *Ecological Politics: Ecofeminists and the Greens.* Philadelphia: Temple University Press, 1998.

Mayer, Margit, and John Ely, eds. *The German Greens: Paradox Between Movement and Party.* Philadelphia: Temple University Press, 1998.

Resenbrink, John. *Greens and the Transformation.* San Pedro, CA: R&E Miles, 1992.

Reynolds, David. *Democracy Unbound: Progressive Challenges to the Two Party System.* Boston: South End Press, 1997.

Richardson, Dick, and Chris Rootes, eds. *The Green Challenge: The Development of Green Parties in Europe.* New York: Routledge, 1995.

Spretnak, Charlene, and Fritjof Capra. *Green Politics.* Santa Fe, NM: Bear & Company, 1986.

Tokar, Brian. *The Green Alternative.* San Pedro, CA: R&E Miles, 1987.

HUMAN RIGHTS PARTY
(MICHIGAN)
1960s–1980s

The social movement of the 1960s was actually a widely diverse collection of movements, the remnants of some of which—women, gays, blacks, ecology, peace—are with us today. For the most part, however, the 1960s left no legacy of permanent organizations. For whatever reason, the politics of the 1960s was primarily that of anti-institutional protest. As such, it emphasized demonstrations, rallies, marches, and other forms of non-party politics based on short-term mass mobilizations to present lists of "demands" to government. Such "direct action" was thought more authentic than engaging in party-building or legislative struggle, which was seen as a "sell out." Because it was based on such ad hoc mass mobilizations, the 1960s left no institutions of oppositional power, such as the trade unions that emerged from the 1930s.

Exceptions to this tendency were the myriad of local radical third parties that sprang up all across the nation in the late 1960s and early 1970s. These local third parties—all of which viewed the Democratic party as unsalvageable—moved beyond protest to organize for the political defeat of the government. They wanted permanent political power. In California, there was the Peace and Freedom party, in Vermont the Liberty Union, in the District of Columbia the D.C. Statehood party, in Alabama the New Democratic party, in Texas, La Raza Unida party, and in Arizona the New party. In other states, numerous smaller such parties were loosely allied under the national umbrella of the People's party, which ran Dr. Benjamin Spock for president in 1972 and for vice president in 1976. Most of these parties flourished briefly and then died.

One of the more successful of these local third parties was the Michigan Human Rights party (HRP), which not only obtained statewide ballot status, but also elected city councillors in Ann Arbor and Ypsilanti. In Ann Arbor, the municipal elections, like most in Michigan, were partisan based, which encouraged thoughts of third-party activity. Additionally, council elections were ward based instead of at-large. Thus, candidates with strong support among certain interest groups—such as among students or blacks—could hope to gain some representation in the districts that were dominated by those groups.

Young radicals unhappy with the Democratic party's prosecution of the war in Vietnam, as well as its domestic policies, therefore formed the Radical Independent party. Under that name in the April 1971 municipal elections, they unsuccessfully ran a write-in candidate for mayor and Jerry DeGrieck (a former student government vice president) as their sole write-in candidate for city council.

Following their defeat, the party spent a year in intensive organizing. In the 1971 election, a total of 27,000 voters had gone to the polls. As the April 1972 election drew near, the party had registered 15,000 new student voters alone. A university poll, taken before the campaign, showed one-third of the student voters already favoring the party, with another third undecided. Between the two elections the party also affiliated with the new statewide HRP, which gave them automatic ballot status.

Thus, in April 1972, DeGrieck was on the

ballot and this time was elected to city council representing the first ward, a district dominated by students and poor blacks. The neighboring second ward, which contained most of the town's student dorms, elected HRP candidate Nancy Wechsler, a long-time activist in the local women's and tenants' rights movements. In addition, the HRP also "spoiled" the election of Democratic candidates in two other wards, ensuring that no Democrats were elected in Ann Arbor that year. For the next two years, the eleven-person city council consisted of five Republicans, four Democrats, and the two HRP members.

Inspired by the success of HRP in Ann Arbor, activists in Ypsilanti's Students for a Democratic Society (SDS) and the anti-war and environmental movements joined with other veterans of the Ypsilanti Left to form a local chapter of the HRP in the summer of 1972. In the April 1973 municipal elections the new chapter of the HRP ran a slate of candidates—including local SDS activist Eric Jackson—for council, all of whom lost. They tried again in April 1974 and sent two HRP candidates to the city council, Eric Jackson and Harold Baize, the latter active in the local environmental movement.

Meanwhile, in Ann Arbor, both DeGrieck and Wechsler "came out" as gay, although their sexual orientation was not known at the time of their election. In April 1974, however, council candidate Kathy Kozachenko became the first candidate in American history to openly run as a gay. Not only did Kozachenko run as an open lesbian, but she won. Later that year, Democrat Elaine Noble of Boston was elected state representative as an open lesbian. Indeed, Kozachenko's out-front lesbianism was seen as a major aspect of her campaign. Thus, her election to the council was seen as a victory not only for the HRP—which by this time had come to identify itself as a "socialist-feminist" party—but for the women's and gay movements as well.

DeGrieck and Wechsler had declined to run for re-election in 1974. Therefore, Kozachenko was the third and last Ann Arbor HRP councilperson, serving from 1974–76. By April 1976,

the Ann Arbor HRP, like most of the other similar local third parties around the country, had ceased to exist in all but name, and Kozachenko, feeling isolated and abandoned, decided not to run for re-election. In Ypsilanti, however, Jackson and Baize decided together to run for re-election as HRP candidates, and both were elected to two-year terms.

In November 1976, however, the statewide HRP put the presidential and vice-presidential candidates of the People's party—with which it was affiliated nationally—on the Michigan ballot. The People's party ticket, composed of Margaret Wright and Dr. Benjamin Spock, did so poorly (garnering just over 3,000 votes) that the HRP lost its ballot status, from which it never recovered. By the time the municipal elections of 1978 arrived, Jackson and Baize were officeholders without a party. They and the remnants of the Ypsilanti HRP entered the Democratic party and waged a strong campaign in the primary. They elected Peter Murdock (former leader of the Ypsilanti SDS), black socialist Jerome Strong, and Baize, in their respective districts, with Jackson losing his Democratic primary battle by thirteen votes.

In 1980, Jerome Strong was defeated, and Baize decided, after six years, to retire from the council. Thus ended the run of the Michigan Human Rights party. Murdock went on to become mayor in 1981 and again in 1983, but as a Democrat. The failure to endure of the HRP and the myriad local third parties like it across the country was a result of their marginal status within a larger social movement that did not take the acquisition of political power seriously. It thus represents a promising road not taken by the movement of the 1960s.

ERIC LEIF DAVIN

There have been no books or articles written about the Human Rights party. This article is based upon interviews with activists.

See also: District of Columbia Statehood Party; La Raza Unida Party; Liberty Union Party of Vermont; Peace and Freedom Party; People's Party, 1971–1978.

HUNKER DEMOCRATS

1840s

The Hunkers were the conservative faction of the New York Democratic party of the 1840s, opposing the radical Barnburners. The intra-party struggle between the two allowed the Whig candidate Zachary Taylor to win the 1848 presidential election. The term "Hunker," of Dutch origin, became common around 1843 as opponents (Whigs and Barnburners) accused them of unprincipled "hunkering" after public office. According to historian Denis Tilden Lynch: "Hunker is a corruption of *hunkerer*,—one who desires, a selfish person. *Hunkerer*, in turn, is derived from *hunkeren*, the infinitive of 'desire' *ik hunker* is 'I desire.'"

The emergence of the Hunkers (and Barnburners) resulted from the failure of the Albany Regency, America's first political machine, a party built on patronage and favoritism for its supporters. Built by Martin Van Buren in "the partyless period after the War of 1812," the Regency was a group of patronage-bound, highly disciplined editors, politicians, and officeholders who practiced party loyalty, organization, and discipline. By the 1840s, the main difference between the two factions was their views on slavery, but their struggle initially arose over development of New York's canal system. By 1827 the Erie Canal (completed in 1825) was generating enough income to allow the legislature to suspend direct taxation. However, by the mid-1830s public funds, in particular for popular new canal projects, were running low. "Conservatives" (who became Hunkers) favored continued development, borrowing if need be; "radicals" (who became Barnburners) advocated building within the state's means. In 1838, a Whig assembly authorized borrowing $4 million for canal projects; Democratic governor William Marcy, against expectations, signed the bill.

It was Marcy, later a Hunker leader, who had earlier coined the phrase that would become associated with the "spoils system" of patronage politics: "It may be, sir, that the politicians of the United States are not so fastidious as some gentlemen are, as to disclosing the principles on which they act. . . . They see nothing wrong in the rule, that to the victor belong the spoils of the enemy."

Other Hunker leaders included Horatio Seymour; Daniel Dickinson, Marcy's father-in-law; businessman, banker, and Regency leader Benjamin Knower; Edwin Croswell, editor of the Albany *Argus* (the Regency newspaper); longtime Canal Commissioner William C. Bouck; and Henry Foster and Samuel Beardsley, state legislators from canal districts.

DEMOCRATIC PARTY FACTIONALISM

By the late 1830s, state and national bank policy had become highly divided by factions. Many Hunkers profited from connections "between state-chartered 'pet' banks and Jackson's Federal funds deposited in them" and, led by Marcy, opposed President Van Buren's plan to remove the banks and establish an independent treasury. Hunkers also favored stronger tariffs and were less sympathetic to various popular movements and third parties, such as the Workingmen's party, the Equal Rights party, and the anti-rent and abolition movements. Known to some as the "pro-slavery Democrats of New York," their desire for party unity meant they were opposed to the Wilmot Proviso (the non-extension of slavery) and favored Texas annexation. Hunker support was strong in canal districts (or prospective canal districts), New York City, Buffalo, and Albany, weaker in the west and non-existent in the far north. Support was more transitory as time went on, increasingly tied to specific politicians with shifting loyalties. For example, comparing vote distribution from the Democratic state convention of September 1847 and gubernatorial returns a year later illustrates this perfectly.

By 1842 canal expenses were ruining state finances and credit. In 1843 a Democratic legislature passed the "Stop and Tax" bill, which halted canal development and substituted taxing for borrowing. This was the first public expression of party differences; battle lines were being hardened. By 1843 the Albany *Atlas* became a Barnburner paper: Each faction now had its own newspaper, destroying a critical element of the Regency machine. Control of the party machinery became increasingly important; the party handled patronage poorly. Resentment mounted as Hunker Horatio Seymour saw legislation through, which partially undid "Stop and Tax." Then, in 1844, Van Buren made his opposition to the immediate annexation of Texas public. At the Democratic National Convention he was denied the presidential nomination; Hunkers were lukewarm in their support. Eventually Benjamin Butler (Van Buren's Barnburner manager) withdrew his candidacy for president and gave his (and New York's) support to James Polk.

New York Democrats, including Van Buren, campaigned actively for Polk's victory, and Barnburners believed they were instrumental in Polk's win, especially since Van Buren had controlled a large bloc of delegates, and Barnburner Silas Wright was offered and declined the vice presidency. They saw top cabinet positions and other choice spots as "theirs." Circumstances intervened, however, and Polk (somewhat inadvertently) slighted them. Most insulting was

when Marcy was given the War Department, a position that would have been Butler's were it not for communications problems. Marcy lobbied to get other Hunkers appointed to both federal and state jobs. Polk belatedly tried to correct his mistake by appointing Barnburners to other positions, but in the end, Hunkers remained in control of leadership positions in New York State government.

INFLUENCE OF HUNKERS IN DEMOCRATIC NATIONAL POLITICS

The rift progressively widened. In 1845 the Democratic slate for state legislature was split for the first time. In 1846, Hunkers (unsuccessfully) opposed the renomination of Barnburner Governor Silas Wright and, with the Whigs, passed a bill that all but negated "Stop and Tax." But by now the main issue dividing the two factions was slavery. Hunkers favored Polk's expansionist Texas policy while preferring to remain silent on slavery and the Wilmot Proviso. Wright was considered a prospect for the presidency in 1848, but died in 1847, increasing conflict among Democrats at the Texas state convention in September 1847. Though Barnburners were in the majority at the convention, Hunkers controlled the party machinery and quickly nominated their candidates, refusing to allow for discussion of the Wilmot Proviso. Angry remarks, in particular one by Hunker James Wadsworth concerning Wright, insured that the convention would break up with the party badly divided. The Barnburners held their own convention, and while they did not nominate a separate ticket, the Hunkers (i.e., Democrats) were outpolled by a ratio of ten to one in several traditionally Democratic counties that fall. In spite of this, the Barnburner defection legitimized Hunkers nationally as the true Democratic party in New York.

The climax was reached at the 1848 Baltimore Democratic National Convention. Both factions sent the New York allotment of thirty-six delegates. While the convention body was

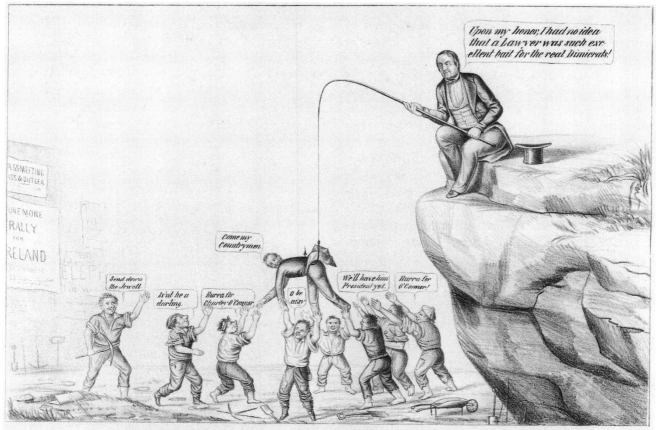

AN OLD HUNKER FISHING FOR VOTES.

A conservative breakaway faction of the Democratic party, the Hunkers struggled with the anti-slavery Barnburners for control of the party in the 1840s. Hunker presidential candidate Martin Van Buren is shown in this 1848 lithograph desperately trying to win New York votes by dangling the popular Lieutenant-Governor Charley O'Connor as bait. *(Courtesy of the Library of Congress)*

inclined to support the Hunkers because of their acquiescence to the South on slavery issues, much of the balance of the convention time was the taken up by a fight over credentials. By a close vote it was decided that each New York delegate would receive half a vote (as opposed to one); neither side was satisfied. Barnburners refused to participate and bolted after Lewis Cass was declared the party nominee: Thus, Hunkers were the New York Democratic party. The Barnburners subsequently supported Martin Van Buren and the Free Soil party, virtually assuring Whig candidate Zachary Taylor of a win in New York, since a substantial majority of Free Soil voters in New York were Democrats before the election. In fact, New York's thirty-six electoral votes (the largest bloc in the nation) were Taylor's exact margin of victory in the electoral college. Democrats (Hunkers) were routed in the state polls.

DEMOCRATIC UNITY AND DECLINE OF HUNKERS

Rapprochement began in the spring of 1849. Hunkers softened their position on the extension of slavery but remained opposed to it being a party-wide principle. They nominated a slate of candidates that fall but (in spite of great opposition) resolved to withdraw half of them and support Barnburners. Marcy was instrumental in formulating a compromise position that papered over their differences. The union was strained, and though Democrats won a majority of the state vote, they took only half of the contested state offices and barely lost the legislature. By 1850 there were two Hunker factions: pro-southern Hards, led by Daniel Dickinson, and conciliatory Softs, led by Marcy and Horatio Seymour. Marcy's attempt (backed by former Barnburner John Van Buren) to secure the 1852 Democratic presidential nomination signaled the end of the Hunker Democrats.

JODY C. BAUMGARTNER

See also: William Marcy; Horatio Seymour; Zachary Taylor; Martin Van Buren.

Bibliography

Alexander, DeAlva Stanwood. *A Political History of the State of New York.* Vols. 1 and 2. New York: Henry Holt, 1906.

Binkley, Wilfred E. *American Political Parties, Their Natural History.* 4th ed., enlarged. New York: Alfred E. Knopf, 1962.

Blue, Frederick J. *The Free Soilers: Third Party Politics, 1848–1952.* Urbana: University of Illinois Press, 1973.

Cole, Donald B. *Martin Van Buren and the American Political System.* Princeton: Princeton University Press, 1984.

Donavan, Herbert D.A. *The Barnburners: A Study of the Internal Movements in the Political History of New York State and of the Resulting Changes in Political Affiliation, 1830–1952.* New York: New York University Press, 1925.

Lynch, Denis Tilden. *An Epoch and a Man: Martin Van Buren and His Times.* New York: Horace Liveright, 1929.

Niven, John. *Martin Van Buren: The Romantic Age of American Politics.* New York: Oxford University Press, 1983.

Paul, James C.N. *Rift in the Democracy.* Philadelphia: University of Pennsylvania Press, 1951.

Polakoff, Keith Ian. *Political Parties in American History.* New York: Wiley, 1981.

Spencer, Ivor Debenham. *The Victor and the Spoils: A Life of William L. Marcy.* Providence: Brown University Press, 1959.

INDEPENDENT DEMOCRATS
1832–1833

The Independent Democrats, a short-lived breakaway group from the Democratic-Republicans, was the direct result of the nullification crisis of 1832, in which South Carolina briefly challenged the federal government's right to impose a high tariff on imports. Largely engineered by vice president and the former and future South Carolina senator John C. Calhoun, it quickly fell apart after South Carolina backed down from its challenge and the nullification controversy passed.

SLAVERY AND TARIFFS

According to recent scholarship, the nullification crisis had as much to do with slavery as it did with tariffs. More than any other state in the union, South Carolina was dominated by its slave population. Indeed, it was the only state at the time that had a slave majority—at some 56 percent of the population. And in the wealthy lowland plantation districts where most of the political elite of the state lived and did business, the ratio was far higher. Thus, more than anywhere else, the planter class of South Carolina felt vulnerable to any challenges to the "peculiar institution."

There were many challengers in the 1830s. The abolitionist movement had become more vocal and active: William Lloyd Garrison's *Liberator* newspaper had been launched in Boston in 1831; the largest slave uprising in American history—led by Nat Turner of Virginia—had occurred in that same year; and the British Parliament was moving toward the abolition of

slavery in the empire, which it would declare in 1833. Many South Carolina planters, then, were highly fearful that the federal government might move against slavery.

The more immediate threat, however, was the tariff. As one of its last acts, the John Quincy Adams administration had passed a system of high tariffs in 1828—a system southerners disparagingly called the "tariff of abominations." As a center of manufacturing for the American market and a minor exporting region, the North had several reasons to push for high tariffs: They protected infant industries against more sophisticated British competition and helped raised revenues for a government actively involved in internal improvements. For southern planters, however, tariffs forced them to pay more for the imports they relied upon. The 1828 tariff essentially shifted wealth from South to North. It also underlined the basic problem of federalism. Could a politically and economically dominant region of the country force its agenda on the rest of the republic? And could that dominance come to affect slavery?

During the early years of the Andrew Jackson administration in the late 1820s, South Carolinians remained hopeful. After all, Jackson was a southern planter himself and showed no great love for the manufacturing interests of the North. But Jackson was under pressure from a House dominated by northerners, and he needed to offer something to them in order to assure that his war against the Bank of the United States—his political *bete noire*—would proceed. Thus, in 1832, in an act seen as betrayal by many southerners, Jackson signed off on a new tariff system that was pretty much a continuation of the 1828 system.

NULLIFICATION CRISIS

The reaction across the South was immediate, vociferous, and angry—doubly so for South Carolina. In November 1832, the South Carolina legislature passed an ordinance of nullification, declaring that the tariffs of 1828 and 1832 would not be enforced in the state after February 1, 1833. Moreover, the act stated, South Carolina would secede from the union should the federal government try to enforce payment of the tariffs inside the state. Though Jackson's vice president in his first term and thus in Washington, John C. Calhoun was the ideologue behind the nullification movement, even as he was a moderating influence in bringing it to a peaceful conclusion.

In 1828, he had published *The South Carolina Exposition and Protest,* a tract in which he laid out his theories of federalism. According to Calhoun, the union was not essentially composed of the people, but of the states, and thus ultimate sovereignty lay there. If a state judged a law was unconstitutional, they had the right to nullify it. Moreover, just as the people had the right to overthrow a tyrannical government, so the states had the right to leave a tyrannical union. While Calhoun first published his tract anonymously, his speeches of the time led many to believe he had written it, a fact he acknowledged in 1831.

With Jackson overwhelmingly elected to a second term in early November 1832, Calhoun, who resigned as vice president in December and was immediately appointed to the Senate by the South Carolina legislature—was thus free to effect opposition to the tariff, which included organizing a breakaway faction of the Democratic party called the Independent Dem-

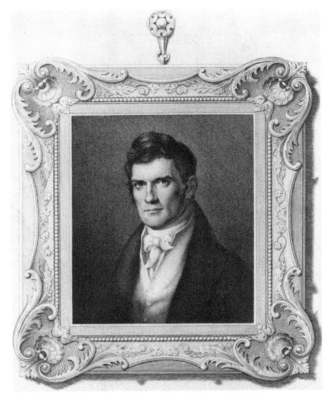

Vice president and South Carolina Senator John C. Calhoun is depicted in this portrait (ca. 1810s) decades before he would lead the Independent Democrats, a brief breakaway faction organized around the nullification controversy of 1832. *(Courtesy of the Library of Congress)*

ocrats. Widely supported in South Carolina, it soon gained potential adherents across the South, threatening to break the party apart along sectional lines, as would happen twenty-eight years later in 1860.

This time, both the party and the union held together. There were several reasons for this. First, Jackson was careful to apply a carrot-and-stick approach to the South Carolina rebels: promises to reduce the tariff and a strong show of force, including the dispatch of federal troops. Second, Calhoun—along with pro-tariff Henry Clay—was able to quickly work out an effective compromise tariff that largely satisfied North and South. Third, South Carolina was isolated, as the rest of the South did not see the tariff issue as a reason to threaten to break the union apart. By March 1833, the nullification crisis was over and the Independent Democrats had faded away. Most of them—including Calhoun—would find that the Democratic party was more and more to their liking in the 1830s and 1840s, largely because they increasingly came to control it as their pro-tariff opponents left to form the Whigs.

JAMES CIMENT

Bibliography

Holt, Michael. *Political Parties and American Political Development from the Age of Jackson to the Age of Lincoln.* Baton Rouge: Louisiana State University Press, 1992.

Livermore, Shaw, Jr. *The Twilight of Federalism: The Disintegration of the Federalist Party, 1815–1830.* New York: Gordian Press, 1972.

INDEPENDENT PROGRESSIVE PARTY

1948–1952

ORIGINS OF THE PARTY

Approaching the 1948 presidential election, liberals in the Democratic party were unhappy with the "accidental presidency" of Harry Truman. This was especially true in California, where resentments against Truman ran deep. Not only had Truman been the anointed choice for vice president by the allegedly corrupt city bosses and party regulars at the 1944 Democratic National Convention, but Truman, despite his Missouri roots, represented to many liberal westerners the dominance of conservative, anti-labor, and anti-growth northeastern financial interests. Many Californians also felt that Truman's posture toward the Soviets was too aggressive and a betrayal of Franklin Delano Roosevelt's more conciliatory foreign policy.

HENRY WALLACE'S INDEPENDENT CAMPAIGN

For liberal Californians, as with other liberals across the country, Henry Wallace was the personification of all their hopes for a return to "true" New Deal policies in the post-war era. Wallace served in the first two Roosevelt administrations as secretary of agriculture and in Roosevelt's third term as vice president. Wallace lost his bid for a second term as vice president when Harry Truman won the nomination at the 1944 Democratic National Convention. As

a conciliation, Roosevelt appointed him secretary of commerce where he served until breaking with the Truman administration over its hard-line policy toward the Soviets in autumn of 1946. Wallace remained active in politics, however, serving as editor of the *New Republic* and delivering speeches to political and civic groups across the country. In the spring of 1947, Wallace addressed crowds in Los Angeles, San Francisco, and Oakland at events organized by the Progressive Citizens of America (PCA), a liberal group that was critical of the Truman administration's cold war policies.

Wallace's enthusiastic reception on his California speaking tour publicly exposed a divide within the Democratic party between party regulars and liberals that had opened with Roosevelt's death in 1945. California state politics in the 1930s and 1940s was notoriously fluid and unstable. Cynical about the leadership of the major parties, many Californians sought political reform through single-issue organizations such as the Townsenders—a grassroots movement that advocated the adoption of a generously financed old-age pension system—and through insurgent campaigns within the major parties that could, and often did, leave their mark. In 1934, for example, the socialist author Upton Sinclair, an insurgent, won the Democratic nomination for governor but lost to the Republican candidate in the general election. Liberal Democrats blamed conservatives within the party for not supporting Sinclair with enthusiasm. In subsequent years, there was enduring enmity between the two factions that was mitigated only in part by the enthusiasm among all Democrats for the New

Deal and FDR. After the war, the strains between liberal and conservative Democrats were evident when James Roosevelt (FDR's son) served as Democratic state party chairman in the late 1940s. Roosevelt gave voice to liberal and progressive discontent with his criticism of Truman's foreign policy and by distancing himself from Edward Pauley, the leader of Truman supporters within the California Democratic party.

Emboldened by James Roosevelt's critical posture toward Truman and heartened by the support Wallace was receiving nationally as a potential challenger to Truman, liberal Democrats in California were convinced that sufficient support could be generated among progressives to send a Wallace delegation from California to the 1948 Democratic National Convention. In July 1947, Robert Kenny, former state attorney general and a leader of the southern California PCA, organized a statewide committee to select a slate of Wallace delegates. Kenny's early efforts enjoyed widespread support from the state's Democratic coalition. Leading members of California's congressional delegation, including prominent liberals Helen Douglas and Chet Holifield, approved of Kenny's efforts, as well as James Roosevelt, left-leaning unions, the PCA and many county Democratic organizations in southern California.

FORMATION OF THE PARTY

Against the wishes of Robert Kenny, but with the blessing of C.B. "Bennie" Baldwin (Henry Wallace's political advisor), a faction of Wallace supporters organized the Independent Progressive party of California (IPP) in August 1947. The leaders of the IPP adopted a "dual strategy"—namely, a campaign to send a Wallace delegation to the 1948 Democratic National Convention while simultaneously organizing a drive to get the IPP on the ballot in California. This two-pronged plan was to serve as a platform for Wallace's bid for president in the event that the campaign to win the Democratic nomination failed. When Wallace announced that he would run for president as a third-party candidate in late 1947, the focus of Wallace's California supporters turned exclusively to collecting enough signatures to qualify for official status before the March 1948 deadline.

The core supporters of the IPP were seventy locals of the Congress of Industrial Organizations trade unions. Hugh Bryson, president of the Marine Cooks and Stewards Union, served as state chair of the IPP. The most important organizational force behind the new party were the Townsendites, who had the grassroots resources to organize the petition drive needed to get the IPP on the state ballot. Unionists were attracted to Wallace's strong commitment to labor and the Townsendites were attracted to the new party's embrace of their pension plan, as well as the endorsement of the IPP by their leader, Robert Townsend.

The IPP billed itself as the true successor to the New Deal, and as a party that, according to its campaign literature, would "fight for the policies of Franklin D. Roosevelt." Promising to "fight against depression, halt reaction at home, and preserve world peace," the IPP fused national liberalism with western populism. The IPP advanced human rights principles and a conciliatory stance toward the Soviets in foreign affairs while embracing anti-monopolistic reforms for the domestic political economy.

As the IPP gathered strength, the prospects for Kenny's "Democrats for Wallace" campaign dimmed in late 1947 when James Roosevelt decided that an insurgent Wallace campaign for the nomination could never topple Truman. Truman moved to the left in late 1947 as part of a campaign to shore up the groups within the New Deal coalition, including western progressives and unions. Wallace's public pronouncements on foreign policy alienated many centrist Democrats amid speculation that communists held influence within his camp. Meanwhile, due to the im-

California congresswoman and activist in the Independent Progressive party, Helen Gahagan Douglas addresses a youth rally in New York City, March 21, 1945. *(Courtesy of the Library of Congress)*

pressive efforts of the Townsendites, the IPP collected the 275,000 signatures needed to get the new party onto the 1948 ballot. The IPP's reach was extensive enough to field candidates in almost every congressional and state assembly and senate race. Ten Democratic candidates cross-filed on the IPP ticket. The IPP raised nearly $39 million for the Wallace campaign, lagging behind only New York, Pennsylvania, and Illinois among Wallace's state organizations.

DECLINE OF THE PARTY

But in the end, the failure of Wallace's presidential campaign destroyed the prospects for

the long-term viability of the IPP. Although Wallace's campaign swing through California in the autumn of 1948 was enthusiastically received, the outcome of the November election was disappointing. Under the sponsorship of the IPP, Wallace won only 190,381 votes in California, 4.73 percent of the votes cast in the state. Wallace's showing compared unfavorably to previous third-party campaigns in California. Robert La Follette's Progressive party won 33.1 percent of the vote for president in California in 1924 and Theodore Roosevelt won 41.8 percent of the presidential vote in 1912. The IPP won no congressional seats or state offices. The new party could not harness California's natural bent for insurgency nor could it exploit the weakness of the state's major-party organizations.

In 1952, the IPP sponsored a San Francisco lawyer, Vincent William Hallinan, to run a national campaign for president. Hallinan conducted a thirty-state tour, but received only 140,416 votes nationally. Soon after the 1952 election, the IPP disbanded in a political atmosphere that was increasingly hostile toward left-wing political movements and a policy of rapprochement toward the Soviets.

RICHARD FLANAGAN

See also: Progressive Party, 1948; Henry Agard Wallace.

Bibliography

McWilliams, Carey. "California's Third-Party Donnybrook." *The Nation,* April 13, 1948.

Schmidt, Karl M. *Henry A. Wallace: Quixotic Crusade 1948.* Syracuse: Syracuse University Press, 1960.

Independent Progressive Party of California. *Of the People,* October 27, 1947.

☆☆☆☆☆☆☆☆☆☆☆☆☆☆☆☆☆☆☆☆☆☆☆☆☆☆

INDEPENDENT REPUBLICAN PARTY

1864

The Independent Republican party was formed from the radical elements of the Republican party and only existed during the presidential campaign of 1864. Although it had a very short life as a distinct political party, the constituent groups that formed this party continued to be important groups in shaping electoral politics of the Republican party. In many respects, it was what the Independent Republican party did not do that was its most important contribution.

The election of 1864 occurred in the most turbulent and violent period of electoral politics since the Revolution. The party system of the Jacksonian period had dissolved and a new, more modern party system was in its early development. The Independent Republican party existed in the early part of this third party system, and it was only during this early period of the third system that the Republican party would attain presidential electoral majorities across all sections of the United States. The ability to avoid factionalism in this early period was mandatory for the Republicans to achieve this electoral success in a very critical period for the nation.

The formation of the Independent Republican party can be understood as a continuation of a political movement, the members of which, during other periods, had supported other political parties. These were very issue-driven interests with limited partisan loyalty that demonstrated preference for change over tradition. Many of these interests had been active in the Liberty party, the Free Soil party, the Conscience Whigs, and the Republican party that was formed in 1856. The Independent Repub-

lican party had an issue-driven focus reflecting its constituent interests and was thereby committed to abolitionist principles and opposed to many aspects of the Lincoln administration's conduct of the war. If the Independent Republican party had continued campaigning through the general election, it would have continued the previous disposition to factionalism and exacerbated the electoral cleavages of the early period of the third party system. Based on this hypothesis, it seems reasonable to assume that the Republican party's capacity to pursue victory in the war, to guide Reconstruction, and to dominate national politics as it did during the remainder of the nineteenth century would all have been compromised had the Independent Republican candidates not withdrawn. It was very significant that the Independent Republican party leadership was persuaded to endorse the Lincoln-Johnson ticket and did not challenge the Republican party, which was calling itself the Union party during this election. This persuasion included the capitulation of Republican leadership with some of their concerns, which in turn shaped the Union party's position on Reconstruction and impacted the political crisis that unfolded with President Johnson.

The issues that defined the Independent Republican party were largely the issues of the Civil War itself, most particularly slavery and emancipation. The Independent Republican party was associated with the Radical Republicans in Congress, from whose ranks were drawn many of the leaders and strongest supporters of the Independent Republican party.

On May 31, 1864, there were 350 people who

John C. Frémont—shown in this daguerreotype from the 1850s—served as the Republican party's first presidential candidate in 1856. Eight years later, he became the favored choice of the Independent Republicans, a brief-lived breakaway faction of radical congressmen seeking an alternative to Lincoln in the 1864 election. (*Courtesy of the Library of Congress*)

attended the first and only Independent Republican convention held in Cleveland, Ohio. The chairman of the convention was General John Cochrane of New York, who would be the party nominee for vice president. John C. Frémont of California was selected as the party nominee for president. Frémont was born in Georgia and was educated at Charleston College, but was expelled and thus never graduated. He moved westward in search of adventure and can be variously characterized as a soldier, explorer, tycoon, failed-businessman, adventurer, and politician. In 1850, he was elected to the U.S. Senate from California.

Frémont had been the Republican party nominee in 1856 and, at the age of 43, had been one of the youngest men to ever be nominated for president. In 1860, he was a rival to Lincoln for the Republican nomination. Frémont was an outspoken opponent of slavery, and when the Independent Republicans gathered in Cleveland, he was the obvious choice for the nomination. Frémont was not present and did not actively seek the nomination, though he reluctantly accepted it for a brief period. In September 1864, Frémont and Cochrane were persuaded by Lincoln and the national Republican leadership to withdraw in support of the Lincoln-Johnson ticket.

The Independent Republican party platform included provisions that called for the preservation of the union, observance of the rule of law, use of force to suppress rebellion and that suppression of rebellion be without compromise, recognition that Reconstruction is primarily a congressional issue, demand that the Monroe Doctrine be enforced against any anti-republican government in North America, and a general endorsement of confiscation and redistribution of property held by those in rebellion. Slavery being a paramount issue, the platform argued for de facto constitutional interpretation that "the rebellion has destroyed slavery" and now an "absolute equality before the law" should be established. Included in the platform were calls for constitutional amendments that would protect the equality of all men before the law, place a one-term limit on the presidency, and allow for the president and vice president to be elected by direct popular vote. Many of these issues would form a substantive policy basis for Republican administrations throughout the remainder of the period and would be important components of later progressive and governmental reform efforts.

MICHAEL HAIL

See also: Free Soil Party; Liberty Party.

Bibliography

Havel, James T. *U.S. Presidential Candidates and the Elections,* Vol. 1. New York: Simon and Schuster, 1996.

Johnson, Donald Bruce. *National Party Platforms,* Vol. 1. Urbana: University of Illinois Press, 1978.

Kleppner, Paul. *The Third Electoral System, 1853–1892.* Chapel Hill: University of North Carolina Press, 1979.

Kruschke, Earl R., ed. *Encyclopedia of Third Parties in the United States.* Santa Barbara: ABC-CLIO, 1991.

Mazmanian, Daniel A. *Third Parties in Presidential Elections.* Washington, DC: Brookings Institution, 1974.

McKee, Thomas Hudson. *The National Conventions and Platforms of All Political Parties, 1789–1905.* New York: Burt Franklin, 1906.

Schapsmeier, Edward L., and Frederick H. Schapsmeier. *Political Parties and Civic Action Groups.* Westport, CT: Greenwood, 1981.

Zornow, William F. *Lincoln and the Party Divided.* Norman: University of Oklahoma Press, 1954.

INDEPENDENT-SOCIALIST PARTY

1958–1960s

High hopes that were not quite realized marked the history of the Independent-Socialist Party (ISP), which launched a gubernatorial slate on the New York ballot in 1958. The candidates in the race were all former officials of the American Labor party (ALP), including John T. McManus, editor of the progressive newsweekly, *The National Guardian*, who ran for governor, and Corliss T. Lamont, an active progressive civil libertarian who ran for senator. The Socialist Workers party (Trotskyists) was significantly involved in the organization, and the hope was to combine forces so as to put the party permanently on the ballot by polling over 50,000 votes throughout the state. Enough nominating signatures were gathered to put the party on the ballot (over 26,000), but the final vote fell slightly short of the 50,000 votes for governor needed to secure a ballot position for the following year. Former ALP leaders Henry Abrams and Morris Goldin sent a letter announcing the organization of the United Independent-Socialist Campaign Committee after much of the preliminary work had been finalized. Their letter dates the initiation of the united effort as January 17, 1958, and was addressed to "some 40 prominent individuals representing the various tendencies on the left." An important participant in the series of meetings that followed, described by Abrams and Goldin as a "Continuations Committee," was the Socialist Workers party, the primary representative of which was Murry Weiss.

The formation of the ISP may have begun with the Twentieth Congress of the Communist party in Moscow when Premier Nikita Khrushchev revealed the crimes of the Stalin regime, causing many American Communists to abandon the Communist Party USA (CPUSA). The CPUSA had maintained a position of supporting "progressive" Democratic party candidates. The Socialist Workers party (SWP), with a long tradition of fielding independent, openly socialist candidates wherever possible, approached former leaders of the ALP and together joined a call for a nominating conference at the Great Northern Hotel, June 13–15, 1958. In addition to a large number of former ALP leaders, including Dr. Annette T. Rubinstein, various representatives of left-wing organizations were invited to participate. Vincent Hallinan of California, who had been presidential candidate on the 1952 Progressive party ticket, was principal guest speaker. Approximately 500 people registered for the conference, which was to decide on candidates and the platform of a possible new electoral coalition. Another 200 sent in absentee registrations of support. African-American philosopher and writer Dr. W.E.B. Du Bois was an initial sponsor, and the artist Rockwell Kent supported the campaign. The CPUSA sent Arnold Johnson as its spokesperson, and heated debates marked the three-day conference. The Socialist Party–Social-Democratic Federation (SP-SDF) had been invited to participate, but declined. In fact, the word "United" had to be removed from the original name of the United Independent-Socialist party, under threat of suit from the SP-SDF. The Socialist Labor party declined outright any invitation to participate.

The primary issue was whether to launch a full slate with McManus in the gubernatorial position, or to confine efforts to a senatorial race, with the possibility of running Corliss Lamont in that spot. Lamont had polled over 100,000 votes as the ALP senatorial candidate in 1952. The chief point of the Communist spokespersons was that to withdraw Left workers from the bid of the official labor leadership to support W. Averell Harriman as the Democratic party nominee would be "sectarian." A July 27 editorial in *The Worker* put it clearly: The challenge to the gubernatorial bid by W. Averell Harriman was "destined to come into a frontal clash with the labor movement." The CPUSA supported the position of running just the senatorial candidate, possibly Lamont, not a full ticket. Those in favor of mounting a full ticket argued that a real challenge that would be avowedly socialist was necessary as a "peace" effort in the campaign.

Those officially speaking at the 1958 conference included Henry N. Abrams; former ALP leader McManus; Joyce Cowley, SWP 1957 mayoral candidate; Richard DeHaan of the Young Socialist Alliance (YSA); Dr. Rubinstein; and Muriel McAvoy, widow of ALP leader Clifford McAvoy. The debate over the issue of the single-candidate slate was a heated one, but ultimately a resounding majority voted to launch a full slate. Arnold Johnson withdrew from the conference after the defeat of the one-candidate proposal. The door, however, was held open by the anti-CPUSA victors for the CPUSA's participation in the selection of a slate and possible compromise amendments to the platform.

The final slate, a full one, was headed by McManus, who had a record of active organizing experience in the Newspaper Guild. Other candidates included Dr. Annette T. Rubinstein, former head of the Robert Louis Stevenson School and editor of *I Vote My Conscience*, the speeches and writings of Vito Marcantonio. Well-known for her work as a Marxist literary authority and for her ALP and Progressive party political activity, Dr. Rubinstein was the only woman in a major position in the race. Similarly, the candidate for comptroller, Hugh N. Mulzac, was the only African American in the statewide field. Mulzac had been promoted to captain of the merchant marine ship *Booker T. Washington*, a World War II "Liberty" ship with an integrated crew. Mulzac served as its skipper from 1942 to 1947, when he had been blacklisted for radical activity. Also a former ALP candidate, Scott K. Gray, Jr., an upstate farmer and lawyer, ran for attorney general.

To some, it seemed strange for the SWP to throw all its support into getting the ISP onto the ballot. After all, everyone on the ISP slate was a former member of the ALP and the Socialist Workers had never supported the ALP. One possible explanation was the wartime antifascist popular front. With the CPUSA backing liberals and left-wing Democrats—per instructions from the Communist International—the SWP might have seen the ALP as a means to bring socialists into the Democratic party. Indeed, Roosevelt headed the ALP ticket as a fusion candidate and many Democratic candidates frequently received ALP backing.

As McManus pointed out in a published radio address: "The Independent-Socialist party is evidence of the hope of a core of [the American Labor Party's] former voters to re-establish a political voice in our state, independent of the two old parties. But there is this difference: that whereas the American Labor party did not embrace socialist objectives, the Independent-Socialist party does, in the conviction that wars, depressions, and exploitation of minorities cannot be ended in an economic system run solely for profit, and not primarily for the people's benefit."

The SWP greeted the move in an editorial in *The Militant*, its newsweekly: "For our part, we pledge our unstinting support to a campaign that marks a big step forward in the revitalization of the socialist movement. We are confident the campaign will help to unite a long-divided socialist camp." Invitations to participate in the organization of the coalition were sent to leaders and members of all socialist tendencies and to independents. Subsequent meetings resulted in the call for the campaign and program.

The Militant editorial continued: "The campaign will bring presently inactive socialists back to active duty and it will win many new adherents to socialism. Its salutary effect will not be limited to New York. It will help rebuild the socialist movement across the country."

The next step was to put together a platform that all could agree on. The Mideast offensive—air attacks on Lebanon—was the deciding factor for Corliss Lamont. Uncertain whether he could run, due to other commitments, Lamont, son of millionaire Thomas W. Lamont and long-time civil liberties and pro-peace educator, announced his candidacy at a press conference on July 18. The landing of American and British troops in the Middle East, gravely increasing the threat of World War III, caused him to put aside all other considerations in order to speak out for peace. Lamont had polled better than 120,000 votes as ALP candidate for U.S. senator in 1952.

The final platform was composed and put forward by a steering committee made up of the former ALP leaders, SWP and YSA leaders, and a coalition of independent socialists. The preamble to the platform hit hard against the Democratic party, especially incumbent governor W. Averell Harriman. The main point was to establish the ISP as a "peace" party in the wake of air strikes in Lebanon, cold war politics, witch-hunt attacks on the Left, and the worsening recession. The platform declared that the Democratic and Republican parties promoted "bi-partisan Truman and Eisenhower 'doctrines.' " The platform accused the Democratic and Republican parties of being "committed to brink-of-war policies which cannot fail to involve the world in catastrophic conflict unless reversed," and being responsible for the cold war atmosphere, the danger of nuclear buildup, and, close to home, for anti-labor legislation.

In a direct hit at labor leadership support for Harriman, the ISP platform noted that Democratic Governor Harriman and the Republican majority in the state legislature were continuing the reactionary policies of the previous Republican administration under Dewey, including the Security Risk Law, the Feinberg Law, and the Condon-Wadlin Act—all of which targeted left-wingers, liberals, and trade unionists.

The platform took special note of the need for civil rights for minority peoples and for special facilities for working mothers. Of great importance was the fact that the last third of the platform was devoted to delineating reasons why the failure of capitalism pointed to "the socialist alternative to the greed, brutalization, repression, economic insecurity, and war-making tendency of capitalism." Still, the platform called for the voters to register a "protest" vote against the two major parties and the capitalist system. The point was not to promise that socialism could be achieved through the ballot box; rather, the importance of the campaign was to shore up independent forces. As the platform cited, "Throughout the house of labor is heard the repeated demand for an independent political course that will open the way to a labor party able to offer America the choice of a labor government."

The ISP was hit, especially by the SP-SDF and some major newspapers, for blaming all ills of the cold war era on the United States and for being uncritical of the Soviet system. To this one ISP spokesperson replied, "We're citizens of this country—not Russia. It's here that we can exert more influence—not there." Lamont added: "I have been critical of civil liberties in the Soviet Union, . . . but despite the dictatorial aspects of the Soviet regime, I think we can work out agreements in international affairs." McManus summed up the ISP position in reply to charges that all involved were pro-Soviet: "Our common denominator is peace. Our collective hope lies in a search for socialist alternatives to the eternal profit system's cycle of boom, bust, and war."

To get on the ballot in New York State required arduous work by SWP and YSA crews, helped by independent socialists. Signature-gathering was organized by Mrs. McAvoy, Morris Goldin, and SWP local leader Richard Garza. Because teams had to be fielded to all sixty-two Upstate counties to obtain signatures, it was inevitable that former independent progressives close to the pro-Soviet camp came in close proximity with Trotskyists. New friendships and alliances formed, some of them lasting. Ultimately, the ISP did garner more than

26,000 nominating signatures and overcame two challenges to establish its name on the New York ballot. As a result, the ISP was granted more than $100,000 in radio and television air time with which to spread the socialist message. McManus's citywide vote was 23,538; Lamont received 37,992 citywide and better than 50,000 statewide. However, since the senatorial vote does not decide ballot status in New York, the failure of the gubernatorial candidate to poll the necessary 50,000 meant that the party had not achieved ballot status for the following election.

However, the elan of the joint effort carried through the elections. As the *New York Post* noted, although the ISP "did not receive the 50,000 votes necessary for it to be listed on the next election ballot, McManus said it would 'stay in business.'" Specifically, a nationwide call went out for a convention in Cleveland on November 28–30, 1958, featuring McManus and Vincent Hallinan, intended to consider a possible merging of forces for the 1960 election campaign. That electoral merger failed to materialize on a nationwide basis, but united electoral actions spun off in Seattle and in several centers in the Midwest. ISP campaigner Elinor Ferry noted that British Labour Member of Parliament Harold Davies reported that the British were watching the American amalgam closely. Reverberations in the United States led to joint actions among various tendencies on the Left— many of whom had first come together in the ISP. Some of these actions included support of free travel to Cuba, opposition to the Vietnam War, opposition to Jim Crow laws in the South, and support of voter registration drives among African Americans there; however, no further direct unified electoral action occurred among the same or similar forces. In short, the ISP disappeared as an electoral force and party.

NORA RUTH ROBERTS

See also: American Labor Party; Progressive Party, 1948; Socialist Workers Party.

Bibliography

Abrams, Henry P., and Morris Golden. General letter in behalf of ISP, August 1958. (Tamiment Library holdings).

"Answer to a Dilemma." Editors. *The National Guardian,* June 2, 1958.

"The CP and Corliss Lamont." Editors. *The Militant,* July 24, 1958.

"Excerpts from Floor Debate on Electoral Policy." *The Militant,* June 30, 1958.

Feinberg, Alexander. "Leftists to Press for a Full Slate." *The New York Times,* June 16, 1958.

"For Democracy, Planned Economy, and Socialism." Editors. *The National Guardian,* June 23, 1958.

"A Great Step Forward." Editors. *The Militant,* July 18, 1958.

"Group in Seattle Plans United Socialist Ticket." *The Militant,* August 11, 1958.

"Groups on Left Weigh Unity in 1960 Election." *New York Post,* November 7, 1958.

"Independent-Socialists Vote for a Full Slate in N.Y. State Elections." *National Guardian,* June 2, 1958.

Pilat, Oliver. "Leftist Group to Run Lamont for Senator." *New York Post,* July 27, 1958.

———. "Leftists Change Party Name to Avoid Lawsuit by Socialists." *New York Post,* July 25, 1958.

———. "Leftists Start Choosing Ticket after Walkout by Communists." *New York Post,* June 16, 1958.

"Platform of the Independent-Socialist Party." (Tamiment Library holdings).

Platform Statement, Independent-Socialist Party, August 1958. (Tamiment Library holdings).

Ring, Harry. "Anti-War Ticket Begins Campaign." *The Militant,* July 23, 1958.

———. "Debate Over Socialist Political Action." *The Militant,* June 30, 1958.

———. "Lamont, McManus, Rubinstein to Run; Lebanon Invasion Hit." *The Militant,* July 18, 1958, p. 2.

Wershba, Joseph. "New Party, Led by Ex-ALPers, Seeks 50,000 Votes in State." *New York Times,* October 30, 1958.

☆✶☆✶☆✶☆✶☆✶☆✶☆✶☆✶☆✶☆✶☆
JOBLESS PARTY
1932

The Jobless party was founded in 1932 in St. Louis, Missouri, by Father James Renshaw Cox. The historical context was that of the Great Depression, with high unemployment and great public dissatisfaction with incumbent Republican President Herbert Hoover. The 1932 platform of the Jobless party called for nationalization of all banks, confiscation of personal fortunes, government relief for the poor, and federally financed public works programs to provide employment for the jobless. The Jobless party temporarily joined forces with the Liberty party in the 1932 election campaign, but the two parties were unable to agree on a presidential candidate to represent the joint parties. Father Cox subsequently represented the Jobless party as its presidential candidate, receiving 741 votes (less than 0.01 percent of the overall votes cast in the election). William H. Harvey represented the Liberty party, receiving greater support than Cox with 53,199 votes. The Jobless party was dissolved after the election of 1932. The party never received much support beyond personal support for Father Cox, and the concerns of the Jobless party were largely addressed by programs implemented by Democratic President Franklin Delano Roosevelt following his election in 1932.

The Jobless party held one convention in its brief history. The convention was in St. Louis on August 17, 1932, and it was planned to be a joint convention with the Liberty party. When the two parties disagreed over leadership, however, they held separate conventions. The Jobless party convention was scheduled for two days, but when Father Cox faced no opposition as presidential nominee, the convention ended after the first day. Father Cox, who was from Pittsburgh, brought about 500 supporters with him from Pennsylvania to St. Louis, and he received a fifteen-minute ovation when his name was put forward for the presidential nomination. Dr. V.C. Tisdal of Elk City, Oklahoma, accepted the nomination as the Jobless party's candidate for vice president. Convention delegates adopted Father Cox's eighteen-point platform for social relief and economic reform, and Father Cox focused on his economic platform in his acceptance speech. The Jobless party's campaign for the presidency was cut short, ending in September 1932 when the party ran out of money.

The Jobless party was one of many third parties that represented the view that the Republican and Democratic parties were inadequate to cope with the problems of the Great Depression and that a state of national emergency required bolder actions than either of the major parties were likely to consider. The party received far fewer votes than the other third parties on the ballot in 1932, including the Socialist, Communist, Prohibition, Liberty, Socialist Labor, and Farmer Labor parties, whose presidential candidates each received at least twice as many votes as Father Cox. The Jobless party received most of its support from Father Cox's supporters from Pennsylvania. Most voters who were attracted to the social and economic recovery programs proposed by the Jobless party voted for Roosevelt. The concerns represented by the Jobless party were largely addressed by the New Deal programs of President Roosevelt, and Cox was appointed by Roosevelt to serve on the Pennsylvania State Board of the

National Recovery Administration, a central element of President Roosevelt's plan for economic recovery. President Roosevelt's Works Progress Administration, a national program that provided jobs for workers engaged in building roads, schools, bridges, and other projects, embodied the concerns of the public works plank of the Jobless party.

Father Cox was born in Pittsburgh in 1886, and he died in 1951. As a child, Cox believed that he was saved from going blind by a miracle from God. Cox had promised that he would become a priest if his sight was saved, and he followed through with his promise. Father Cox became pastor of St. Patrick's Church in Pittsburgh, and he became well known in Western Pennsylvania. From 1925 until his death in 1951, Father Cox delivered a series of radio addresses in Western Pennsylvania; 101 of his later addresses remain available. Father Cox's radio addresses reflect the commitment to social action on behalf of the economically disadvantaged that marked the 1932 presidential campaign of the Jobless party and Father Cox's work on behalf of the National Recovery Administration during the presidency of Franklin Delano Roosevelt.

VIRGINIA A. CHANLEY

Bibliography

"Jobless Name Cox, End Convention." *New York Times,* August 18, 1933.

Rosenstone, Steven J.; Roy L. Behr; and Edward H. Lazarus. *Third Parties in America: Citizen Response to Major Party Failure.* Princeton: Princeton University Press, 1996.

Schapsmeier, Edward L., and Frederick H. Schapsmeier. *Political Parties and Civic Action Groups.* Westport, CT: Greenwood Press, 1981.

Witt, Sally A. "Hell Was Not Made for Us: Father James R. Cox and the Catholic Church of Pittsburgh in the 1940s." Master's thesis, Duquesne University, 1989.

KNOW-NOTHING PARTY
1850s

ORIGINS OF THE PARTY

The Know-Nothing party was founded in the early 1850s. It began as a secret society, the Order of the Star Spangled Banner, whose members, when asked about anti-immigrant and anti-Catholic activities in their neighborhood, replied, "I know nothing." It originally drew its support largely from highly fearful evangelical Protestant groups, mostly in the northeastern states. Antagonisms between different ethnic and religious groups, a deeply embedded anti-Catholicism, and much nativist-driven wariness about the dangers of continued immigration into the United States had long been significant aspects of American culture. These inchoate feelings exploded into organized and sustained political resistance, first at the local level in the 1840s, when, against the backdrop of outbursts of intense awakenings of religious spirit, anti-Catholicism was reinvigorated and became more focused among many Americans.

Specifically, some political activists became increasingly aware of what they perceived as a very dangerous threat to dominant American values and forcefully articulated the need to organize a native American political movement to thwart the dangers they confronted. What they believed to be an uncontrollable, dangerous flood of immigrants, particularly Catholics from Ireland and Germany, had begun to enter the United States in the mid-1840s, when severe crop failures and ensuing famine in Western Europe caused the number of immigrants from Ireland and Germany to swell to record numbers.

These immigrants brought with them both their commitment to their faith and the growing apparatus of the Catholic church, with its priests, nuns, and bishops alike. Such posed an ominous threat to Protestant America, particularly since priests, nativists believed, so clearly controlled the voting decisions of the new immigrants and would use that control to advance a Catholic agenda, not to protect American values. Catholic voters, according to one nativist newspaper, "band together naturally" at the polls. "Religious superstition, hatred of the Protestants, and the commands of their Roman leaders, keep them together under all circumstances." In this context, the extended visit of a papal nuncio, Gaetano Bedini, to the United States in 1853, allegedly to settle an internal church dispute, provoked extreme reactions and fears among those quick to note evidence of growing papal power on American soil.

Immigrants also brought great social evils with them from the "hellholes" of Europe, evils that, after a decade, could clearly be seen, particularly in the major eastern cities of the United States. The increasing social decay could be seen in the immigrant-filled prisons and poor houses; in the rapid decline of many neighborhoods due to the expansion of saloons and the loutish public behavior, even on the Sabbath, that usually accompanied them; in the economic distress caused by labor competition; and in the powerful political agenda manifested by the immigrants and their spokesmen, an agenda seeking to promote state aid for parochial schools and laws allowing the church to expand its control of property, and its power, in the United States.

A proto-eugenics message characterizes this American Party (Know-Nothing) print of the ideal Anglo-Saxon American. Produced in 1854, it was meant to contrast the ideal (native-born) American with Catholic Irish immigrants, usually depicted in cartoons at the time as snub-nosed, apelike creatures. (*Courtesy of the Library of Congress*)

FORMATION OF THE PARTY

These fears first galvanized organized political reaction at the local level. In the early 1840s, candidates of the nativist National Republican party did well in New York City elections. The party also had some success in Philadelphia, electing a congressman, Louis Levin, three times beginning in 1844 on an anti-immigrant platform. But these victories were only the beginning of what nativists believed needed to be done. A decade later, the situation and the threat posed had grown worse in nativist

eyes, far beyond the boundaries of a single locality. Something was going wrong in America, and, to them, its cause was self-evident. It seemed clear, therefore, that the time had come for a national political organization that would aggressively promote and protect American values and American freedoms against the Catholic-immigrant menace. The Know-Nothing party was the result.

The Know-Nothings' determination to challenge and destabilize the existing political system was promoted as well by what they saw as the misbehavior of both major parties and the sagging fortunes of the Whig party, once considered friendly to nativist impulses and capable of winning national power. Part of the Know-Nothing appeal was their challenge to the way politics had been traditionally organized and implemented in the United States since the Jackson period. Politics, as practiced by the old parties, had grown complacent and accommodating; it had lost its bite, succumbed too readily to compromise, and avoided the critical issues. The dominant old parties were increasingly out of step with the needs of the nation faced with danger and disruptive change.

OPPOSITION TO MAJOR PARTIES

In particular, the political problem, as the emerging Know-Nothings saw it, was that both of the old parties seemed indifferent and certainly unresponsive to the alien threat posed to American life. They were too committed to their traditional ways, particularly their need for immigrant support at the polls. The Democrats' role was clear. From the beginning of the republic, they had enjoyed the votes of Irish Catholics, and they would never willingly turn away from them. In fact, the Democrats would always encourage further immigration and promote the achievement of the Catholic program in every way that they could, whatever the consequences for America. Furthermore, the party had come under the thumb of southern slavery expansionists, intent on their own destructive purposes, in need of immigrants' votes to accomplish their goals, and little interested in the problems posed by the great wave of Catholics flooding the streets and alleys of the Northeast.

The Whigs, in the meantime, seemed to have lost their ability to win significant national power and their willingness to confront the "demonic" Democrats with their Catholic and slave-state support. Shamefully, Whig leaders had also begun to make overtures to the Irish as well (in the presidential election of 1852). Apparently they believed that this was the only means they had of winning national elections. Nativists saw that there was no political salvation to be had there. Dedicated, therefore, to replacing dated political parties and dispensing with the anti-democratic political practices the parties pawned, and with new vigor and insight drawn from fresh faces in the political world, nativist leaders stressed an anti-party argument that denounced the old ways of doing things in American politics.

The increasing political restiveness on the national landscape exploded into a significant electoral standing in 1854, as two new parties, the Know-Nothings and the antislavery Republicans, emerged to challenge the status quo, attracting significant support from voters drawn away from the old parties and from new voters, turning out to protest the dominant Democrats and the weakened Whigs. Both new parties did well; both had enthusiastic supporters. It was not clear, at first, which of these new parties could replace the increasingly reeling Whigs to become the second major party in the American political system.

Unlike their Republican adversaries, the emerging Know-Nothings drew strength in the southern states. In some of them—Maryland and Louisiana, for example—clusters of Catholic immigrants stimulated nativist anti-Democratic responses. Elsewhere in the South, the party drew significant support from those seeking a non-Democratic and non-sectional alternative to the fast-expiring Whig party. The Know-Nothings offered to these people a means of remaining active in electoral politics,

a weapon with which they could continue their twenty-year war against the hated Democrats.

Surprisingly, despite their claims of being non-traditional, the Know-Nothings organized themselves in similar fashion to the other political parties of the day, with an institutional apparatus of committees, caucuses and conventions, an apparatus that allowed the rank and file to express themselves and provided room for party leaders to select and sharpen the components of their advocacy and to use their skills to mobilize voters to their side. Using strident and exaggerated rhetoric in their newspapers, printed pamphlets, and speeches at campaign rallies—a tactic also borrowed from the existing parties—the Know-Nothing leaders attracted voter attention, raised the political temperature, and prepared the ground to bring out their armies on election day. Their leaders kept careful tabs on their supporters, drawing up voter lists and endeavoring to ensure that all those sympathetic to the cause came out to vote. All of these organizing and electioneering techniques had infused the old party system as the best way to accomplish their specific electoral and legislative purposes. They continued to be at the center of activities in the emerging party system as well.

KNOW-NOTHING PLATFORM

The Know-Nothings' policy agenda reflected their claim that they were a reform movement. Their leaders exploited the idea that America's republican institutions and its social stability were in great danger from the alien influx. They pushed, therefore, for a series of local and state policies to contain the threat before them and to establish means that would change the outlook and behavior of the dangerous classes. Their reform agenda advocated the use of the Protestant King James Version of the Bible in public schools, schools that were to be taught by native-born, impartial, professional teachers, not Catholic nuns. They wanted legislatures to enact Sunday "blue laws" designed to restrict what they believed to be the excessive liquor consumption and other anti-social behavior of the threatening immigrants on the Lord's day.

Most of all, they wanted to limit, even proscribe, the immigrants from active involvement in American politics. Nativists argued that immigrant electoral practices were dominated by fraud that corrupted the whole political process: Some northern states permitted aliens to vote if they indicated an intention to become citizens—a practice that infuriated and frightened those who were drawn to the Know-Nothings. The latter advocated an end to that practice and, at the national level, a twenty-one-year period of residence in the United States before one could become a citizen. They demanded electoral registry laws to keep the lists of eligible voters pure and to prevent non-citizens from voting. They insisted that voters be able to read and write English and sought to limit office-holding to American citizens. Their pamphlets frequently repeated their belief that "Americans must rule America," which would never happen under Democratic or Whig control.

KNOW-NOTHING POLITICAL CAMPAIGNS

All of this paid off significantly at the polls at a number of critical moments in the mid-1850s. At first, nativists secretly supported sympathetic candidates of the two major parties. In 1854, they went public, running their own tickets, vigorously contesting a range of national, state, and local elections. They did very well at the state level that year and again in 1855, drawing support from erstwhile Whigs and Democrats and attracting previous non-voters. In New York State in 1855, the Know-Nothings came in second in a three-party race getting 34.1 percent of the vote, compared to the Democrats' 34.5 percent and the Republicans' 31.3 percent.

The Know-Nothings drew their support in the northern states largely, as was to be expected, from those Protestant groups, mainly lower- and middle-class artisans and small shopkeepers, whose commitment to their religious tradition made them particularly sensitive to the dangers posed by a growing Catholic presence in the United States. Such feelings were not limited to the large seaport cities where the number of immigrant Catholics had grown, and their "peculiar" lifestyles had become so evident to their immediate neighbors. People in small towns and rural areas in the religiously sensitive "Burnt Over" district of Upstate New York and in similar areas of New England, Pennsylvania, and Ohio witnessed a number of religious revivals over the past half-century, which reasserted the truth of the Protestant way and reminded people of the constant dangers posed by the Catholic threat to the Protestant religion and to the American republic.

The Know-Nothings showed much strength in the northwestern states as well, but not as much as the Republican party. There, concern for the territories and opposition to further southern expansion west of the Mississippi were the issue priorities among those politically involved. Whatever the anti-Catholicism in these states (and there was a great deal in Ohio, Indiana, and Michigan), the Know-Nothing policy agenda never took hold as widely and as prominently as it did further east. Still, the nativists remained, in these states as elsewhere, a force to be reckoned with by both Democrats and Republicans.

As a result of their strong showing in the polls in 1854 and 1855, the Know-Nothings were a significant element in a number of New England state legislatures and actually controlled the Massachusetts legislature while winning the governorship there as well. In the confused aftermath of the elections to Congress in those years, with anti-Democrats of different party identification in a majority, Nathaniel P. Banks, elected as a Know-Nothing from Massachusetts, was chosen as Speaker of the U.S. House of Representatives in late 1855. In the presidential election of 1856, the Know-Nothing candidate, Millard Fillmore from New York, who was the former Whig congressional leader, vice president, and president, won the electoral votes only of the state of Maryland, but garnered over 20 percent of the national popular vote, which was the largest third-party vote up to that time in an American election. Their vice-presidential candidate was Andrew Jackson Donelson, nephew of the great Democratic leader of an earlier generation, Andrew Jackson, and emblematic of the Know-Nothings' appeal across former party lines.

Given all that was occurring in these elections, some political observers believed that, with the strength they were already showing, the Know-Nothings would become the nation's second major party, easily outrunning the Republicans. Historian Michael Holt quotes one Cincinnati Whig in 1854 as saying that "the people do hate Catholics, and what happiness it was to thousands to have a chance to show it in what seemed like a lawful and patriotic manner"—that is, successfully at the polls. That powerful and persistent sentiment clearly was driving the growing strength behind Know-Nothing candidates and the party's emergence as a major national force.

DECLINE OF THE PARTY

The Know-Nothings, however, had reached their high-water mark. They had successfully contributed to a major disruption of American political patterns in 1854 and 1855, but they could not hold the field. They were unsuccessful in sustaining the strong position they had achieved at the outset of the electoral realignment. Too many things started to go wrong for them. Once in office, for example, Know-Nothing legislators were able to accomplish little, bedeviled by their own divisions over policy and competing priorities and by the active and clever resistance of their opponents. They were able to enact a few of their nativist-oriented policies in a number of states, including a suffrage law in Massachusetts that barred immigrants from voting for two years *after* they became citizens; other initiatives were deflected or defeated by their opponents. In Congress, the Know-Nothings were never numerous enough,

or effective enough, to make much headway against the hated immigrants. Having helped upset the political apple cart at the electoral level, Know-Nothings were unable to take as much advantage of the situation in which they found themselves as they and their supporters wanted and expected.

At the same time, despite their strength and appeal, Know-Nothing electoral support began to fade in the face of renewed confrontation over the further extension of slavery into the territories. In 1855, sectional tensions first rocked the party and severely compromised its potential. The same antislavery extension and anti-southern impulses that were drawing other northerners into the Republican party in the mid-1850s influenced many of the Know-Nothings. A number of these nativists, led by Henry Wilson of Massachusetts, pressed for a coalition of the two new parties combating the Democrats. Other Know-Nothing leaders resisted strongly and stressed the priority of the Catholic danger. It was not clear, however, which issues were the more central ones among voters and which party could find ways to win out among these northern constituencies.

The Know-Nothing leadership guessed wrong on these matters. At the meeting of the party's national council—its equivalent of a national convention—in Philadelphia in 1855, the assembled delegates fell in behind what many of the northerners among them saw as too much of a pro-southern position on slavery extension and the current difficulties in the territories, including supporting the highly controversial Kansas-Nebraska Act. Some, therefore, walked out in protest, to form, at first, a Northern American party, the Know-Somethings, dedicated to opposing the extension of slavery and resisting the power of the Catholic church and its too pliant minions.

The Know-Nothings were also hurt by their developing reputation for violence, thanks to a number of highly publicized incidents that their opponents played on repeatedly to good effect. Fairly or otherwise, Know-Nothings were blamed for bloody election-day riots at the polls in 1854 and 1855, directed against would-be Catholic voters. Politics in the United States had always had a violent edge to it, with occasional confrontations and the disruption of orderly electoral proceedings. In the Know-Nothing years, this, it was claimed, had grown much worse with increased reports of voter intimidation and mob disruptions, including some episodes in which would-be voters were killed.

As a result of these incidents, and the fact that the Know-Nothings were blamed for them, some "respectable" nativists reacted in horror, with many looking elsewhere for an effective, but more acceptable, political means of dealing with the growing threats to the republic's stability and liberties. The association of nativists with such violence was clearly overblown by the party's opponents for political purposes, but its effect on the Know-Nothings' fortunes was no less important whatever the exaggeration.

At the same time, after 1855, Know-Nothing prospects were hurt when a sharp dropoff in immigration into the United States occurred. The European economy had begun to recover from its severe downturn of the previous few years, and increasingly Irish and Germans elected to stay at home rather than emigrate to the United States. As the number of immigrants entering the country fell, so did much of the concern among many Americans over the consequences of their numbers and presence. Know-Nothing leaders kept up their warnings of the prime danger as vigorously as they had ever done, but the immediate situation no longer worked to their advantage.

In 1856, the extreme violence, murder, and arson in Kansas between free-state and slave-state settlers, and the caning of the antislavery Senator Charles Sumner on the Senate floor by a southern congressman, all on behalf of sectional claims and rights, seemed to demonstrate the extremism of the southerners and their willingness to do anything necessary in pursuit of their own interests. Sectional tensions increased significantly as the fallout from Kansas and subsequent controversies further fueled confrontation between the North and South over the nation's future. Those tensions had been on the scene since 1854, but now they came full force to the center of the political stage. In the face of such southern determination, other matters be-

gan to seem less potent politically, at least to some of those who had loyally supported the Know-Nothings in 1854 and 1855.

Republican leaders shrewdly began to take advantage of the shifting political environment, using the North's rising anti-southernism to increase their wooing of Know-Nothing voters. They desperately attempted to reduce the number of anti-Democratic parties in the field by uniting the various pieces under their banner. As the editor of the *Chicago Tribune* wrote, the Republican party was "the avowed and mortal enemy" of slavery, but it was "not less the opponent of partisan schemes of political Catholicism." Therefore, another Republican spokesman suggested the party should have as its central principle "opposition to Despotism—whether the seat of its power be in the papal chair of Rome or on a Cotton Plantation of the South."

The Republicans increasingly pressed such notions. More to the point, in particular, the Republicans' willingness to support Know-Nothing initiatives helped ease the transition and draw many into the Republican coalition. Republicans nominated Know-Nothings for office on their tickets; Republican platforms, especially at the state level, adopted Know-Nothing planks; and Republican-controlled state legislatures pushed to enact Know-Nothing proposals. As a result, a sympathetic interaction between the different groups began to dominate matters, an interaction that allowed voters to combine nativism and antislavery, successfully drawing more and more Know-Nothings into the Republican ranks.

Southern Know-Nothings could not follow a similar path. Many of them, pained by the increasing defections of their northern brethren to the Republicans, continued to work through a separate organization to challenge the dominant Democrats and to keep the opposition flags of nativism, conservatism, unionism, and Whiggery alive throughout the South. In the late 1850s they continued to draw varying levels of support from Maryland and Virginia southward, but with little help from their former northern colleagues who were increasingly disconnected from them. At the same time, given the party's stumbling, many of its supporters in both the North and South dropped out of participation in active politics entirely.

As a result, by 1860, the Know-Nothings had disappeared as a national party, or as an effective independent political force despite the vigorous efforts of some of them to maintain their institution and their stance. Some continued to fight as Constitutional Unionists, or as members of other parties in that year, but times had moved beyond the Know-Nothings as an independent organization. The sorting-out process had gone in favor of the Republicans. Nevertheless, the underlying impulses that had led to their organization as a political party still remained cogent to many Americans in that year and were a prominent part of the nation's political discourse and combat through the rest of the nineteenth century, with the Republicans identified, among other things, as the Know-Nothing party's successor.

In the best Know-Nothing manner, Republican campaign rhetoric unrelentingly assailed the Democrats throughout the 1870s and 1880s for their continued support of Irish immigration and the Catholic church, regardless of the danger that such rhetoric posed to inflaming ethnic hatred. The Democrats responded in kind, marking the Republicans as the enemy of outsiders in America, the successors to the departing Know-Nothings, equally determined to use national power to impose what Democrats called narrow Yankee, or "Puritan" (i.e., New England), values and restrictions on the nation's pluralist population. As is often the case, in short, while the Know-Nothings' brief history had ended and the party had disappeared, the basic elements of the party's platform had been absorbed into the existing party system to remain an important part of its outlook and attraction to the voters.

JOEL H. SILBEY

See also: Millard Fillmore; National Republican Party; Whig Party.

Bibliography

Anbinder, Tyler. *Nativism and Slavery: The Northern Know-Nothings and the Politics of the 1850s.* New York: Oxford University Press, 1992.

Baker, Jean. *Ambivalent Americans: The Know-Nothing Party in Maryland.* Baltimore: Johns Hopkins University Press, 1977.

Billington, Ray. *The Protestant Crusade, 1800–1860: A Study of the Origins of American Nativism.* Chicago: University of Chicago Press, 1964.

Gienapp, William. *The Origins of the Republican Party, 1852–1856.* New York: Oxford University Press, 1988.

Holt, Michael. "The Anti-Masonic and Know-Nothing Parties." In *History of the U.S. Political Parties,* Vol. 1. Ed. Arthur M. Schlesinger, Jr. New York: Chelsea House, 1973.

Knobel, Dale T. *Paddy and the Republic: Ethnicity and Nationality in Antebellum America.* Middletown, CT: Wesleyan University Press, 1986.

Mulkhearn, John R. *The Know-Nothing Party in Massachusetts: The Rise and Fall of a People's Movement.* Boston: Northeastern University Press, 1990.

Overdyke, W. Darrell. *The Know-Nothing Party in the South.* Baton Rouge: Louisiana State University Press, 1950.

Rayback, Robert J. *Millard Fillmore: Biography of a President.* Buffalo: Buffalo Historical Society, 1959.

☆☆☆☆☆☆☆☆☆☆☆☆☆☆☆☆☆☆☆☆☆☆☆☆☆☆☆☆☆☆☆☆☆☆☆☆☆☆

LABOR PARTY MOVEMENT

1930s

The standard political accounts of the labor movement in the 1930s emphasize labor's swing from a nonpartisan stance to support of President Franklin D. Roosevelt and the Democratic party in exchange for pro-labor legislation. Forgotten is the fact that a major section of organized labor attempted—for the last time in American history—to forge a labor party in America at that time. Built on the innumerable local labor party campaigns of 1932–36, which sprang spontaneously and simultaneously into existence and groped toward national coordination, the movement suggests that the loyalty of organized labor could by no means be taken for granted by Roosevelt and the Democrats, even as late as the summer of 1936.

All told, a remarkable number of independent labor and farmer-labor parties sprang up between the years 1932 and 1936. The list of towns where such groups fielded their own candidates for local office includes Cambridge, New Bedford, and Springfield, Massachusetts; Berlin and Lincoln, New Hampshire; Danbury and Hartford, Connecticut; Buffalo and New York City, New York; Allentown, Philadelphia,

and the Beaver Valley of Pennsylvania; Akron, Canton, and Toledo, Ohio; Detroit, Hamtramck, and Port Huron, Michigan; Chicago and Hillsboro, Illinois; Sioux Falls, South Dakota; Everett and Goldbar, Washington; and San Francisco, California. Moreover, in at least ten other communities central labor unions endorsed the idea of a labor party, as did the state federations of Labor of Rhode Island, Connecticut, Vermont, New Jersey, and Wisconsin. In Berlin, New Hampshire, a strong local Farmer-Labor party based in the French-Canadian pulp workers elected a mayor and majority of the city council and dominated the industrial town into the 1950s. Over 150 union locals in Connecticut endorsed the formation of a labor party, as did the Maine Textile Council and two top Federation of Labor officials in Maine. In Indiana the Gibson County Central Labor Union, the first labor body in the state to endorse the movement, won the support of nine locals and the Kokomo Central Labor Union for the formation of a local labor party. In 1935, fourteen trade unions and farm organizations in South Dakota founded a state Farmer-Labor party. Theatrical troupes from Brookwood Labor College, the

This panoramic shot shows delegates to the first national convention of the Labor party, Chicago, November 22, 1919. *(Burke and Friedmann, November 22, 1919, courtesy of the Library of Congress)*

foremost labor educational institution of the time, toured industrial centers performing plays that promoted the creation of an independent labor party. National unions such as the United Textile Workers, the Brotherhood of Sleeping Car Porters, and the American Newspaper Guild endorsed the formation of an independent labor party, as did the Southern Tenant Farmers Union. At the 1935 convention of the American Federation of Labor—the convention at which the Congress of Industrial Organizations (CIO) was born—no less than thirteen national unions submitted proposals for the endorsement of a labor party. The CIO unions sought to organize workers on an industrial basis—challenging traditional notions of craft unionism that were prevalent in AFL unions. Indeed, the labor party resolution almost passed, with a vote of 104 (including a majority of delegates representing central labor unions and state federations of labor) to 108 against the resolution.

Labor moved toward independent politics in the early 1930s after the state intervened to smash strikes. What energized the creation of local labor parties from coast to coast were the great strike wave of 1934 and the repression of those strikes. There were 1,856 strikes and over 1,470,000 workers on strike in 1934. These strikes included a big Auto-Lite strike in Toledo, a violent teamster strike in Minneapolis, a general strike in San Francisco, national strikes in auto and steel, and a strike of 400,000 textile workers in New England and the South, which was the largest single industrial conflict in the history of American organized labor.

Democratic governors in New England and the South crushed the textile workers' strike, which taught mill workers to distrust the Democratic party. The same thing happened to workers across the country. As a result, every major center of industrial unrest in 1934, from Toledo to San Francisco, witnessed labor party activity in 1935.

The young workers in auto, rubber, textiles, and steel who poured into the CIO, which was organizing them into unions for the first time, were the same people who were demanding a labor party. This was seen as a se-

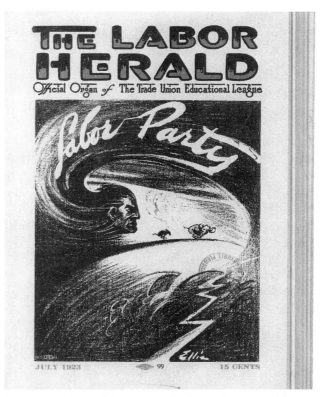

By 1923, when this cover of *The Labor Herald* ran, the Trade Union Educational League had been incorporated into the new Communist Party USA. Its support for the Labor party shows, perhaps, a bit of wishful thinking, as unions and labor politics grew increasingly stunted in the 1920s. *(Courtesy of the Library of Congress)*

rious problem for many in the CIO leadership. John L. Lewis (head of the Mine Workers), Sidney Hillman (head of the Clothing Workers), David Dubinsky (head of the Ladies' Garment Workers' Union), and other top CIO leaders wanted to align the labor movement with Roosevelt and the Democrats. With reactionaries ganging up on Roosevelt, they felt labor could not afford to let him lose. The vehicle they developed for combating the labor party promoters within their unions and swinging them behind Roosevelt was labor's Non-partisan League. The League leadership held out the possibility that this was the long-awaited move toward an independent labor party for which many of the rank and file had been clamoring. Instead, it was a device for lining up recalcitrant labor votes for Roosevelt by defeating labor party sentiment in the CIO and in the labor movement as a whole and wedding labor to the Democratic party.

In this they were successful. In union after union, Nonpartisan League leadership turned back labor party sentiment to obtain endorsement of Roosevelt in 1936. The victorious CIO leadership finally signed the death certificate of their labor party rivals in their constituent unions at the first official convention of the CIO held in Pittsburgh in 1938. There, with the exception of New York's American Labor party, the CIO mandated that all future political activity was henceforth to take place within the established two-party system.

The labor party movement of the early 1930s was the last time that significant elements in organized labor struggled hopefully to create an independent national labor party. For the last half-century and more, since the great realigning election of 1936, organized labor has been married, albeit somewhat shakily, to the Democratic party.

ERIC LEIF DAVIN

See also: American Labor Party; Communist Party; Minnesota Farmer-Labor Party; Nonpartisan League; Socialist Party; Social Democratic Party.

Bibliography

Davin, Eric Leif. "The Very Last Hurrah: The Defeat of the Labor Party Idea, 1934–1936." In *We Are All Leaders: The Alternative Unionism of the Early 1930s,* ed. Staughton Lynd. Urbana: University of Illinois Press, 1996.

Davin, Eric Leif, and Staughton Lynd. "Picket Line and Ballot Box: The Forgotten Legacy of the Local Labor Party Movement, 1932–1936." *Radical History Review* 22 (Winter 1979–80): 43–63.

LABOR PARTY
1990s

LABOR AND AMERICAN POLITICS

Of all the social movements in the United States, the ranks of organized labor hold the largest pool of resources. In 1990 alone, union political action committees spent over $84 million on political candidates—almost entirely for Democrats. Just one labor publication, the United Auto Workers' national magazine *Solidarity*, reaches 1.3 million readers. In other countries, such resources have been used to build strong labor, socialist, or social democratic parties. While the U.S. political system does present several unique legal and structural obstacles, an important reason why no such party exists in our official political spectrum is that the U.S. labor movement—as a whole—has never committed to building one. By contrast, Canada, which has many of the same legal obstacles as found in the United States, has a viable social democratic party, the New Democratic party, because in 1963 the Canadian labor movement threw its might behind the new party.

The collapse of the New Deal social contract has highlighted the costs of limiting union activity to collective bargaining and unwavering electoral support for Democrats. When employers went on the offensive in the 1980s, organized labor suffered defeat after defeat. While the Republicans worked to undermine what legal rights workers had remaining, centrist Democrats awkwardly strove to distance themselves from their former labor ally. Certainly, the party of the New Deal offered no pro-worker, pro-

active agenda for the 1990s and beyond. Having pursued a narrow agenda for decades, unions now found themselves without many allies or active support within the general population. By servicing rather than mobilizing their rank and file, many unions found their members tuned out of politics despite growing feelings of economic insecurity and frustration. A study commissioned by the AFL-CIO in the early 1990s showed that most union members were largely disconnected from their union's political action efforts and saw little connection between politics and their everyday lives. As a steadily declining proportion of workers found themselves in unions, some business leaders gleefully began talking of the death of the labor movement.

SHIFT IN AFL-CIO LEADERSHIP

While typically not covered by the evening news, the labor movement has begun to show significant signs of change. The election of John Sweeney to the presidency of the AFL-CIO on a reform platform has helped legitimize the task of rethinking labor's strategies and practices. A greater emphasis on movement-building has even begun to develop within the federation's political activities. In 1996, for example, when the AFL-CIO spent $35 million on electoral activity, most of these resources were not used for the traditional promotion of labor-endorsed candidates, but for targeted issue ads that highlighted the adverse impact of the Republican

Contract With America. This shifting emphasis from candidates to issues reflected an awareness that asking union members to support some middle-of-the-road Democrat was not motivating them to vote. In 1994 only 16 percent of actual voters were union members. By focusing on issues rather than personalities, the federation helped raise labor membership's turnout to almost one-quarter of the electoral vote two years later. The AFL-CIO has also called on unions to move from choosing between existing candidates to running their own for office. The federation aims to have 2,000 newly recruited union members run for local offices in the year 2000. The AFL-CIO's union cities program also has a strong political component. Sweeney has called on local and national unions to make organizing their number-one priority by diverting a full 30 percent of their resources into organizing. At the same time, the union cities agenda calls on unions to hold their elected officials accountable by demanding that they publicly support organizing and promote legal changes that make the decision to join a union a fair choice.

These changes at the national level have been foreshadowed by events at the local and regional level. In New England, for example, innovative labor-community coalitions have been recruiting activist candidates and developing a progressive electoral agenda since the 1980s. More recently, the fledgling New party has built active local chapters with substantial labor movement involvement in every community in which it has planted roots.

ORIGINS OF THE PARTY

The founding of the Labor party offers an important component of this new labor activism. In 1991, delegates of the Oil, Chemical, and Atomic Workers Union (OCAW) passed a resolution to launch Labor Party Advocates (LPA) as a vehicle to agitate within the ranks of labor for the founding of a labor party. LPA organizers had broad vision. In working for a labor party, they sought not simply to establish a po-

litical party that would genuinely represent working people. They also hoped to help transform the labor movement itself. LPA activists shared a vision of organized labor that went back to the social unionism of the early CIO, when the labor movement represented and fought for working people generally. A labor party could help redefine the labor movement by embodying this broader social vision.

Speaking from her long personal experience with the Canadian labor movement's participation in their New Democratic party, Elaine Bernard, writing in the *Boston Review*, has drawn out the lessons for U.S. labor activists:

> We commonly use the term "labor movement" to describe the world of organized labor. In most advanced industrial countries, that world includes organizations of working people in both the workplace and community. While unions are the main form of organizing in the workplace, labor-based political parties organize in the community. In these countries, when people talk about a "labor movement" they are talking both about trade unions and about this wider spectrum of organizations often including much of the progressive community.
>
> In the United States today there are trade unions . . . but there is really no wider social and political labor movement at all.

LPA activists hoped that their political organizing would help broaden the American labor movement. In particular, it would encourage the process of developing a comprehensive agenda that would allow unions, and working people generally, to move from the defensive battles of the 1980s to an offensive reply to the corporate agenda. And since any labor party would embody the ideals of labor reformers, it would bring to the forefront the best tendencies found within the movement. In short, by working to transform the nation's politics, organized labor could transform itself.

LPA activists used a variety of tactics to promote the idea of a labor party. With very modest resources at the national level, LPA sent its national organizer, former OCAW secretary-treasurer Tony Mazzocchi, around the country to speak on behalf of a labor party. Officers of endorsing unions, such as OCAW president Bob Wages, also contributed their share of public speaking. Most LPA activity, however, came from the grassroots. Within local unions, activists surveyed union members, asking them about their views on politics and the desirability of forming a new party of workers. Conducted in union locals across the country, such surveys consistently revealed widespread dissatisfaction with both major parties and repeated majorities of workers who supported the formation of a new political party of working people. At the most formal level, LPA activists asked unions and labor council assemblies to pass resolutions endorsing the idea of a labor party. More informally, LPA members promoted the labor party idea among their co-workers and union members.

The LPA also tried to gain attention by setting up and participating in public events. LPA activists could be seen handing out literature and talking with fellow workers in Labor Day parades, strike picket lines, and worker rallies across the country. Local LPA groups also sponsored activities of their own. For example, many locals organized public events to support ongoing labor struggles—such as the "War Zone" in southern Illinois involving striking and locked out workers from Staley, Caterpillar, and Firestone. LPA groups set up public hearings and conferences to discuss issues of concern to working people. For example, in December 1994 activists in Ohio and Michigan pulled together a two-day "Labor Education Conference" in Toledo, Ohio.

LABOR UNION SUPPORT

Between 1991 and 1995, the LPA experienced some success. In addition to the OCAW, three other national unions endorsed the LPA: the United Electrical Workers, the Longshoremen, and the Brotherhood of Maintenance of Way Employees. None of these are among the most powerful of the nation's unions; however, the LPA never hoped to pull in such national leadership. The true testing ground of the LPA's message lay at the grassroots. Success in this regard varied, depending upon the area. In California, for example, the LPA won the official endorsement of such bodies as the San Francisco Labor Council and the 75,000-member California Council of Carpenters, as well as a dozen more local councils and unions. In Boston, the 12,000-member Service Employees International Union Local 285 voted to endorse the LPA as did the 18,000-member New England Health Care Employees Union, District 1199, and a 20,000-strong Teamster Local in Chicago. All told, unions and labor councils representing roughly one million total members had formally given their support to the idea of a labor party by June 1996. More informally, and often much more quietly, other groups within major unions had lent support to the LPA. The Service Employees International Union, one of the country's largest unions, while not endorsing the LPA, did pass a broad resolution expressing support for the LPA's campaign for a labor party. The LPA had these successes with relatively few resources and a loose organization.

Despite such considerable activity, by 1995 the LPA had reached a turning point. When originally founded in 1991 the group aimed to recruit as many as 100,000 people and 10,000 elected union officers to endorse the founding of a labor party. This ambitious goal would have produced the founding of a new party with an already-established mass base. The LPA never came close to this goal. The modesty of the LPA's actual membership rolls reflected, in part, a scarcity of resources. But it also reflected the limitations of the project itself. LPA activists had asked people to join an organization that supported the eventual formation of a party that did not yet exist. The LPA explicitly neither ran nor endorsed political candidates; nor did it establish a formal platform or issue campaigns. Only the most politically involved individuals seemed willing to actively join such an abstraction.

In short, five years of organizing had clearly revealed strong sentiment among union members, and the general public, for a new party of working people. It was time to launch such a party. On June 6–9, 1996, 1,500 delegates elected from unions and local LPA chapters across the country met in Cleveland, Ohio, to establish the Labor party.

FOUNDING CONVENTION

The convention set up a formal organizational structure and debated and approved a basic sixteen-point platform. The platform focused on the theme of economic justice, including the right to a job at a living wage, fundamental labor law reform, the reduction of the work week, universal health care, environmental protection, revitalizing the public sector, tax fairness, as well as other progressive reforms. Delegates also debated two questions that run to the heart of the Labor party project.

The first involved the sharply debated decision not to run candidates for at least two years. Critics charged that it strained their credibility to ask people to join a party that did not participate in elections. Defenders of the proposal argued against mounting premature electoral bids that would simply result in failure. The party had to first establish a critical membership base so that when its members ran for office, they did so as credible candidates. The debate cut to a core dilemma faced by any group seeking to recruit progressive organizations—labor unions in particular—into independent politics. While a strong case can be made for bold independent politics, most unions and other progressive organizations with political action committees are understandably not willing to leap into the unknown of third-party organizing. This is especially true if such a project requires them to jettison or jeopardize their ongoing political action working with the Democrats. Unions and other progressive groups have developed substantial relationships with elected Democrats, especially at the local level. No labor leader wants to be politically isolated while giving opportunities to Republicans.

Fledgling new political projects must avoid throwing down a gauntlet that asks unions to choose between the Democratic party and an uncertain alternative. The Labor party's unwillingness to engage in electoral work illustrates a desire not to confront unions with a choice between their traditional Democratic work and Labor party candidacies currently seen as hopeless and premature. (For a contrasting approach to this same dilemma see the entry on the New party.)

In place of electoral campaigns, the party called for ongoing issue and education work to continue the task of building the party's base. The issue of this base, however, leads to the second major question facing the party. The Labor party stands on two legs: 1) the local to national labor bodies that have formally endorsed the party and the individual members of those bodies who have joined and 2) the geographical chapter organizations built on individual membership. The convention debated the relative authority to assign to each of these legs within party decision-making. The delegates' decision to assign representatives of chapter organizations a combined single vote on the Interim National Council reflects the relative strength of the two legs.

Like the LPA, the Labor party has been most successful in its outreach to formal labor bodies. In addition to the four national unions that had joined by the time of the Labor party's founding, the United Mine Workers, the American Federation of Government Employees, and several smaller national unions have formally affiliated with the Labor party. By May 1998 almost 250 local unions and regional labor bodies had endorsed the Labor party. The list includes the Farm Labor Organizing Committee, the California State Nurses Association, the United Needletrades Industrial and Textile Employees (UNITE) Midwest Regional Joint Board, and several central labor councils. Today, the bulk of the Labor party's individual membership has come from recruitment through local unions.

With notable exceptions, the forty-four chapter organizations have experienced general decline. While activists debate the causes of chapter weakness, the party's scarce resources have

Launched in 1996, the Labor party decided to build an organizational framework before running candidates. Still, with the backing of organizing labor, it has significant electoral potential, as this rally at its first national convention—held in Pittsburgh in 1998—attests. *(Courtesy of Michael Kaufman, Impact Visuals)*

not permitted many opportunities to back up local chapter growth. Furthermore, in some cases the people attracted to active participation in local chapters have come from leftist groups or unaffiliated left-leaning individuals with little institutional connection or influence with the labor movement. However, most important, with the possibility of running candidates forestalled, chapter organizations desperately needed viable issue campaigns to organize around. To aid this process the national leadership developed a Twenty-eighth Amendment

campaign in which local activists collected petition signatures calling for a constitutional amendment recognizing the right to a job at a living wage. The campaign had the advantage that, since it was primarily an educational effort, any Labor party group, no matter how big or small, could organize on a grassroots level at whatever level they were capable of mounting. However, while people were willing to sign the petition, the abstract nature of the campaign's formal demand weakened activists' ability to build coalitions, recruit new members, or establish their chapters as serious players in local progressive activism.

The struggle of the local chapters reflects the general challenge the Labor party faces to translate the substantial interest it has organized in favor of independent politics into concrete political activity on the ground. At its second convention in November 1998 delegates passed a proposal to allow the party to begin running local Labor party candidates. The proposal's fairly stringent criteria are designed to ensure that Labor party electoral bids are only mounted as serious undertakings with solid community support and a well-developed plan of action.

PROSPECTS FOR THE FUTURE

If the Labor party can succeed in channeling its supporters into viable candidacies and targeted issue work, it faces a promising future. Other experiences that have combined electoral and issue activism (such as the New party and the Greens) have shown that when activists organize effectively in local communities, working people have responded. The challenge has not been to convince people of the need for change, but to pull together the grassroots resources needed to spread success from one community to another. The Labor party has sown important seeds among the labor movement. Those seeds must now bear fruit.

DAVID REYNOLDS

See also: New Party; Working Families Party.

Bibliography

''Labor and Political Action.'' *Labor Research Review* 22 (1994).

Reynolds, David. *Democracy Unbound: Progressive Challenges to the Two Party System.* Boston: South End Press, 1997.

Sweeney, Sean. ''The Labor Party's Alternative Politics.'' *New Labor Forum* 1 (Fall 1997).

The Labor party publishes the *Labor Party Press* six times a year. The Labor party Web site has the party's program, constitution, and other materials (www.igc.apc.org/lpa).

LABOR REFORM PARTY
1872

Throughout the second quarter of the nineteenth century, labor unions and trade groups were multiplying and pointedly avoiding political involvement. Early attempts at building an independent political party had foundered and failed to address worker's immediate practical concerns. The General Trades Union, founded in 1833, issued a statement that "the Trades Union will never be political, because its members have learned from experience, that the introduction of Politics into their Societies has thwarted every effort to ameliorate their conditions." The Industrial Congress of 1851, a meeting of unions from across the country, hoped to "eschew partyism of every description." During the prosperous 1850s, unions were concluding trade agreements with employers, federating along craft lines, and organizing on a national basis. Unions were agitating primarily for a reduction of the hours of labor, about which government could do little except in the comparatively small public sector. At the same time, a number of groups formed cooperative associations for the purchase of commodities and the notion of producer cooperatives took hold.

The period of the Civil War brought rapid changes in American society, vastly sharpening the disparity between wealth and poverty. While some businessmen and adventurers became very rich, wages remained relatively stagnant. At the same time, prices in the North more than doubled, largely due to the Union government's issuance of $400 million in paper money. (These "greenback dollars," which were not exchangeable for gold, remained in circulation until the government returned to the gold standard in 1879.) Existing labor organizations grew, and several new and powerful unions emerged.

To unify the various groups, delegates of the labor organizations met in Baltimore in 1866 and formed the National Labor Union. Promotion of the eight-hour day was the primary concern, but the federation also decided to form a political party "as soon as possible" and further issued a demand for the formation of a national bureau of labor statistics. In the years following, all of the trades attempted to form producer cooperatives, the concomitant need for capital bringing members first-hand experience with credit problems. The post-war deflation was bringing hardship to all debtors. While labor leaders and the labor press began listening to the monetary theories of farmers who wanted an expansion in the number of greenbacks in order to stabilize prices or generate a mild inflation, there was still no move toward forming a political party. By 1870, the depression was easing and most unions resumed more local activities, distancing themselves from the National Labor Union. The National Labor Union Convention of 1870, which came to be dominated by intellectuals and reformers rather than actual representatives of labor, called for the formation of the National Labor Reform party for the presidential election of 1872.

Some 200 delegates, representing seventeen states, gathered in Columbus, Ohio, in February of 1872 for the convention of the National Labor Reform party. The convention ratified a platform that called for a "purely national circulating medium" (greenbacks) to be issued directly by the government without the intervention of any banks (perceived as money monopolies) to be a legal tender in payment of all debts, public and private, and to be interchangeable with "government bonds bearing a rate of interest not to exceed 3.75 per cent, subject to future legislation by Congress." It called for government to pay the national debt in good faith (in greenbacks) and to stop issuing tax-exempt bonds. It resolved that public lands should not be sold to individuals or corporations, but should be granted to landless homesteaders in amounts not to exceed 160 acres. Other planks called for enactment of legislation to standardize an eight-hour workday, to prohibit the importation of Chinese laborers, and to abolish the use of contract labor in prisons and other reformatories. The platform also resolved that there should be regulation of railroads and telegraph corporations and reform of the civil service so as to remove partisan influence. In recognition that "power ever seeks to perpetuate itself by any and all means," the platform favored limitation of the president to a single term. Finally, a general amnesty for all former Confederates was endorsed.

As candidates, the party considered nine prominent men; several of whom were also being mentioned for the Liberal Republican ticket. In the hope that their selection would also be the choice of the Liberal Republicans, the Labor Reform party nominated David Davis, a Supreme Court justice who had been Lincoln's campaign manager in 1860. Joel Parker of New Jersey was chosen to be the vice-presidential nominee. When both of these candidates had been passed over by the Liberal Republicans, both declined the nomination by the Labor Reform party. A poorly attended second convention named Charles O'Conor, who was also the choice of the Straight-Out (Taproot) Democratic party to lead the ticket without a running mate.

Charles O'Conor (1804–1884) was a member of the New York Bar specializing in corporation cases. He had been a Democratic candidate for lieutenant governor of New York in 1848 and was appointed U.S. attorney for the southern district of New York in 1853. He served as counsel for Jefferson Davis in 1866–67, and at the time of his presidential nomination was special deputy attorney general of New York in the Tweed Ring prosecution cases. (He would go on to write a book about the cases in 1875.) O'Conor was the first Roman Catholic to run for the presidency of the United States. In November, he received a total of 18,602 votes in what has been termed "a fiasco" and a "shipwreck" for the Labor Reform party. Richard T. Ely wrote in 1886 that the National Labor Union, which in 1868 had approximately 640,000 members, "expired in a few years of the disease known as politics. Fatal malady!"

Although the Labor Reform party never again held a national convention, it continued on the state level and eventually made common cause with the Greenback party. Third parties continued to arise, undeterred by the experience of 1872. The National Labor Union and the party it founded are considered to have energized the movement toward an eight-hour workday as well as the eventual creation of a national bureau of labor statistics.

MYRA BURT ADELMAN

See also: David Davis; Liberal Republican Party; Charles O'Conor.

Bibliography

Congressional Quarterly, *Presidential Elections Since 1789*, 4th ed. Washington, DC: Congressional Quarterly, 1987.

Ely, Richard T. *The Labor Movement in America.* New York: Thomas Crowell, 1886.

Havel, James T. *U.S. Presidential Candidates and the Elections.* New York: Simon and Schuster Macmillan, 1996.

Heseltine, William B. *Third-party Movements in the United States.* Princeton: D. Van Nostrand, 1962.

Porter, Kirk H., and Donald Bruce Johnson. *National Party Platforms, 1840–1964.* Urbana: University of Illinois Press, 1966.

Roseboom, Eugene H. *A History of Presidential Elections.* New York: Macmillan, 1964.

☆★☆★☆★☆★☆★☆★☆★☆★☆★☆★☆★☆★☆★☆★☆★☆★
LA RAZA UNIDA PARTY
1970–1981

*I*n the midst of the turbulent early 1970s emerged the first all-ethnic third party in the history of American politics—La Raza Unida party (United People's party, hereafter referred to as RUP). As the nation was caught up in the vortex of protest politics, Chicano (Chicano denotes Mexican Americans born in the United States) activists took to the streets to fight decades of oppression, exploitation, and impoverishment brought on by an Anglo-dominated and -controlled society. Out of this activism, a political and cultural awakening occurred that gave rise to the Chicano movement. During the years 1965–74, the Chicano movement became more militant, and a plethora of leaders and organizations sought redress and change from a society that had relegated them to a second-class and politically powerless status. The nation's Chicano barrios (enclaves) became permeated by an unprecedented climate of change characterized by discontent, rising expectations, and activism.

In 1970, Chicano activists took their protest into the electoral arena, revolting politically against what they perceived as the nation's "two party dictatorship"—meaning that both the Democratic and Republican parties exercised total political hegemony. Furthermore, to these activists the two-party system was one animal with two heads that ate from the same trough.

The RUP's emergence was in great part a product of two major Chicano movement leaders: José Ángel Gutiérrez, Texas leader and cofounder of the militant Mexican American Youth Organization (MAYO), and Rodolfo "Corky" Gonzáles leader and founder of the separatist-oriented Crusade for Justice based in

Denver, Colorado. Gutiérrez at the time was a young graduate student who had become the most prominent and controversial Chicano leader in Texas. A former professional boxer, businessman, and Democratic politician, Gonzáles, by 1970, was also one of the three major leaders of the Chicano movement (the other two were César Chávez, leader of the United Farm Workers, and Reies López Tijerina, leader of the Federal Alliance of Land Grants). An ardent nationalist, he espoused the formation of a separate Chicano nation. For years RUP's pattern of leadership was that of two competing *caudillos* (strong leaders) at the national or regional level complemented by a host of state, regional, or local *caciques* (chieftains or bosses).

Under the leadership of Gutiérrez and Gonzáles, efforts to organize RUP into a third party began in 1970. Using the organizing momentum produced as a consequence of a successful school boycott in Crystal City, Texas, Gutiérrez in January launched the RUP, as part of MAYO's empowerment- and social-change-oriented Winter Garden Project.

In what was tantamount to an electoral rebellion against what MAYO perceived as being an oppressive and unrepresentative two-party system, RUP that year ran several candidates for the city council and school board in Crystal City, Cotulla, and Carrizo Springs. The outcome was politically unprecedented: A total of fifteen candidates were elected with RUP gaining community control of Crystal City's school board and city council as well as Cotulla's city council. As a result of numerous major political, educational, social, and economic changes made by RUP elected officials, Crystal City became the

The first major Hispanic party in American history, the La Raza Unida party ran strongly in Texas, where it was founded in 1970. Here, Texas gubernatorial candidate Ramsey Muñiz addresses the party's 1972 convention in El Paso. *(Courtesy of Armando Navarro)*

symbolic capital of the emerging RUP third-party movement. During the next five years, a number of other local seats were won in other communities in South Texas.

By 1972, the organizing momentum in Texas led RUP to gain official party status and became the first statewide all-ethnic third party in the nation. In 1972 and 1974, RUP unsuccessfully ran statewide candidates for state and federal offices. In both elections, RUP gubernatorial candidate Ramsey Muñiz ran on a very populist Chicano-oriented platform that called for a major redistribution of wealth and bilingual education, among other reforms. In both races he succeeded in capturing only 6 percent of the total vote. None of the other RUP candidates running for state and federal offices were able to surpass Muñiz's 6 percent. However, a few RUP candidates for county commissioner were elected in 1972 and 1978. In 1978, Mario Compean and a few other RUP candidates ran

unsuccessfully for governor and other state offices. Not able to secure a minimum of 2 percent of the vote, RUP was decertified as a political party in Texas, spelling the end of RUP in Texas.

Meanwhile, in 1970, Gonzáles's Crusade for Justice launched the formation of RUP in Colorado. RUP's development in Colorado was very much impelled by "El Plan Espiritual de Aztlán" (The Spiritual Plan of Aztlan)—a product of two youth liberation conferences that were sponsored by the Crusade for Justice. Both were held in 1969 and 1970 in Denver, Colorado. The "Plan" became the Chicano movement's ideological cornerstone of cultural nationalism. For the next six years, Gonzáles sought to organize RUP into a Chicano political party that would be at the vanguard of the struggle to build a Chicano nation.

In 1970, RUP unsuccessfully ran several candidates as independents for federal, state, and county offices. RUP gubernatorial candidate Al Gurrule garnered 1.8 percent of the vote; while others received between 1.3 and 7.5 percent of the votes cast. Without having a large and concentrated Chicano population base, no victories were secured. For the next six years, RUP continued to run unsuccessfully a number of candidates for local, state, and federal office. By 1976, only three candidates ran under RUP's aegis. Because of the small Chicano population base, the intent of RUP candidates was not necessarily to win, but rather to use their campaign to politicize and organize Chicanos throughout the state.

With the rise of RUP in both Texas and Colorado, efforts to organize RUP quickly spread throughout much of the Southwest and parts of the Midwest. During the next few years, in Arizona, California, and New Mexico, RUP committees were organized. Several candidates ran unsuccessfully for local offices, and in some cases, they ran as independents for state and federal offices as well. In none of these three states did RUP succeed in getting on the ballot, but ran as write-ins instead.

Likewise, in the Midwest, even though Chicanos did not have large population concentrations to run effective electoral campaigns, by 1972 activists responded to the call to form RUP. The influences of RUP's organizing in Texas and Colorado were instrumental in fomenting an interest in building a Chicano political party. However, with very few exceptions (e.g., Chicago, Illinois), RUP organizing efforts were more directed toward dealing with issues and developing and providing social service programs. As a result, RUP took on the appearance in some states as either an advocacy-oriented pressure group or as a social service provider and seldom that of a political party.

From RUP's rise to its decline, it was riddled by ideological and strategic schisms. Some activists perceived themselves as nationalists, while others pursued a myriad of sectarian Marxist perspectives (e.g., Socialist Workers party, Communist party, Communist Labor party). RUP's ideological development was such that during its rise it was essentially nationalist and more socialist during its decline

and demise. As a result, RUP's platform reflected an ideological eclecticism that ultimately proved to be detrimental. In 1972, at the national RUP convention in El Paso, Texas, a platform was created that was essentially populist and reform oriented. This was in part attributable to the influence of the Gutiérrez delegates, who were influenced by the Texas populist platform and Gutiérrez's more militant, reformist orientation.

The presence of leadership and ideological conflicts contributed to divergences in state platforms. Colorado's platform, for example, was rather eclectic—ardent nationalist, populist, with socialist overtones, and anti-capitalist—while Texas's was less sectarian, more reformist, somewhat populist, and quasi-nationalist. Overall, by the latter part of the 1970s, RUP's platform became much more separatist and socialist in orientation. Nation-building and networking with other struggles for liberation became the focus of RUP's new leadership.

This diverse and multifunctional posture was in part influenced by the diversity of political agendas or ideologies that permeated its activist ranks. RUP never was able to bridge the diversity of ideas or overcome the conflicts developed by competing leaders. Efforts to foster a unified national platform and party occurred in September 1972 when RUP held its first and last national convention in El Paso, Texas. With some 3,000 persons in attendance from eighteen states, the convention became the locus of a major power struggle between the two competing major leaders—Gutiérrez and Gonzáles. In the end, Gutiérrez prevailed and was voted in as RUP's national chairman.

At no point in time did RUP have a cohesive, unified, and well-defined compatible structure. In part this was ascribable to the fact that only in Texas did RUP become an official political party, meaning that it was successful in gaining ballot status. For purposes of structuring RUP nationally, at the El Paso national convention in 1972, a steering committee called "El Congreso," comprised of representatives from various states, was formed. By 1975, however, after a few conflict-plagued meetings as a result of the power struggle between Gutiérrez and Gonzáles, it collapsed and was replaced by a smaller executive committee comprised of three state chairpersons. Some of the RUP organizing committees functioned more like pressure groups—taking on a variety of issues—rather than a political party.

At the local and regional levels, some states sought to follow the traditional political party structure that included a state central committee and county committees. In California and some other states, initially a diversity of structures existed. Some RUP entities were called chapters, others committees, while still others focos (local units). In some cases RUP's structure was influenced by the orientation of those intent on using their local structures to promote revolution or a Chicano nation. In Texas, RUP activists formed community-based organizations (e.g., Ciudadanos Unidos [United Citizens] in Crystal City) that functioned like pressure groups and were the counterparts to local Democratic and Republican clubs. These organizations were formed in order to buttress RUP's day-to-day organizing efforts. Thus, RUP never succeeded in developing organizational uniformity.

RUP was a product of not only the times but of the young Chicano activists who were by and large at the vanguard of its formation. In Texas, for example, initially its major organizing strength came from MAYO, comprised of students and barrio youth. In Colorado, the Crusade for Justice and its admixture of barrio youth, barrio resident workers, and a few middle-class teachers, administrators, and businesspersons made up its support. In most other states, students and a few intellectuals were at the forefront of organizing RUP. With some rare exceptions (e.g., Crystal City), RUP never developed a mass-based posture capable of co-alescing politically the heterogeneity of the Chicano community. The majority of Chicanos were not willing to break their affiliation with the major parties, particularly the Democratic party. After years of Democratic party socialization, they perceived RUP as being too radical or militant in its politics. Consequently, it never seriously threatened the hegemony of the two major parties. Both the Democrats and Republicans, aided by an often-hostile media, were successful in character assassinating the fledgling Chicano third-party movement. In conclusion, it is important to note that although RUP as a third-party movement became moribund by 1981, a few RUP zealots have continued to keep the struggle and dream of building a Chicano party alive. Thus, if a climate of change develops to where discontent is chronic, once again, impelled by a burgeoning population and depending on their strategic agenda, Chicanos and Latinos could very well opt to form their own political party.

ARMANDO NAVARRO

See also: Rodolfo "Corky" Gonzáles; José Ángel Gutiérrez.

Bibliography

Garcia, Ignacio. *United We Win: The Rise and Fall of the Raza Unida Party.* Tucson: Mexican American Studies Center, 1989.

Gutiérrez, José Ángel. *The Making of a Chicano Militant: Lessons from Cristal.* Madison: University of Wisconsin Press, 1999.

Muñoz, Carlos. *Youth, Identity, Power: The Chicano Movement.* New York: Verso, 1990.

Navarro, Armando. *Mexican American Youth Organization: The Avant-Garde of the Chicano Movement in Texas.* Austin: University of Texas Press, 1995.

☆☆☆☆☆☆☆☆☆☆☆☆☆☆☆☆☆☆☆☆☆☆☆☆☆☆☆☆☆☆☆☆☆☆☆☆☆

LAW AND ORDER
PARTY OF RHODE ISLAND

1841–1842

The United States was the first country to begin to distribute the franchise widely to its citizens. This reform movement began at the turn of the nineteenth century and continued throughout the antebellum period. Moreover, the extension of the franchise was primarily initiated at the state level—the federal government played little or no part and was actually pulled along with the sweeping changes occurring in both North and South in the antebellum republic. Whereas most states in the Confederation and Federalist years required some type of property qualifications for voting, the United States, by the middle decades of the nineteenth century, had more or less achieved what no other country had—universal white male suffrage. As early as the 1830s, writers such as Alexis de Tocqueville were extolling the virtues of "Democracy in America," a term that the Federalists only a generation earlier had used pejoratively.

While universal white male suffrage swept across both the northern and southern United States in the antebellum period, a more complex situation existed for black males living in the North. In short, the franchise was granted to black males on an extremely uneven basis. Some northern states placed no restrictions on black males, some placed a property restriction higher for black males than for white males, and some explicitly restricted the vote to white males—either through state constitutional revision or statute. In Rhode Island, the right to vote was first granted to blacks who met property qualifications. It was then taken away in 1822 and finally restored to them after Dorr's Rebellion in 1842. It is within this larger context

of race and democracy that one needs to place the establishment of the Law and Order Party of Rhode Island in order to understand its importance.

In 1822, Rhode Island altered its franchise law so that only white male adults were allowed to be "freemen"—that is, those who met the freehold qualification were allowed to vote. This change came in the wake of an influx of foreign-born industrial workers into the state after the War of 1812. By 1833, only one-third of all white men were eligible to vote in the city of Providence. Throughout the 1830s, white, propertyless, and foreign-born workers continually agitated for the franchise. Their efforts led to the founding of the Rhode Island Suffrage Association in March of 1840. Within a year, the newly created Suffrage party held its first meeting—known as the People's Convention—in the fall of 1841.

The People's Convention proposed to liberalize the franchise to all white males, including foreign-born, but excluded blacks. Despite the efforts on the part of the Rhode Island Antislavery Society, the People's Convention voted to retain the word "white" in its suffrage clause. In January 1842, the Suffrage Constitution was approved overwhelmingly by the voters of Rhode Island. However, the success of the Suffrage party sent shock waves through the freeholding and nativist communities of the state; they quickly convened their own convention and drafted their own version of a state constitution, which they called the Legal Constitution.

The Legal Constitution was put to a vote before the entire state in March 1842. It was de-

The Law and Order Party of Rhode Island and most of its Whig allies stood opposed to the radical politics of Governor Thomas Wilson Dorr. This 1845 cartoon ridicules Whigs and Law and Order men of that state who broke with their parties and supported Dorr's release from jail. *(Courtesy of the Library of Congress)*

feated by only 676 votes. One month later, the People's election was held, and Thomas Dorr was elected as their governor. While the legal government of Rhode Island did not recognize the People's government, it also did not move to stop them. In May, Dorr led an attempt to seize the Providence Arsenal, but his attack was quelled. The Dorrites who composed the People's Legislature resigned, and Dorr fled the state. Amid the chaos, the freeholders moved in to calm the situation and called for a constitu-

tional convention to be assembled in September 1842. Firmly in control of the situation, the freeholders began to call themselves the Law and Order party.

The Law and Order party scheduled elections for delegates to the convention in August and opened the voting to all native male citizens who could meet a three-year residence requirement. The black community, having been rebuffed by the Suffragists, happily aligned themselves with the conservative Law and Order party. The decision was strategic. As Frederick Douglass explained at the time: "We cared nothing for the Dorr party on the one hand, nor the 'law and order party' on the other. What we wanted, and what we labored to obtain, was a constitution free from the narrow, selfish, and senseless limitation of the word *white*."

The Law and Order party sought the help of blacks in order to keep the foreign-born disenfranchised. When Dorr returned during the summer of 1842 and led a rebellion of almost 1,100 men against the state government, the black community turned out in droves to support the Law and Order party's cause. Dorr's Rebellion was quelled with the help of the state's black population. The Law and Order party knew it was indebted to blacks in Rhode Island, and they rewarded their loyalty by dropping the word "white" from the suffrage clause in their convention. In November 1842, the constitution was approved overwhelmingly; blacks regained the right to vote in Rhode Island, and the Law and Order party was the chief reason.

CHRISTOPHER MALONE

Bibliography

Lemons, J. Stanley, and Michael A. McKenna. "Reenfranchisement of Rhode Island Negroes." *Rhode Island History* 30, no. 1 (1971): 3–13.

Rammelkamp, Julian. "The Providence Negro Community, 1820–1842." *Rhode Island History* 7, no. 1 (1948): 20–33.

LIBERAL PARTY

1944–

New York State has been the site of much third-party activity over the years. While most other states can also make this claim, New York is an anomaly in that some of its third parties have been able to achieve official ballot status—that is, the law guarantees they will appear on the election ballot. New York State election law states that if a party can garner 50,000 votes in the quadrennial gubernatorial election, it is guaranteed a ballot spot in all New York elections for the next four years (the time of the next gubernatorial election), as long as the party in question chooses to field a candidate. Coupled with this rule, the state has what is known as the cross-endorsement rule, a relatively unique provision that simply states that parties are allowed to nominate other parties' candidates for the same office in the same election. Only two other states, Vermont and Connecticut, have provisions similar to New York's cross-endorsement rule. Third parties in New York often cross-endorse one of the major parties' gubernatorial candidates in an effort to gain the 50,000 votes necessary to achieve official ballot status. When they are successful in this tactic, New York's third parties have been able to gain political prominence rarely achieved by third parties in other states or at the national level. One such party is the Liberal party of New York State, the longest existing third party in the United States.

The Liberal party was founded in May 1944 when some members of the American Labor party (ALP) became dissatisfied with Communist influence within the ALP and withdrew to form their own non-communist, left-of-center party. David Dubinsky, president of the International Ladies' Garment Workers' Union, and Alex Rose of the United Hatters, Cap, and Millinery Workers Union were the principals behind the formation of the Liberal party. They were assisted by leading intellectuals, academics, union leaders, and theologians, including Adolph A. Berle, an advisor to Franklin D. Roosevelt during the New Deal, and Reinhold Niebuhr, professor of applied Christianity at Union Theological Seminary.

The founders wanted a vehicle through which to support the re-election campaign of Roosevelt in 1944, but were dissatisfied with the state Democratic party because of its control by the Tammany Hall machine, unhappy with the national Democratic party because of the influence of southerners within the party, and unwilling to remain with the ALP for reasons already mentioned. Roosevelt encouraged the formation of the party, as did prominent academic and philosopher John Dewey, who served as an honorary vice chairman in the party for several years. Besides actively working for the re-election of Roosevelt, the party adopted a platform that called for, in part, the achievement of full employment; the right of workers to join free, independent trade unions and bargain collectively; the abolition of poverty in the United States, the conservation of natural resources; increased unemployment benefits; and the provision of a decent home for every American.

The party's platforms have changed little in ideology over the years, although they have expanded somewhat in scope. The party still calls for policies to protect the rights of workers and the environment, but they have added planks of a more well-rounded liberal agenda to their platforms. Opposition to capital punishment, calls for gun control, protection of reproductive freedom, the assurance of civil rights for all citizens, less stringent immigration quotas, expansion of social welfare programs, and opposition to government funding for private schools have become consistent party positions.

As can probably be determined by the original 1944 platform goals listed above, the Liberal party was designed to appeal to the working class in New York State. The party usually had a small group of left-leaning academics serving in party organization and leadership capacities, but relied on organized labor and the working class as its primary base of support during its founding period. Dubinsky's Garment Workers represented one of the larger unions in New York (peak membership of 450,000), and their membership provided a rather substantial base upon which to build. The party still sees itself as an advocate for workers in New York, but the decline in union membership in the state has made organized labor a less central part of the party's membership in recent years.

The Liberal party has always been a mostly regional party, with almost all of its strength located in New York City. In the past, much of the state's union membership resided in the city, and the New York metropolitan area has long been the bastion of liberalism in the state, with much of the rest of the state being conservative in its ideology. Of the 92,001 votes cast for governor in 1994 on the liberal line, 52,316 came from voters living in New York City. Outside of New York City, the party barely exists, having hardly any formal organization at all in the rest of the state. Party headquarters is located in New York City, and almost all party events take place there.

PARTY LEADERSHIP AND STRUCTURE

The Liberal party has always had an elaborate organizational structure, theoretically headed by the state chairperson, with numerous vice chairpersons, honorary vice chairpersons, and an executive director; however, the position of state chairperson, with one exception that will be discussed somewhat below and in detail later, has always been a titular one. In fact, the party has been almost entirely controlled by three men throughout its history, all of whom have held the formal title of vice chairman, the traditional position in the party for the de facto leader. From the outset, Dubinsky and Rose held almost total control of the party, with other party officials falling in line with the wishes of these two men. Dubinsky usually dealt with the party's membership and other officials while Rose served as the party's chief political tactician, dealing with prospective candidates, elected officials, and the leaders of other parties. This relationship continued until Dubinsky's retirement from the Garment Workers' Union in 1966, after which he was still involved in party affairs, but on a much more limited basis. From this point, until his death in 1976 at the age of 78, Rose single-handedly controlled the party. Rose used his skill as a political tactician to turn the party into a force in local, state, and national politics, many times successfully positioning the party so that its line on the ballot could decide elections.

A system of leadership by committee existed for approximately six months after Rose's death, but by the end of 1977, Raymond B. Harding had taken control of the party, although his power was not as absolute as that of Rose or the team of Rose and Dubinsky. Harding exerted shaky control over the party until 1982, when a rift developed between him and the Reverend Donald Harrington, the party's state chairman, and James Notaro, the party's executive director. The rift expanded into a four-year-long war for control of the party, a war Harrington and Notaro seemingly won in 1984 when they were elected by the party committee to leadership positions and Harding was ousted as a party official. The next two years, however, saw the bitter continuation of the struggle between Harding and the team of Harrington and Notaro, with both sides regularly appealing to the courts to settle their dispute. The feud finally ended in 1986, with Harding regaining his leadership role and Harrington and Notaro leaving the party. Since 1986, Harding has run the party with almost the same total control that Rose possessed during his tenure as party leader, dictating party positions and nominations.

INFLUENCE

The Liberal party has been able to exert considerable influence on the outcomes of elections at the local, state, and national level over the course of its 54-year history. At the local level, Rose masterminded an election victory for incumbent New York City Mayor Robert F. Wagner in 1961. The Tammany Hall machine had decided to deny Wagner a third term, unhappy with some of his reform agenda. Rose designed a "beat the bosses" campaign for Wagner to run on, and while Wagner eventually received the Democratic nomination, it is widely held that the Liberals' extensive campaign effort, coupled with the 213,985 votes Wagner received on the Liberal line, largely delivered the mayor's victory. The party also contributed heavily to John Lindsay's first election as mayor of New York City in 1965, when Lindsay received 244,270 votes on the Liberal line and won by a margin of 136,144 votes. The party then paved the way for the mayor's re-election in 1969, when Lindsay won running only on the Liberal line after the Republican party refused to nominate him for another term. In 1969, Lindsay won re-election by a margin of 159,976 votes. He received 844,023 votes on the Liberal line alone, a total that was sufficient to secure victory.

At the state level, no Democratic candidate in a statewide election has been victorious without also having the Liberal party nomination since the party's founding in 1944. The party has significantly contributed to victory in specific state elections as well. The Liberal line provided 312,595 votes for Herbert Lehman in his 1950 election to the U.S. Senate, an election Lehman won by 246,960 votes. W. Averell Harriman also owed his 1954 election as governor largely to the 264,092 votes he garnered on the Liberal party line, winning the election by just 11,124 votes. Although the party did not provide the margin of victory for Mario Cuomo in his 1982 election as governor, the party's early endorsement of Cuomo over favorite Ed Koch provided the candidate with much needed momentum and legitimacy beyond his home area of Queens.

Despite the fact that it is only a state party, the Liberal party has also played a key role in some presidential contests, delivering 329,235 votes to FDR in 1944. Roosevelt won New York by 316,591 votes that year. The party also substantially helped Harry Truman win in the state in 1948, providing 222,562 votes in an election where Truman's margin of victory in the state was only 39,101. In 1960, John F. Kennedy received 406,178 votes on the Liberal party line in New York and won the state by 383,666 votes.

Of course, the victories of the candidates mentioned above cannot be directly attributed to the Liberal party. As discussed earlier, New York's cross-endorsement rule allows third parties to nominate the candidates of one of the major parties as their own. With the exception of Lindsay in 1969, each of the candidates discussed above also had the nomination of a major party. The presence of a candidate on multiple ballot lines makes it difficult to attribute the margin of victory to one party line over another. It is impossible to determine whether voters who registered their preference for a candidate on a third-party (in this case Liberal party) line would have still voted for the candidate without the presence of the third-party line option. Candidates might very well receive approximately the same number of total votes without possession of a third-party line, but then again, they might not. Citizens wishing to register a specific political message with their vote might possibly vote the third-party line, regardless of the candidate. It is simply impossible to tell. Perhaps more important, candidates in New York *perceive* the lines provided by third parties as important and consequently try hard to obtain certain third-party endorsements. Therefore, while very few electoral victories can be directly attributed to the Liberal party, the vote totals registered on the Liberal party line in the above examples are sizable enough to justify the claim that the Liberal party has played a significant role in selected New York State elections.

The Liberal party has also been able to influence the nomination decisions of the New York Democratic party, by threatening to withhold its nomination from the Democratic designee if it finds him or her unacceptable, a situation some political observers have termed "the tail wagging the dog." Refusing to heed the party's wishes on nominations has proven costly to the Democrats in the past. In 1966, Rose and the Liberal party did not approve of the Democrats' potential nominee for governor, Frank O'Connor. When the Democrats nominated him anyway, the Liberals nominated Franklin D. Roosevelt, Jr., to run on their ticket. Nelson Rockefeller, the Republican gubernatorial nominee, defeated O'Connor in the 1966 election by 392,263 votes. Roosevelt, Jr., received 507,234 votes for governor on the Liberal party line, a number large enough to have given O'Connor and the Democrats a victory.

While the Liberal party has most certainly been influential in the past, that is not the case now. The last date listed for any significant party accomplishment was 1982, the year of Mario Cuomo's first election as governor of New York. Since that time, the Liberal party has been ineffective and inconsequential in the political process, although the decline started much earlier than 1982. As stated earlier, union membership has steadily declined in New York (and the nation) since the late 1950s. In 1969, Louis Stulberg, Dubinsky's successor as the International Ladies' Garment Workers' Union president, ended the union's affiliation with the Liberal party after a three-year dispute with Rose over his management style. In 1966, the party lost its third position on the state ballot to the upstart Conservative party when the Conservative party's gubernatorial candidate got more votes than the Liberal party's candidate. Despite these setbacks, Rose's presence and political skill kept the party in a relatively powerful position, at least in New York City and state politics.

CONCLUSION

Upon Rose's death in 1976, the party began to completely fall apart. Party enrollment numbers began to tumble, and in 1978 the party dropped to the fifth position on the ballot behind the new Right-to-Life party. In 1980, then New York City mayor Ed Koch said he would refuse the Liberal nomination if it was offered, declaring, "The Liberal party died when Alex Rose went to heaven." On top of all these troubles, the aforementioned feud between Harding and Harrington and Notaro was carried out in a very public manner over the course of four years, further tarnishing the party's image and reducing its political clout. By 1986 the Liberal party was at least $100,000 in debt, evicted from its headquarters for prolonged failure to pay rent, and essentially moribund.

Harding clearly had his work cut out for him when he resumed control of the Liberal party in 1986. Despite the dire straits he inherited, and was at least partly responsible for, Harding has managed to keep the party afloat. His methods, however, have left many wondering if, as political observer Joseph Laura put it, "the party chose to barter its soul." During the tenure of Dubinsky and Rose, and continuing throughout the period of Rose's leadership, the Liberals always backed liberal candidates who agreed with the party's agenda. This has changed in recent years under Harding. In 1989, Harding chose to give the Liberal nomination for mayor of New York City to Rudolph Giuliani, whose liberal credentials were questionable at best. The move was widely viewed as a gamble to save the party by attracting some voters back and a maneuver to place the party in a position for some much needed patronage should Giuliani win. Giuliani lost in 1989, but again received the Liberal party nomination for his 1993 campaign for the mayor's office. The move was again seen as a desperate attempt to save the party and receive access to power and patronage appointments. Bill Lynch, campaign manager for Giuliani's Democratic opponent, David Dinkins, said, "Liberal Rudy Giuliani is an oxymoron." This time Giuliani won the election, and Harding received the patronage he was after, with both of his sons and many top Liberal party officials receiving jobs from Giuliani.

Having supplied some of his party's loyal members with jobs, Harding moved to ensure that the Liberals remained on the ballot in New York. For the 1998 gubernatorial election, Harding gave the Liberal party nomination to Betsy McCaughey Ross, who in 1994 was elected lieutenant governor on the Republican and Conservative lines. McCaughey Ross's liberal credentials are almost non-existent. The Liberal party, however, needed its candidate for governor to poll at least 50,000 votes so the party could keep its spot on the ballot, and McCaughey Ross was the only one of four potential Democratic candidates who promised Harding to campaign hard even if she did not receive the Democratic nomination.

McCaughey Ross accomplished what Harding hoped she would, garnering 77,509 votes for governor in the 1998 election. This ensures that the Liberal party will stay on the ballot in New York State until 2002; however, many observers now view the Liberal party with derision and see the party as being on its way out in state politics. The *New York Times* recently ran an editorial terming the Liberals a "party for hire" and calling for an end to the cross-endorsement rule and a companion rule that allows parties to nominate candidates who are not party members. Judith Hope, chairwoman of the New York State Democratic Committee, believes we are currently witnessing the last days of the Liberal party: "They are on the way out. Their days are numbered. It's bye-bye Liberal party, and that's a very good thing." Whether or not Hope's prediction comes true remains to be seen; however, it is clear that the party is no longer the force in New York State politics that it once was. At best, the future of the Liberal party of New York State is cloudy and uncertain.

MARK D. BREWER AND JEFFREY M. STONECASH

See also: American Labor Party; Communist Party; Conservative Party (New York); David Dubinsky; Raymond B. Harding; Right-to-Life Party; Alex Rose.

Bibliography

Behn, Dick. "Liberals and Conservatives: The Importance of New York's 'Third' Parties." *Empire State Report* (April 1977): 164–169.

Gillespie, J. David. *Politics at the Periphery: Third Parties in Two-Party America.* Columbia: University of South Carolina Press, 1993.

Jewell, Malcolm E., and David M. Olson. *American State Political Parties and Elections.* Homewood, IL: Dorsey Press, 1978.

Laura, Joseph. "A Tale of Two Parties." *Empire State Report* (July 1986): 62.

Lynn, Frank. "The Liberals—Is the Party Over?" *Empire State Report* (October 1983): 26–28.

Moscow, Warren. *Politics in the Empire State.* New York: Alfred A. Knopf, 1948.

Scarrow, Howard A. *Parties, Elections, and Representation in the State of New York.* New York: New York University Press, 1983.

Schapsmeier, Edward L., and Frederick H. Schapsmeier. *Political Parties and Civic Action Groups.* Westport, CT: Greenwood Press, 1981.

Spitzer, Robert J. "Third Parties in New York State." In *Governing New York State,* ed. Jeffrey M. Stonecash, John Kenneth White, and Peter W. Colby, pp. 103–116. Albany, NY: State University of New York Press, 1994. (New edition forthcoming, 1999).

Storozynski, Alex. "Two Ends of the Spectrum." *Empire State Report* (October 1989): 17–20.

Wilson, David McKay. "Under The Influence." *Empire State Report* (July 1998): 19–21.

Zimmerman, Joseph F. *The Government and Politics of New York State.* New York: New York University Press, 1981.

Other References

Liberal Party of New York State Web page at http://www.liberalparty.org.

LIBERAL REPUBLICAN PARTY
1872

A BRIEF EXISTENCE

The life of the Liberal Republican party was brief. It was spawned by the dissension that percolated within the Republican party following the Civil War. Prominent Republican patriarchs, dissatisfied with the administration of Republican President Ulysses Grant, nurtured it. It reached maturity in the presidential campaign of 1872. The outcome of that election was its death knell.

The United States of the early 1870s was trying to adjust to the changes occasioned by rapid industrial growth and the economic, social, and political changes that accompanied that growth. In addition, efforts to "reconstruct" the post–Civil War South were ongoing. Disputes over how best to accomplish that objective continued. The federal government under Grant's leadership, (or the lack thereof as some would argue) was still heavily engaged in the business of Reconstruction. The continued presence of federal troops in the southern states would be a reminder of the unsettled state of affairs for several more years.

The Civil War settled the issues of slavery and nullification—issues that provided an adhesive for the Republican party of the 1850s. The political agenda of the 1870s was quite different from the one with which "old guard" Republicans such as Senators Charles Sumner, Lyman Trumbull, and Carl Schurz had been concerned. New Republican leaders such as New York's Roscoe Conkling and Maine's James G. Blaine were taking the party in new directions with different priorities and a different view of politics. This "new" Republican party emphasized the need for a federal government that pro-actively supported capitalistic economic growth and the industrial interests that promoted that growth. Erecting protective tariffs, making generous land grants to railroads and extensive appropriations for improvements to rivers and harbors are examples of the actions advocated by this new breed of Republican party leaders.

Sumner, Trumbull, Schurz, and their cohorts disapproved of these policies and the political values they represented. They feared that the federal government was becoming too big, too powerful, and too intrusive upon local interests and prerogatives. It was not states' rights *per se* that they championed. Their concern was that "big government" posed a threat to the constitutional principle of federalism. They wanted the Grant administration to disengage the federal government from its Reconstruction involvement. Their dissension was also fueled by the perception that the new breed of professional politician had cast its lot with the new breed of industrial "robber barons," such as Jay Gould and Cornelius Vanderbilt. In concert, they were destroying the moral fiber and integrity of America. Furthermore, these old-guard patriarchs were disappointed and dismayed by the corruption, ineptness, and cronyism that characterized President Grant's first term of office.

The mid-term elections of 1870 suggested increasing dissatisfaction with Grant's administration. The Republicans lost seats in both houses of Congress—from 149 to 134 in the House and from 56 to 52 in the Senate. The Democrats gained forty-one seats in the House and six seats in the Senate. The success of Republican dissidents in Missouri was particularly noteworthy. With the aid of Democratic votes they succeeded in electing B. Gratz Brown as governor and Carl Schurz as U.S. senator. These men would soon be instrumental in leading other disenchanted Republicans away from the party of Lincoln to form the Liberal Republican party.

MEMBERSHIP OF LIBERAL REPUBLICANS

The leaders of the Liberal Republican party were highly educated members of society's "upper crust." Political activism was not strange to any of this cadre. Most had been active in the abolitionist movement. Many were old Free-Soilers. Many were founders of the Republican party. Their ranks included former members of Lincoln's cabinet and three of the four then living Republican senators who had refused to vote for the conviction of Andrew Johnson at his impeachment proceedings. Many of those who led the Liberal Republican movement did so because of their opposition to the Reconstruction policies of the Grant administration.

Division within the Republican party grew as the election year of 1872 approached. This schism was actualized when disgruntled Republicans, now calling themselves Liberal Republicans, organized a mass meeting at the Cooper Institute in New York on April 12, 1872. Four powerful newspaper editors—Samuel Bowles of the *Springfield Republican* (Massachusetts), Murat Halstead of the *Cincinnati Commercial*, Horace White of the *Chicago Tribune*, and Colonel Henry "Marse" Watterson of the *Louisville Courier-Journal*—came out in support of the Liberal Republicans. This group came to be known as "the Quadrilateral." Other prominent newspaper moguls such as Whitelaw Reid of the *New York Tribune* added their support. One notable exception to the press's support of the Liberal Republican efforts was E.L. Godkin,

editor of *The Nation*, who characterized the split in the Republican party as the biggest disaster since Bull Run. The support of the Quadrilateral provided much of the impetus for the Republican dissidents to plan an independent national campaign in 1872.

At a national convention held in Cincinnati in May 1872, the Liberal Republicans chose Horace Greeley as their presidential candidate. In the first round of voting at the convention, however, Charles Francis Adams (son of John Quincy Adams and ambassador to Great Britain during the Civil War) received 205 votes, Greeley received 147, Trumbull (senator from Illinois) 110, B. Gratz Brown (governor of Missouri) 95, and David Davis (associate justice of the U.S. Supreme Court) 92. By the fifth ballot, only Adams and Greeley remained in contention receiving 309 and 258 votes respectively. Greeley turned the tide on the sixth and final ballot gaining the nomination with 482 votes to Adams's 187.

Greeley's nomination is perhaps emblematic of the lack of cohesion within the Liberal Republican party. His nomination undoubtedly drove some supporters back to the ranks of the Republican party and discouraged some potential supporters from joining the cause. Greeley's nomination was intended to lure the support of Democrats, who knew they could not defeat Grant on their own. Also, because of his post–Civil War support for Jefferson Davis, Greeley was thought to sympathize with southerners in their efforts to regain political efficacy. (He was a supporter of Jefferson Davis during his trial and offered to bail him out of jail.) The problem with this cast for Democratic support was that Greeley had developed a reputation for being an adamant "Democrat basher." He once wrote, "All Democrats may not be rascals but all rascals are Democrats." Thus, the nomination of Greeley further weakened the already tenuous coalition between Liberal Republicans and Democrats. Furthermore, his previous equivocation on the issue of slavery caused trepidation in both Liberal Republicans and southern Democrats.

The party did not exhibit ideological coherence. While party members were generally op-

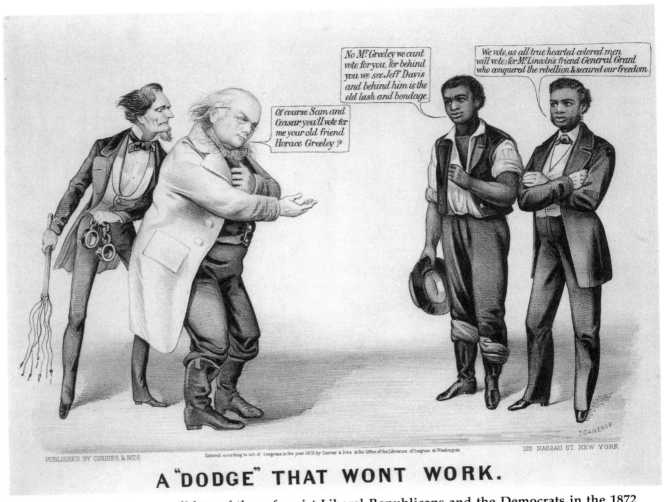

A "DODGE" THAT WONT WORK.

Horace Greeley, fusion candidate of the reformist Liberal Republicans and the Democrats in the 1872 presidential campaign, could not shake the latter's image as the anti–civil rights party of white southerners, as this 1872 Currier and Ives print makes clear. *(Courtesy of the Library of Congress)*

posed to protective tariffs and in favor of civil service reform, it did not provide any uniform, comprehensive policy position on the economy nor on political reform. The party's greatest unifying element was the desire to defeat President Grant. Furthermore, Greeley, the party's presidential candidate, did not particularly favor civil service reform—the Liberal Republicans' main platform proposal—and he had openly opposed lower tariffs. Ultimately, reduction in tariffs was dropped as a plank in the party platform because no agreement could be reached on the issue. Civil service reform was a weak issue that did not capture the public's attention.

Susan B. Anthony attended the convention in hopes of gaining support for women's suffrage. The Liberal Republicans, however, decided that women's rights would not be an issue they would champion in the campaign.

Democrats realized that their only hope for defeating Grant was to capitalize on the division within the Republican ranks. At their convention in Baltimore, Maryland, on July 9–10, the Democrats nominated Greeley, albeit reluctantly. They also adopted the Liberal Republican platform in its entirety. Ultimately, many Democrats did not even bother to vote, much less actively support the ticket.

1872 CAMPAIGN

The general tenor of the presidential campaign of 1872 was dirty and nasty. Greeley's eccentricities (including his rumpled and somewhat peculiar appearance) and his inconsistencies provided fodder for the Republican press. For example, his pronouncements on slavery and Reconstruction were ambivalent. He was anti-slavery, yet he refused to condemn the southern culture. Illustrative of the lambasting that Greeley received is the cartoon by Thomas Nast in *Harper's Weekly* showing Greeley extending his hand over the grave of John Wilkes Booth. There also was concern by those who might otherwise have sympathy for the Liberal Republican causes that, if Greeley were elected, it would mean that the southern Democrats would take over the government.

The Liberal Republicans (and their uneasy Democratic allies) mainly tried to focus the American public's attention on President Grant's appointment of incompetent cronies, his incompetence, his inattention that allowed corruption to permeate his administration, and his intemperance (Greeley was a teetotaler). Other Liberal Republican positions included reconciliation with white southerners and providing amnesty for all, an end to Grant's interventionist Reconstruction policies, civil service reform, tariff reduction, an end to preferential treatment of industrial concerns (for example, land grants for railroad companies), controlling inflation, and reduction in the national debt.

The Liberal Republicans were poorly organized. There was a serious lack of campaign funds. Nonetheless, Greeley campaigned actively and vigorously. He gave more than 200 speeches. Unfortunately for the Liberal Republicans many of these speeches were disastrous. Greeley was constantly saying the wrong things to the wrong audience. In the South, he argued for equal rights for African Americans, not a position that was likely to engender enthusiastic support from southern Democrats. In the North, he argued for universal amnesty for Confederate officers and the withdrawal of troops from the South. This allowed Republi-

cans to reinforce the perception that Greeley was overly sympathetic to the South.

The Liberal Republicans had little, if any, "grassroots" organization. White voters in the South and middle-class reform-minded groups elsewhere provided the bulk of Liberal Republican electoral support. It was expected that dissatisfaction with the ineptness and cronyism of the Grant administration would cause defection of rank-and-file Republicans. However, this did not occur.

Many Democratic/Liberal Republican issues were nullified by the Republican administration's actions during the course of the campaign. Grant made sure that tariffs were lower; the national debt was reduced; income tax was repealed; civil service reform was enacted; and amnesty was granted to most Confederates.

While there was a fair degree of turmoil within and swirling about the political structures and politics of the early 1870s, the general climate of the country was quiescent. The economy was strong and vibrant; financial conditions were stable and prosperity widespread. When the nation is enjoying good times of this sort, worker and employer, farmer and merchant, alike tend to favor the status quo. While the Liberal Republican party was born out of sincere concern for maintaining the political priorities and values upon which the Republican party was originally founded, as was to be demonstrated by the election of 1872, most of the public did not share that concern.

The Liberal Republican/Democratic ticket was defeated soundly. Many southern Democrats stayed home rather than vote for either Greeley or Grant. Some Liberal Republicans simply became disenchanted with the party's ticket and returned to the Republican party fold. Greeley took only six states, all were either border or southern states—namely, Georgia, Kentucky, Maryland, Missouri, Tennessee, and Texas (votes in Louisiana and Arkansas were challenged because of alleged electoral improprieties and subsequently disallowed). He garnered only 2,834,761 (43.83 percent) popular votes to Grant's 3,598,235 (55.64 percent). The Liberal Republicans had very modest success in electing members to Congress. Five were elected to the Senate and fourteen Liberal Republicans were sent to the House of Representatives.

With that, the Liberal Republican party departed the American political scene. Most of its members remained active in politics and went on to champion their causes in other venues. However, like the Liberal Republican party, Horace Greeley did not survive the election of 1872. He died on November 29, 1872, after the election but before the electoral college voted.

In spite of their failure, the Liberal Republicans' challenge unsettled the Republican party leadership. The campaign had revealed renewed Democratic strength. The Republicans took only 50.1 percent of the vote in the South. As a result, rather than retain a rigorous form of Reconstruction, Republicans now resolved to attempt some reconciliation with the South. Thus, it can be argued that the Liberal Republican party, while accomplishing little at the polls, did much to influence the Republican party to move toward national reconciliation. On the other hand, it did little to curb corruption in business and government or to temper economic protectionism that continued to char-acterize politics and public policy during this era.

DONALD E. GRECO

See also: B. Gratz Brown; David Davis; Free Soil Party; Horace Greeley; Carl Schurz; Charles Sumner; Lyman Trumbull.

Bibliography

Binkley, Wilfred E. *American Political Parties,* 2d ed. New York: Alfred A. Knopf, 1949.

Cashman, Sean Dennis. *America in the Gilded Age,* 3d ed. New York: New York University Press, 1993.

Maisel, L. Sandy, and Charles Bassett, eds. *Political Parties and Elections in the United States.* New York: Garland, 1991.

Nash, Howard P., Jr. *Third Parties in American Politics.* Washington, DC: Public Affairs Press, 1959.

Polakoff, Keith I. *Political Parties in American History,* New York: John Wiley and Sons, 1981.

Ross, Earle Dudley. *The Liberal Republican Movement.* Seattle: University of Washington Press, 1910.

Simpson, Brooks D. *The Reconstruction Presidents.* Lawrence: University Press of Kansas, 1998.

LIBERTARIAN PARTY
1971–

EARLY GROWTH

The Libertarian party was founded in David Nolan's living room in Westminster, Colorado, on December 11, 1971. The eight individuals who attended the founding convention included John Hospers, a philosophy professor at the University of Southern California; Edward Crane, the party's first national chair; *Reason* magazine editor Manuel Klausner; economist Murray Rothbard; author R.A. Childs; Theodore Nathan, a businessman from Oregon; and Jim Dean of the *Santa Ana Register* newspaper. By the presidential election of 1972, the party had grown to eighty-five members and the party's nominee, John Hospers, was on four state ballots. He received less than 3,000 votes.

The party had grown to be the third largest political party by the 1976 presidential election. Since 1972, the Libertarian party has nominated a candidate in each presidential election. Numerous Libertarian candidates have campaigned for state and local elected offices, and several have served in appointed posts. The growth of the party is related to the growing dissatisfaction with both the Democrats and Republicans.

The founders of the Libertarian party had been meeting for about four months as the Committee to Form a Libertarian Party. There was some disagreement whether it was the right time for the creation of a party to espouse libertarian principles. Murray Rothbard, for example, did not believe that libertarianism could ever be implemented through the party system. A significant impetus for the creation of the party was the imposition of wage and price controls by the Nixon administration in 1971. According to David Nolan, the early party activists saw that the Democrats and Republicans had drifted away from the libertarian vision of the country's founding fathers. The activists saw Nixon's actions as proof that the government had become authoritarian.

Party founders believed in a unique political philosophy that mixed a strong attachment to capitalism with social Darwinism and its conception that society functions like nature, with rewards to the strongest, and the objectivism of Ayn Rand and its belief in the power of the individual will. The *Libertarian Party News* described the philosophy of the party as a mix of left-wing-style defense of civil liberties and right-wing-style advocacy of free markets, overlaid with a healthy distrust of government power. In short, party members believe that government should just leave them alone.

A number of people have been important to the growth and development of the Libertarian party. A Republican member of the electoral college from Virginia, Roger MacBride, cast a vote for the new party's ticket. MacBride became a celebrity among Libertarians and was the party's 1976 presidential nominee.

Another significant player in the development of the Libertarian party was David Koch, who contributed money to the party. On principle, the Libertarians refuse to accept public campaign financing from the Federal Election Commission. Unfortunately, one fact of modern campaigns is that voters will not accept a party until they know the party's message, and communication costs money. Sharing the ticket with California lawyer Edward Clark, Koch was the party's vice-presidential nominee in 1980. He was nominated to take advantage of the personal campaign spending loophole in federal election campaign law. His contribution of over $2 million helped the party run a respectable campaign and achieve ballot access in all fifty states, the first third party to do so since the Socialists in 1916. Koch's money also allowed the party to establish institutions such as the Cato Institute to develop and communicate libertarian ideas. According to *Mother Jones* writer Mark Paul,

> Until Koch opened his wallet, the movement was a ragtag collection of obscure academics, gold bugs, science fiction nuts, and cranks, united only by their hatred of the state and their joy of squabbling with one another. His money transferred the Libertarian movement from a doughty band of true believers into a political force that is on the verge of becoming the first party since the Socialists to offer a serious challenge to the "Republicrat" monopoly.

One critic of Koch's influence over the party referred to the institutions created with Koch's money as the "Kochtopus."

Koch was brought to the Libertarian party largely through the efforts of Edward Crane, the party's first national chair. Crane had been a financial advisor in California and the California Libertarian party vice chair before being elected national chair in 1974. As national chair, Crane is credited with building the party, primarily with the infusion of Koch's money. Crane and Koch left the party in 1983 after their more pragmatic approach to politics was repudiated in the presidential nominating convention that year.

LIBERTARIAN PRINCIPLES

The principles of the Libertarian party are encapsulated by a declaration on the membership application. The form states, "I hereby certify that I do not believe in or advocate the initiation of force as a means of achieving political or social goals." While Libertarians appear to be anarchists, the Libertarian party does not advocate the end of government. Libertarians are better described as "min-archist," that is, minimal government. The government exists to protect the rights of each individual. These rights include the right to life (anti-abortion), the right to liberty of speech and action, and the right to property. The government must take action when some entity tries to infringe upon these rights.

The 1996 Libertarian national campaign platform applied these principles to many current issues. If elected, Harry Browne, the 1996 Libertarian presidential nominee, promised to reduce the size of government. Government is not inherently bad, but the federal government is big and does not work effectively. Most of the other platform planks emerge from this idea of reducing the size of government.

The income tax would not be necessary with a much smaller government. In fact, according to the Libertarian party, tariffs and excise taxes would provide enough revenue to fund a Libertarian government. Social Security also would be ended. Retirees currently receiving Social Security benefits would receive annuities from private companies purchased with the proceeds from a sale of unnecessary federal assets. Of course, a smaller government requires less spending. Browne proposed cutting 50 percent of the federal budget during his first year in office. He also called for a balanced budget.

Ending welfare has been a Libertarian platform plank for many years. Libertarians also called for the end of federal involvement in education. There is no constitutional requirement for the federal government to be involved in education. With the repeal of the income tax, citizens would be able to afford to send their children to private, or religious schools, or to home school.

The Libertarian position on crime and the "War on Drugs" has attracted significant public attention, and criticism. The platform states that before there were drug laws in the United States, there were no drug problems. Ending the War on Drugs will reduce crime by taking the profit out of the illicit drug trade. In addition, the Libertarians call for the pardon of all persons convicted of non-violent drug offenses to free prison space to hold truly violent criminals.

The platform called for more control over the federal judiciary. If elected, Browne would appoint only those judges who consider the Bill of Rights "a literal, absolute document." Judges would not make decisions that infringe upon any of the rights specified in the Constitution or the Bill of Rights. In general, the Libertarian platform called for Americans to regain their right to choose and act on their own personal values.

The Libertarian party also developed positions on immigration, national defense, and foreign policy. The party sought to end immigration restrictions. Such quotas keep productive and skilled workers from immigrating to this country. The end of welfare would remove the incentive for non-productive people to immigrate to the United States. A Libertarian president would bring all American troops back home and remove the country from all entangling alliances such as NATO.

Abortion has been an issue that the Libertarian party has found difficult to fit into its principles. The party first considered the issue in its 1984 platform. Delegates debated the rights of the woman versus the rights of the unborn child, eventually placing the issue in the context of a woman's property rights. Since a woman's body is her property, she can do with it what she pleases. The party, however, stated that government should not allow tax dollars to be spent on abortions. The abortion issue, combined with the issue of legalizing drugs, has hindered the party's acceptance by voters who might otherwise agree with the notion of limited government.

The Libertarian party is a national party with affiliates in each state and the District of Columbia. The affiliates' status as parties is determined by the ballot access laws in each state.

The party's bylaws govern who may be a member. To become a member, one must pay dues of about $25 and certify opposition to the use of coercion to further political or social goals. At the end of 1996, the party reported about 11,000 dues-paying members. Of course, party membership in the United States is unimportant as voters may cast ballots for any party on election day. In 1996, the party had about 163,000 registered voters in those states that allow registration as a Libertarian.

The party appeals to educated people typically in the computer or engineering fields. Most identify with the need to have the freedom to do what they want. These people are less likely to follow a strict moral code, and political scientists John Green and James Guth found that most do not have a religious affiliation. A number of Libertarian activists surveyed reported an open hostility to religion. Unfortunately, most research focuses on party members and activists with less attention given to those people who vote for Libertarian candidates.

PRESIDENTIAL POLITICS

The Libertarian party's first presidential candidate, John Hospers, appeared on the ballots of four states in 1972, receiving 3,671 popular votes. In 1976, Roger MacBride's name was on thirty-two ballots. He received 173,011 popular votes, or 0.2 percent of the total vote. Most of his support was in Alaska, Hawaii, Arizona, Idaho, California, and Nevada.

The Libertarian ticket of Clark and Koch appeared on ballots in all fifty states and the District of Columbia in 1980. Despite the large expenditure of campaign funds, the ticket garnered only 921,299 votes (1.1 percent). Internal disputes weakened the party by 1984. David Bergland, the nominee, appeared on only forty ballots and received 228,314 votes (0.25 percent). Former congressman Ron Paul (Republican, Texas) was the nominee in 1988. Party leaders thought that the party would benefit from a candidate with an established campaign organization. Paul received 421,720 votes (0.5 percent). In 1992, the party was challenged by the candidacy of Ross Perot. Andre Marrou, a

One of the most successful third parties of the post–World War II era, the Libertarian party did particularly well in 1996 with its national ticket headed by Harry Browne, pictured here at the party's July 4 nominating convention in Washington, D.C. (*Courtesy of the Libertarian party*)

former Libertarian member of the Alaska House of Representatives, received 291,612 votes (0.3 percent). Economist and author Harry Browne garnered 485,586 votes (0.5 percent) in the 1996 election. This total put the Libertarian candidate in fifth place behind Perot and Green party nominee Ralph Nader.

The Libertarian party has enjoyed success in state and local elections. In 1996, more than 800 Libertarian candidates ran for public office. By the end of 1996, the party had 171 members serving in elected or appointed office, primarily at the local level.

Two major obstacles block the Libertarian party's road to major party status. The first challenge is money. The party's most significant growth occurred during the late 1970s when David Koch provided financial resources. In 1996, the party spent $3 million on the Harry

Browne campaign, not enough to adequately communicate the Libertarian message. Ross Perot spent $30 million communicating his critique of the federal government, taking some potential support away from the Libertarians. Perot also accepted public financing for his campaign in 1996.

The second major obstacle the Libertarians must confront is a problem that has plagued other third parties in American history. The two major parties regularly adopt third-party proposals as their own. For example, President Ronald Reagan worked to reduce government, end welfare, and cut taxes—all important items on the Libertarian program. While his proposals were not completely adopted, Reagan's actions took some of the attention away from the Libertarians. In the 1994 elections, the Republican party regained control of both houses of Congress by advocating many Libertarian proposals. The only Libertarian ideas not typically adopted by the other parties are items such as legalizing drugs and decriminalizing victimless crimes. When reducing government and ending welfare become part of mainstream politics, the media focuses on the Libertarian party's more radical ideas. This has the effect of discouraging potential supporters, while it makes an interesting news story. Many who have libertarian views choose to remain in the Republican party; in fact, the Republican Liberty Caucus is an organization of libertarian Republicans.

Despite the inability to achieve more than 2 percent of the presidential popular vote, the Libertarian party has contributed to the American party system. For example, many ideas that were considered radical in the 1970s have become topics of mainstream political debate. One such idea is privatizing government services. The Libertarians were talking about privatizing Social Security at their first presidential nominating convention in 1972.

The Libertarian party also has changed the political map in America. At one time, most observers discussed American politics as left to right. Now, political scientists must consider a four-way matrix that includes libertarianism and authoritarianism.

Libertarian candidates have affected the outcome of a number of important races. In 1992, the Libertarian candidate for U.S. Senate in Georgia captured enough votes to keep incumbent Senator Wyche Fowler, a Democrat, from winning an absolute majority. Since Georgia law requires that a candidate must receive more than 50 percent of the vote to be elected, Fowler and Paul Coverdell, the Republican candidate, were forced into a unique general run-off election. Coverdell was elected.

The party has turned adversity to advantage and helped other third parties in this country. Most states have ballot access regulations that make it difficult for parties other than the Democrats and Republicans to achieve ballot status. In many states, third-party candidates must circulate petitions and/or pay filing fees not required of the two major parties. The Libertarian party, through lawsuits and lobbying, has made it easier for other parties to appear on the ballot. Ironically, many of these other third parties have attracted the support of Americans who are dissatisfied with the two major parties. These dissatisfied voters are the key to the growth of the Libertarian party.

JOHN DAVID RAUSCH, JR.

See also: Harry Browne; **Map 8:** Libertarian Party (1980); **Map 9:** Libertarian Party (1984); **Map 10:** Libertarian Party (1988); **Map 11:** Libertarian Party (1992); **Map 12:** Libertarian Party (1996); Reform Party.

Bibliography

Bergland, David. *Libertarianism in One Lesson*, 6th ed. Costa Mesa, CA: Orpheus Publications, 1993.

Boaz, David. *Libertarianism: A Primer*. New York: Free Press, 1997.

Browne, Harry. *Why Government Doesn't Work*. New York: St. Martin's Press, 1995.

Green, John C., and James L. Guth. "The Sociology of Libertarians." *Liberty* (September–October 1987).

Hazlett, Joseph M. *The Libertarian Party and Other Minor Political Parties in the United States*. Jefferson, NC: McFarland, 1992.

Hospers, John. *Libertarianism: A Political Philosophy for Tomorrow*. Los Angeles: Nash, 1971.

Kelly, John L. *Bringing the Market Back In: The Political Revitalization of Market Liberalism*. New York: New York University Press, 1997.

MacBride, Roger L. *A New Dawn for America: The Libertarian Challenge*. Ottawa, IL: Green Hill, 1977.

Paul, Mark. "Seducing the Left: The Third Party that Wants You." *Mother Jones* (May 1980).

Raimondo, Justin. *Reclaiming the American Right: The Lost Legacy of the Conservative Movement*. Burlingame, CA: Center for Libertarian Studies, 1993.

☆☆☆☆☆☆☆☆☆☆☆☆☆☆☆☆☆☆☆☆
LIBERTY PARTY
1840–1848

ANTISLAVERY ROOTS

The Liberty party was founded in 1840 as the electoral wing of the movement to abolish slavery. It nominated James G. Birney for president in 1840 and 1844 and also nominated several candidates for the U.S. House of Representatives and for a scattering of local offices. Although its candidates were never elected, and most received few votes, the party's presence may have affected the outcome of the 1844 presidential election and some congressional elections in New England. The party's formal existence ended in 1848, when it joined with dissident Barnburner Democrats and "Conscience" Whigs to form the Free Soil party, abandoning its 1847 nomination of John P. Hale of New Hampshire. However, a dissident faction continued as the Liberty League for several more years.

The Liberty party ranks included many antislavery luminaries. Among these, in addition to Birney and Hale, were found at one time or another Gerrit Smith, Salmon P. Chase, Joshua Leavitt, Henry Stanton, Lewis Tappan, and Birney's two running mates, Thomas Earle (1840) and Thomas Morris (1844). Others opposed it, however, from both ends of the antislavery spectrum. On one hand, the followers of abolitionist William Lloyd Garrison objected strongly to the party's willingness to use state action, rather than moral suasion alone, to bring slavery to an end, as well as its refusal to endorse full political rights for women. Matters came to a head at the 1840 convention of the American Antislavery Society, held soon after the founding of the Liberty party. Garrison and

his supporters won resolutions to seat women as delegates and to oppose electoral action. His opponents, including Birney and Stanton, the society's corresponding secretaries, then left the organization and founded the competing American and Foreign Antislavery Society.

On the other hand, most of those antislavery activists who did support electoral action believed that such action would be most effective if directed toward supporting antislavery Whigs. Liberty party members believed it was wrong to vote for a party that included slaveholders within its ranks, as the Whigs certainly did, so they ran candidates against even such strongly abolitionist Whigs as Joshua Giddings of Ohio (although they did support Giddings in 1842, after the House of Representatives had expelled him for a speech in favor of the slaves' right to revolt on the brig *Creole*). Giddings was strong enough to survive the Liberty challenge, but in some Massachusetts districts, where a majority was required for election, Liberty campaigns sometimes caused congressional seats to go to candidates with a plurality rather than a majority. Many committed abolitionists objected to a practice that undercut antislavery officeholders of other parties, so the Liberty vote was always far below the membership of the antislavery societies.

However, for most Liberty voters political effectiveness was at best a secondary concern. In their view, it was far more important to vote in accordance with one's conscience than it was for that vote to have an effect on state action. Once Birney had been nominated in 1840, together with his running mate, Thomas Earle of Pennsylvania, very little attempt was made to actually mobilize voters. Birney himself spent the entire length of the campaign traveling to and from the World Antislavery Convention held that summer in London (where he was elected a vice president of the convention and helped to argue successfully against Wendell Phillips's motion to accept women as delegates). Birney and Earle received only 6,797 votes, with many of their supporters arriving at the polls to find, at a time when ballots were printed and distributed by the parties, that Liberty ballots were not available.

Despite this seemingly weak beginning, the party forged ahead with little self-doubt. Birney was nominated again for the 1844 election, this time with Thomas Morris of Ohio, a former Democratic senator, as his running mate. The Liberty presidential vote swelled to 62,103. This was only 2.3 percent, but enough to constitute the margin of victory in three states—Ohio, Michigan, and New York. Ohio was carried by the Whig candidate, Henry Clay, but Michigan and New York by the Democrat, James Polk. Had one-third of the Liberty voters in New York supported Clay instead, Clay would have won both the state and the presidency. Both Polk and Clay were slaveholders, but Polk was committed to the annexation of Texas and other pro-slavery causes, while Clay was more inclined to compromise. When Texas was admitted as a slave state in 1845, antislavery Whigs blamed the Liberty party; Liberty supporters retorted that the Whigs should have offered a better candidate. Whether it was condemned or praised, Birney's 2.3 percent demonstrated the reality that the issue of slavery could no longer be compromised or ignored in American politics.

Initially, the Liberty party had no platform. Its "one aim" was hostility to slavery and to the slave power. Since most of the party accepted the view that the federal government had no power to abolish slavery in the states, this meant in practice that the party opposed slavery in the territories and the District of Columbia, and the admission of new slave states. The party also vowed to appoint only opponents of slavery to federal office and, following the defeat of Chase's more moderate position at its 1843 convention, declared that the fugitive slave laws were null and void.

However, as the party took up its work, it discovered that a single-issue stance did not satisfy many of the antislavery voters; it responded by explaining that slavery was at the root of most other national problems, so that abolition was the best solution to them all. At its 1841 convention, which renominated Birney for the 1844 campaign, it issued an eight-point platform: new world markets for the products of free labor, tax-free imports of cotton and manufactured goods, opposition to a national bank, disposal of public lands to free immigrant settlers rather than slaveholders, an end to war on the American Indians, support for human rights and republican principles, universal public education, and direct election of the president and vice president. In 1842, Birney ran for governor of Michigan on a program endorsing the opening of world markets (so that trade with the slave states would not be necessary), public education of all classes and races, and a sound currency.

REGIONAL STRENGTHS

The Liberty party's strength was highly regional. It did not exist in the South and not much in the border states. (However, in 1844, Birney received 4,836 votes, or 5.7 percent, in Maryland.) Although some abolitionists had lived in the South, few were able to remain there; Birney himself was forced to leave Alabama for Kentucky, and later to leave Kentucky for Ohio, because of his views. Most of its votes came from New England, New York, and the states of the old Northwest. The 1844 Birney-Morris vote was above 8 percent in Massachusetts, New Hampshire, Vermont, and Michigan. The percentages were lower in New York (15,812 votes, or 3.3 percent) and Ohio (8,082 votes, or 2.6 percent), but in absolute numbers these populous states were at the core of Liberty support and activism.

The party's support everywhere had a strong religious component. Many members had been influenced by such revivalist preachers as Charles Grandison Finney and saw political activity for justice as a moral duty. Many ministers were party members, and entire congregations sometimes joined.

At the congressional level, Liberty offered candidates for the House of Representatives in every year but one from between 1840 and 1847: 2 in 1840, 3 in 1842, 11 in 1843, 17 in 1844, 1 in 1845, 21 in 1846, and 8 (all but one from Maine) in 1847. The Liberty view was that it was wrong to remain in a party with slaveholders. Hence, it did not hesitate to put up candidates against abolitionist Whigs. Edward Wade ran three times against Joshua Giddings; his vote grew from 7.5 percent in 1843 to 12.9 percent in 1846.

No Liberty congressional candidate was elected (although one was appointed to the Senate for a short term); none ever finished ahead of a Whig or Democrat. Occasionally, as with the 1844 presidential election, the party held the balance of power. Its impact was particularly great in New England, where the laws at that time required a candidate to get a majority of all votes cast in order to be elected. In 1841, the small Liberty vote kept some eighty seats in the Massachusetts legislature vacant; the next year, seven out of the ten Massachusetts congressional seats were similarly unfilled.

Beginning in 1841, the Liberty party worked to develop a party organization similar to those of the Democrats and Whigs, with committees at every level down to the smallest ward. The party also developed a lively but struggling press. By 1844, it published three daily, twenty weekly, and two semi-monthly papers, with a total circulation of about 35,000 copies per week.

The election of 1844 made it clear that the antislavery vote would have to be reckoned with. However, it was also clear that many antislavery voters, abolitionists included, were not willing to give their vote to a candidate or party limited to one idea. This situation created great pressure for the Liberty party to broaden its appeal. Many activists sought to do so, while others insisted that only a pure antislavery message, rooted in moral force rather than appeals

to the interests of white voters, could bring slavery to an end.

A complex struggle developed within the party. First, Birney and his allies attempted to broaden the Liberty platform itself. They proposed a program of universal reform, including cuts in the pay and perquisites of the president and members of Congress, free trade, unlimited liability for stockholders, and an end to the standing army and navy. Despite Birney's support, this proposal was rejected by Liberty conventions in Michigan and Chicago.

Another group, led by William Goodell of New York, chose to form a new party rather than struggle within the old one. Goodell had proposed a broader program to the New York Liberty party convention in 1845, where it had been defeated; in 1847, however, Gerrit Smith, long a defender of "one idea," was converted to the idea of a broader platform. Goodell then organized an unauthorized national convention in June 1845 in Macedon Lock, New York. The convention launched a new party, the Liberty League, and nominated Smith for president.

Finally, a group led by Salmon Chase sought to merge the Liberty party with antislavery Whigs and Democrats to form a new antislavery party with a broader platform. Such an alliance had taken control of the state of New Hampshire in 1846, electing as governor an antislavery Whig, Anthony Colby, and sending both the antislavery ex-Democrat John P. Hale and, for a short term, Joseph Cilley of the Liberty party to the Senate.

Chase's strategy prevailed. The annexation of Texas, the resulting war with Mexico, and the congressional battle over the Wilmot Proviso made it more and more difficult for either the Whigs or the Democrats to bridge the division over slavery. Chase failed to convince the October 1847 Liberty convention in Buffalo to defer a nomination pending negotiations with the antislavery elements of the other parties, but Hale, who was nominated, indicated that he would withdraw should a broader coalition come into being. Such a coalition came together in August 1848, when some 10,000 to 20,000 people assembled in Buffalo to found the Free Soil party. Henry Stanton read a letter from

MARRIAGE OF THE FREE SOIL AND LIBERTY PARTIES.

The alliance of the antislavery Free Soil party, as depicted by its presidential candidate Martin Van Buren, and the openly abolitionist Liberty party, as portrayed by a caricature of an African-American woman, is the subject of ridicule in this 1848 cartoon. *(Courtesy of the Library of Congress)*

Hale withdrawing as a Liberty candidate, and Martin Van Buren was nominated. A small group of Liberty men tried to keep the party going, but failed, and the Liberty party was effectively at an end.

The merger of the Liberty party into the Free Soil party meant the abandonment of many of the former's principles. In particular, while Liberty had always held that the fundamental evil of slavery was its injustice to the slave, and had upheld racial equality as well as the end of slavery, Free Soil's emphasis was squarely on the interests of northern white people in ending the power of the slaveowners over the rest of the nation. Some scholars have argued that the change constituted a failure for the Liberty party. In one sense it was, and some of the Liberty leaders left politics because of this failure. However, given the structure of American elec-

tions it is difficult to see how the party could have done otherwise. Moreover, by 1848, the economic and political contradictions around slavery had reached a point where even the moderate Free Soil program could have no other result than the emancipation of the slaves.

JOHN C. BERG

See also: James Gillespie Birney; Salmon P. Chase; Free Soil Party; Joshua Giddings; John P. Hale; Whig Party.

Bibliography

Blue, Frederick J. *Salmon P. Chase: A Life in Politics.* Kent: Kent State University Press, 1987.

Bretz, Julian R. "The Economic Background of the Liberty Party." *American Historical Review* 24 (1929): 250–264.

Fladeland, Betty. *James Gillespie Birney: Slaveholder to*

Abolitionist. Ithaca, NY: Cornell University Press, 1955.

Friedman, Lawrence J. *Gregarious Saints: Self and Community in American Abolitionism 1830–1870.* Cambridge: Cambridge University Press, 1982.

Harlow, Ralph Volney. *Gerrit Smith, Philanthropist and Reformer.* New York: H. Holt, 1939.

Kraditor, Aileen S. "The Liberty and Free Soil Parties." In *History of U.S. Political Parties,* ed. Arthur M. Schlesinger, Jr. New York: Chelsea House, 1973.

Kraut, Alan M. "The Forgotten Reformers: A Profile of Third Party Abolitionists in Antebellum New York." In *Antislavery Reconsidered: New Perspectives on the Abolitionists,* ed. Lewis Perry and Michael Fellman. Baton Rouge: Louisiana State University Press, 1979.

———, ed. *Crusaders and Compromisers: Essays on the Relationship of the Antislavery Struggle to the Antebellum Party System.* Contributions in American History, no. 104. Westport, CT: Greenwood Press, 1983.

Maizlish, Stephen E. *The Triumph of Sectionalism: The Transformation of Ohio Politics, 1844–1856.* Kent: Kent State University Press, 1983.

Middleton, Stephen. *Ohio and the Antislavery Activities of Attorney Salmon Portland Chase, 1830–1849.* Distinguished Studies in American Legal and Constitutional History. New York: Garland, 1990.

Niven, John. *Salmon P. Chase: A Biography.* New York: Oxford University Press, 1995.

Sewell, Richard H. *Ballots for Freedom: Antislavery Politics in the United States, 1837–1860.* New York: Norton, 1980.

Sorin, Gerald. *The New York Abolitionists: A Case Study of Political Radicalism.* Contributions in American History, no. 11. Westport, CT: Greenwood Press, 1971.

Volpe, Vernon L. *Forlorn Hope of Freedom: The Liberty Party in the Old Northwest, 1838–1848.* Kent: Kent State University Press, 1990.

———. "The Liberty Party and Polk's Election, 1844." *The Historian* 53 (1991): 691–710.

☆☆☆☆☆☆☆☆☆☆☆☆☆☆☆☆☆☆☆☆☆☆☆☆☆☆☆☆
LIBERTY UNION PARTY OF VERMONT

1970–1976

While traditionally conservative in nature, Vermont has had a long history of third-party activity. Perhaps this is due to the nationalistic spirit existing in the people of the state, something which is rarely found in states outside the South. Vermonters are proud of their independent political culture and never tire of reminding out-of-staters that Vermont, like Texas, was an independent republic before joining the Union. "Vermont is a way of life" reads one bumper sticker. It was precisely amid this independent spirit, during the heady days of anti-war protests and demonstrations for the creation of a Vermont nation, that the Liberty Union party was formed in 1970.

After Eugene McCarthy's presidential bid in 1968, a group of his anti-war activist-volunteers returned to Vermont to take up their liberal and radical causes. In 1970, Bernie Sanders and political science professor Michael Parenti formed the Liberty Union party. A year after its founding, the Liberty Union party ran its first candidate for office as Bernie Sanders sought election to the U.S. Senate—a seat made open by Winston Prouty's death. He won around 2 percent of the vote. In 1972, Sanders ran for the governor's office. This time the Liberty Union candidate received only 1 percent of the vote total.

While not successful in electoral politics in its early days, the Liberty Union party was much more successful in its work *between* elections. In 1973, the Liberty Union party organized a statewide campaign to defeat a constitutional amendment that would have extended the term of many state offices from two years to four years. Liberty Union activists saw this as a way of centralizing power away from the people; not coincidentally, both major parties supported the amendment. The Liberty Union faithful went from town to town distributing leaflets, appeared on radio talk shows, spent every cent of their $200 war chest, and got their message out. In the end, they had won: The amendment went down to defeat.

By 1974, the party's profile had been raised considerably. Marches on the state capital to protest cuts in services to low-income people were quite successful. One major factor in the success was the involvement of organized labor in the protests. Construction workers who had been abandoned by Democratic Governor Tom Salmon joined with Liberty Union; they had come to realize that "welfare" was not a dirty word for those unemployed. Later that year, the party ran forty-three local and statewide candidates. Parenti ran on the Liberty Union ticket for the state's only congressional seat; Sanders again ran for governor. Both polled around 7 percent of the popular vote. During the election, pundits were arguing that Vermont was fast becoming a three-party state. Liberty Union had reached its zenith in influence.

However, the party's influence waned in the years after 1974. Bernie Sanders ran once more on the Liberty Union ticket in 1976 for governor. He received 6 percent of the vote. Sanders left the party shortly thereafter, arguing that the party lacked sufficient activists and resources to be successful. He later went on to be elected to the U.S. House of Representatives as an independent, where he currently serves. Yet, faced with declining support at the polls and few resources, the Liberty Union party lost its backing

349

and the public profile it had fought hard to maintain in the previous years.

While Liberty Union's upswing can be attributed to several factors, the cause of its decline can certainly be found in its lack of resources. As Parenti says, "The lifeblood of electoral politics is money." The party was not able to compete with the major parties in fundraising; furthermore, funds are sure to dry up when performance at the polls weakens, especially in the winner-take-all system of American electoral politics. Although some want to continue registering a protest vote, many people do not want to continually vote for a loser. And Liberty Union activists found it difficult to support themselves while engaged in the difficult full-time work of politics. Despite this, Liberty Union sought to provide Vermonters an alternative to the mainstream politics of the 1970s, which, as Parenti pointed out, was "left to the likes of George Wallace and Ronald Reagan."

CHRISTOPHER MALONE

See also: Bernard Sanders; Vermont Progressive Coalition.

Bibliography

Parenti, Michael. "A Third Party Emerges in Vermont." *Massachusetts Review* 16, no. 3 (1975): 490–504.

LOWNDES COUNTY FREEDOM ORGANIZATION

1966–1967

The Lowndes County Freedom Organization (LCFO) was founded in Alabama in 1966 by the Student Non-violent Coordinating Committee (SNCC), which consisted of idealistic college students with a dream that the promise and spirit of American democracy could be extended to each and every person in society. These students coalesced in the early 1960s with like-minded allies to make these principles and precepts real in the nation's segregated South, where the embedded values of white supremacy made democracy a limited and race-based reality. Hence, in the bedrock counties of the region—the black-belt counties—where democracy for some faded and for others became shaded into racial tyranny, SNCC entered to empower the disenfranchised.

SNCC VOTER REGISTRATION AND PARTY FORMATION

Even before they formed political parties such as the LCFO, the SNCC immediately encountered stiff, stubborn, violent, and brute resistance to their voter registration drives of the 1960s. Hence, they quickly came to realize that mere idealism and moral suasion alone wilted before long-entrenched white power. The political ideology of the South and its elected officials were prepared to defend their secular religion—segregation. Hence, the moral crusaders of SNCC decided to organize and tackle the problem another way.

In Mississippi in 1964, SNCC activists, along with local white moderates and northern white college students, created the Mississippi Freedom Democratic party (MFDP) and with it launched an assault on segregation at the 1964 National Democratic Convention, hoping that white liberals and well-placed moderates would not let the principles and precepts of democracy be so flagrantly violated and set aside. However, the liberal and white moderate politicians at the national convention did what politicians do best: They compromised. The SNCC activists, however, believed they had compromised on principles, and the SNCC Mississippi workers, despite appeals from civil rights leaders such as Martin Luther King, Jr., rejected the compromise. As they saw it, national party leaders had let the values of the nation-state slip away, even in the glare of national coverage on television. Nevertheless, the SNCC activists decided to give the national political elites one more opportunity. This time, instead of party elites, SNCC turned to Congress. Few understood that SNCC was seeking to expose the complicity of national institutions and national liberal and moderate leaders with the southern system of racial exclusion.

To test Congress, MFDP ran candidates against most of the incumbent white Democrats who supported white supremacy and segregation, both of which denied democracy and undergirded racial tyranny in Mississippi. These candidates promptly and predictably lost in the 1964 November general election. In 1965, SNCC filed with the House of Representatives seating challenges that could have overturned the election results for four of the five re-elected congressmen and the one re-elected senator. And although congressional public hearings were held, Congress dismissed the seating challenges, plainly denying African Americans participation in the political system. SNCC activists had now seen their cherished idealism fail on three different and separate occasions: first, the extreme white resistance to the voter registration drives; second, at the Democratic National Convention; and third, in the halls of Congress. They predicted from these three experiences, especially the latter two, that their white liberal and moderate allies, and their tactic of political goodwill, would vanish should a crisis arise such as an intense political conflict with the white majority.

THE LOWNDES COUNTY FREEDOM ORGANIZATION

After much soul searching, SNCC concluded that a new strategy to realize democracy in America would be one of self-reliance and self-determination. African Africans would have to carry their own cause and burden. To effect this change in political strategy, they chose to build and organize a county-level political party at the grassroots level. Hence, they chose a single county in Alabama, with an African-American population majority, Lowndes County, in which to launch this county-level political party.

On March 3, 1966, SNCC activists held an organizing convention in Lowndes County. Due to the high illiteracy rate in the state, the new political entity, the Lowndes County Freedom Organization (LCFO), used a symbol of the black panther so that it would be easily recognized by the African-American electorate. Immediately before and after the organizing convention, the white state Democratic leaders, led by Governor George Wallace, attempted to cripple the fledgling political party.

Under direction of Governor Wallace in 1965, the state legislature had passed a law that

extended the length of each white elected official's term of office in black-belt Bullock County. This action was designed to preempt any possible takeover and to serve as a model of what would happen if such an effort was made. The Bullock County model served as a harbinger of things to come. Within a month and a half after the founding convention of the LCFO, on May 3, 1966, the Lowndes County Democratic party executive committee upped the qualifying fee for the upcoming state Democratic primary by 1,000 percent. For the majority of offices, the fee went from $50 to $500. By way of justification, party chairman, Robert Dickson, Jr., said that a new party meant more competition, and more money was needed to compete.

Reacting to this new obstacle, the party's leadership urged blacks in the county to boycott the state's upcoming Democratic primaries. Given that Governor Wallace was backing his wife to succeed him, other African-American leaders in the state felt that the boycott strategy was ill advised. They requested that Martin Luther King, Jr., visit the state under his organizational banner, the Southern Christian Leadership Conference (SCLC), and urge primary participation. During his tour of the state, King consciously avoided Lowndes.

LCFO ELECTION RESULTS

Nonetheless, the LCFO held its own primary and nominated candidates for the 1966 general elections. By October 1966, the chairman of the LCFO announced that the party would place eight candidates on the ballot. Eventually, seven ran: One each for sheriff, coroner, tax assessor, tax collector, and three for the Board of Education. Just prior to the election, Stokely Carmichael, the incoming chairman of the SNCC and popularizer and chief spokesperson for "black power," declared that this party's forthcoming victory would be a perfect example of the slogan. His support, however, may have set into motion a political backlash, for the

LCFO did not achieve victory in its initial political contest.

In the election, the vote for the LCFO candidates stood at 1,630 while that for the white incumbents stood at 2,170. This implied that numerous African-American voters supported white candidates. This was partly true because of the economic dependence of these voters upon white merchants, businessmen, and farmers, some of whom, according to Justice Department observers, intervened and had their field hands vote as instructed.

The election outcome severely hindered and handicapped the LCFO. In the next year, however, the LCFO merged with a new African-American statewide party—the National Democratic Party of Alabama (NDPA). Then, in 1970, the LCFO chair, John Hulett, was elected sheriff; Alma Miller was elected circuit clerk; and Ed McGhee became coroner. By the time that the NDPA faded from the state in 1982, African Americans held most of the power in Lowndes County.

LEGACY OF THE LCFO

The simple achievement of the LCFO was the eventual empowerment of African Americans in a county where they had a popular and political majority. The party eventually was absorbed into the NDPA, which would go on to help reform the state Democratic party from an exclusive to an inclusive organization.

One unique aspect of this county-level political organization reached well beyond the confines of the county and ultimately the state. The party symbol, the black panther, would go on to become the symbol and name for one of the most distinct and unique African-American political groups in the nation, the Black Panther party. This organization still reverberates in the nation's psyche and consciousness.

HANES WALTON, JR.

See also: Black Panther Party; Stokely Carmichael (Kwame Toure); Mississippi Freedom Democratic Party; National Democratic Party of Alabama; George C. Wallace.

Bibliography

Analavage, R. "A Victory in Defeat in Lowndes." National Guardian, November 19, 1966.

Carson, Clayborne. In Struggle: SNCC and the Black Awakening in the 1960s. Cambridge: Harvard Univesity Press, 1981.

Cook, Samuel DuBois. "The Tragic Myth of Black Power." New South (February 1966).

Hulett, John; Stokely Carmichael; and J. Benson. The Black Panther Party. New York: Merit, 1966.

Kopkind, Andrew. "Lair of the Black Panther." New Republic, August 13, 1966.

Toure, Kwame, and Charles V. Hamilton. Black Power: The Politics of Liberation. New York: Vintage Press, 1967.

Walton, Hanes, Jr. Black Political Parties: An Historical and Political Analysis. New York: Free Press, 1972.

☆☆

MINNESOTA FARMER-LABOR PARTY

1916–

Among the many portraits of Minnesota's governors that hang in the white-marbled gallery in its state capitol is one of Governor Floyd B. Olson, one of several third-party governors which that state has now had. The canvas shows him holding a radio microphone as he confidently holds one's gaze. But apart from the visual reference to a new communication technology, the picture cannot really capture how exceptional a politician the man and his movement were. Unlike the independent entrepreneurs who have recently occupied American governorships in such diverse states as Alaska and Connecticut, Olson instead headed an organizationally robust party—indeed, the most successful example of a state-level, radical third party in American history.

The Minnesota Farmer-Labor party emerged during the domestic stresses of World War I. It was an amalgam of the state branch of the national Nonpartisan League (a farm protest movement that originated in North Dakota), the Minneapolis Socialist party (then locally strong), and the Minnesota State Federation of Labor (which soon formally voted an ongoing affiliation with the party's slating organization, the Farmer-Labor Association). The Farmer-Labor party grew rapidly until the mid-1920s and enjoyed particular success in capturing a share of the state's congressional delegation. The party advocated the defense of worker and farmer rights as a means of mobilizing voters in urban and rural regions of the state. In 1924 it played a key role in the third-party presidential campaign of Robert La Follette. But as the nation began to "keep cool" with Calvin Coolidge, the party faltered, losing attractive candidates, voter enthusiasm, and eventually the formal support of the Minnesota Federation of Labor.

Then in 1930 the party's 1924 gubernatorial candidate, Floyd B. Olson, decided to run again. Olson was intelligent, handsome, and evidently charismatic, a gifted speaker who could establish a rapport with angry farmers crowded outside his office as well as with the party faithful in a convention hall. In the early 1920s he fought his way into the Minnesota legal establishment with a degree from a night law school. He was an early leader in the American Civil Liberties Union, whose founders sought to protect the right of free political speech for left-wing radicals in the Nonpartisan League, the Socialist party, and the Communist party, and to protect the civil liberties of labor organizers and strikers. Olson was also an experienced litigator and criminal prosecutor who served for many years as Hennepin County Attorney, a jurisdiction that includes Minneapolis.

Olson's political heyday ran from 1931 to August 1936, when he died in office from stomach cancer. During this period the Farmer-Labor party prospered, as shown by the table displaying key aspects of Farmer-Labor electoral strength. (See table on page 355.)

The party grew to control the state's congressional delegation and by 1936 had elected, for the first time, two full-term senators (though twice before it had briefly controlled Minnesota's senate delegation, in 1923–24 and 1935–36). As the right-most column in the table shows, the party also made rapid progress in mobilizing voters to support its candidates for all statewide executive offices, including state treasurer, secretary of state, attorney general,

FARMER-LABOR ELECTORAL STRENGTH, 1930–36

Year	Farmer-Labor Vote for Governor (%)	U.S. House Seats Won by Farmer-Labor Party (%)	Number of U.S. Senate Seats Held by Farmer-Labor Party	U.S. House Districts Contested by Farmer-Labor Party (%)	Change in Mean of Total Absolute Number of All Voters, All Executive Offices (%)	Change in Mean of Total Absolute Number of Farmer-Labor Voters, All Executive Offices (%)
1930	59.3	10	1	80		
1932	50.6	55	1	*	+33.6	+33.1
1934	44.6	33.3	1	100	+2.0	+5.5
1936	60.7	66.6	2	100	+9.5	+25.0

Source: Richard M. Valelly, *Radicalism in the States: The Minnesota Farmer-Labor Party and the American Political Economy.* Chicago: University of Chicago Press, 1989, pp. 119–120.

*Election at large

and lieutenant governor, as well as the governorship. This column shows the percent increase from election to election in the average of the total absolute number of Farmer-Labor voters for all statewide executive offices, and it can be compared to the column immediately to the left. Comparing the two columns suggests that all Minnesota voters increasingly cared about the other statewide executive offices besides the governorship and Farmer-Labor voters cared even more than the electorate as a whole about the entire set of state executive posts.

Of course, Olson does not deserve the entire credit (or even the lion's share of it) for these changes. As the table indicates, his own electoral performance actually declined. It was his highly controversial successor, Elmer Benson, who put in the better performance. Olson's leadership, however, was doubtless a factor in the party's growth spurt between 1930 and 1936—a record that makes it the best-known example of a cluster of organizations that, with the exception of the Wisconsin Progressive party (1934–48), emerged west of the Mississippi in the 1920s and 1930s.

These political formations combined agrarian populism, Debsian socialism, militant trade unionism, and middle-class progressivism, in various mixes and degrees. Other examples of

similar organizations in other states were the North Dakota Nonpartisan League (1915–56), the Washington Farmer-Labor party (1920–24), the Idaho Progressive party (1920–26), and the Oklahoma Farmer-Labor Reconstruction League (1922). Other more ephemeral organizations existed in Montana, South Dakota, and Texas. All mounted gubernatorial and congressional campaigns. The North Dakota Nonpartisan League and the Oklahoma Farmer-Labor Reconstruction League succeeded in electing governors, as did the Minnesota Farmer-Labor party and the Wisconsin Progressive party.

THE POLICY ACCOMPLISHMENTS OF THE FARMER-LABOR PARTY

Of these various vehicles for activist, radical government, the Minnesota Farmer-Laborites did the most to affect local, state, and national policy. The party changed collective bargaining in Minnesota, and it slowed the rate at which farmers were forced off the land by economic crisis during the second half of the Hoover ad-

Rural poverty, like this scene from the Lake of the Woods region in 1939, led many Minnesota farmers to join the Farmer-Labor party in the 1920s and 1930s. *(John Vachon, September 1939, courtesy of the Library of Congress)*

ministration, before passage of the 1933 federal Agricultural Adjustment Act. Two other constituencies of the Farmer-Labor party that joined its coalition in the late 1920s and early 1930s were small businessowners facing competition from chain stores and rural bankers facing the prospect of sale of their establishments to large banks in better condition. For them, the Farmer-Laborites backed anti–chain store legislation and discouraged the acquisition of independent banks by Twin Cities or out-of-state banks.

The Farmer-Labor party's role in both industrial relations and agricultural income security involved party-movement collaboration: In both policy areas very militant social movements pushed for policy outcomes that they did not achieve, but due to the Farmer-Labor party's assistance there was nonetheless real policy change in the direction preferred by these movements.

As governor, Olson used the state's police power, specifically his command of the state National Guard, to recast industrial relations in the Twin Cities and elsewhere in the state (such as in Duluth, on the Iron Range, and in meatpacking and processing in southeastern Minnesota). American governors have often used, or been called upon to deploy, state National Guards in order to break strikes. Either they have enforced anti-picketing injunctions that allow employers to withhold recognition of strike leadership or they have used military force to assault strike pickets and labor marches directly. Olson instead used the National Guard during the 1934 truckers' strike in Minneapolis to subtly break apart an "open-shop" anti-union system that had thrived in the Twin Cities for two decades.

Essentially Olson relieved the pro-employer and trigger-happy Minneapolis police force of its peacekeeping duties. Olson also met with President Franklin D. Roosevelt to propose a way to force employer recognition of the strikers' Trotskyist-led union leadership. He persuaded Roosevelt to threaten withdrawal of federal funds from Twin Cities banks. Olson's actions set a precedent for a second deployment of the Guard in Minneapolis in 1935 and for quite similar use of the Guard by the other two Farmer-Labor governors who succeeded Olson— Hjalmar Petersen (the lieutenant governor who assumed the governorship at Olson's death in office and served until 1937) and Elmer Benson (1937–39).

The Farmer-Labor governors thus made the state National Guard a more neutral (and thus less pro-employer) instrument for preserving public order during labor strikes. In so doing, in a context of increased labor militancy, they promoted a rapid increase in trade unionism within the state's borders and the development in Minnesota of modern collective bargaining.

A similar pattern of party-movement collaboration occurred in agriculture in 1932 and 1933. Commercial farmers in Iowa, the Dakotas, Minnesota, and elsewhere in the North Central states and the Plains increasingly faced mortgage foreclosure as prices for corn, milk, and other commodities rapidly sank in the general deflation. In Iowa and Minnesota protest emerged partly through the Farmers Holiday Association, an offshoot of the Farmers Union that named itself after the presidential moratorium on bank transactions, the Bank Holiday.

Farmers began blocking roads, both to dramatize their plight and to cause shortages at regional farm markets. They also gathered at public foreclosure sales of farms. There they would either prevent completion of sale (through a mix of intimidation and pleading) or force sale at a nominal price that the original farmer could easily afford. Third, they organized protest marches on government officials, in addition, of course, to lobbying public officials more quietly.

One important response, taken jointly by the Republican and Farmer-Labor parties, was tax relief through "homestead exemption" legislation, which provided a standard property tax exemption. Another was to slow down the rate at which creditors dispossessed debt-ridden farmers of their land and property until some measure of economic recovery set in.

Thus, in February 1933, after several months of issuing sometimes fiery statements of sympathy for the farmers' plight, Olson proclaimed a one-year moratorium on foreclosure sales in Minnesota, acting on the basis of the state's police power. This placed considerable pressure on the legislature to call for a moratorium. The Farmer-Labor party did not control the legislature, not enjoying a state senate majority. It did control the house of representatives, however, and on April 18, 1933, Olson was able to sign the Minnesota Mortgage Moratorium Act.

The Minnesota attorney general, elected as a Farmer-Laborite, then participated in the defense of the Minnesota Mortgage Moratorium Act when the U.S. Supreme Court accepted an appeal brought from the Supreme Court of Minnesota, which had upheld the statute. In describing the scope and depth of economic distress in Minnesota, the resulting distortion of mortgage contracts undertaken in different times, and the public interest in restoring order and confidence in property rights, the Minnesota attorney general played a key role in the case's presentation. The U.S. Supreme Court was persuaded to break from a tradition of strict construction of the contract clause. In an opinion for the Court written by the Chief Justice it affirmed the judgment of the Minnesota Supreme Court. The Court's decision gave support to the large number of moratoria enacted throughout the country. It is today a basic undergirding of government regulation. In fact, its doctrine of what is constitutional official action under a state's police power in emergency circumstances is a potent precedent, for better or for worse.

In contrast to this legal contribution to the national policy process, the Farmer-Labor party had little effect on congressional politics despite its control of the Minnesota delegation in both the House and the Senate. The one exception is its role in the Depression-era debate over unemployment insurance, in which a Farmer-Labor congressman, Ernest Lundeen, defined the radical end of the policy debate.

Lundeen used his assignment to the subcommittee on unemployment insurance of the House Committee on Labor to publicize his plan for government and employers to replace fully all wages lost to unemployment, with the administration of insurance funds to occur through local workers' and farmers' councils. Thousands of American Federation of Labor locals expressed support for the Lundeen bill, which applied to all workers and farmers "without discrimination because of age, sex, race, color, religious or political opinion or affiliation" and covered workers unemployed due to maternity, sickness, accident, or old age. Amazingly, the House Committee on Labor reported favorably on the bill after hearings on it in 1934 and 1935; however, it never received a rule for floor consideration once the Roosevelt administration denounced it and soon died when it was defeated as a proposed amendment to the Social Security Act.

EXPLAINING THE FARMER-LABOR PARTY'S HISTORY

Given this record, several questions about the Farmer-Labor party's history seem pertinent: Why and how did the party emerge? What explains its persistence (as either Minnesota's leading party or as its second party) for over a quarter of a century? Why did it go as far as it did, and why did it eventually collapse when it did?

A plausible answer to these questions is that the Farmer-Labor party expressed deep social and economic aspirations in the 1920s but that it was eventually overshadowed by the New Deal, which ultimately handled those concerns. Leadership troubles in 1937 and 1938, after Olson's death, and growing left-wing sectarianism within the party accentuated the New Deal's eclipse of the Farmer-Labor party. So, too, did Republican acceptance of New Deal liberalism—specifically, collective bargaining—which was led by such younger Minnesota Republicans as Harold Stassen (elected governor in 1938).

The rapid increase in the party's electoral strength during the New Deal underscores the surprising complexity of the party's evolution. Far from the New Deal stealing the Farmer-Labor party's thunder, the Minnesota electorate became more attached to the Farmer-Labor party.

As the New Deal grew stronger, particularly after the 1934 "mid-term" elections (when the Democrats experienced a jump in congressional strength that has never been replicated in any other mid-term national elections), the Farmer-Labor party itself became a much larger and busier tent. It boasted a dense infrastructure of ward clubs in the cities (some of which operated regular weekend dances and other social gatherings), a separate network of women's activists grouped within the Farmer-Labor Women's Federation who exercised considerable influence on local government and relief expenditures, a scattering of youth clubs, dozens of county organizations and out-state political clubs, and a continuously operating formal party organization and newspaper grouped within the Farmer-Labor Association, whose personnel and expenses were supported by state patronage, individual dues, and labor union contributions.

In the end, the New Deal era development that probably most troubled the Farmer-Labor party was the transformation of the "group system." The New Deal generated far-reaching change in how farmers and workers were organized in formal interest-group associations, in turn generating new organizational dynamics and loyalties that tugged against historic farmer and worker linkages to the Farmer-Labor party.

For instance, the New Deal's 1933 labor legislation (the famous Section 7a of the National Industrial Recovery Act) encouraged previously obscure left-wingers in the small Minneapolis labor movement to confront employer power in that city. The result was the Minneapolis general strike of 1934, one of several city-wide strikes that year that erupted along a broad swath stretching from the West Coast to the Midwest. With the Farmer-Labor party's support, American Trotskyism suddenly acquired a significant labor base—the only state in the country, in fact, where it actually had labor union strength. Yet the Minneapolis Trotskyists, despite their respect for Olson and the Farmer-Labor party, understood themselves as affiliates of the Farmer-Labor party, not as loyal followers.

When the Wagner Act of 1935 later encouraged rapid organization among Congress of Industrial Organizations (CIO) unions in the state under Communist leadership, the stage was set for bitter discord within the labor movement. The Farmer-Labor leadership had trouble negotiating the schism between the Minnesota State Federation of Labor and the state CIO. Indeed, Governor Benson and his circle probably preferred the Minnesota Communist party and the Minnesota CIO to the state Federation of Labor and the Trotskyist labor heroes of 1934. In the end, after violent clashes in the Twin Cities between rival union gangs and the Benson administration's disturbingly tepid response to the gangland-style execution of a pro-Trotskyist labor leader, the Benson administration deeply alienated the Federation and the Minneapolis Trotskyists.

In agriculture, the design and administration of the Agricultural Adjustment Act advantaged the Farm Bureau Association. The Farm Bureau, however, was nonpartisan, suspicious of labor militancy, and opposed to collective bargaining at out-state dairy and grain processing facilities. These stances represented a new tension between organized farmers and organized workers.

By the mid-1930s, at the height of the Farmer-Labor party's electoral strength, the Farmer-Labor party's "base" of auxiliary movements and associations was filled with novel enmities. Labor was split down the middle; farmers and workers were split from each other.

The Farmer-Labor party never recovered from this crisis, instead sorting itself into opposing factions that struggled for several years to control the formal organizations of the party. In 1940 and 1942 it averaged only about 37 percent of the gubernatorial vote and fared about 10 points worse in the 1942 regular and special senate elections. In 1940, U.S. Senator Henrik Shipstead switched to the Republican party and won re-election; by then only one of the state's congressional seats remained in Farmer-Labor hands. Finally, in 1944, former governor Benson led his party into the Democratic party, resulting in the formation of the Democratic-Farmer-Labor party (DFL). A rising generation of Democratic liberals preferred a ballot line that could still appeal to a sizable core of Farmer-Labor loyalists.

The last electoral contest in Minnesota waged by an old-line Farmer-Laborite was the 1950 gubernatorial contest in which the former Farmer-Labor attorney general, Harry Peterson, ran on the DFL line. As late as 1972 there were former labor leaders who ran for (and won) house elections on the DFL line and who first entered politics when the Farmer-Labor party still defined the state's political spectrum. Today, there are very few Farmer-Laborites left. What remains is a strong progressive tradition that continues to define the way liberal Minnesota politicians seek to influence state and national politics.

To sum up, the Farmer-Labor party was truly a going concern. It had a vital impact at the state level, and it left a lasting imprint on national regulatory doctrine. Today its vision of social security still inspires scholarly comment and research.

RICHARD M. VALELLY

See also: Communist Party; Nonpartisan League; Socialist Party.

Bibliography

Faue, Elizabeth. *Community of Suffering & Struggle: Women, Men, and the Labor Movement in Minne-*

apolis, 1915–1945. Chapel Hill: University of North Carolina Press, 1991.

Gieske, Millard. *Minnesota Farmer-Laborism: The Third Party Alternative.* Minneapolis: University of Minnesota Press, 1979.

Haynes, John Earl. *Dubious Alliance: The Making of Minnesota's DFL Party.* Minneapolis: University of Minnesota Press, 1984.

Valelly, Richard M. *Radicalism in the States: The Minnesota Farmer-Labor Party and the American Political Economy.* Chicago: University of Chicago Press, 1989.

MISSISSIPPI FREEDOM DEMOCRATIC PARTY

1964–1980s

ORIGINS OF THE PARTY

In the annals of American history, sociologist James Silver dubbed Mississippi a "closed society" that segregated white and black residents in a caste system. Perpetuating and continuing segregation, one Alabama newspaper, whenever segregationists received a constitutional setback from the courts, would run headlines such as "Thank God for Mississippi," implying that segregation and white supremacy were safe as long as Mississippi existed. It was the most defiant of the southern states. In fact, in its own image of itself, Mississippi was unreconstructed since the Civil War, and it had withstood every conceivable challenge to make it democratic.

It was this embedded and ingrained defiance that attracted the idealistic college student summer volunteers and the equally idealistic members of the Student Non-violent Coordinating Committee, a multiracial organization dedicated to equality for black Americans. The feeling and the high spirits in this new group was that if one could crack Mississippi, the rest of the South would fall. Shatter the citadel of white supremacy and the region could finally start all over again. For in Mississippi, the African-American population and voting-age electorate had been pressed to the wall and beyond. They had no rights that white society had to observe. In Mississippi, African Americans were the clear victims of democracy.

In July 1961, C.C. Bryant, a leader in the McComb County National Association for the Advancement of Colored People (NAACP), invited civil rights organizer Robert Moses to launch a voter registration drive. As Moses moved quietly to start the wheel turning, he envisioned a mock election—to be called a Freedom Election—to activate the masses. But before he could set the Freedom Election in place, two local black ministers announced their candidacy for congressional seats. In the second congressional district, which was composed of a majority of black-belt counties, Reverend Merrill Lindsey entered the Democratic primaries, and in the third congressional district Reverend Robert L.T. Smith of Jackson ran against the incumbent. Both men, while well meaning, were defeated. The masses were not ready to besiege the registration hall and emerge as new voters in the state. However, their experience did indicate to Moses that the task he had taken on was much greater than one man could effectively deal with. He would need help. During the early 1960s Freedom Rides in Mississippi, a Council of Federated Organizations (COFO) had been developed to unify and coordinate the efforts to secure the Freedom Riders' release from jail. The Freedom Rides were organized efforts to register African Americans, primarily college students from the North. When the riders were arrested, Governor Ross Barnett would not talk with any official of any of the civil rights organizations. The COFO was a confederation of the NAACP, Southern Christian Leadership Council (SCLC), Congress of Racial Equality (CORE), and the Student Non-violent Coordinating Committee (SNCC) formed specifically to be a liaison with the governor. After the release of the riders, COFO was disbanded. Moses revitalized the organization and created a crash program to educate the masses of unregistered voters in the state. During the numerous voter-training sessions that COFO conducted, two mock Freedom Elections were held.

By the end of 1963, however, the inspired voter registration effort, even with incredible hard work and creative tactics, had only marginal success. When the training sessions and the mock elections were over, less than 6 percent of the African-American voting-age population had been added to the rolls. Much more would be needed if democracy was to shine in the state.

FORMATION OF THE PARTY

Moses devised a new tactic: a "Freedom Summer," wherein white college students from the eastern elite schools would be invited down to help conduct the voter registration drives. Simultaneously, the birth of a new political entity would dramatize the plight of African Americans in Mississippi to the nation and the world. On April 26, 1964, COFO delegates met and fashioned the Mississippi Freedom Democratic party (MFDP). At the end of the founding meeting, the delegates agreed to make party-building their number-one agenda item, since voter registration drives were already under way, and to nominate candidates to run in the June 1964 state Democratic primary.

Knowing that their candidates would likely lose, the MFDP tried to attend and participate in the regular party's local, county, and state conventions. At the ward and precinct meetings they were harassed, disrespected, deliberately misled, and harshly treated. At the county meetings, where more sophisticated Democrats were present, they were not badly treated but simply ignored and not permitted to participate in the proceedings. On July 24, 1964, when the state convention was held, no African-American delegates could attend since none had been elected at the county level (hence, the state's delegation to the national convention

was all white). The MFDP delegation had four white delegates out of a total of forty-four.

At the state convention, the credentials committee heard the state delegation deny that voting discrimination played any part in the state's political process. The MFDP delegates refuted the charge, and leading civil rights leaders appealed to the credentials committee to seriously consider the group's seating challenge. During the hearing, President Lyndon Johnson sent Senator Hubert Humphrey (later revealed to be his choice for vice president) and Tom Finey (whom the president had sent earlier that year to the state to gather background materials on the dispute) to also make presentations to the credentials committee on what to do about the dispute. All of their proposals undercut any ruling that would give the MFDP a legal base and standing. Eventually, it was their proposal that prevailed. It offered the MFDP an honorary status and special delegate-at-large positions for the MFDP chairman and national committeeman. Once this proposition was made, Dr. Martin Luther King, Congressman Charles Diggs, CORE Chairman James Farmer, activist Bayard Rustin, and a host of others attempted to persuade the MFDP to accept it. Although this proposal was approved by the credentials committee and the full convention on August 25, the MFDP rejected it as being too little recognition for the rigid system of segregation that African Americans in the state had to endure.

Although even Congresswoman Edith Green (Democrat, Oregon) said that "the black people in Mississippi deserved better than mere consideration as honored guests," this compromise was too much for the regular white state delegation. Upon hearing the credentials committee decision, sixty-five of the sixty-eight members walked out. One of the remaining three was a personal friend of the president.

Following this setback in their convention strategy, MFDP went back to the state and prepared their candidate and ticket for the fall general election. However, the Mississippi State Election Commission ruled against the MFDP petition to get on the state ballot for the fall election, declaring that the party petition did not have enough registered voters' signatures.

Martin Luther King, Jr., gives the funeral oration for freedom marcher Armstead Phipps, an activist in the Mississippi Freedom Democratic party, who died of a heart attack during a freedom march in 1966. (*United Press International, 1966, courtesy of the Library of Congress*)

At this point, the MFDP was left with only another Freedom Election to make its presence and influence seen in the presidential contest. In the mock elections held by the party over a three-day period, some 68,029 individuals voted. The Johnson-Humphrey ticket received more votes in the Freedom Election than they did in the official state election. Once the results were in, the MFDP used the results to set in motion their congressional seating challenge.

HOUSE SEATING CHALLENGE

On December 4, 1964, the MFDP filed their seating challenge to overturn the election (due to the exclusion of blacks) with the clerk of the House of Representatives in accordance with the procedure for contesting elections. Despite the MFDP filing, the House of Representatives voted to seat the Mississippi congressmen pending the outcome of the hearing. Here is where the seating challenge started to run into serious trouble. The first brief filed by the MFDP argued that its congressional candidate had been duly elected in the Freedom Elections, and they were therefore legal and bona fide contestants. This brief was severely attacked by even some of the strongest party supporters and eventually it was withdrawn. A second brief was prepared. This one made its case on moral instead of legal grounds, suggesting that new elections should be called and the MFDP candidates put on the ballot. But because this brief did not meet certain procedural requirements, the clerk of the House at first refused to have it sent to the subcommittee. Under pressure from several sources, the clerk did print the brief, and the subcommittee finally got to consider the case. Although the Subcommittee on Elections and Privileges, which heard the case, was headed by and dominated by southerners, the decision was rendered strictly along legal lines (i.e., were election rules, procedures, and processes violated in the election). As the subcommittee report put it, while it was quite

unfortunate about the disenfranchisement and the plight of African Americans due to the circumstances, this did not constitute a breach of the election laws and rules. Thus, the Subcommittee on Elections and Privileges report recommended a dismissal of the MFDP congressional seating challenge. A minority report recommended further study and analysis and not an immediate dismissal. On September 17, 1965, the full House voted 228 to 143 to accept the report. Although the report was amended to indicate that the Mississippi congressmen were not "entitled to the seat," the seating challenge ordeal was over.

In the aftermath of this effort, SNCC became disillusioned, withdrew its support from the MFDP, and moved into Lowndes County, Alabama, to create another type of African-American party. Without the SNCC, the local MFDP supporters and indigenous leaders moved into continued mobilizing for the 1966 elections.

ELECTORAL EFFORTS

Under the direction of Lawrence Guyot, who was now the MFDP chairman, the party ran candidates in the first, third, and fourth congressional districts and one for the U.S. Senate. Despite the fact that in the interim between the seating challenge and these elections, Congress had passed the 1965 Voting Rights Act, the MFDP candidates were poorly supported. The mean percent for the four candidates was 12.3 percent. The range ran from a high of 24 percent for the candidate in the third congressional district to a low of 2 percent in the fourth district. However, in terms of overall votes, the white MFDP senatorial candidate received the greatest number—27,863. The lack of resources, skills, and money meant that statewide mobilizing was difficult and entrenched power stubborn. The MFDP was feeling the loss of the SNCC.

Undaunted, the MFDP prepared for the 1967 statewide elections by putting a host of candidates in the field. Competing with the MFDP was the NAACP under the leadership of civil rights activist Charles Evers. Both groups had slates and in some counties and townships, they were in direct competition. But it was in this election that the four-year-old party would win its first victories. Six MFDP candidates won office. Five captured county-level posts, and Robert Clark, a part-time college instructor and former local antipoverty official, was elected to the state legislature. He became the first African American to be elected to the state legislature since Reconstruction. But before the upstart party could savor its hard-won victory, Mississippi Democrats reacted.

First, the ten-year incumbent whom Clark beat, James P. Lowe, filed an election challenge declaring that the legislative district was comprised of two counties and that Clark had only qualified in one. Then came the real explosion. None of the bonding companies in the state would approve surety bonds for any of the candidates except two. Mississippi law required that all elected officials be bonded. Here was the defiant state at its best.

To solve the first problem, the incoming governor, John Bell Williams, personally interceded and asked the 65-year-old Lowe to withdraw his challenge. He complied and Clark was sworn in. In the bonding matter, both the MFDP and the NAACP had to combine forces and go outside of the state to get surety bonds. The victory was now final.

While 1967 was the year of initial victory, 1968 started with the assassination of Dr. King and another 1968 Democratic National Convention delegate seating challenge. To improve its chances, the MFDP merged with several like-minded groups in the state, including the NAACP, the AFL-CIO, and the Young Democrats, and formed a biracial coalition. From this group came the Loyal Democrats of Mississippi (LDM). In order to stave off this challenge, the regular Democrats named three African Americans to their delegation. However, two of these African Americans withdrew. The LDM carried an almost racially balanced delegation to the convention with Aaron Henry as chairman. This time the credentials committee seated the LDM over the regular state party.

ABSORPTION INTO THE DEMOCRATIC PARTY

In the 1968, 1969, and 1971 elections the MFDP ran separate slates of candidates and continued to win local- and county-level offices. The NAACP also went its separate way, running candidates in the state for local, county, congressional, and statewide offices. In 1972 the MFDP and NAACP once again coalesced and went back to the Democratic National Convention. Slowly, shades of cooperation started to appear, and as the decade wore on, activities became more and more easily merged. For once inside the state's political institutions, MFDP candidates acted as Democrats, particularly if they wanted to have any policy-making influence. Thus, by the election of Republican Ronald Reagan in 1980 and the movement of southern-elected officials into this reborn party, absorption into the Democratic party was made much easier. And with absorption, the MFDP lost its separate political identity.

The idealists won a tough victory. They increased African-American voter registration in the state. They eventually unseated the regular state Democratic party. They transformed from an exclusive white-only vehicle to one of inclusion. And they elected African Americans to offices where none had been before. It was not a complete victory: The state's defiant attitude did not completely yield, but it was nonetheless modified. And part of that modification can be seen in the state's realignment with the Republican party.

Because of the MFDP's arrival, African-American voters are participants in their own and the state's political future. The MFDP made a significant start.

HANES WALTON, JR.

See also: Lowndes County Freedom Organization.

Bibliography

Coleman, Mary D. "The Black Elected Elites in Mississippi: The Post–Civil Rights Apportionment Era." In *Black Politics and Black Political Behavior:*

A Linkage Analysis, ed. Hanes Walton, Jr. Westport, CT: Praeger, 1994.

———. *Legislators, Law and Public Policy: Political Change in Mississippi and the South.* Westport, CT: Greenwood, 1993.

Guyot, Lawrence, and Mike Thelwell. "The Politics of Necessity and Survival in Mississippi." *Freedomways* (Spring 1966).

———. "Toward Independent Political Power." *Freedomways* (Summer 1966).

McLemore, Leslie Burl. "The Effect of Political Participation Upon a Closed Society—A State in Transition: The Changing Political Climate in Mississippi." *The Negro Educational Review* 23 (January 1972).

———. "The Freedom Democratic Party and Changing Political Status of the Negro in Mississippi." Masters thesis, Atlanta University, 1965.

———. "The Mississippi Freedom Democratic Party." *Black Politician* (October 1971).

———. "The Mississippi Freedom Democratic Party: A Case Study of Grass Roots Politics." Ph.D. thesis, University of Massachusetts at Amherst, 1971.

Minnis, Jack. "The Mississippi Freedom Democratic Party." *Freedomways* (Spring 1965).

Walton, Hanes, Jr. "Black Political Parties and Congress: The Role of the *Congressional Records.*" In Walton, Jr., ed., *Black Politics and Black Political Behavior: A Linkage Analysis.*

———. *Black Political Parties: An Historical and Political Analysis.* New York: Free Press, 1972.

NATIONAL DEMOCRATIC PARTY OF ALABAMA

1967–1980s

*A*t the 1964 Democratic National Convention, the state of Mississippi had two contesting delegations, the regular state party delegation and a new one—the Mississippi Freedom Democratic party (MFDP). The credentials committee heard the arguments of the two groups and due to the urging of President Lyndon Johnson seated the regular delegation and offered the MFDP two honorary seats in the balcony, which they refused. After the convention a reform commission urged state parties to use a fair procedure in selecting future delegates.

In the neighboring state of Alabama, civil rights activists were watching the bold and strategic action of the MFDP and their new convention politics. In the midst of the civil rights movement, it had become obvious to some that elimination of segregationist laws were not enough, institutions such as political parties also had to be transformed. In Alabama, the Democratic party was under the leadership of Governor George Wallace, and while state law prevented him from succeeding himself, he supported his wife, Lurleen, for governor in 1966.

However, prior to her victory in 1966, the civil right activists Dr. John Cashin, an African-American dentist in Huntsville, and Charles Morgan, Jr., a white American Civil Liberties Union (ACLU) lawyer, took a proposal to the statewide African-American organization, the Alabama Democratic Conference (ADC), at its annual meeting in November 1965. The chairman of the ADC felt that the call for a new political party was much too hasty and did not give the regular state party enough time to re-

form itself and remove all of its symbols and rules supporting white supremacy, including the whites-only primary. Two years after the 1964 convention, and just prior to the state Democratic primaries, the executive committee of the state party met on January 22, 1966, and decided to remove all references to white supremacy from its constitution and bylaws and from its ballot emblem. After this action, the state party's emblem read: "Democrats of the Right." However, these changes notwithstanding, Wallace backed his wife for governor in the Democratic primaries, and despite opposition funded by the Nixon administration, she won.

Despite this victory, the Democratic primaries had split the ranks of the ADC when the chairman supported a little-known candidate and the executive committee of the ADC supported the former attorney general Richard Flowers. The split in the ADC led to a split in the African-American electorate and enabled the Lurleen Wallace victory. Thus, the state party emblem may have changed its wording, but George Wallace was still in power.

This outcome was more than the civil rights activists could take. On December 15, 1967, Cashin and Morgan filed for a state charter for the National Democratic Party of Alabama (NDPA) and received it four weeks later. Then, they held their first organizing convention in Birmingham on July 20, 1968, and selected a delegation to go to the 1968 Democratic National Convention. At that convention, the credentials committee heard the seating challenges of the three contesting groups from Alabama: (1) the NDPA, (2) the regular party delegation with two black delegates and, (3) the American

Independent Democratic party (AIDP), whose all-white membership did not support George Wallace's newly created third party, the American Independent party. Plus, the ADC pledged to sign loyalty oaths to support the convention's eventual nominee. The credentials committee voted not to seat either the NDPA or the AIDP.

After losing its seating challenge, the NDPA returned to the state and entered the fall election campaign. In fact, the NDPA would run candidates for national, state, and local offices in every election from 1968 until 1982. In the 1968, 1972, and 1976 presidential elections, the NDPA placed the nominees of the National Democratic Convention on its ballot. However, in 1976, nominee James E. Carter sent a telegram to the Alabama secretary of state asking that his name be removed from the NDPA's ballot. The support for the presidential nominees on the party ballot was nearly 46,000 votes, approximately 5 percent of the vote cast in the 1976 elections.

At the senatorial level, the party entered candidates in the 1968, 1972, and 1980 elections. Its greatest support came in the first election where the white candidate captured 72,699 votes, 22 percent of the total vote cast. In its second effort, it received 31,421; its votes declined to 2,973 votes in the third and final outing. In the party's House of Representatives races (1968 until 1976 and again in 1980), the vote totals went from a high of 83,818 in 1968 to a low of 1,743 in 1980.

At the statewide level, the party ran gubernatorial candidates in 1970 and 1982. The NDPA received 13 percent of the vote in its initial effort with 125,000 votes but received 4,693 votes in 1982, less than one-half of one percent of the total vote cast. Hence, the party's national and statewide efforts were impressive but nonetheless unsuccessful. That would change, however.

In the heavily "black-belt" African-American counties that run across the middle of the state, the party's candidates were swept to victory. In the November 1968 general elections, the party elected seventeen of its members in three black-belt counties and one individual to the Alabama State Legislature— one of two African Americans elected. By 1970,

the Lowndes County Freedom Organization, the other African-American party in the state, merged with the NDPA, and this enlarged NDPA would, before the end of the decade, elect the majority of all black elected officials in ten of the state's black-belt counties. Although the party did have white participation and it supported white candidates for office, its voting constituencies in Wallace's Alabama were essentially an African-American electorate.

With the decline of Wallace in national politics and his born-again racial repentance at the state level, the regular Democratic party reformed itself with significant pressures from other statewide black leaders. Victories in the ten counties were not enough to offset African Americans who ran on and won seats under the regular Democratic banner. Racial competition from within the regular party undercut the upstart NDPA. Leadership troubles in the NDPA internally weakened it and the Republican victories nationally forced the local factions to close ranks.

By 1982, in the middle of President Reagan's first term, the NDPA was a shell of its former self. Its voter support had dissipated, many returning to the state party. But before it collapsed, the NDPA had increased voter turnout in the state to unprecedented levels, forced the reform of the regular party, empowered African Americans in the black-belt counties, and energized the African-American Democrats in the regular party to displace the old segregationist party elites. The NDPA had transformed the old state party.

HANES WALTON, JR.

See also: Lowndes County Freedom Organization; Mississippi Freedom Democratic Party; George C. Wallace.

Bibliography

Carter, Dan T. *The Politics of Rage: George Wallace, the Origins of the New Conservatism, and the Transformation of American Politics.* Baton Rouge: Louisiana State University Press, 1995.

Frye, Hardy T. *Black Parties and Political Power: A Case Study.* Boston: G.K. Hall, 1980.

Walton, Hanes, Jr. "Black Political Parties and Congress: The Role of the *Congressional Record.*" In *Black Politics and Black Political Behavior: A Linkage Analysis,* ed. Hanes Walton, Jr., pp. 41–48. Westport, CT: Praeger, 1994.

———. *Black Political Parties: An Historical and Political Analysis.* New York: Free Press, 1972.

———. "The National Democratic Party of Alabama and Party Failure in America." In *When Parties Fail: Emerging Alternative Organizations,* ed. Kay Lawson and Peter Merkl, pp. 365–388. Princeton: Princeton University Press, 1988.

Walton, Hanes, Jr., and William H. Boone. "Black Political Parties: A Demographic Analysis." *Journal of Black Studies* 5 (September 1974): 86–95.

NATIONAL REPUBLICAN PARTY

1820s–1830s

The National Republican party emerged out of the political chaos marking the transition between the first and second party systems in the late 1820s and early 1830s. Essentially composed of former Federalists and anti-Jacksonians—before they found a home in the rising Whig party—it gained most of its support in the northeastern states. Short-lived and volatile, the National Republicans largely stood for the same ideas and programs of the Whigs: that a political elite, based on merit not birth, should run the nation's government, and that same government should be actively involved in the regulation and promotion of economic growth.

BACKGROUND

The origins of the National Republicans lay in the collapse of the Federalist party in the late 1810s. Despite a host of causes, the Federalists were essentially doomed for a simple reason: They could not cope with the era's rising mass politics, wrought by the new laws that expanded the suffrage to more and more white men, regardless of how much property they owned. By the late 1810s and early 1820s, the Federalists had essentially folded, with its members gravitating toward the all-encompassing Democratic-Republicans. (Confusingly, the Democratic-Republicans, known at the time as the Republicans, would eventually become known as the Democrats, a name they continue to have. To simplify, the term "Republican" will be used throughout this entry to signify the Democratic-Republicans.) But a single party for a country with such diverse interests as America was likely to see its omnipresence doomed and quickly, as was indeed the case with the Republicans of the day.

In the 1824 presidential election, five candidates of varying political stripes ran—all as Republicans. These included Secretary of State John Quincy Adams, Secretary of War John C. Calhoun, Treasury Secretary William Crawford, Speaker of the House Henry Clay, and Indian-fighter and hero of the War of 1812 Andrew Jackson, who actually took the most electoral votes. With none of the candidates winning an outright majority, the final decision went to the House of Representatives, where a deal was struck between Adams and Clay whereby the latter threw his votes to the former. Jackson's supporters cried foul and vowed political revenge. Over the next four years, they built up the nation's first mass political organization, the Jacksonian Democratic-Republicans, took control of Congress and eventually won the presidency for their candidate in 1828.

The victory was overwhelming and left the former Federalists within the Republican party feeling as if they no longer had a home, since Jackson now controlled the party. This sense of political alienation was exacerbated by the many proto-populist actions taken by the Jackson administration, most especially its destruction of the economy-regulating national bank, its cutting back of funds for internal improvements, and its continuing hostility to high tariffs. Added to these actions were the symbolic issues; Jackson and his followers, to many of these well-bred men, seemed crude and vicious and unnecessarily racist toward Indians and blacks.

NATIONAL REPUBLICANS

Several political groups emerged to challenge Jackson's leadership, albeit not very effectively. First, there were the old New England Federalists under New Hampshire Senator Daniel Webster, who dreamed of a radical realignment of parties that would lead to higher tariffs and internal improvements. Another group arose around Adams and Clay that believed that the Republican party had been hijacked by extremists around Jackson, who were destroying its Jeffersonian ideals in the name of appealing to the common man at the lowest common denominator of whiskey-led campaigning. They also suspected the Jackson administration of fraud, since it had appointed so many old Federalists to posts of power. Indeed, many members of the Adams-Clay wing tried to keep their distance initially from unreconstructed Federalists who approached them.

Finally, another anti-Jackson force emerged around the Anti-Masonic party. A rather strange political organization—based as it was on opposition to a Masonic conspiracy to rule America—the party was, in fact, a collection largely of small farmers and businessmen, most of whom lived in the rural areas of New England, New York, and Pennsylvania, and were opposed to the big-money power of the eastern cities, as well as the rude proto-populism of the Jacksonians. In general, both the Webster and Adams-Clay factions were wary of joining the Anti-Masons in a grand anti-Jackson coalition, and the Anti-Masons were equally wary about them.

Gradually, however, an uneasy coalition of Webster and Adams-Clay Republicans, as well as some old Federalists and new Anti-Masons came together into the National Republican party in 1831, when they held a nominating convention (the second in American history; the Anti-Masons had just hosted the first). Clay was nominated for president and John Sergeant, a Pennsylvania congressman, for vice president. The party—its ticket barely holding together its divided and often hostile factions—did poorly in the Jacksonian Republican sweep of 1832. The National Republicans fell apart over the next few years, with most of their members and leadership forming the core of the newly rising Whig party, which would successfully challenge the Republicans for the next twenty or so years.

JAMES CIMENT

See also: Anti-Masonic Party; Federalist Party; Whig Party.

Bibliography

Holt, Michael. *Political Parties and American Political Development from the Age of Jackson to the Age of Lincoln.* Baton Rouge: Louisiana State University Press, 1992.

Livermore, Shaw, Jr. *The Twilight of Federalism: The Disintegration of the Federalist Party, 1815–1830.* New York: Gordian Press, 1972.

NATIONAL SILVER PARTY

1880s–1904

ORIGINS OF THE PARTY

The National party, otherwise known as the National Silver party, originated as a single-interest group advocating the free coinage of silver and monetization of silver at pre-1873 silver-to-gold ratios. Lobby efforts to re-establish silver as a currency failed during the 1880s, and so western silverites began to pursue state and federal legislative representation. These strategies worked in the western state legislatures, but the party's success at the national level came largely from silverites' willingness to join with silver advocates from the major parties to form a fusion party or a fusion ticket. The National Silver party's best opportunity for national influence came in the 1896 election, but when the Democratic party chose a silver platform and William Jennings Bryan as its candidate, the silver movement's national platform was lost. The election of Republican William McKinley doomed the cause of silverites. Although the National Silver party made inroads in Congress in the 1896 elections, its power had faded by 1900. With the economic boom of 1898 through 1904, the silver movement eventually faded from national attention.

Although it called itself a national party, the National Silver party's primary influence was largely limited to the western states, especially the newly admitted states of Nevada, the Dakotas, Nebraska, Colorado, and Idaho. The silver movement received its impetus from two related historical developments. First, the discovery of gold deposits in the East, coupled with the reduction of silver production in the West, led to an increase in the value of silver.

During the 1860s and 1870s, silver coins were worth more melted down than they were as currency. Therefore, a rush on silver currency began. To rectify this imbalance, Congress passed the Demonetization Act of 1873, eliminating silver as a recognized currency.

Second, late in the 1880s, new silver deposits were discovered in Nevada and other western states. These new silver mines meant that silver was now more plentiful, but it also mean that the price of silver had declined in relation to gold. Western developers and miners advocated a return to a bimetallic standard (parity between gold and silver) in which silver was valued at 16 ounces to an ounce of gold, instead of the existing ratio of 22 to 24 ounces of silver to an ounce of gold. Since most gold was controlled by eastern business interests, the battle over silver was not just a battle to protect the price of a western metal, it was a battle over the economic center of the nation, pitting eastern bankers against western farmers and miners. Moreover, as more western states entered the union, the existing congressional power base in the eastern seaboard became less tenable. The move toward bimetallism was not only a move to support silver, but was also a move to assert the independence and growing power of the newly admitted western states.

The National Silver party was based in western states, primarily Nevada, Colorado, and Iowa. Its leadership was drawn from silverites who found themselves alienated in their own parties: The key figures in the National Silver party had often been very active in the Republican, Democratic, and Populist parties before trying to form a silver party.

PARTY LEADERSHIP

Perhaps the most influential leader of the National Silver party was U.S. Senator William Morris Stewart from Nevada, a former Silver Republican. Stewart believed that the economic and monetary issues surrounding silver would overwhelm partisan conflicts and create a new political structure in the United States. His efforts on behalf of a National Silver ticket and in 1896 for William Jennings Bryan was both important for Bryan and perhaps instrumental in his defeat. Because the Democratic convention had adopted a silver platform, eastern papers such as the *New York World* painted Bryan and other silver supporters as captives of the "Silver Trusts" and played on people's fear of trusts. Another leader of the National Silver party was William Dallas Bynum from Indiana. Bynum represented silver interests in the House of Representatives from 1885 through 1895. His electoral defeat in 1894 reduced the number of silverites in the Congress and deprived the House of one of its most powerful advocates for silver. During the 1896 presidential campaign, Bynum, Stewart, and other silverites rallied for Bryan and Arthur Sewall, the Democratic nominees for president and vice president.

1896 ELECTION

The National Silver party's most important impact on national politics came during the tumultuous 1896 election. Like the Silver Republicans, the National Silver party leadership expected that both major parties would adopt a gold standard platform. When Democrats chose Bryan and advocated free silver, the National Silver party faced a tactical decision. They could try to run their own candidate; they could support Bryan and Sewall; or they could support part of the ticket. Most of the leadership and the party chose to support Bryan at first. At the National Silver Party Convention, held in St. Louis (the home of the Republican National Convention) on July 24, the party endorsed Bryan for president, but insisted on the nomination of Thomas Watson of Georgia as the vice-presidential candidate. This move further divided silverites, as many silverites believed their best chance to influence the election was to present a unified front with the Democratic ticket.

The National Silver party convention eventually endorsed the Bryan-Sewall Democratic ticket but adopted its own platform. The silver platform was a simple document, calling for a bimetallic currency standard, with silver valued at 16 ounces to one ounce of gold. The platform also advocated that all currency "intended to circulate as money" should be legal tender, opposed the issuance of interest-bearing bonds in peacetime, and opposed a federal policy of borrowing gold internationally to finance domestic programs. The platform supported a tariff that would keep foreign silver from trading at different rates than domestic silver. Because of the increased supply of U.S. silver, the metal had fallen in value in relation to gold; however, numerous nations still supported a bimetallic standard, which meant that these nations could trade silver in the United States at a higher profit than could domestic silver producers. By supporting a tariff, the silverites intended to establish trade parity with these nations.

THE PARTY'S INFLUENCE

The National Silver party was a single-interest party, focusing entirely on monetary policy; as a result, the party lacked a broad voter base to capture more than a few seats in Congress and had little chance of affecting presidential politics. In fact, other than its ability to elect a few senators and state legislators, the party was largely ineffective in national politics. Its influence was limited to Nevada (electing one U.S. senator and a number of state legislators) and Iowa (where the party was able to broker the Democratic convention and guarantee itself one U.S. congressman and one state official).

The party was more effective in state and national races by operating as a "fusion" party.

Instead of running its own candidates and organizing its own campaigns, the party would ally with silver supporters in the major parties and try to combine influences to oppose gold candidates, primarily of the Republican party. The strategy failed because while the silver factions in the major party agreed on the need for a silver standard, they could not overcome other differences. Moreover, efforts to fuse with the Populists led to charges that the Populists were only interested in converting other candidates to the full Populist ticket. Most National Silver party members, Silver Republicans, and Silver Democrats rejected many tenets of Populism, and so fusions involving the Populists were usually full of tension.

The end of the National Silver party came after the election of 1896. Not only was McKinley's election to the presidency a signal for a more conservative policy in the United States, but shortly afterward the U.S. economy recovered and the currency issue became less relevant. In the end, the National Silver party failed to make a lasting impact on American politics because of its own internal conflicts, the ability of the Democratic party to capitalize on the silver issue, and the limited goals party members pursued. By 1904, the National Silver party had ceased to exist.

MICHAEL P. BOBIC

See also: William Jennings Bryan; Populist Movement/People's Party; Silver Party of Nevada; Silver Republicans.

Bibliography

Argersinger, Peter H. *Populism: Its Rise and Fall.* Lawrence: University Press of Kansas, 1992.

David, Paul T. *Party Strength in the United States: 1872–1970.* Charlottesville: University Press of Virginia, 1972.

Durden, Robert F. *The Climax of Populism: The Election of 1896.* Lexington: University of Kentucky Press, 1965.

Haynes, Frederick Emory. *Third Party Movements Since the Civil War.* Iowa City: State Historical Society of Iowa, 1916.

Hopkins, James H. *A History of Political Parties in the United States.* New York: G.P. Putnam and Sons, 1900.

Schlesinger, Arthur M. *History of U.S. Political Parties.* Vol. 2. New York: Chelsea House, 1973.

NATIONAL SOCIALIST WHITE PEOPLE'S PARTY

1967–

NAZI ORIGINS

The National Socialist White People's party (NSWPP) was the successor to the American Nazi party (ANP). The first neo-Nazi organization in the United States, the ANP was founded by George Lincoln Rockwell in 1958. After Rockwell's assassination in 1967 and the ensuing power struggle, Matthias Koehl, one of Rockwell's top deputies, took control of the party and changed the name to the National Socialist White People's party. In 1983, the party's name was changed to the New Order. By the mid-1980s, Koehl had moved the party's headquarters from Arlington, Virginia, to suburban Milwaukee, Wisconsin.

If third parties are on the periphery of the American party system, the NSWPP is located on the margins of that periphery. The party has entered the electoral arena, primarily in local elections, but the most successful candidates, such as David Duke in Louisiana and Ralph Forbes in Arkansas, have been former NSWPP members who ran as a candidate for another party. Considering its minuscule political influence, many observers do not consider the NSWPP to be a party; however, the party has been able to attract much publicity despite its lack of electoral success.

The ANP emerged from the vision of George Lincoln Rockwell. Rockwell, a World War II naval aviator, was first introduced to right-wing political thought and anti-Semitism while serving at the San Diego naval base during the Korean War. A strong anti-communist, he had supported Senator Joseph McCarthy's actions to rid the military and government of communist sympathizers. He also belonged to a group that wanted to draft General Douglas MacArthur to run for president. One of the other members of the group gave Rockwell some right-wing pamphlets to read. He found some of the material fascinating and intriguing. After reading Hitler's *Mein Kampf*, Rockwell began devising plans to institute national socialism in the United States with himself as the *Führer*.

Rockwell, known as Commander because of his naval rank, opened the headquarters of the ANP in Arlington, Virginia, in 1958. The party was small, with less than twenty members, and had little financial support. Despite an apparent lack of resources, the ANP managed to attract media attention to its demonstrations against Jews and blacks. Getting attention was easy for a small group of men organizing and marching in brown uniforms with swastikas and saluting each other with "heils."

Commander Rockwell was assassinated in 1967 by a mentally unstable former party member. The NSWPP, under the leadership of Matthias Koehl, emerged from the ensuing power struggle. Koehl considered the NSWPP to be the "second generation" of the national socialist movement begun by Rockwell. In Koehl's scheme, the goal of the first generation was to gain publicity for the movement. The second generation would work to develop small local cadres of committed party members to begin building the Aryan new order. By the early 1980s, the second generation had renamed Koehl's party the New Order.

The NSWPP was a paramilitary organization with a hierarchical structure. At the highest level was the commander, first Rockwell and then Koehl. Regional units were commanded by a captain. Each unit had "soldiers" who served as bodyguards and protection for the leadership. The party was a top-down organization.

As the party's first leader, Commander Rockwell worked to bring public attention to the ANP. He and his followers marched in demonstrations opposing Jews, blacks, and communists. He published a number of pamphlets and a book titled *This Time the World*. In an audacious move, Rockwell unsuccessfully worked to create a relationship with Elijah Muhammad's Nation of Islam. He spoke on college campuses in the United States and tried to export national socialism to Great Britain and Australia. In 1962, Rockwell established the World Union of National Socialists, an organization headed at one time by Matthias Koehl. In 1965, Rockwell ran for governor of Virginia. At the time of his assassination, he was developing a plan for the ANP to run a candidate for president in 1972 under the slogan, "The Jews Are Through in '72!"

Matthias Koehl, the party's second commander, was able to increase party activities for a time after Rockwell's assassination. Koehl moved party headquarters into a new building in Arlington, Virginia, in 1968. He expanded party activities further into the electoral arena. In 1976, the party planned to run a number of candidates for local offices in several cities. Arthur Jones, a NSWPP member, was an unsuccessful candidate in the nonpartisan election for mayor of Milwaukee. Several other NSWPP candidates ran for the Milwaukee Board of Education. Koehl also tried to develop ties with former Nazis in Germany. He traveled to Germany in 1975 and 1986, meeting with former Nazi leaders. In the mid-1980s, party headquarters were moved to suburban Milwaukee because Koehl wanted to be in the "more Aryan environment" of the Midwest. Under Koehl's leadership, the party continued in its attempts to recruit new members in the 1990s.

The political program of the NSWPP was a combination of white supremacy, socialism, rural populism, and "Christian identity" beliefs (the belief that America should be a Christian-based republic). Creation of a "National Social-ist Aryan Republic" on the North American continent was the party's primary goal. Only persons with "unmixed, non-Semitic, Caucasian European" ancestry would be allowed to become citizens of the new republic. All Aryan peoples, regardless of national origin, would be eligible for citizenship.

Among the rights enjoyed by citizens would be the right to decent housing, including a right to affordable home ownership. Citizens would also be free from excessive taxation and would have the right to a living wage sufficient to support oneself and his family. The NSWPP program also called for free quality medical care.

The family was an important pillar of the NSWPP program. To maintain the traditional, two-parent family, with the "gainfully employed husband and father as head of the family and the home-making wife and mother as its heart," the party proposed interest-free state mortgage loans to allow young married couples to immediately purchase a home. The amount of these loans would be reduced depending on the number of children. In addition, homes containing growing children would not be required to pay property taxes. Divorce would be made much more difficult. Such "social perversions" as homosexuality, feminism, and pornography would be suppressed. Abortion would be allowed only with a court order specifying that medical science determined the unborn child to be deformed or mentally retarded.

The Aryan republic would have an "honest and efficient economy" based on actual production, not the speculation or manipulation of money and pieces of paper. Among the economic ventures encouraged by the republic would be family farms. "Mass plantation-style agribusiness" would be prohibited in favor of small family farms. According to the NSWPP, the family farm provides social, racial, and environmental stability. To encourage family farming, the Aryan republic would abolish agricultural commodity speculation and provide interest-free loans for equipment and supplies required by farmers.

The NSWPP's views on foreign policy were relatively straightforward. The Aryan republic would work to encourage the development of national socialism among Aryan peoples world-wide. The republic would protect all Aryans from persecution, discrimination, or threatened genocide. Universal military conscription and military training for all young men would be established. All males between the ages of 18 and 50 would be part of the military reserve. Military pride and tradition would be a major aspect of the educational system.

In sum, the goal of the NSWPP was to promote a better race. The improvement of the Aryan race would occur through the utilization of "positive eugenic measures." All defects, including racially impure blood in the gene pool would be removed. As one NSWPP document stated,

Our people must be turned away from their present path of materialism, cynicism, and egotism and become inspired by the racial idealism and rebirth of traditional Aryan values. By these values we mean such ideals as the strong nuclear family unit; the love and cherishing of White children; personal responsibility for self and family; fortitude in adversity; physical courage in the face of the enemy; a sense of patriotism and racial community; generosity to those of our race who are sick or hurt or in need; and the concept of rights and privileges as the earned rewards of social responsibility fulfilled.

The NSWPP, and its successor the New Order, have continued the policy of denying the existence of the Holocaust and promoting anti-Israel sentiments.

The membership of the ANP, and later the NSWPP, has never been large. Most observers, including the Anti-Defamation League and the Federal Bureau of Investigation, estimate membership at from 100 to 200 nationwide in the late 1990s. Using newsletter subscriptions as a less rigorous measure of party support, there were only about 1,200 supporters. The media regularly saw a larger party because the party was able to mobilize sizable numbers of followers for demonstrations and marches. The actual number of dues-paying members, however, was quite small.

The party finds its greatest constituency among racists and other individuals outside the accepted boundaries of American politics. People attracted to the NSWPP have been described by experts as "hatemongers with real or potential personality disorders." Despite the small size of the party's actual membership, the potential membership is quite large. In general, the party might appeal to people who are disgruntled with the current state of affairs, who see the government as the tool of Jewish internationalists, or who are unemployed or underemployed and believe that minority groups get the "good" jobs.

A search of the World Wide Web suggested that, in 1998, most of the NSWPP political activity was taking place in the South, the Midwest, and Idaho. Tracking the political activity of the NSWPP is difficult because different groups are using the name, perhaps illegitimately.

Nazi parties in the United States have not been electorally successful. In addition, they have been plagued by internal strife and government regulation. In the 1964 New Hampshire presidential primary, Rockwell was unable to obtain the 100 signatures necessary to get on the ballot. None of the local candidates who ran under the party label in 1976 were elected.

The most successful candidates have been former NSWPP members running as candidates of other parties. Chief among these is David Duke, though it is unclear when he left the NSWPP. In 1989, as a Republican, Duke was elected to the Louisiana House of Representatives. He was a Republican candidate for the U.S. Senate in 1990. His most successful campaign was the 1991 gubernatorial race, when Duke defeated the mainstream Republican in the open primary and lost the general election to Edwin Edwards, the Democratic former governor. Interestingly, Koehl's New Order party was highly critical of Duke's more "mainstream" campaigns, challenging Duke's claims that he no longer believed in white supremacy.

In Arkansas, Rockwell associate Ralph Forbes won the 1990 Republican primary for lieutenant governor with 46 percent of the vote. Forbes lost the run-off election, however, to a

The National Socialist White People's party—with its white supremacist ideology—was often closely allied to the Ku Klux Klan, as indicated by this party rally at an unidentified location in the South in the late 1950s. *(Courtesy of the Library of Congress)*

black candidate. In 1996, Forbes was the presidential candidate for the America First party.

The party has historically lacked financial resources. Few Americans of means would want anyone to find out that they had contributed to an organization that idolizes Adolf Hitler. Most party members cannot afford to contribute money to the party. The finances of the party also have been reduced by the many legal actions taken against it. The party has been charged with violating the federal tax code a number of times, once causing the IRS to padlock the Arlington headquarters. In addition, the violent history of party members has resulted in expensive legal action.

The ANP and the NSWPP have been training grounds for future right-wing extremist leaders. This status has proven to be a shortcoming for the leadership of the New Order. A number of other groups claim the mantle of national socialism in the United States. William Pierce, head of the National Alliance and author of *The Turner Diaries*, was a member of the ANP. Frank Collin founded the National Socialist Party of America (NSPA) after being expelled from the ANP by Rockwell. In 1978, Collin and the NSPA attempted to march in Skokie, Illinois, the residence of a large number of Holocaust survivors.

In 1983, a former member of the NSWPP, Harold Covington (aka Winston Smith), adopted the NSWPP's name and formed his own group in the Carolinas. By 1998, there was confusion as to which group was the legitimate champion of national socialism. This confusion, and the culture of violence, seem to doom the party to continued insignificance as an electoral vehicle.

The ANP and the NSWPP brought the concept of "white power" into the political arena. Almost all white supremacist organizations rely on George Lincoln Rockwell's writings. Rockwell also introduced Christian identity thought into political discussion. Many of his theories of race relations are based in Christian identity beliefs.

It is doubtful that any party claiming national socialist ideals could ever gain significant political support in the United States. Even other white supremacist groups, such as the Ku Klux Klan, find it difficult to work with the NSWPP. In part, this is a result of the Ku Klux Klan's opposition to the socialist and communitarian nature of the party—the socialist aspect of national socialism. It also seems unlikely that the NSWPP, or the New Order, could move into the mainstream.

JOHN DAVID RAUSCH, JR.

See also: America First Party; David Duke; Matthias Koehl, Jr.; Douglas MacArthur; National States' Rights Party; George Lincoln Rockwell.

Bibliography

Anti-Defamation League. *Hate Groups in America: A Record of Bigotry and Violence,* 2d ed. New York: Anti-Defamation League, 1988.

Berlet, Chip, ed. *Eyes Right! Challenging the Right-Wing Backlash.* Boston: South End Press, 1995.

Dobratz, Betty A., and Stephanie L. Shanks-Meile. *"White Power, White Pride!" The White Separatist Movement in the United States.* New York: Twayne, 1997.

George, John, and Laird Wilcox. *American Extremists: Militias, Supremacists, Klansmen, Communists and Others.* New York: Prometheus Books, 1996.

Gillespie, J. David. *Politics at the Periphery: Third Parties in Two-Party America.* Columbia, SC: University of South Carolina Press, 1993.

Haley, Alex. "Playboy Interview: George Lincoln Rockwell." *Playboy* (April 1966).

Langer, Elinor. "The American Neo-Nazi Movement Today." *The Nation,* July 16–23, 1990.

Rose, Douglas D., ed. *The Emergence of David Duke and the Politics of Race.* Chapel Hill: University of North Carolina Press, 1992.

Simonelli, Frederick J. "The American Nazi Party, 1958–1967." *The Historian: A Journal of History* 57 (1995): 553–566.

★★★★★★★★★★★★★★★★★★★★★★★★★★★★★★★★★★

NATIONAL STATES' RIGHTS PARTY

1958–1984

Founded in 1958 and lasting well into the 1980s, the National States' Rights party (NSRP) was the most successful post–World War II, neo-Nazi party in the United States. The party was founded by Dr. Edward Fields and Jesse B. Stoner and remained on the extreme Right fringe of the U.S. political party system for nearly three decades.

A direct descendant of several extremist groups (the Columbians [1946], the Christian Anti-Jewish party [1952], and the United White party [1956]), the NSRP formed from a paramilitary group and promised to save the United States from any and all internal threats of destruction by ridding the country of Jews, Blacks, Catholics, and other groups deemed undesirable. Throughout its tenure, the party was able to incorporate several other fringe groups into its fold, including the Conservative party (Florida), the National White American party, the North Carolina Knights of the Ku Klux Klan, and the Seaboard Citizens' Council.

The NSRP found success in the South by appealing to southern racial traditionalists. The party was first headquartered in Jeffersonville, but was quickly moved to Birmingham, Alabama, and then to Augusta, Georgia, before finally settling in Marietta, Georgia. At its height, the organization claimed a membership of over 12,000 members. However, by most accounts, actual membership was most likely 1,500–2,000 members, spread across thirty individual chapters.

The two most important people in the NSRP were its founders Fields and Stoner. Fields provided the business sense and organizational skills to keep the party running from day to day, and Stoner was the flamboyant politician and stump speaker who took the group's controversial and extreme messages to the public.

Fields, a chiropractor and strident anti-Semitist, truly was the primary figure responsible for the NSRP. Serving as the national secretary of the party and the editor of the party's newsletter, *The Thunderbolt* (the symbol of the German Nazi party), Fields was the reason that the NSRP enjoyed stability and longevity, which was uncommon for most neo-Nazi parties in the United States. Fields began his political career in the 1940s with another organization of the extreme Right—Christian Anti-Jewish party. He served as chief secretary of the Christian Anti-Jewish party. It was during this time that he met Stoner, and the two organized the NSRP. Additionally, Fields often traveled abroad and is well known in European neo-Nazi circles. In the late 1970s, Fields organized a short-lived Ku Klux Klan group in Georgia, known as the New Order Knights of the Ku Klux Klan. During the last days of the NSRP in 1983, a group of NSRP members (States' Rights Voters League), who did not like Fields's personality or his alleged womanizing, voted him out of the party and published various allegations against him. During this time, the friendship between Fields and Stoner began to wane, and Fields was arrested for breaking into Stoner's home while attempting to retrieve some of his belongings. Eventually, Fields abandoned the NSRP and concentrated his full attention on publication of *The Thunderbolt* (he changed the name in 1988 to *The Truth at Last*).

Stoner served as national chairman of the NSRP and was the most visible public person-

Seen here leaving a September 14, 1957, meeting with President Dwight D. Eisenhower, Arkansas Governor Orval Faubus accepts the dispatch of federal troops to Little Rock to quell white violence surrounding the integration of the city's Central High School. Faubus was a key leader of the anti-integration National States' Rights party of the 1950s. The photo was originally captioned "An Amiable Meeting." (*United Press, September 14, 1957, courtesy of the Library of Congress*)

ality of the organization. Initially a lawyer, Stoner began his political career in the 1940s by serving first as a kleagle (organizer) for the Ku Klux Klan and then as archleader of the Christian Anti-Jewish party, where he met Fields. People associated with extreme Right politics often characterized Hitler as a moderate when compared to Stoner. In 1966, while appearing before a congressional committee investigating the Ku Klux Klan, Stoner pleaded the Fifth Amendment and refused to answer a single question about the organization. In 1969, he was one of several lawyers representing James Earl Ray in his appeal of his conviction in the assassination of Martin Luther King, Jr. Stoner was an ambitious politician. He ran for political office often, and on several occasions, he was moderately successful. He performed best in state-level campaigns for the offices of lieutenant governor and governor in the state of Georgia. However, Stoner's downfall began in 1977, when he was indicted and charged in Alabama as a co-conspirator with an unknown person in the 1958 bombing of a Birmingham church. Several African-American children perished in the explosion, but the indictment and conviction by white authorities said that the church was empty. Convicted in 1982, Stoner served three and a half years in prison. While he was in prison, the NSRP disbanded. Upon his release from prison in 1986, Stoner formed a new group, the Crusade Against Corruption. The organization is nowhere near the scale of the NSRP and is more like a typical extreme-right one-man operation.

The platform and policy proposals of the NSRP remained consistent throughout the party's nearly thirty-year existence. Like all neo-Nazi organizations, the party desired an all-white America. However, most of the party's statements fell just short of avowing pure nazism, but its principles and symbols exhibited this desire. Written in 1958, the party's platform remained unchanged until its demise in the 1980s. The party called for a "white folk" community, whites-only government, complete racial segregation, laws banning interracial marriages, and voluntary repatriation of blacks to Africa. However, unlike many other parties of the Right, the NSRP did not oppose government spending programs such as Medicare and Social Security, which led to criticism of the group by other rightist organizations such as the John Birch Society. Ultimately, the party appealed to racially traditional southerners as well as workers and farmers.

The NSRP exhibited a stability and longevity uncommon to other neo-Nazi organizations in the United States. The NSRP played an active role in the presidential campaigns between the years 1960 and 1972. In 1960, the NSRP chose Governor Orval Faubus (against his wishes) of Arkansas to run under its banner. The party selected Admiral John G. Crommelin, an ex-naval officer as its vice-presidential candidate. On the ballot in six states, the NSRP received 214,541 votes. The party nominated John Kasper for president and Jesse Stoner for vice president in 1964. The pair, on the ballot in only three states, performed poorly, especially when compared to the performance of Faubus and Crommelin in 1960. They received less than 7,000 votes. In 1972, rather than run their own candidate, the NSRP concentrated its support and resources on George Wallace's bid for the presidency.

Stoner often used the NSRP label in runs for state public office and, surprisingly, performed moderately well in these campaigns. In 1948 (under the Stoner Anti-Jewish party) he ran for Congress in Tennessee and received 500 of 30,000 votes cast. In 1970, he ran against Jimmy Carter in the Democratic gubernatorial election in Georgia and received 18,000 votes. In 1972, he ran in the Georgia Democratic primary for U.S. senator and garnered 40,000 votes. In 1974, he ran in the Democratic primary for lieutenant governor in Georgia and received 71,000 votes. He campaigned using the slogan, "You can't have law and order and niggers too—Vote White!" Finally, he ran in the Georgia Demo-

cratic primary for governor in 1978 and finished third.

The NSRP officially disbanded in 1984. After Stoner was jailed in Alabama, Fields was unable to keep various factions in the party united. After the collapse of the party, the friendship between Fields and Stoner ceased and each went their separate ways.

NANCY MARTORANO

See also: Edward Fields; National Socialist White People's Party; Jesse (J.B.) Stoner.

Bibliography

George, John, and Laird Wilcox. *American Extremists: Militias, Supremacists, Klansmen, Communists, and Others.* Amherst, NY: Prometheus Books, 1996.

———. *Nazis, Communists, Klansmen, and Others on the Fringe.* Buffalo, NY: Prometheus Books, 1992.

Gillespie, J. David. *Politics at the Periphery: Third Parties in Two-Party America.* Columbia: University of South Carolina Press, 1993.

Havel, James T. *U.S. Presidential Candidates and the Elections: A Biographical and Historical Guide,* Vol. 2. New York: Macmillan Library Reference USA, 1996.

Kruschke, Earl R. *Encyclopedia of Third Parties in the United States.* Santa Barbara, CA: ABC-CLIO, 1991.

Lipset, Seymour Martin, and Earl Raab. *The Politics of Unreason: Right-Wing Extremism in America, 1790–1970.* New York: Harper and Row, 1970.

O Maoláin, Ciarán. *The Radical Right: A World Directory.* Santa Barbara, CA: ABC-CLIO, 1987.

☆☆☆☆☆☆☆☆☆☆☆☆☆☆☆☆☆☆☆☆☆☆☆☆☆☆☆☆☆☆☆☆☆☆☆☆☆☆☆

NATIONAL UNITY CAMPAIGN

1980

The candidacy of John B. Anderson in 1980 represented one of the most successful independent or third-party presidential bids in the twentieth century. Running against incumbent Democratic President Jimmy Carter and Republican challenger Ronald Reagan, Anderson succeeded in getting on the ballot in all fifty states and the District of Columbia and in winning over 5.5 million votes nationwide.

ROAD TO 1980 ELECTION

When Jimmy Carter was elected in 1976, he won by temporarily reassembling the Democrats' New Deal coalition, a coalition that made the Democrats the majority party for much of the twentieth century. In the 1960s, members of this coalition began to desert the Democrats for both philosophical and economic reasons. At the same time, more and more voters became independent and came to view both political parties as increasingly irrelevant—trends that grew through the 1970s. By 1980, 37 percent of Americans embraced the independent label, creating a large pool of voters potentially sympathetic to a third-party or independent presidential candidate.

Political turmoil and partisan fractiousness marked the 1980 presidential contest. Jimmy Carter's re-election efforts were hampered by two seemingly intractable national problems: the Iranian hostage crisis and a serious economic downturn. Moreover, Carter faced an intra-party challenge from the Democratic left,

represented by Massachusetts Senator Edward M. Kennedy. On the Republican side, former California governor Ronald Reagan marshaled the party's growing conservative forces and bested a series of challengers to win his party's nomination.

One of these challengers was Representative John B. Anderson of Illinois. Anderson had been a member of the House of Representatives since 1961. In his early years in Congress, Anderson espoused some traditional, conservative positions. He sponsored a constitutional amendment that acknowledged the authority of Jesus Christ; he voted against liberal social welfare programs such as food stamps and Medicare; and he supported funding for the Vietnam War effort, for the B-1 bomber, and for the neutron bomb. In 1969, Republicans in the House elected Anderson as chair of the House Republican conference; he thus became the third ranking Republican in the lower chamber of Congress.

In the 1970s, Anderson's position on a slew of issues began to evolve. He had turned against the American war effort in Vietnam, calling it "the most tragic error in diplomacy and military policy in our nation's history." He supported an open housing policy, busing, abortion rights, the equal rights amendment, gun control, and the SALT II (Strategic Arms Limitation Talks) arms control treaty with the Soviet Union. At the same time, he expressed opposition to school prayer, to the MX missile, and to the Kemp-Roth proposal for an across-the-board tax cut. Earlier in the decade, he had gained notoriety when he became the first Republican in Congress to publicly call for President Richard Nixon's resignation during the Watergate crisis. All of these positions isolated Anderson from the conservative philosophy of his Republican party. By 1978, the New Right targeted Anderson for defeat in the Republican primary in his home district, a challenge that proved unsuccessful.

REPUBLICAN PRIORITIES

When Anderson entered the Republican presidential primaries of 1980, he was still a virtual unknown outside of Congress. But he quickly made a name for himself as the only Republican candidate willing to speak out on behalf of the party's moderate wing. Anderson further reinforced this image as an outsider within his own party—and as an honest and straight-talking politician—by taking what might be called courageous positions. He defended President Carter's grain embargo in the farm state of Iowa, and he spoke out in favor of gun control at a forum organized by the New Hampshire Gun Owners' Association. All of this contributed to what became known in the media as "the Anderson difference."

Anderson did well in some of the early primaries. Although he finished fourth in New Hampshire, he won 10 percent of the vote in a crowded field and his performance was hailed by the press as a victory of sorts. Anderson finished a strong second in two subsequent Republican primaries—Massachusetts and Vermont—but then lost to Reagan in his home state of Illinois (by a margin of 49 percent to 38 percent). Anderson's strategy in the primaries was to appeal to a segment of the electorate that was not typically part of the Republicans' coalition: young people, women's groups, and gun control advocates. This strategy, alongside his liberal policy positions, earned him the enmity of his party. Fellow Republican Congressman Philip Crane once said to him, "You're in the wrong party, John."

On April 24, 1980, John Anderson announced that he would seek the presidency as an independent. He formed the National Unity Campaign as the party vehicle for his run for president. His decision was predicated on a number of factors. He obviously was not going to win the Republican presidential nomination—he had won barely 10 percent of the necessary delegates. He had, however, demonstrated that there was a constituency out there for a candidate with Anderson's particular philosophy of fiscal conservatism and social liberalism—although this constituency no longer felt welcome in a Republican party aligned with the New Right. Anderson's decision to run was further buoyed by poll findings that suggested that voters were unusually dissatisfied with the candidates offered to them by the major parties. In fact, at the end of April, right after Anderson declared his intention to run, a variety of polls placed Anderson's support level at around 20 percent. Anderson's entry into the presidential race was also facilitated by a report from campaign aide and fundraising expert Tom Mathews that millions of dollars could be raised from thousands of centrist voters—the "alienated middle"—by way of direct mail appeals.

Anderson's campaign organization, in the words of a campaign aide, "was something less than a well-oiled political machine." His campaign manager, William Bradford, was Anderson's former colleague from their days in the Foreign Service and thus had relatively little campaign experience. Control of the campaign was eventually given to prominent media consultant David Garth. Television producer Norman Lear also acted as an informal advisor and fundraiser for the campaign. Many staffers and volunteers were young collegians who were drawn to Anderson on the strength of his Republican primary performance.

Anderson's polling numbers peaked early. He stood at over 20 percent in the weeks after he announced his intention to run, but over the next two months, his numbers fell. By mid-July, about 15 percent of voters expressed an intention to vote for him. His poll numbers dropped for a variety of reasons. The Republican convention was held in mid-July and Ronald Reagan successfully rallied the party around his conservative candidacy amid a barrage of national media coverage. To compensate for the loss of media attention, Anderson embarked on a tour of Europe and the Middle East—the purpose of which was to maintain some media attention and to display Anderson's qualities as a foreign policy expert. But media coverage of the foreign tour was quite negative. Anderson's prospects were also undermined by the media's "horse-race" coverage of the campaign. Polls showing Anderson trailing contributed to a public perception that the candidate could not win. Media coverage—so favorable during the primaries—began to depict Anderson's campaign as drifting toward conventionality.

THE STRUGGLE FOR BALLOT ACCESS

The campaign faced a far more fundamental problem—access to the ballot. By the time Anderson had declared his intention to run as an independent, the filing deadlines for presidential candidates had already passed in five states. Moreover, each state had different requirements—rules governing the number of signatures required to get on the ballot, who could sign petitions, and deadlines for submission of petitions. Some states had "sore loser" laws whereby a candidate defeated in a major party presidential primary could not get his/her name placed on the ballot for the presidential election. The Democrats, fearful that an Anderson candidacy would hurt Carter's re-election, fought legal battles to keep Anderson off the ballot. At a time when Anderson's campaign organization should have been devoting its resources to campaigning—as were the major party candidates—it instead devoted huge amounts of time, energy, and money to contesting ballot access rules across the country. By the end of the summer, before the traditional Labor Day campaign kick-off, Anderson's campaign was already $1 million in debt. Although Anderson did ultimately succeed in his efforts to get on the ballot in every state—he collected 1.2 million signatures nationwide toward that end—his failure to campaign alongside the

major parties ultimately cost him much public support.

A number of developments in late August and September brought new momentum to the campaign, albeit a momentum that proved to be fleeting. On August 24, 1980, Anderson named former Wisconsin governor Patrick Lucey to be his vice-presidential running mate. Lucey was a liberal Democrat and a former supporter of Senator Edward Kennedy's challenge for the Democratic nomination. The Anderson-Lucey National Unity ticket also released its platform, a series of commitments that, in Anderson's own words, reflected his "wallet on the right, heart on the left" political philosophy. The platform's centerpiece was a 50 cents a gallon gasoline tax, designed to encourage energy savings and to allow for a reduction in Social Security taxes. The platform advocated an Urban Reinvestment Trust Fund, to be paid for by federal excise taxes on alcohol and tobacco; tax incentives for companies and labor unions that would voluntarily hold the line on prices and wages, respectively; and tax-based investment incentives for businesses, especially small businesses. "Sacrifice" was a theme frequently associated with Anderson's economic policies; the candidate was adamant in his opposition to tax cuts, especially Reagan's across-the-board tax cuts. On social issues, such as school prayer, the equal rights amendment, abortion, and gay rights, Anderson's positions were, in his own words, "unabashedly liberal." What was striking about Anderson's platform and his entire candidacy was the absence of an intense, emotional issue, the kind that typically drives third-party candidates to run.

In the weeks following the release of the platform, Anderson received welcome news from three different sources. The New York Liberal party gave Anderson its presidential line, thus ensuring him ballot access without a legal battle in one of the largest states. The League of Women Voters announced that it would include Anderson in the televised presidential debates if he maintained a 15 percent poll rating. And perhaps most significantly, the Federal Election Commission (FEC) ruled that for the purposes of campaign finance laws, the National Unity ticket would be treated as a political party. This meant that if Anderson received at least 5 percent of the popular vote on election day, he would be eligible for federal funding after the election. Compared to the large lump sums that the major parties would get to wage their campaigns, Anderson's prospective payoff was quite minor. But the promise of federal funds enabled Anderson to borrow money from both banks and donors and use his expected election-day performance as collateral.

Money proved to be the bane of Anderson's candidacy. Over the course of the presidential election campaign, Anderson raised $17.1 million dollars. The Reagan and Carter campaigns each received about $30 million from the federal government (plus millions more in funds from parties, political action committees, and independent expenditures; Reagan's funds totaled $64 million, Carter's were $54 million). Nearly $10 million of Anderson's funds came from individual contributors, and $4.2 million came by way of the federal government, but only after the election. The campaign ended up borrowing $2.23 million, only $400,000 of which came from banks.

Anderson's campaign spent over $16.5 million. But these funds were disbursed in ways that hindered the candidate's ability to wage a competitive campaign. The single largest expenditure item was fundraising ($3 million); over $2 million was spent on gaining access to the ballot. Anderson spent only $2.29 million on media. By way of contrast, the Reagan campaign spent over $17 million alone on the purchase of media time. In the media age, a candidate who cannot spend considerable resources on media is doomed to failure. This is precisely what happened to John Anderson.

ELECTORAL RESULTS

Anderson's efforts to gain exposure were hampered not only by his lack of money but also by the strategy of Democratic candidate Jimmy Carter. Although the League of Women Voters ruled that Anderson could participate in the candidate debates if he maintained a 15 percent standing in public opinion polls, President Carter refused to appear in any debate with Anderson. Carter's campaign had previously fought Anderson's quest to get on the ballot, and a Carter financier had urged the FEC not to grant federal funding to the National Unity ticket. Carter's campaign felt that Anderson's presence in the race was disproportionately harmful to the president. And so on the date of the first scheduled debate (September 21), Anderson debated Reagan one-on-one. By October 28, when the final candidate debate was scheduled to take place, Anderson's poll rating had slipped well below 15 percent; thus the League of Women Voters withdrew its invitation.

On November 4, 1980, Republican Ronald Reagan defeated Democrat Jimmy Carter by a margin of 50.8 percent to 41 percent. John Anderson finished third, winning 6.6 percent of the vote, or over 5.7 million votes. He did not win any electoral votes. His greatest area of strength was New England where he won nearly 14 percent of the vote. He also did well on the West Coast, and in the upper Midwest, Colorado, and Arizona. Surveys suggest that young white voters were more likely than their older counterparts to vote for the National Unity ticket (15 percent of 18- to 25-year-old whites voted for Anderson), as were the most affluent whites (15 percent among whites whose income exceeded $50,000) and the most educated whites (13 percent of white college graduates). It is also instructive to examine some of Anderson's greatest areas of weakness: African Americans (1 percent voted for him), white southerners (4 percent), and white working-class Americans (5 percent). Anderson's appeal clearly did not resonate with some of the traditional members of the New Deal coalition.

In ideological terms, Anderson's voters were not all that distinct from the rest of the electorate. Like their candidate, they tended to be more liberal on social issues (such as aid to minorities, women's rights, and abortion), and in this respect they resembled Carter voters. On economic questions, they were generally hostile to government intervention and thus resembled

Reagan voters. And in terms of partisanship, it should come as no surprise that Anderson drew disproportionately from the ranks of independents—12 percent of independents reported an Anderson vote.

ANDERSON'S LEGACY

Anderson's success can be attributed to a number of factors. First, by most accounts, his campaign performance during the Republican presidential primaries was outstanding and propelled him to national prominence. Second, he identified a constituency that was receptive to his twin messages of social liberalism and fiscal prudence. Third, his tenacity won him ballot access across the country. Fourth, since the 1960s, more voters have displayed weakened partisan attachments and have become susceptible to the appeals of third-party or independent candidates. And fifth, Anderson benefited from the fortuitous fact that many Americans viewed both Jimmy Carter and Ronald Reagan as rather unappealing candidates.

Yet, it is worth noting that Anderson's campaign never realized its early potential. With poll ratings hovering above 20 percent in the spring of 1980, Anderson failed to build on this substantial core and indeed saw it mostly disappear. What contributed to the failure of the National Unity ticket?

There are at least three factors that kept Anderson from seriously contending. First, there are institutional barriers to all third parties—the National Unity ticket was no exception. The electoral college discriminates against candidates with geographically diffuse support, such as Anderson had. Moreover, restrictive ballot access rules across the country forced the campaign to spend a disproportionate amount of money merely to get on the ballot. The rules governing campaign finance also hinder the ability of third parties to wage competitive campaigns. Anderson's campaign was unusually fortunate in that it received some federal funding after the election; however, alongside the

subsidies accorded to the major parties, Anderson's grant was too little, and far too late.

Alongside these institutional barriers, the Democratic party embarked on a deliberate strategy to delegitimize the Anderson candidacy. This strategy—especially Carter's refusal to debate Anderson before a national audience—effectively reduced Anderson's visibility as a serious third-party contender for president. The upshot of this strategy—along with changing media coverage—was to create a public perception that Anderson could not win the election. Surveys taken before the 1980 election found that less than 1 percent of the electorate felt that Anderson would win. Moreover, among Reagan and Carter voters who had considered voting for Anderson (27 percent of the electorate), 45 percent stated that they decided not to vote for Anderson because he had no chance of winning. More than anything else, these perceptions harm an independent candidate's ability to break through.

There is a third factor that made Anderson different from most other third-party presidential aspirants and helps explain why he ended up losing support throughout the campaign. Anderson's campaign did not have an intense, emotional issue that carried the candidate and seized the electorate. The candidate ran a centrist campaign. During the primaries, this strategy worked to some extent, as Anderson, on his party's left, identified a core constituency that brought him some success. But in the general election, running from the center is what the major parties try to do. So Anderson no longer looked so "different."

In the end, Anderson was doomed by the very nature of his own appeal and by the character of his constituency. The evidence suggests that many voters were attracted to him not on the strength of his own qualities but rather out of discontent with the major-party candidates. He ran against the major parties but his centrist appeal lacked an emotional chord. In fact, the most significant electoral development in the 1980 election was the conversion of many working-class, ethnic, and southern voters—the bedrock of the Democrats' New Deal coalition—into Reagan Democrats. Anderson's supporters tended to be young, independent, and affluent, and held little emotional investment in politics.

Although John Anderson won over 6 percent of the vote, his presence in the election was not a decisive factor in Ronald Reagan's victory. That is not to say, though, that his candidacy had no impact. Anderson's run for the presidency exposed the tension between the socially conservative Republican party and its traditionally moderate wing. His success in striking down ballot access restrictions ensured that future third-party and independent candidates would face far fewer hurdles. And by capturing 5.7 million votes, Anderson's campaign signaled the presence of a large pool of voters with little prior attachment to the political parties—a bloc that could again be mobilized by a strong independent or third-party candidate.

HOWARD GOLD

See also: John B. Anderson; **Map 3:** John Anderson (1980).

Bibliography

Abramson, Paul R.; John H. Aldrich; Phil Paolino; and David W. Rohde. "Third Party and Independent Candidates in American Politics: Wallace, Anderson, and Perot." *Political Science Quarterly* 110 (1995).

Abramson, Paul R.; John H. Aldrich; and David W. Rohde. *Change and Continuity in the 1980 Elections.* Washington, DC: Congressional Quarterly Press, 1982.

Alexander, Herbert E. *Financing the 1980 Election.* Lexington, MA: D.C. Heath, 1983.

Anderson, John B. *Between Two Worlds: A Congressman's Choice.* Grand Rapids: Zondervan, 1970.

Bisnow, Mark. *Diary of a Dark Horse: The 1980 Anderson Presidential Campaign.* Carbondale: Southern Illinois University Press, 1983.

Candidates '80. Washington, DC: Congressional Quarterly, 1980.

Drew, Elizabeth. *Portrait of an Election: The 1980 Presidential Campaign.* New York: Simon and Schuster, 1981.

Gold, Howard J. "Third Party Voting in Presidential Elections: A Study of Perot, Anderson, and Wallace." *Political Research Quarterly* 48 (1995).

Greenfield, Jeff. *The Real Campaign. How the Media Missed the Story of the 1980 Campaign.* New York: Summit Books, 1982.

Pomper, Gerald, et al. *The Election of 1980: Reports and Interpretations.* Chatham, NJ: Chatham House, 1981.

Rosenstone, Steven J.; Roy L. Behr; Edward H. Lazarus et al. *Third Parties in America.* 2d ed. Princeton: Princeton University Press, 1996.

Schneider, William. "The November 4 Vote for President: What Did It Mean?" In *The American Elections of 1980,* ed. Austin Ranney. Washington, DC: American Enterprise Institute, 1981.

Smallwood, Frank. *The Other Candidates: Third Parties in Presidential Elections.* Hanover, NH: University Press of New England, 1983.

West, Darrell M. *Making Campaigns Count: Leadership and Coalition-Building in 1980.* Westport, CT: Greenwood Press, 1984.

Whittle, Richard. "John Anderson Still Trying to Dump His 'Spoiler' Image." *Congressional Quarterly Weekly Report,* September 27, 1980.

NATIONAL WOMAN'S PARTY

1916–1980s

The National Woman's party was founded in Washington, D.C., in 1916 by members of the Congressional Union for Woman Suffrage and the National American Woman Suffrage Association. The central focus of the National Woman's party at its inception was the passage of the Susan B. Anthony amendment to the U.S. Constitution. The Nineteenth Amendment extended the right to vote to women and was successfully passed in 1920. Alice Paul, a lifelong leader of the National Woman's party, wrote the first equal rights amendment (known as the Lucretia Mott amendment) and first introduced this amendment in Congress in 1923. The National Woman's party was at its strongest in the 1920s, with some 50,000 members. The party lost influence in the women's movement after the 1920s, although it maintained an office in Washington, D.C., and continued to support passage of the equal rights amendment and to urge women to run for political office as late as the 1980s.

The National Woman's party is more appropriately classified as an interest group rather than a political party, as the group never put forth candidates for office on a party ticket. Rather, the National Woman's party first focused its efforts on securing passage for the Nineteenth Amendment and then turned attention to attempts to convince both Democratic and Republican parties to support an equal rights amendment to the Constitution.

In advocating women's suffrage, the National Woman's party was active in picketing the White House and criticizing President Woodrow Wilson for a lack of action in extending the right to vote to women. The tactics of the National Woman's party were more militant than other feminist groups, and many of its women supporters were arrested and jailed for civil disobedience. The National Woman's party argued that the Democratic party, as the party holding the presidency and the majority in Congress in 1916, should be held responsible for the lack of women's suffrage at the national level. The 1916 platform of the National Woman's party expressed support for the Susan B. Anthony amendment and pledged to secure passage of the amendment without reference to the interests of any national political party. Because of its intense opposition to Democratic party candidates in the 1918 election, the National Woman's party is credited with being partially responsible for the election of a Republican majority in the U.S. Senate that year. Shortly thereafter, Congress voted in favor of a women's suffrage amendment, and the amendment was ratified by a sufficient number of states to become the Nineteenth Amendment to the U.S. Constitution.

Alice Paul and Lucy Burns, founders of the National Woman's party, first met in England in 1909. They became involved in the women's suffrage movement in England and became friends and admirers of Emmeline Pankhurst, leader of the British Women's Social and Political Union. Both Paul and Burns were arrested for civil disobedience and participated in hunger strikes several times while in England, and they put the more militant tactics of the English effort to work in the United States upon their return home. In 1913, the National American Woman Suffrage Association (NAWSA) asked

Alice Paul and Lucy Burns to form what they called a congressional committee to focus on a drive for a federal amendment to extend suffrage to women. From the 1890s through 1910, five states (Wyoming, Colorado, Utah, and Idaho in the 1890s and Washington in 1910) had granted women the right to vote, but there was little effort focused on the national level. The congressional committee of the NAWSA, based in Washington, D.C., would begin to change this.

The congressional committee and the National Woman's party that followed it were strongly influenced by the experiences of Alice Paul, Lucy Burns, and other women who had been involved in the British effort for women's suffrage. In England, women suffragists experienced outright hostility and violence. In the United States in 1913, apathy and indifference were the more pressing concerns for advocates of women's suffrage. The progressive era focus on reform made change seem more likely in the United States. Thus, Paul and Burns did not believe that U.S. suffragists needed to become as militant as those in Britain. However, they became more pessimistic about the pace of change after a couple of years in Washington, D.C., and their commitment to the necessity for forceful action by women ultimately led them to break with less militant NAWSA suffragists to form the National Woman's party.

The National Woman's party reflected the views of British suffragists, including the belief that the party in power should be held responsible for the lack of national women's suffrage. The party pressured for change in government policy, engaging in marches and parades, street meetings, distribution of pamphlets, chalking slogans on sidewalks, and candidate heckling. The party did not go so far as to engage in the violence and guerrilla tactics that were used in Britain, although in 1917 218 women from twenty-six states were arrested for picketing and obstructing traffic and nearly 100 women were jailed. The women protested with hunger strikes and were force-fed in response. Negative publicity led to release of the prisoners and invalidation of their arrests. The NAWSA publicly denied approval for the tactics of National

Woman's party members, and the public was wary of challenges to the government, particularly at a time when the nation was involved in World War I. Although the relative importance of the National Woman's party in the passage of the Nineteenth Amendment is indeterminate, it seems clear that the strength of their commitment helped to speed its passage.

The National Woman's party turned its attention to passage of the equal rights amendment to the U.S. Constitution in the 1920s. Party members also supported international efforts to achieve legal equality for women, working on behalf of the Equal Rights Treaty and the Equal Nationality Treaty in the United States, Europe, and Latin America. Militant confrontation and challenge to the party in power became less successful tactics as times changed and divisions in feminism hampered efforts on behalf of improving conditions for women. The National Woman's party came to focus on endorsing women for both elective and appointive offices in government, promoting writing and teaching women's history, and remembering women's past achievements. With divisions between leaders of the National Woman's party, American social feminists, and groups such as the League of Women Voters, the Women's Trade Union League, and the Consumer's League (which struggled against the National Woman's party for influence with women's organizations), the party never regained the support it had in its early years. Further, the equal rights amendment supported by the party has never been ratified.

The leaders of the National Woman's party came primarily from wealthy, upper-middle-class backgrounds from the Northeast. They were highly educated women who successfully sought support from other wealthy and prominent women. The central goal of the party after 1920 was the achievement of equality before the law. The National Woman's party differed from other women's organizations who supported laws on behalf of women and children, laws associated with both Progressive and New Deal reforms. Such laws, they argued, implied that women were unequal or even inferior to men and needed special protection. The National

Members of the National Woman's party celebrate the passage of the Nineteenth Amendment, granting women the right to vote in 1920, by unfurling a banner outside their Washington headquarters. The woman on the balcony is unidentified. *(Courtesy of the Library of Congress)*

Woman's party held the position that economic and social equality for women were necessary goals, but members argued that these would follow once equality before the law was achieved.

National Woman's party co-founder Alice Paul was born in 1885 in Moorestown, New Jersey, and she died in Moorestown in 1977. Paul, the eldest of four children, came from an upper-middle-class, reformist Quaker background. She was taught that women were equal before God and that it was important to address social problems. Alice Paul attended Swarthmore College, a Quaker institution that her maternal grandmother had helped to found. Paul graduated from Swarthmore in 1905, and she received a master's degree in 1907 and a Ph.D. in social work in 1912 from the University of

Pennsylvania. After achieving the main goal, passage of the Nineteenth Amendment, Paul went back to school for three different law degrees. She received a Bachelor of Laws from Washington College of Law in 1923 and a Master of Laws and Doctor of Civil Laws from American University in 1927 and 1928. Paul never married, and she devoted her life's work to the cause of equality for women. Paul served as the chair of the national council of the National Woman's party in the early years of the party, and she remained a member of the national council or served as vice president or advisory chair of the party in later years. In 1938, Alice Paul organized the World Party for Equal Rights for Women, known as the World Women's party. Further, Paul was influential in the inclusion of references to equality for the sexes in the preamble to the United Nations charter and the 1964 U.S. Civil Rights Act.

Co-founder Lucy Burns was born in Brooklyn, New York, in 1879, the fourth of eight children. Burns died in 1966. Burns's family was Irish Catholic and upper middle class, and Burns remained close to her family throughout her life. In 1902, Burns received a B.A. in English from Vassar, followed by graduate studies at Yale and a brief period teaching English at Erasmus High School in Brooklyn. Bored and restless, Burns left the United States for graduate studies in Bonn and Berlin from 1906 to 1909. She was on vacation from study in Berlin when she became involved in the suffrage movement in England. In 1913, Burns became co-chair with Alice Paul of the congressional committee of the NAWSA, followed by leadership roles in the National Woman's party. Burns never married nor had children of her own, although she raised an orphaned niece. In her later years, Burns devoted herself to family and church.

VIRGINIA A. CHANLEY

See also: Lucy Burns; Alice Paul.

Bibliography

Becker, Susan D. *The Origins of the Equal Rights Amendment: American Feminism Between the Wars.* Westport, CT: Greenwood Press, 1981.

Flexnor, Eleanor. *Century of Struggle.* Cambridge: Harvard University Press, 1959.

Ford, Linda G. *Iron-Jawed Angels: The Suffrage Militancy of the National Woman's Party, 1912–1920.* Lanham, MD: University Press of America, 1991.

Irwin, Inez Haynes. *The Story of the Woman's Party.* New York: Krause Reprint, 1971.

Schapsmeier, Edward L., and Frederick H. Schapsmeier. *Political Parties and Civic Action Groups.* Westport, CT: Greenwood Press, 1981.

☆☆☆☆☆☆☆☆☆☆☆☆☆☆☆☆☆☆☆☆☆☆☆☆☆☆☆☆☆☆

NATURAL LAW PARTY

1992–

Claiming to be America's fastest-growing political third party, the Natural Law party (NLP) was founded in 1992 in Fairfield, Iowa, by "a group of educators, business people, and concerned citizens who had grown tired of politics as usual and gridlock between the two major parties." Although the party is young and has yet to elect any candidate to office, it has become active in all fifty states and rivals the Libertarian party in electoral breadth, ideological depth and organizational development.

The philosophical basis of the NLP is a belief that the natural, scientific laws that govern the universe can be successfully applied by government to cure the problems of society. NLP platforms have emphasized "prevention-oriented government, conflict-free politics and proven solutions to America's problems designed to bring the life of the nation into harmony with natural law." At the root of the party's positions on most social and economic issues is a belief in the therapeutic power of Transcendental Meditation (TM), which natural law advocates contend reduces stress and improves personal happiness—leading to a healthier populace, less crime, and greater productivity in schools and the workplace. The costs saved from reduced social problems, in turn, contribute to a more efficient government and more robust economy. The party even contends that TM will improve American foreign policy, by reducing conflicts with other countries.

Overall, the party's "prevention-oriented" and TM-based approach translates into policy positions that do not easily fit on a traditional Left-Right ideological spectrum. On crime, the party is opposed to conservative approaches, such as building prisons, expanding the death penalty, and increasing the number of police, but is also opposed to social programs, such as drug treatment and education, which are favored by liberals. Concerning the economy, the party is strongly in favor of cutting taxes, believing that cuts can be offset by the savings gained from a healthier and happier populace. Unlike the classic laissez-faire approach, however, the party puts a premium on reducing unemployment and creating jobs. On abortion, the party says it is "committed to substantially reducing the number of abortions in America," but believes that this should be done "through education, not legislation." On a similarly controversial issue—gay marriages—the party says it neither supports nor opposes such legislation. The party supports affirmative action "as a necessary evil," but does not support quotas. It supports NAFTA and similar agreements, supports work-oriented welfare reform, and opposes the legalization of drugs.

The NLP's most visible positions have been on agricultural issues and food production. Recently, the party has waged an active media and petition campaign against genetically engineered foods, arguing that such products should be more rigorously tested and labeled by the federal government. At the heart of NLP opposition to genetic engineering is the belief that such manipulation of genetic structures in organisms violates natural order, which could have grave consequences for the balance of the ecosystem.

Among the events considered to be most significant in the party's short history are: quali-

393

Physicist John Hagelin and Mike Tompkins, the Natural Law party's presidential and vice-presidential candidates respectively, garnered 113,668 votes in forty-four states in the 1996 elections. Here, a campaign bus leaves from Washington in July 1996. *(Courtesy of the Natural Law party)*

fying for national party status and federal matching funds in the 1992 election; qualifying for ballot access in California in 1996 (which required the party to register 104,000 voters); and the 1998 publication of a book, *The Natural Law Party: A Reason to Vote,* by Robert Roth, the national party's press secretary.

John Hagelin, a Harvard-trained quantum physicist, is the party's two-time presidential candidate and its most visible leader. In 1992, along with vice-presidential nominee Mike Tompkins, Hagelin ran in thirty-two states and received 39,179 votes, the largest share of which came from Iowa (the party's base), New York, Ohio, and Michigan. Hagelin was the only candidate other than the major-party candidates that year to receive federal matching funds. In

1996, Hagelin and Tompkins nearly tripled their vote, garnering 113,668 ballots in forty-four states. More than 15,000 votes came from California, and the ticket also did well in Massachusetts and Illinois. Throughout the campaign, Hagelin was included in national third-party candidate debates and forums that were broadcast on national cable television.

Sub-presidential candidate recruitment is a major initiative of the NLP. The party sponsors frequent candidate training programs, and party literature indicates that their candidates "consistently [report] remarkable increases of happiness, energy, knowledge and success in their lives as a direct result of running for office on the Natural Law party ticket." Although the 1992 elections saw 125 candidates running along with Hagelin, four years later the party, according to its literature, recruited close to 400 candidates who gathered 760,000 votes in congressional races alone. Twelve candidates garnered more than 4 percent of the vote. In 1998, their best-known candidate was Harold Bloomfield, a nationally recognized psychiatrist and best-selling author of self-help books, who ran for governor of California. He finished with 28,467 votes. In the same year, the NLP candidate for governor of Ohio, Zanna Feitler, a teacher of the TM method, got substantial recognition for her performance in a debate with the major-party candidates that was later aired on C-SPAN.

The NLP of the United States is the largest of sixty Natural Law parties organized throughout the world. Industrialized countries such as Canada, France, Italy, the United Kingdom, Russia, Japan, and Australia have active members and organizations, and the party extends to less developed countries such as India, Malaysia, Estonia, and the Philippines. Some, such as the NLPs of Canada and France, have run ample slates of candidates in recent parliamentary elections garnering small percentages of the vote. The international Natural Law parties congregate annually for a convention and to discuss global issues such as electoral system reform, human rights, environmental protection, and food safety.

CHRISTIAN COLLET

See also: John Hagelin; Libertarian Party.

Bibliography

Roth, Robert. *The Natural Law Party: A Reason to Vote.* New York: St. Martin's Press, 1998.

NEW PARTY

1992–

FOUNDATION OF THE PARTY

While according to the statistics a majority of Americans have seen their standard of living eroded by the economic restructuring of the 1980s and 1990s, the nation's inner cities have suffered the worst fate. Indeed, the United States is one of the few industrially developed countries in which official policy has largely abandoned its cities—leaving many urban neighborhoods the victims of wholesale disinvestment and decay. While current U.S. politics often pits suburban voters against city populations, the problems that face the nation's cities have not remained confined to their borders. Indeed, urban decay, corporate flight, low-wage jobs, eroded public services, and social crisis show a clear spread into the suburbs—radiating from the inner to the outer rings.

The founders of the New party believed that the key to national power lay in building a new political base that unites the nation's cities with their inner-ring suburbs. Both face similar economic forces. Both contain populations disenchanted with "politics as usual." As the most recent of the current national third-party efforts, the New party is still a fledgling organization. By the end of 1997 it had established active local chapters in ten states (Wisconsin, Minnesota, Maryland, Arkansas, Texas, New York, Massachusetts, Illinois, Montana, New Jersey) plus the District of Columbia.

ECONOMIC AND SOCIAL JUSTICE

From its beginning, the New party has articulated a distinct brand of progressive third-party politics. Its strategy revolves around six central elements: the combination of issue and electoral work, grassroots activism, local focus, ballot flexibility, coalition politics, and resource-supported organizing. These elements have paid off in clear New party successes. Some parts of the New party's strategy, however, have also drawn controversy from among third-party activists.

Like other third-party groups, but with its own distinct spin, the New party was founded to break the isolation of electoral politics from issue activism. "We don't wait until five months before the election to start to groom voters," stresses Milwaukee organizer Tammy Johnson. "We are building a movement 365 days a year." Thus, for example, in several cities New party activists became key organizers of successful Living Wage campaigns. These efforts have enacted laws requiring companies receiving taxpayer money, either through city contracts and/or financial assistance, to pay a living wage—typically defined as above the federal poverty line for a family of four ($8.30 an hour in 1998). Living Wage campaigns have united broad and lasting labor-community-religious coalitions around basic economic issues. The New party's early commitment to Living Wage organizing has made it one part of this mushrooming movement. By 1998, Living Wage campaigns had won local ordinances in over sixteen cities with new campaigns under way in over three dozen others.

Combining issues with electoral organizing has not meant simply pursuing both types of activities simultaneously, but developing ways so that they reinforce each other. For example, in Little Rock, Arkansas, the New party won a police accountability ordinance following a controversial killing of three African-American men. The victory came in a context of several years of New party electoral campaigns that placed eighteen New party candidates into local and state offices committed to this issue. New party activists have directly combined issues and elections by placing initiatives on the ballot. In 1997, for example, a successful New party–sponsored ballot initiative placed the Minneapolis police department under the jurisdiction of the city's civil rights ordinance. Minneapolis activists also passed a ballot initiative to block public funds from being used to help build a sports stadium developed by a local billionaire.

GRASSROOTS ORGANIZING

The New party has also made organizing issues out of the undemocratic obstacles found in the U.S. electoral system. In Minnesota, for example, the Twin Cities New party succeeded in getting a bill called the "New Democracy Act" introduced into the state legislature. It included provisions to allow more than one party to endorse the same candidate, permit 16-year-olds to vote in school board elections, shorten campaign seasons, establish a Citizen's Campaign Jury to monitor political advertising and convene public debates, and a proposal to provide free public television air time to candidates who agree to spending limits. In the November 1996 elections, two Massachusetts communities passed New party campaign finance reform advisory ballot initiatives. That same year, the Arkansas New party helped pass the state's new tough campaign finance reform law and has worked to make Little Rock the first city in the state to fully implement its provisions.

Also, like other progressive political groups, the New party emphasizes grassroots organizing. A great myth of American politics portrays the current money-driven, media-focused tactics used by the major parties as the only possible way to conduct modern politics. Yet, the two parties began developing their advertising style of election well before the rise of television and radio as dominant sources of public information—the two mediums that supposedly dictate the format of our political campaigning. Indeed, with over half the electorate routinely staying home on election day, old grassroots methods to get out the vote can prove decisive. As the famous political scientist E.E. Schattschneider wrote over three decades ago: "Anyone who finds out how to involve the forty million [non-voters] in American politics will run the country for a generation." Decades of research suggest that media advertising campaigns, if anything, reduce voter turnout. Grassroots campaigns behind candidates that represent a genuine break from politics-as-usual provide a consistent way to remobilize the marginalized majority. Indeed, successful New party election campaigns consistently reveal significant voter turnout increases—the direct result of community-based campaigns that literally go door to door.

The New party's grassroots focus extends beyond increasing the vote, however. In theory, all political parties should organize at a grassroots level. Yet, in the United States the Republicans and Democrats abandoned serious local structures almost a century ago. The New party believes that strong parties must be built through grassroots organizing at the local level, so that party organizations are controlled by ordinary people. Most scholarship on American electoral politics assumes that this two-party evolution represents the natural modernization of party organizations in general, rather than a distinct model driven by elite interests. By contrast, the New party's strategy assumes that neighborhood-based, membership-driven political organizations still provide the foundation of an active democracy.

The Precinct Leadership Action Network (PLAN) model illustrates how New party organizers have sought to recruit leadership at a block-by-block level. The New party has used electoral bids, house parties, and targeted issue work to develop PLAN. In Milwaukee, for example, the New party started its first Living Wage campaign by targeting one city neighborhood, chosen for its racial and economic diversity. Volunteers went door-to-door systematically throughout the area. In speaking with residents, activists both built support for the local Living Wage ordinance while also identifying people willing to volunteer in the campaign. Through PLAN organizing, local New party chapters expanded their activist base beyond the "usual lefty suspects" to include many residents not normally politically active but concerned about the economic future for themselves and their community. The first Living Wage campaign during the summer of 1995 grew well beyond the initial neighborhood. By the end of the summer, Milwaukee organizers had developed a base of eighty-six precinct leaders and several hundred volunteers who signed "activist contracts." National membership figures suggest that the Milwaukee experience is not unique. Between 1992 and 1997, New party membership grew from almost zero to 10,000. In 1997 this doubled to 20,000.

A strategy that combines issue work with elections and organizes at the grassroots is hardly unique to the New party. Indeed, this twin focus has provided the foundation for every significant progressive third party since the founding of the country. In contrast to the narrow electoral focus of the major parties, progressive political action conceives of itself as a social movement along the same lines as union organizing or the civil rights movement. What makes the New party distinct is the particulars of how it pursues these two basic ingredients. These details form the fault lines of debate over third-party strategy. New party activists point to several strategic decisions as key to their success. Each flows logically from the others.

NEW PARTY ELECTORAL STRATEGY

The starting point lies with the New party's decision to grow from effective, localized organizing. All third-party groups must debate whether electoral or issue work should target concrete victories or look toward more general educational aims. This question often takes the form of whether a group should focus primarily on local elections, which are more winnable, or run candidates for state and national offices, which provide a higher profile. More than any other current progressive third-party group, the New party has decidedly favored winnable, local contests. New party organizers believe that both the disenchanted majority and local progressive groups are only going to join third-party projects that offer concrete changes in policies and which seriously contest for immediate political power. Thus, the New party only enters electoral contests in which its candidates can either win or have a strong, credible showing. This means that most New party candidates have run for local offices. Of the over 100,000 offices up for election during a typical presidential election year, 90,000 are local contests while 8,000 of the remaining are at the state level. Most local contests are nonpartisan—meaning that no party line appears on the ballot. Third-party candidates can thus run on an equal footing with those from the major parties.

Reflecting this bottom-up focus, the New party nationally did not support Ralph Nader's 1996 bid for the U.S. presidency. As New party staff person Daniel Cantor argued in a statement reflective of the party's central strategy:

> There won't be a serious third-party challenge from the left this year; nor should there be. The base can't sustain it. We have to build our base at the local level before we try a presidential run. Over time we can move up. But there's no substitute for building our power. It has taken the American left a long time to get as weak as it is. To think we can rebuild our strength by

running for president is just unpersuasive. There is just no substitute for the unglamorous work of building a base city by city, state by state.

THE PARTY'S ELECTORAL EFFORTS

The New party's track record reflects its bottom-up focus. Of the 231 New party candidates to enter elections, 152 have won office. Most of these, although not all, have been for local offices. By late 1997 in Wisconsin, for example, the New party had elected nine country commissioners around Madison and three in Milwaukee, eleven members to the Madison city council and one in Milwaukee, four local school board members, two state senators, and one state assemblyperson. In Washington, D.C., nineteen New party members had won election to the city's Advisory Neighborhood Committees. The November 1998 elections saw thirty-two out of thirty-nine New party candidates elected including state representatives in Maryland, Arkansas, Montana, and Illinois. Seven out of seven candidates won in Little Rock for city council, state legislature, and county court.

Prioritizing winnable elections has led the New party to choose tactical flexibility in its use of the ballot line when running for partisan offices. In Wisconsin, the New party has run statewide candidates to maintain a third-party ballot status inherited from the Farm-Labor party. However, when New party members have won state assembly seats, they did so on the Democratic party's ballot line. Similarly, New party member Danny Davis won his election to the U.S. Congress by challenging the Chicago machine in the Democratic primaries. While the New party ultimately aims to run candidates on its own ballot line, organizers have concluded electing someone using the Democratic line can, at times, offer more concrete opportunities for expanding grassroots organization than simply running a marginal third-party ticket. The Chicago New party, for example, saw Danny Davis's campaign for the Democratic congressional nomination as a clear opportunity to organize within black neighborhoods. By contrast, running a third-party candidate at that moment would have been viewed as a futile gesture by most activists in the African-American community. All told, roughly 15 percent of New party electoral bids have used the Democratic ballot line; 80 percent have entered nonpartisan contests; and 5 percent have used an independent or third-party ballot.

The New party's openness to tactically using the Democratic party ballot has proven quite controversial among third-party activists. Until recently, much of the argument focused on the New party's advocacy of electoral fusion. Under this tactic, two parties can endorse the same candidate. Thus, for example, the Greens and New party could run common candidates using both their ballot lines. The controversy surrounding fusion comes from its application to the Democratic party. Historically, the Populists used fusion candidacies with the Democratic party to varying degrees of success. In Kansas, for example, fusion helped elect a Populist state legislature that remained true to the movement's ideals. However, the Populists' controversial decision to endorse Democrat William Jennings Bryan for U.S. president in 1896 sparked the movement's final collapse. Today, critics fear that fusion would similarly jeopardize a third party's political independence and identity. Some even charge that the New party is not serious about third-party politics, but simply aims to become a progressive bloc within the Democratic party.

In reply, fusion advocates argue that the tactic offers a way of avoiding the "wasted vote" syndrome that plagues third-party candidates. Under fusion, voters could select a winning candidate, but do so on a third-party ballot line that reflects their true political leanings. Given the open primary system common in this country, fusion could also allow third-party candidates to capture a rival ballot line by simply entering and winning a major party's primary. Fusion proponents also point to the fact that most states outlawed the tactic long ago in direct response to third-party organizing. Recently, the U.S. Supreme Court upheld these laws, in a case brought to it by the New party, arguing explicitly that states had the right to enact laws bolstering the two-party system.

Fusion has also been attractive to the New party because it offers a tool for working with genuine progressives within the Democratic party. Since until recently the Democrats have offered the only electoral game in town for working people, many committed progressive activists have run as Democrats for local offices. Their loyalties focus on their grassroots supporters more than the Democratic leadership. Changes in the AFL-CIO's political emphasis to one of organizing—especially among women, people of color, and new immigrants—promise to generate even more such local progressive Democrats. In most other industrialized countries these people would be members of a Left party. Fusion and ballot flexibility allows the New party to reach out to such activists and their supporters.

As with its advocacy of fusion, the New party's willingness to use the Democratic party ballot line has drawn criticism that such tactics compromise its third-party aims. Critics wonder how a group can build a third party if it does not run candidates on its own ballot line. The New party defends this tactic, arguing that the ballot name used by specific candidates does not in and of itself provide the defining element in third-party building. For New party activists, establishing lasting political independence requires effective local groups that grow over time. The ballot line used by a particular candidate represents a tactical, rather than strategic question. The New party is different from, for example, the successful labor-community coalitions found in New England (called the Legislative Electoral Action Program in Connecticut, the Commonwealth Coalition in Massachusetts, and the Dirigo Alliance in Maine). These groups aim to transform their local Democratic parties into tools of progressive activism by recruiting and running progressive activists for offices on the Democratic ticket. By contrast, the New party sees its use of the Democratic ballot as a tactical tool to build its own independent political organization.

The New party views its prioritizing of winnable elections and its ballot flexibility as elements necessary for building broad coalitions. Any mass progressive political movement in this country must bring together a broad array of progressive groups and mobilize diverse communities. The New party has sought and won formal endorsements and membership from local progressive groups. However, the New party has also entered broad coalitions centered around specific projects rather than party membership. In Milwaukee, for example, the same people who were key to establishing the local New party chapter also helped to launch a bold jobs coalition called Sustainable Milwaukee. The project has pulled together community, labor, and religious groups to develop a community-driven, progressive economic plan for the city's future. Out of this planning has come several projects including ongoing Living Wage campaigns, a central-city workers training center, job access campaigns to open large construction projects to significant minority hiring and union prevailing wages, toxic site cleanup, and plans to shift significant government money from highway construction to public transportation. The local New party benefited from the coalition contacts and the opportunities for grassroots activism provided by projects such as the Living Wage campaigns. The economic coalition gained from the local chapters' people-to-people organizing.

LABOR PARTICIPATION

Wherever they have been active, New party groups have tried to open new political paths for local union activism. Some local unions have outright affiliated with New party chapters. These include the National Education Association (NEA) and United Food and Commercial Workers (UFCW) in Montgomery County, Maryland; Teamster Local 705 and Service Employees International Union (SEIU) Local 800 in Chicago; and American Federation of State, County, and Municipal Workers (AFSCME) Local 994 and SEIU Local 100 in Little

Rock, Arkansas. In Houston, Texas, leaders from the Association of Community Organizations for Reform Now (ACORN), the Houston Federation of Teachers, the National Association for Women (NOW), UFCW, AFSCME, the local plumbers unions, and the Houston Central Labor Council recently formed an organizing committee to build a local New party chapter. In Portland, Oregon, a similar group includes leaders from the Rainbow Coalitions, Jobs with Justice, the Oregon Public Employees Union, and the Sierra Club. Many other unions have joined New party–sponsored electoral and issue coalitions. Roughly two out of five New party members are either in unions or in some way connected to the labor movement.

The New party sees its commitment to winnable candidacies, issue work, and flexible ballot lines as key to gaining union support. Fledgling political projects must avoid throwing down a gauntlet that asks unions to choose between the Democratic party and an uncertain third-party alternative. No labor leader wants to be politically isolated while giving opportunities to Republicans. For the New party, its electoral flexibility has allowed it to go to local unions and ask them to support specific winnable candidacies, rather than a wholesale break with their traditional Democratic political action work. As local New party chapters gain success they hope to build stronger ties and credibility with local unions, becoming increasingly relevant vehicles for union political work.

DIVERSITY IN MEMBERSHIP

The New party would also point to its basic strategic focus as aiding its notable success in multiracial organizing. One-third of the party's membership is black, Latino, or Asian American. A significant number of black and Latino candidates have been elected through its efforts—including several notable cases in which the New party candidate proved to be the first person of color elected to that particular posi-

tion. Success in this regard has come from deliberate and ongoing attention to fostering diversity. The New party would also argue that its flexibility on ballot selection has helped by allowing it to participate in electoral insurgencies seen as serious by communities of color. The party has also benefited from its close connection to ACORN—an organization with a long history of activism within low-income, minority neighborhoods.

BUILDING COALITIONS

In building coalitions, the New party has sought unity on concrete projects rather than comprehensive ideology. Among current progressive third-party efforts, the New party is the only progressive third-party group that has not held a national convention or adopted a formal platform. Critics charge the New party with not having a clear ideology or political agenda. New party organizers argue that an effective national convention can only happen once the party has established a significant number of active local chapters. In this way, a national platform would reflect concrete, on-the-ground experience and debate. In the place of a detailed platform, the party has established a core set of principles that include: domestic investment in people and infrastructure, urban reconstruction, fundamental political reform, sustainable development, family-supporting jobs, lifelong learning, economic democracy, progressive taxes, fair trade, and genuine equal opportunity through universal access to quality health care, education, and housing.

In addition to these principles, the work done around Sustainable Milwaukee and a related study entitled Metro Futures provides the basic intellectual framework for a high-road, sustainable economic municipal platform. The New party sees the nation's cities as the foundation for a progressive future. As the repositories of over a century of investments in human and physical infrastructure, cities offer the building-blocks of an alternative and sustainable economy. The population of the nation's cities and inner-ring suburbs also includes much of the racial and ethnic diversity that is our nation's future.

Coalition-building has also provided the resource base to fund staff-supported grassroots work. The New party has been selective in establishing local chapters—looking to support local groups with paid organizers. The New party has concluded that effective, local groups need staff to establish themselves over the long term. This focus explains why many areas that have members in the national New party do not yet have organized local chapters. The New party's strategy involves a long-term focus in which patient grassroots organizing expands into greater political power over a ten- to twenty-year time horizon.

With such a horizon, only time will tell where the New party will ultimately end up. Thus far, the New party has succeeded in establishing active local groups that it can point to as model examples of how to organize among politically neglected and disenfranchised groups. The New party's goal is simple. Remobilize the locked-out majority into a mass democratic movement for fundamental change. Drawing from their experience, New party organizers argue that most Americans, and especially those living in or close to the nation's cities, already feel the need for change. Progressive organizers simply need to accumulate the human and financial resources necessary to reach out to these people with a believable alternative. Uniting the city with its inner-ring suburbs offers a majority-seeking strategy. If followed to its logical conclusion the New party's strategy seeks outright political power and the basic reconstruction of American democracy.

DAVID REYNOLDS

See also: Green Party; Labor Party, 1990s; Working Families Party.

References

The *New Party News* is published twice a year and offers detailed overviews of chapter activity and strategy. The New Party Web site has biweekly updates, documents, lists of elected officials, and so on at www.newparty.org. "Reviving American Politics: A Debate on the New Party" (*Boston Review* 18, no. 1 [January–February 1993]) provides a detailed presentation and discussion of the New Party's strategy by one of its founders and several commentators. "Saving Our Cities" (*Boston Review* [February–March 1997]) offers a debate over the urban agenda formulated by intellectuals closely associated with the New Party.

Bibliography

Cantor, Dan, and Wade Rathke. "A Non-partisan Party: The New Party Model." *New Labor Forum* 1 (Fall 1997): 37–42.

Reynolds, David. *Democracy Unbound: Progressive Challenges to the Two-party System.* Boston: South End Press, 1997.

★★★★★★★★★★★★★★★★★★★★★★★★★★★★★★★★★★

NEW ALLIANCE PARTY

1979–1994

The New Alliance party (NAP), founded in 1979 and disbanded in 1994, was at once the most eccentric yet visible electoral campaign to emerge from the factional stew of Vietnam-era New York City radicalism. Occupying an idiosyncratic meeting ground between psychotherapy and politics, the NAP fielded candidates for offices ranging from city council to president (most often party chair Lenora Fulani) and gained significant media attention.

The NAP's history began in 1970, when a tiny radical collective on Manhattan's Upper West Side began organizing political activity around a profit-making experimental encounter therapy practice. Eventually dubbed "Social Therapy," the scheme proved both an effective recruiting tactic and lucrative business, generating steady streams of adherents and revenue.

The intellectual and emotional leader was Fred Newman, who held a Ph.D. in the philosophy of science from Stanford University and abruptly turned to Marxism in the mid-1960s. Newman and his small band of followers—physically occupying a communal apartment, intellectually occupying the tumultuous intersection of confrontational sectarian politics and radical psychology—became convinced they could concoct a psychotherapy that would challenge not just individual neurosis but structural injustice in society. Newman and his original associates argued that only a revolution of the working class could resolve the individual psychic crisis; at the same time, like practitioners of *est* and other distinctly un-Marxist products of the nascent human potential movement, they believed that the road to their revolutionary

new age lay in an extreme version of confronting the oppressor within, stripping the ego of its bourgeois, individualistic core. Virtually every aspect of existing life—sexual orientation and partners, domestic arrangements, employment—could be challenged at the whim of the therapist, with accommodation a condition of remaining in therapy. Much of the "revolution" urged upon clients involved recruiting adherents among friends, lovers, and neighbors, and making large financial donations to the movement's work.

By the mid-1970s, Newman and his associates formed the International Workers' party, its leadership indistinguishable from the Social Therapy collective. The Newmanites (then numbering perhaps thirty committed members) moved in and out of coalitions and vicious factional struggles with other marginal groups. The most notable coalition was with Lyndon LaRouche, already well on his journey to fascism and feared on the left for his followers' history of violent thuggery. Newman embraced LaRouche in 1974 as an ally and mentor, and then broke with him several months later.

The Newmanites began running for local political office on an independent slate. In 1977 one Social Therapy client-turned-practitioner, Nancy Ross, won an Upper West Side school board seat. That success led the Newmanites further into electoral politics, where they emerged in 1979 as the neutral-sounding New Alliance party, articulating a "more democracy" political agenda far more likely to win allies—and donations—than their neo-Trotskyist rantings of the preceding decade. Particularly high on the NAP's agenda was ballot access, challenging New York's notoriously restrictive election laws. At the same time, the NAP adopted an electoral strategy that Newman and party chair Lenora Fulani (another Social Therapy client-turned-practitioner) eventually called "Two Roads Are Better Than One"—supporting not only the party's own electoral line but also the campaign of any Democrat who would accept their endorsement. Although some New York Democrats who were awarded the NAP's support eyed the party uneasily, the dedication of its volunteers often proved irresistible.

Starting in the early 1970s, Newman and his then all-white collective embraced the notion that while they would form an intellectual vanguard, the black community would produce "organic" leaders of its own for whom they would be allies and strategists. In practice, that theory justified the NAP'S penchant for alliance with some of the most controversial and polarizing African-American leaders, ranging from Brooklyn Democratic machine boss Vander Beatty, eventually jailed for election fraud, to Louis Farrakhan of the Nation of Islam. The Reverend Al Sharpton worked closely with the NAP early in his career but eventually distanced himself from the Newmanites.

In 1984, when Jesse Jackson first ran for president as a Democrat, the party supported Jackson (whom Newman had ridiculed just a few months earlier in explicitly sexual terms) but also ran a presidential candidate in the general election—a black socialist-turned-NAP member named Dennis Serrette. Serrette was on the ballot in thirty-three states and received 35,000 votes. A year later Serrette broke with the NAP, giving an embittered account of his years in the party to a black-owned newspaper in Mississippi. He described his frustration with what he termed the party's all-white leadership and the control he said Newman imposed on him through Social Therapy. The NAP's response was a $2 million defamation lawsuit against the newspaper, which was ultimately thrown out of court.

In the early and mid-1980s the NAP began seeking ballot status around the country, sometimes (as in North Carolina and Mississippi) moving its existing members into a community

One of the more successful third-party candidates for president in recent years, Lenora Fulani was on the ballot in all fifty states in 1988, garnering nearly a quarter-million votes nationwide. (*Courtesy of the Patriot party*)

just long enough to qualify to run for some local office and conduct a fundraising canvass. Social Therapy offices and party organizing drives were established in Washington, Boston, Chicago, Atlanta, and other cities. Encountering the often daunting ballot access requirements imposed on alternative parties by two-party state legislatures, the NAP sued, time and again, occasionally convincing courts to cast aside restrictions. In 1985, shortly after Jesse Jackson founded his Rainbow Coalition, the NAP started its own lobbying arm called the Rainbow Alliance, later the Rainbow Lobby. In 1988, thanks to an ever-larger pool of therapy clients-turned-volunteers and an ever-larger pool of contributions, the NAP managed to qualify for matching funds and place Fulani, its new presidential candidate, on the ballot in all fifty states. Fulani—an accomplished public speaker with a sure instinct for the soundbite—won 225,934 votes. In 1992, the party backed marginal Democratic candidate Larry Agran, a former mayor of Irvine, California.

In its fifteen years on the electoral map, the NAP was controversial on several fronts. Fulani and Newman were both criticized as anti-Semitic, particularly in their defense of Farrakhan and their own provocative statements about Jews (whom Newman, himself Jewish, once called "the stormtroopers of capitalism"). Within the American Left, the NAP gained a reputation for disrupting the activities of other organizations, either by flooding them with NAP adherents or setting up competing, similarly named groups. Financially, the NAP and Fred Newman's numerous affiliated enterprises were criticized as a complex, profit-making shell game. But the most enduring criticism was of the NAP's cult-like character, a charge leveled by the Anti-Defamation League among others. Though less insular than many totalistic organizations, numerous accounts by former adherents depicted the NAP and the Social Therapy organization exerting close, manipulative control over the private, political, and financial lives of its members. As with many cults, real political attainments were less important than the constant appearance of activity, with founder Newman's pronouncements, writings, plays, and sexual choices at the center.

Although the NAP at its peak claimed to have 10,000 members, its core activists never numbered more than a few hundred. In 1994, Newman, Fulani, and other New Alliance leaders formed a coalition with Ross Perot loyalists to form the Patriot party. They ultimately disbanded the NAP, continuing political activity through the Patriot party, Perot's Reform party, and other independent formations.

BRUCE SHAPIRO

See also: Lenora Fulani; Lyndon Hermyle LaRouche, Jr.; Fred Newman; Reform Party.

Bibliography

Berlet, Chip. *Clouds Blur the Rainbow: The Other Side of the New Alliance Party.* Somerville, MA: Political Research Associates, January 1987.

Shapiro, Bruce. "Dr. Fulani's Snake-oil Show." *The Nation,* May 4, 1992.

"A Cult by Any Other Name: The New Alliance Party Dismantled and Reincarnated." Anti-Defamation League, 1995.

NONPARTISAN LEAGUE

1915–1956

*I*n the spring of 1915 a small band of political organizers driving Model A Fords bounced across the prairie grasslands of North Dakota. In a matter of months they created perhaps the most successful third party in American history. Led by a charismatic former Socialist party organizer named Arthur C. Townley, the Nonpartisan League (NPL) put into practice a simple idea: that government should be a positive force in the service of working Americans. Making innovative use of the direct primary to take control of the dominant Republican party, the NPL gained control of all three branches of the North Dakota State government between 1917 and 1921. Once in office, as political scientist Richard Valelly noted, the NPL turned the North Dakota statehouse into "a virtual lab for policy experimentation."

NPL policy-making foreshadowed much of the later New Deal. Taking cues from their constituency of aggrieved wheat farmers, the NPL administration passed far-reaching legislation in 1916 and 1918. This legislation established a system of government-owned banks, mills, and grain elevators, and inaugurated government-sponsored crop insurance and support for farm cooperatives. The NPL also established a state industrial commission with jurisdiction over state-owned business, and a state Home Building Association that was a pioneer in the area of public housing. Although the NPL's domination of North Dakota State government lasted only four years, it had a powerful and lasting effect on regional politics. One of the most important legacies of the NPL's expansion into neighboring states was the Minnesota Farmer-Labor party (also known as the Farmer-Labor Democratic party).

The NPL was a direct byproduct of early twentieth-century wheat-belt politics. When it came time to sell their wheat, North Dakota farmers had few alternatives. There were no terminal markets in North Dakota, so farmers were forced to sell wheat locally or ship it to Minnesota. Either way, their wheat ended up at the Minneapolis exchange, which was dominated by the Minneapolis Chamber of Commerce, an interlocking association of grain shippers, terminal elevators, and commission houses.

Farmers claimed these powerful corporate "middlemen" controlled the wheat market by imposing a number of discriminatory policies. According to John H. Worst, president of North Dakota's agricultural college in 1916, "Fifty-five million dollars a year [was] lost to the farmers of North Dakota through unfair practices in the grain trade." Most important was the practice of grading and inspecting wheat. Farmers and other observers claimed they were often cheated by inaccurate weights or swindled by dishonest agents and inspectors who rated much of the wheat produced in North Dakota below its actual grade. In what historian Robert L. Morlan called a "mystical transformation," many tons of lower grade (and thus less expensive) wheat was somehow transformed into top-grade wheat somewhere between the elevator and the terminal in Minneapolis—in other words, after it was purchased from North Dakota farmers. An estimate of the cost to farmers of unfair grading was provided by Dr. Edwin F. Ladd, a professor at the state agricultural college and state food commissioner, who showed that, for a 100-million-bushel crop, farmers were underpaid by $5,271,398.23. In addition to unfair grading, banks charged interest rates that often exceeded 20 percent and railroad lines charged exorbitant shipping rates.

The effect of this system on North Dakota farmers was calamitous. Between 1900 and 1910, tenancy rates in North Dakota increased from 8.5 percent to 14.3 percent, while the percentage of farms that were mortgaged increased from 31.4 percent to 50.9 percent. In response, farmers turned to their political representatives for relief. In 1914, North Dakota voters endorsed a referendum for a state-owned terminal elevator, but it was never built. Instead, the executive committee commissioned a study, which concluded that such an elevator was unnecessary, while the state legislature voted against construction of the elevator the following year.

By 1915, farmers' grievances over the prevailing system of wheat production and marketing—as well as the refusal of the major parties to reform this system—were sufficient to overwhelm the existing regional party system. In addition, there existed a strong tradition of agricultural protest in the region, which provided the foundations for the NPL's rapid rise to power. In the late nineteenth century, for example, the Grangers and the Farmers' Alliance had been active in the Dakotas. After their demise, many Dakota farmers joined the American Society of Equity, a regional marketing cooperative that was the driving force behind the unsuccessful effort to build a state-owned terminal elevator. Competing with the Society of Equity was the Socialist party, which was popular with many farmers because of its agrarian platform. Upholding the legacy of the Farmers' Alliance, individual planks in the Socialist platform endorsed a system of government-sponsored mills, elevators, and crop insurance.

Arthur C. Townley was a large farmer who joined the Socialist party after being forced into bankruptcy following a bad harvest. Based upon his own experience, Townley had a keen sense of the injustices inherent in the current system of grain production. In 1914 the Socialist party hired Townley, who possessed the zeal of a door-to-door salesman, to organize farmers who were sympathetic to the Socialists' agrarian platform but were reluctant to join the party. Socialist leaders, however, discontinued the program when he and other organizers signed up more sympathetic farmers than the entire party membership. Party leaders feared the new recruits would take over. Released from his duties, Townley's next act was to establish a separate organization dedicated to the principle of non-partisan political action on behalf of farmers. In 1915 he founded the farmers' Nonpartisan Political League (NPL) of North Dakota and set out in a Ford Model A to spread the NPL gospel. Townley later claimed that the NPL "was built on 'an idea, a Ford, and sixteen dollars.'"

The early growth of the NPL was nothing short of phenomenal. On Townley's first day in the field, he signed up all nine farmers he visited; in subsequent months, NPL organizers, many recruited from the Socialist party, had similar success. The NPL sales pitch was simple. Farmers paid their dues of $2.50 a year (eventually raised to $16 biannually) and signed a pledge and platform card. The pledge proposed that the NPL gain control of the state government by endorsing farmer-friendly candidates in the state's direct primary, regardless of party affiliation. The NPL platform was drawn from Populist and Socialist notions of activist government mobilized in the service of working people. Individual planks called for the creation of state-owned terminal elevators, flour mills, packing houses, and cold storage plants; state inspection of grain and grain dockage; exemption of farm improvements from taxation; and state-sponsored crop (hail) insurance and rural credit banks. In the early years, farmers' checks (often post-dated until harvest) came in fast enough to support a legion of stump speakers, and in September 1915, the NPL began publishing its own newspaper, the *Nonpartisan Leader*.

NPL organizers next trained their sights on the state legislature. The big question was whether the party's thousands of new farmer-

The Nonpartisan League won control of the North Dakota state government in the late 1910s and early 1920s through its appeals to the needs and concerns of farmers. The rural nature of the state is captured in this picture of the capital, Bismarck, during this period. *(Capitol Bookstore, 1910s, courtesy of the Library of Congress)*

members, with little experience in party-building, would "stick." In other words, would NPL members stand together in the face of increasingly vehement opposition from bankers, agents, and other prominent citizens? In December 1915, the NPL sponsored meetings across the state to plan for the upcoming campaign. Precinct meetings were held in February 1916, which provided the answer to the allegiance question. In enthusiastic meetings around the state, more than 90 percent of NPL members turned out in each precinct. In all, 26,000 farmers attended this extraordinary event in American third-party politics, including hundreds who participated personally in the democratic process for the first time.

On March 29, 1916, forty-five NPL delegates met in the Fargo municipal auditorium to continue their unique experiment in grassroots third-party politics. Delegates wrote the names of prospective candidates on a blackboard and then discussed the merits of each. Nominated for governor was a relatively unknown, college-educated wheat farmer and county commissioner named Lynn Frazier, from the Pembina County town of Hoople. The remaining candidates endorsed by the NPL had more political experience and name recognition and included the current secretary of state, a state's attorney, and various county-level officials.

On primary day in 1916 the NPL shocked the political establishment by electing enough committeemen to control the Republican State Central Committee. In fact, every NPL candidate was elected by NPL voters, some of whom supposedly crossed flooded rivers in order to reach the polls. On election day, the NPL continued its stunning rise to power, gaining control of all three branches of North Dakota State government. Only one NPL-endorsed candidate lost in a statewide race: the candidate for state treasurer, a Democrat. In the state legislature, the NPL held 81 of the 113 seats in the house and 18 of the 49 seats in the senate.

NPL legislators immediately began to enact their program, although Republican holdovers in the senate blocked some of their ambitious agenda. NPL-sponsored legislation passed in 1917 included a state grain-grading system, state deposit insurance, reduced assessments on farm machinery and farm improvements, railroad rate reform, and increased funding for education.

With electoral and policy success, however, came the mobilization of a much stronger counterattack by the NPL's opponents. The basic strategy employed against the NPL had two components: cooptation and confrontation. With the goal of cooptation, NPL opponents organized competing "reform" organizations, such as the well-funded North Dakota Good Government League and the Independent Voters' Association, which offered watered-down versions of NPL proposals to lure away voters. In addition, in 1916 the North Dakota Democratic party changed its platform to mirror that of the NPL, much as the national Democrats did in 1896 in response to the People's party. Confrontation was also effective. In 1917, NPL opponents maligned unelected NPL leaders such as Townley, who met with the new legislators in a tightly controlled daily caucus in a Fargo hotel just down the street from the Capitol. NPL opponents also questioned the motives—particularly the left-leaning political affiliations—of Townley and other NPL organizers. Later, during a climate of war hysteria after the United States entered World War I, NPL opponents employed organized violence by law enforcement or mobs against NPL stump speakers and mass rallies.

As their organization expanded its scope and power, NPL organizers sought to extend the nonpartisan movement into neighboring states. On November 26, 1917, Townley traveled to New York City where he received an enthusiastic reception from farmer and labor representatives in the Great Hall of Cooper Union. Two weeks later, 1,000 members of the Dairymen's League, who had recently staged a successful statewide milk strike, endorsed a resolution calling for the creation of a non-partisan party organization in the Empire State. Eventually, NPL organizations existed in thirteen states across the Midwest and Northwest, and as far south as Texas. The most successful of these organizations—and the one that provoked the most virulent counterattack— was the NPL of Minnesota, which forged alliances with organized labor, laying the groundwork for the more familiar Minnesota Farmer-Labor Democratic party.

In Minnesota, however, severe restrictions upon civil liberties and outright repression were used to curtail NPL activity. NPL opponents disputed the patriotism of the NPL's predominantly foreign-born members and accused NPL leaders such as Townley of traitorous acts. Although the NPL's official position was in support of the war effort, the party's stump speakers were often critical of war profiteering and military conscription. The Minnesota Public Safety Commission, a wartime agency with expansive police powers, created a Bureau of Intelligence charged with enforcing a directive designed to suppress "agitators of disloyalty" and "sentiments bordering on treason." When the NPL began an organizing campaign in Minnesota in 1918, the Commission took part in what Morlan called "a reign of terror" against the party. Law enforcement officials or local mobs, all in the name of enforcing loyalty, disrupted NPL meetings. NPL speakers were tarred and feathered, and many were beaten as nineteen Minnesota counties banned NPL meetings. On February 28, 1918, Townley and NPL organizer Joseph Gilbert were arrested and jailed for sedition in Martin County. Although neither was convicted, such charges undoubtedly cost the NPL votes in the next election.

Despite the increasingly hostile attacks, NPL leaders in North Dakota looked to the 1918 elections as a way to consolidate their hold over the state government. On election day, Governor Frazier was re-elected, and the NPL gained greater majorities in each legislative chamber. In other states, the NPL was less successful. In Minnesota, the NPL candidate for Governor, Charles A. Lindbergh, Sr., lost in the primary when both Democrats and Republicans joined ranks in defense of the political establishment.

The NPL's large majorities in the North Dakota State Legislature allowed its leaders to push through the remaining parts of their legislative program. In 1919, the NPL passed ten constitutional amendments and a number of bills that established an industrial commission to oversee state-owned businesses, a state bank, a state-owned grain elevator, a home building association, workman's compensation, and subsidies to farm cooperatives.

The NPL's string of electoral and policy successes, however, was endangered by internal division and stepped-up opposition by the party's enemies. Within the NPL, two factions emerged: One supported the continued building of state-owned and-operated businesses; the other endorsed independent farmer cooperatives as the preferred road to socialism. Further, three important NPL leaders defected to the opposition in 1919, which, as Morlan explained, "precipitated a series of violent political struggles which were to leave the state in turmoil for years to come." Townley was again indicted for anti-war conspiracy. NPL meetings were continually broken up throughout the region. The most damaging action by NPL opponents was undoubtedly an Eastern bank boycott of North Dakota bonds, which were to be used to finance construction of state-owned enterprises.

In the 1920 statewide elections in North Dakota, Republicans and Democrats cut into the NPL's majorities in the state legislature even as Governor Frazier was elected for a third term. Then, during an extraordinary recall election in 1921, NPL opponents in the Independent Voters' Association were successful in removing from office Governor Frazier and two NPL members of the Industrial Commission. This election marked the first time in American history that a sitting governor had been recalled. In a larger sense, the recall demonstrated that the attacks of NPL opponents, the controversy over the war, and the worsening farm recession had taken its toll on the NPL.

The NPL remained a potent force in North Dakota politics for many years, although the party would never again rival its early successes at the ballot box or in passing legislation. NPL candidates were elected governor in 1924 and 1926, and Lynn Frazier and William Lemke, who were elected to Congress during the Depression, sponsored landmark legislation on farm foreclosure protection. After the decisive recall election, however, the NPL lost its hold on state government, and with it much of its voting base. Scholars argue that the NPL evolved into a progressive faction within the North Dakota Republican party until its final demise in 1956. As a historical phenomenon, the NPL has attracted insufficient attention from historians in proportion to the organization's significance in the annals of American third-party politics.

THOMAS J. KRIGER

See also: Minnesota Farmer-Labor Party; Populist Movement/People's Party; Socialist Party.

Bibliography

Mooney, Patrick H., and Theo J. Majka. *Farmers' and Farm Workers' Movements.* New York: Twayne, 1995.

Morlan, Robert L. *Political Prairie Fire: The Nonpartisan League, 1915–1922.* Minneapolis: University of Minnesota Press, 1955.

Saloutos, Theodore, and John D. Hicks. *Agricultural Discontent in the Middle West, 1900–1939.* Madison: University of Wisconsin Press, 1951.

Valelly, Richard M. *Radicalism in the States: The Minnesota Farmer-Labor Party and the American Political Economy.* Chicago: University of Chicago Press, 1989.

PEACE AND FREEDOM PARTY

1967–

ANTI-WAR ROOTS

The Peace and Freedom Party (PFP) arose in the fractious New Left political environment of the late 1960s as a self-proclaimed "permanent radical political party." Some scholars trace the party's official origin from meetings held in Ann Arbor, Michigan, in 1967, but the party began as and remained (in 1998) a California phenomenon. As early as 1966, a number of dissident, anti-war "peace candidates" waged insurgency campaigns in Democratic party congressional primaries, targeting districts represented by liberal Democrats who had not distanced themselves from the Johnson administration's Vietnam War effort. These candidates, including three editors of *Ramparts* magazine, failed to win a nomination, but they captured between 41 and 47 percent in Alameda, Marin, San Mateo, and Santa Barbara area primaries by attacking the alleged complacency of Democratic candidates.

The 1966 peace candidates' campaigns registered tens of thousands of new voters and packed local California Democratic Councils (CDCs) with anti-war activists. Prior to 1966 the CDC had been home to middle-class reformists, Stevenson liberals (named after the intellectual Democratic presidential nominee of 1952 and 1956, Adlai Stevenson), who had previously captured many county organizations from traditional party workers. Some peace candidates, including at least one using a Peace and Freedom name in his campaign literature, secured local CDC endorsements in 1966. This occurred despite the fact that CDC had a history of supporting the incumbent. Robert Scheer's peace candidacy in Berkeley's seventh congressional district mobilized activists from the University of California at Berkeley's Free Speech Movement and Vietnam Day Committee, as well as prominent African-American community leaders. Scheer and others later stood against their Democratic opponents as independent write-in candidates in the general election.

The effort to establish a party came out of the 1968 presidential election. Activists from the 1966 peace campaigns decided that a serious third-party alternative could be built from the radical anti-war movement in coalition with black nationalist organizations, particularly the Black Panther Party for Self-Defense in California. Since the ideology of black nationalist groups prevented them from joining with white organizations, the PFP and Black Panthers formed only indirect coalitions. The Black Panthers, furthermore, were a relatively small group whose active members may have numbered in the hundreds. A survey of PFP activists taken in early 1968 found they were overwhelmingly white, highly educated, and far younger than activists attending similar meetings of California's major parties. Seventy-two percent identified themselves as radical when asked to place themselves on an ideological scale, and large majorities agreed with planks from the Black Panther party's platform.

The party attained ballot status in California prior to the 1968 election after party workers filed 101,500 registrations in January. The secretary of state documented 64,248 as valid by September. The valid forms constituted only 0.7 percent of all registered voters, but were over 1 percent of those participating in the previous gubernatorial election. This satisfied California's requirements for granting ballot access to new parties. Although PFP strategist Farrel Broslawski joked of those registering that "a lot of them figured it was a new folk-rock group," the PFP maintained a base of registered voters in the state from 1968 through 1998. The number of voters registered with the party declined to just under 27,000 in 1976, but rebounded to over 70,000 by September 1997 (0.48 percent of registrations).

California law stipulates that once granted ballot access, any party can retain its status if one candidate for statewide office polls at least 2 percent. Since 1968, at least one PFP candidate has met this criterion in successive elections. This provides leftist presidential candidates from inside or outside the party with a vehicle for ballot access in the nation's largest state. The PFP has consistently listed a slate of candidates for California's eight statewide offices to ensure a candidate meets the 2 percent requirement. In the mid-1990s, it was also contesting about one-fifth of state and federal legislative districts.

PFP candidates for state office invariably receive more support in California than PFP candidates for president. The 1994 PFP candidate for attorney general, for example, received ten times more votes (259,000, or 3.2 percent) in California than the party's 1996 presidential nominee. Every PFP candidate for state office from 1990 through 1998 out-polled the party's presidential nominees for 1988 through 1996. Candidates for less important state offices and candidates running against relatively safe incumbents tend to gain the most votes. In the 1990s, PFP candidates for lower-level statewide office (e.g., attorney general, secretary of state, controller) occasionally received around 3 percent of the vote, and some legislative candidates received one-fifth of votes in their districts.

These levels of support do not necessarily reflect the party's base of loyalists. Survey data from the 1994 California elections demonstrate that minor parties draw about one-third of their support from their registered voters. But these minor parties regularly draw more votes than they have registered voters. The balance appears to come from others who are dissatisfied with major-party candidates and from those seeing no difference between Democrats and Republicans. The 1994 survey illustrated that most California minor-party voters are not closely aligned with the party they vote for, suggesting that parties such as the PFP have come to serve some voters as an instrument for protest against major parties.

District-level results demonstrate that PFP candidates do better when contesting safe legislative districts, suggesting that some support is due to a form of risk-free protest voting. In safe Democratic districts, voters who might otherwise support a Democrat have little fear of "wasting" their votes by supporting a PFP candidate since a Democrat will inevitably win the seat. Other things being equal, PFP candidates poll best in safe districts and even better in districts without Republican candidates. Three districts where the PFP scored over 17 percent between 1994 and 1996 were safe Democratic districts with no Republican candidates.

The PFP have never won any statewide or national offices, but when combined with other minor parties their votes frequently prevent candidates from winning with majorities. PFP votes might also spoil potential Democratic victories on occasion. For example, support received by PFP candidates would have been enough to swing elections to a Democrat in the first congressional district in 1990 and in the 1994 California secretary of state contest. The party can also claim a handful of victories in local non-partisan races in northern California (e.g., State Party Chair Marsha Feinland was elected to the Berkeley Rent Control Board in 1994 as part of a "pro-tenant" slate).

While having a relatively long but ineffective history in California, the party's influence in national elections has been even more muted. The California PFP nominated candidates for president and vice president from 1968 through 1996 (excluding 1988 when a candidate ran under the PFP label in a few states but not California). The only attempt at a national campaign under the PFP banner, however, was in 1968, when it nominated Eldridge Cleaver, then a 33-year-old convict-turned-writer serving as an official in the Black Panther party. Douglas Dowd, a Cornell academic, was the party's vice-presidential candidate. Cleaver is credited with working to build a party that appealed to elites from the middle-class New-Left movement of the period, as well as black nationalists, and is credited with getting the Black Panthers to assist in registering voters needed to qualify the PFP for ballot status in California. He advocated an unconditional withdrawal from Vietnam, social revolution, and black separatism. The attraction that radical elites felt for Cleaver did not translate into support at the mass level. Although the party was on the ballot in nineteen states, it received only 36,613 votes (about 0.02 percent). Seventy-five percent came from California, where Cleaver was a "write-in" candidate. No PFP presidential candidate has since improved on Cleaver's meager showing.

After 1968, there were some attempts at using the Peace and Freedom banner outside the state, and the California party has also entered into alliances with other small national efforts during presidential election years. This means that California PFP ballot positions have been used by leftist candidates from outside the state. Support for PFP candidates for statewide office in California, by preserving ballot access, provides if not subsidizes a valuable resource for these candidates. Variations in state ballot laws cause small-party candidates to seek the presidency under different party banners in different states and prevent them from qualifying in many states. A California PFP nomination can save them from the arduous task of qualifying in the nation's largest state.

In 1972, for example, People's party candidate Benjamin Spock received the California PFP ballot position, and he received 70 percent of his 78,751 national votes from the state. Spock received just 0.10 percent of the national total. In 1976, People's party presidential candidate Margaret Wright used the PFP's California ballot spot and gained 85 percent of the People's party's votes there. With Spock as her running mate, Wright received less than 0.06 percent of the national vote. The California PFP nominated Sonia Johnson for the 1984 presidential election. Johnson ran in other states as a Citizens party candidate but collected 36 percent

of her 72,200 votes under the PFP label in California. She received less than 0.001 percent of the national vote.

Herbert Lewin of Philadelphia sought the 1988 California PFP nomination for president, after securing the nomination of the micro-sized internationalist workers party. Lewin was listed under the PFP label in Vermont (after seeking the Liberty Union nomination there) and a few other states, but appeared in California as an independent who received only fifty-eight votes. Most of California's 1988 PFP votes went to Lenora Fulani, the New Alliance party candidate who was listed as an independent. Fulani was unable to secure California's PFP's ballot spot in 1992, and was left off California's ballot despite qualifying in forty other states. In 1992, the California PFP's presidential candidate was Ron Daniels, director of Jesse Jackson's 1988 campaign. Daniels was also on the ballot in nine other states, collecting only 27,396 votes (66 percent of which came from California). PFP presidential candidates have twice appeared only in California, in 1980 and 1996, when Marsha Feinland collected all of the PFP's 25,332 votes in California.

After Cleaver's 1968 contest, national elements of the party's organization quickly collapsed. Cleaver left the United States after being injured in a shoot-out with Oakland police in 1969, and the tenuous links between the PFP and the Black Panther party evaporated. Although charges of attempted murder were latter reduced, Cleaver remained in exile from 1969 to 1975. When he returned, he was no longer involved with the Black Panthers or the PFP. The PFP did run several candidates for legislative and statewide offices in California in 1970, but it received only minimal support and won no offices. After these defeats, a number of anti-war activists from the PFP attempted to build another national peace party by joining with the short-lived People's party in 1971. Despite the exodus of many founding members in the early 1970s, the PFP continued as a legal entity in California, contesting state elections while providing People's party presidential candidates with ballot access in 1972 and 1976.

Following the U.S. exit from Vietnam and estrangement between the party and black nationalists, the PFP platform evolved into a more generalized statement of social democratic principles (e.g., free health care, "useful jobs at union pay levels," affordable housing for everyone) and multicultural tolerance. After 1974, party platforms increasingly stressed feminist issues, and through the 1980s and 1990s, platforms also gave attention to environmental concerns. Since its founding, platforms continued to stress the peace issues that originally mobilized the party in the 1960s, including abolition of the CIA and withdrawal of U.S. troops from other countries.

It is difficult to forecast the future of the PFP. One area of uncertainty involves changes in California's election law. A party's ability to control which candidates run under its label changed in 1998. Prior to 1998, California law called for closed primaries that restricted decisions about the nominees to registered members of a respective party. Candidates from the PFP or other leftist groups who sought to run under the PFP name thus had to win support from a majority of registered PFP voters. After the state changed to an open (blanket) primary in 1998, party members have less control over nominations. The open primary allows unaffiliated voters and voters from other parties (major and minor) to participate in one large primary where any candidate can receive votes from any voter. The candidate from each party who receives the most votes goes on to the general election. State law, moreover, prevents parties from controlling who seeks the party's nomination. This means that centrist candidates of either major party can appeal for "cross-over votes" from Democrat, Republican, and independent voters. The effects of open primaries on California's minor parties are less clear. Given the crowd of leftist candidates and small Left parties that campaign in presidential elections, and given the value of ballot access in California, an open primary could be an end to invitations for candidates from outside the PFP fold to compete for the PFP nomination.

Thus far, only one off-year California election has been contested under the open primary. Feinland, the PFP's 1996 presidential

nominee and state party chair, sought the PFP nomination for governor in 1998. She was defeated by Gloria La Riva, who had previously been listed on the Workers World presidential and vice-presidential ticket from 1984 through 1996. It is difficult to determine if La Riva would have been selected as a PFP nominee under a system where decisions were made only by registered party members, as they were prior to 1998.

The Peace and Freedom party was born to contest the 1968 election, a year that produced a fivefold increase in the proportion of California voters registered with minor parties (up from 0.5 percent to 2.5 percent—comprised of 1.7 percent American Independent party and the balance PFP). But by 1976, barely 1 percent of state voters were registered with a minor party and only 0.2 percent with the PFP. In the 1990s, however, support for California's minor parties again began to climb, and combined registration increased to 5.1 percent by 1996. The PFP more than doubled its base of registered voters during this period. Unless these newly registered voters are aging 1960s loyalists returning to their roots, it appears that the party has rebuilt a following among a small group of new voters. Nineteen ninety-four survey data confirm that voters registered with California's minor parties are significantly younger than major-party voters. Combined with the fact that many other voters will occasionally cast a ballot for a minor party out of protest or frustration with the major parties, this should ensure that the PFP continues to reap a small share of votes in California elections. This would guarantee that its candidate (or some minor-party candidate) can appear on presidential ballots in the nation's largest state.

TODD DONOVAN

See also: Black Panther Party; Eldridge Cleaver; Ron Daniels; Lenora Fulani; Benjamin Spock.

Bibliography

Chester, Lewis; Godfrey Hodson; and Bruce Page. *An American Melodrama: The Presidential Campaign of 1968.* London: Deutsch, 1969.

Day, Glenn. *Minor Party Candidates and Parties of 1988.* Jefferson, NC: McFarland, 1988.

———. *Minor Party Candidates and Parties of 1992.* Jefferson, NC: McFarland, 1992.

Donovan, Todd; Tammy Terrio; and Shaun Bowler. "Loyal Attachments and Protest Voting for Third Parties in State Elections." Paper presented at the Western Political Science Association meeting, Tucson, Arizona, 1997.

Elden, James, and David R. Schweitzer. "New Third Party Radicalism: The Case of The California Peace and Freedom Party." *Western Political Quarterly* (1971): 761–774.

English, David. *Divided They Stand.* New York: Prentice Hall, 1969.

Inter-University Consortium for Social and Political Research. *ICPSR Study 7757.* Ann Arbor, MI: Inter-University Consortium for Social and Political Research, 1997.

Jones, Bill. *Report of Registration.* Sacramento: California Secretary of State's Office, 1997.

Lang, Serge. *The Scheer Campaign.* New York: W.A. Benjamin, 1967.

Lee, Eugene, and Bruce Keith. *California Votes: 1960–1972.* Berkeley: Institute for Governmental Studies, 1974.

Maisel, Louis; Sandy Basset; and Charles Basset. *Political Parties and Elections in the United States.* New York: Garland, 1991.

Scammon, Richard; Allice V. McGilluray; and Rhodes Cook. *American Votes,* Vol. 22. Washington, DC: CQ Press, 1996.

PEOPLE'S PARTY

1971–1978

*I*n the late 1960s and early 1970s a myriad of local radical third parties sprang up all across the nation in opposition to the Vietnam War and the domestic policies of the two major parties. These local third parties—all of which viewed the Democratic party as unsalvageable—moved beyond protest to organize for the political defeat of the government. In this sense, they were marginal to the main thrust of the social movement of the 1960s. For whatever reason, the politics of the 1960s was primarily that of anti-institutional protest. As such, it emphasized demonstrations, rallies, marches, and other forms of non-party politics based on short-term mass mobilizations to present lists of "demands" to government. Because it was based on such ad hoc mass mobilizations, no institutions of oppositional power that were created in the 1960s continued into future decades, unlike other decades such as the 1930s from which trade unions emerged. The exceptions to this tendency were the many local radical parties around the country, which wanted permanent political power. For the most part, however, the "movement" of the 1960s ignored them.

Most of these local radical parties were loosely allied under the national umbrella of the People's party, which ran Dr. Benjamin Spock for president in 1972 and for vice president in 1976. The call for the establishment of a national third party—the People's party—was issued by the California Peace and Freedom party in 1971. Itself organized in 1967 by civil rights and anti-war activists, the Peace and Freedom party chose Black Panther leader Eldridge Cleaver as their presidential candidate in 1968. Not only

did Cleaver appear on the ballot in California, but efforts by itinerant California organizers also managed to get him on the ballot in twenty other states. As the 1972 presidential election drew near, however, such "colonizing" was not needed, as a large number of similar third parties had appeared in other states. As it had four years earlier, the Peace and Freedom party sought a national non-sectarian left presence in the upcoming election and invited other state and local parties to join it in a nationwide coalition of like-minded parties.

Thirty-five parties from twenty-five states and the District of Columbia answered the call. The most prominent, besides the Peace and Freedom party, were the Michigan Human Rights party, the (Washington) D.C. Statehood party, the Arizona New party, the Indiana Peace and Freedom party, the Texas New party, and the Wisconsin Alliance party. Over the Fourth of July holidays in 1971, they met in Albuquerque under the auspices of the Independent New Mexican party and voted to maintain their separate identities but to operate at a national level as the Coalition. At a founding convention in Dallas that November, hosted by the Texas New party, the Coalition became the People's party. The platform that emerged described the party simply as "a mass party of the left" seeking to unite all oppressed peoples.

That 1971 founding convention also nominated anti-war activist Dr. Benjamin Spock for president and Julius Hobson, a black educator active in the D.C. Statehood party, for vice president. The rationale for nominating Spock was that, being so few in numbers, limited in funds, and unknown in most parts of the country, the

Presidential candidate of the People's party ticket in 1972, Dr. Benjamin Spock (dark suit and glasses, front row, center) is shown here marching in a 1965 anti–Vietnam War march in New York City. (*Associated Press, 1965, Courtesy of the Library of Congress*)

People's party could not hope to gain any recognition at all with an unknown candidate.

The allied parties of the People's party were pledged to put the Spock-Hobson ticket on the ballot back in their home states. Some important parties in the coalition, however, balked. The Michigan Human Rights party, for instance, decided that it would be suicide for them to put the national ticket on the ballot. Michigan electoral laws required the top candidate of a party to obtain a certain percentage of the vote to maintain ballot status, which the Human Rights party already had. They feared that, with anti-war McGovern on the ballot as the Democratic candidate, their own candidate would not meet the requirement, and they would lose their ballot status. Nevertheless, ten affiliates did put the ticket on the ballot and the People's party candidates garnered 78,751 votes.

Between 1972 and 1976 the constituent state and local parties that made up the People's party coalition began to falter as the movements of the 1960s began to falter. Many ceased to exist. The ones that survived moved further away from the amorphous populism that they, and the People's party, originally espoused. A brochure for the Michigan Human Rights party, for instance, clearly stated their reasoning in calling for a new party: "The old parties have failed.

They exist for power rather than for people. We're at war. We're victims of . . . an unfair tax system, . . . poverty, . . . repression, and decay. Only a new and radical political approach can get at the root causes of these crises. The Human Rights party is determined to take courageous action to solve these problems." By 1974 it became evident that this "courageous action" was to declare one's self a socialist. The Human Rights party became "socialist-feminist." In August of that year the Peace and Freedom party also formally adopted a socialist-feminist platform, prompting a libertarian wing to bolt. The socialist faction of the Peace and Freedom party had also, just the month before at a convention in Indianapolis hosted by the Indiana Peace and Freedom party, succeeded in having the People's party explicitly identify itself as a "socialist-feminist" party.

For the 1976 presidential election the People's party nominated Margaret Wright, a black parent and educational activist from Los Angeles, as its presidential candidate. Ben Spock accepted the party's nomination for vice president. The ticket, presenting itself as "A Socialist Alternative," received only 48,346 votes nationwide. Three thousand of those votes came from Michigan, where the Human Rights party had finally placed the ticket on the ballot. As many had feared in 1972, the vote total was so low it caused the party to lose its ballot status, a blow from which the party never recovered.

The 1976 election was the last hurrah of the People's party. As in Michigan, many of its affiliated local parties had withered and faded away. By late 1977, the People's party essentially consisted of a national office in Washington, D.C., staffed by a single person, Casey Peters; the California Peace and Freedom party; and the New York Working People's party, a small sectarian group which sought to capture the mantle of the People's party. The Peace and Freedom party was not to be captured by New York City, however. By early 1978 the two had gone their separate ways, and the People's party ceased to exist. Casey Peters turned what remained of the party's records over to the Tamiment Institute at New York University and closed the national office.

ERIC LEIF DAVIN

See also: Black Panther Party; District of Columbia Statehood Party; Human Rights Party (Michigan); Peace and Freedom Party; Benjamin Spock.

Bibliography

Davin, Eric Leif. "Dr. Spock, the Campaigner." *Pittsburgh Post-Gazette*, March 21, 1998.

Spock, Benjamin, and Mary Morgan. *Spock on Spock: A Memoir of Growing up with the Century.* New York: Pantheon Books, 1989.

POOR MAN'S PARTY
1949–1966; 1988

The Poor Man's party was founded in 1949 in response to domestic and economic policy initiatives of Franklin Roosevelt and Harry Truman as well as elite attention to threats of communism (the Red Scare). The New Deal and Fair Deal initiatives received severe criticism from the Poor Man's party. The party was founded to provide an alternative vote choice to those who would otherwise support Democratic presidential candidates.

Henry Krajewski and his supporters formed the Poor Man's party as a way to establish a platform critical of the Roosevelt and Truman administrations. Krajewski was particularly critical of the New Deal and Fair Deal programs initiated by these two presidents. His criticism of the New Deal and Fair Deal programs promulgated his own Square Deal. The party symbol, a black and white pig from his own farm, was chosen because it represented the anger (squealing) of the people caused by the New Deal and Fair Deal.

The party functioned as a personal faction for its founder. He was a pig farmer and tavern owner from Secaucus, New Jersey. Born in Jersey City in 1912, Krajewski moved to Secaucus in 1925. He built his political base from his pig farming business as well as from a tavern that he owned in Secaucus. His death in 1966 essentially signaled the end of the party.

Krajewski's political career involved running for office without establishing a formal organization to recruit candidates to run for other offices, save for a running mate when he ran for president. Although he ran for several national, state, and local offices, Krajewski did not enjoy any electoral successes. The party did not func-

tion as an organization but provided a label and associated symbols for its founder to seek public office.

His first run for office was for Secaucus town councilman in 1950. This was followed by a run for Hudson County Freeholder (1951). He also sought the governorship in 1953 and garnered 12,881 votes.

Krajewski did not allow his electoral failures to discourage him from seeking national office. He ran for a U.S. Senate seat in 1954 (35,421 votes) as well as for president in 1952 and 1956. Krajewski did not get on the presidential ballot in any state except his home state of New Jersey.

He also offered President Lyndon Johnson the opportunity to name him as his vice-presidential running mate in 1964. President Johnson's lack of response was deemed a refusal, which encouraged Krajewski to continue his efforts to secure national office. He vowed that he would seek a U.S. Senate seat again in 1966. This campaign was terminated in 1965 due to his poor health.

Krajewski's presidential campaigns focused on both domestic policy and foreign policy. He also advocated a change in the structure of the federal executive office as one of his campaign themes. Krajewski's criticism of the Roosevelt and Truman administrations is well summarized by a statement that he made during his 1952 presidential campaign: "The Democrats have been hogging the administration at Washington for twenty years, and it's about time the people began to squeal." He believed that three specific populations required attention in the domestic policy arena: The young, the elderly, and the poor constituted the party's primary constituencies. He sought tax breaks for the poor and increased spending on behalf of the young and the elderly.

Specifically, Krajewski advocated a one-year moratorium on income taxes for those earning up to $6,000 per year. He argued that this would allow poor people to pay off other bills and use the money for necessities. He also supported excise tax reductions for liquor and gasoline. He favored increased federal spending in order to provide schoolchildren one pint of free milk daily. Other domestic policy initiatives included the proposed requirement that young people work for one year on a farm. He also supported lowering the minimum age from 65 to 60 for receiving Social Security.

On the domestic front, Krajewski sought a shift in the constitutional structure. Specifically, he wanted the checks and balances system to be reinforced in the executive branch through a bipartisan executive. He believed that two co-presidents, one Democrat and one Republican, would impede abuse of power from the oval office.

In foreign policy matters, Krajewski's positions aligned well with the Republican party. He held a strong defensive posture and was a staunch supporter of Republican Senator Joseph McCarthy's attempts to root out communists from political and social institutions. His anti-communist positions reinforced his view that the United States should achieve a total victory in Korea and the annexation of Canada. He argued that the United States should not recognize the People's Republic of China and its communist system.

Krajewski's deteriorating health caused him to give up his campaign efforts and political activities in 1965. He suffered from diabetes-related health problems (which led to a leg amputation) coupled with a heart condition. He died on November 8, 1966, essentially signaling the death of the Poor Man's party. However, the party label was revitalized when Henry Krajewski's son-in-law, Richard Kemly, ran as a Poor Man's party candidate for Congress in 1988. Kemly ran against incumbent Democrat Robert Toricelli for New Jersey's ninth district. He was unsuccessful.

The Poor Man's party was a personal faction for Henry Krajewski, who used timely political issues as the basis for seeking political office at the local, state, and national level. His perseverance was not rewarded with any victories. His campaign themes and political views did not achieve resonance with either major party.

TERRI FINE

See also: Lenora Fulani; Henry Krajewski; Lyndon Hermyle LaRouche, Jr.; Fred Newman; Reform Party.

Bibliography

Congressional Quarterly. *Congressional Quarterly's Guide to U.S. Elections.* 3d ed. Washington, DC: Congressional Quarterly, 1994.

"Heat Fells a Candidate." *New York Times,* July 7, 1952.

"Henry Krajewski: Was Candidate Three Times, of Own Poor Man's Party—Had Tavern in Secaucus." *New York Times,* November 9, 1966, obituary.

"Pig Farmer Asks Votes." *New York Times,* September 11, 1952.

"Pig Farmer Joins Presidential Race." *New York Times,* March 9, 1952.

"A Poor Man and His Run for Office." *The Record* (Bergen County, NJ), November 9, 1988.

"Poor Man's Candidate." *Time* (March 17, 1952).

Schapsmeier, Edward L., and Frederick H. Schapsmeier. *Political Parties and Civic Action Groups.* Westport, CT: Greenwood, 1981.

POPULIST MOVEMENT/PEOPLE'S PARTY

1880s–1890s

The appearance of the People's party, one of the most significant third parties in American history, was the culmination of the large-scale mobilization shaped by the organizers of the National Farmers' Alliance and Industrial Union in the late nineteenth century. The sequential events that connected these two social formations—the Farmers Alliance and the resulting People's party constitute what has come to be called the "Populist Revolt" in America. Collectively, these related happenings provide an interesting test of conventional ideas of how independent political action can be an instrument of social reform in modern societies. It is a test many have not managed to pass: Populism stands as one of the least understood political movements in American history. As for the movement, so for the word itself: In its modern usage, "populism" is one of those vague terms of political description that is sufficiently thin on specific content as to be easily molded into whatever partisan shape its user may wish it to have. A fair measure of explanation is required to sort through this maze.

HISTORICAL BACKGROUND

One begins with a brief review of the economic grievances the agrarian movement endeavored to address. A series of self-help economic experiments created experiences that over time generated a number of political proposals. In finding a way to place these political ideas before the nation, the farmers painstakingly constructed the populist agenda.

What was to become the National Farmers' Alliance first came into existence in the late 1870s as a rural cooperative. Located on the southern fringe of the western farming frontier that stretched from Canada to the Gulf of Mexico, it arose in Texas at a time when the era of industrialization and transcontinental railroad building had created a national market economy. Farmers found themselves caught in elaborate structures of exploitation—by banks and other lending institutions that charged high interest on chattel mortgages and by rural credit merchants who exacted usurious rates on food and supplies advanced to farmers during the growing season. The merchants held liens on the farmers' crops in what was called, straightforwardly enough, "the crop lien system." After the Civil War, the crop lien became the dominant commercial arrangement for southern cotton production, while the chattel mortgage proliferated in the western granary from Kansas and Iowa to the Canadian border. Both the crop lien and the chattel mortgage proved to be effective financial instruments for lending institutions because they were highly profitable. In effect, the fruits of the labor of western and southern farmers were harvested not by farmers but by the institutions financing agricultural production. In a phrase popularized by agrarian reformers, the relationship creditors had with debtors became the means of "farming the farmers." For the nation, the most visible social result was massive debt peonage that slowly engulfed agricultural America in the 1870s and 1880s. Hundreds of thousands and eventually millions descended into landless tenancy. That this fact did not make its way into standard history texts attests to the controlling power the idea of progress has traditionally exerted within American culture, affecting historians as effortlessly as it has affected everyone else.

Whether considered noteworthy or not, these phenomena were not restricted to those advanced societies where capitalism was fully emerging in the late nineteenth century. Rather, among disparate human communities around the globe, peonage has existed in one form or another since pre-Roman times. Whatever the degree of exploitation inherent in each "form," the practice itself became the means through which capital to build cities was extracted from rural people who had no means to feed themselves during the long growing seasons that necessarily preceded income-yielding harvests. As is now becoming somewhat better understood, the culture of capital accumulation that developed in America in the late nineteenth century rationalized widespread exploitation of workers and farmers as a given, whether it occurred on the land or within the emerging factory system. Under these circumstances, the continuing interest in American populism is fueled by the vivid example it provides of sustained self-activity on the part of the victims. American farmers did not go quietly into peonage.

Yet it would be a mistake to see populism as some sort of spontaneous act of mass defiance, or even as a kind of naked expression of will that surfaced because "times were hard." Rather, the People's party was a product of a particular organizing experience that activated upward of two million rank-and-file American farmers. Coming to terms with populism requires a sustained focus on these organizing experiences for they explain how a broad popular movement materialized in America.

AGRARIAN ORGANIZING

After some fruitless experiments between 1878 and 1884 in small-scale cash cooperatives along lines pioneered by the earlier Grange movement, Alliance organizers slowly fashioned a recruiting tool that was so massively appealing to debt-ridden farmers that it offered the prospect of transforming the American countryside. The idea was a broad-gauged credit cooperative. It was a concept that took into account the economic weakness of debt-ridden small farmers and landless tenants. In 1885, organized farmers successfully pioneered what they called the "bulking" of cotton, pooling their product in a cooperative marketing plan designed to produce harvest-time sales direct to British and East Coast American cotton buyers. Mass sales of this kind succeeded in attracting competing buyers, a circumstance that soon brought marginally higher returns to cotton producers. The euphoria was immediate: Some celebrating farmers flew blue flags from their wagons as they went home, and word spread throughout rural districts that the Alliance was "doing something" for the dirt farmer. In little more than six months during the fall and winter of 1886, the Alliance credit cooperative attracted 250,000 Texas farmers desperate to escape the clutches of the crop lien system.

Confident in their now-proven organizing capabilities, cooperative advocates fashioned elaborate plans for a multistate organizing campaign throughout the South and West in 1887–88. The objective was to create structures for cooperative purchasing as well as cooperative marketing. Alliance organizers had learned how to create large-scale co-ops, and they had learned how to explain it: Wherever Americans grew cotton, corn, or wheat, membership in the Alliance soared—from Florida to the Dakotas. Inevitably, the newly organized cooperatives were to be opposed by the financial and commercial institutions that had benefited from exploiting farmers. These ranged from Chicago Livestock Commission houses, trunk-line railroads, and hundreds of country banks in the West to the manufacturers of jute bagging for cotton bales as well as thousands of credit merchants throughout the South. But while the propagandists of commercial America might regale the population about the virtues of self-reliance, self-help farmer cooperatives were perceived as impolite attacks on corporate profits. The resulting tensions that developed between big business and the activities of Alliance co-ops gave organized farmers a first-hand view of how the economy of the late nineteenth century had changed for small farmers—even with group power—against strong business interests.

American populism did not emerge via "rising consciousness," but through education and shared experiences. The "education" gained by large-scale credit cooperatives emerged very early in the founding alliances in Texas and then was repeated as the cooperative movement spread throughout the western granary and the southern cotton belt. The experiences generated within the Alliance cooperative politicized the farmers it had recruited. For example, in 1885 when the fledgling alliances were first experimenting in mass cotton sales, the state organization designated an "Alliance Purchasing Agent" to contact agricultural equipment manufacturers and offer a mass market in exchange for lower prices for plows and other agricultural necessities. The agent, an energetic organizer named William Lamb, was outraged to discover that officials of America's leading farm equipment companies treated him with disdain and even contempt. They told him to go back and tell his members to place their orders through the company's nearest retailers. There would be no discounts. William Lamb pondered the long-term implications of this attitude and decided to make a few plans of his own.

The nation's fledgling labor movement provided Lamb and other cooperative advocates with the kind of opportunity they were looking for. After some difficult organizing experiences in the West, Knights of Labor officials won what they considered to be a breakthrough victory over Jay Gould's Missouri-Pacific Railroad. In 1885–86 they employed the slogan, "We made Jay Gould recognize us," to pyramid national membership from 100,000 to 700,000. In the spring of 1886, however, Gould moved to crush the union by instigating a conflict. The railroad abruptly fired an employee for missing work while attending a union meeting—after having been given permission to do so. The

union's members, their very right to existence challenged, rallied to defend their organization. From beginning to end, the Great Southwest Strike was a series of minor and major battles between armed workers and armed deputies and militiamen, interspersed with commando-like raids on company equipment by bands of workers. In Texas, Louisiana, Arkansas, Missouri, and Kansas, thousands were indicted, hundreds were jailed, and many died. Major newspapers denounced the workers, said their grievances were imaginary, praised the railroad's "magnanimity," and repeatedly predicted the imminent return of the men to their jobs. It was within such emotional currents that the political awareness of the early Farmers Alliances began to take root.

In the West, it was hard to distinguish farmers from workers; they dressed alike, attended the same churches, read the same newspapers, and often hailed from the same families. To William Lamb, the relevant fact was that farmers and workers were held in equal contempt by commercial America. It was time both groups showed they could work together. As president of the Montague County Farmers' Alliance, Lamb issued a boycott in support of the Knights of Labor in order, he said, to "secure their help in the future." This act produced an internal conflict in the Alliance to define the meaning of the farmer movement, provoking a struggle that would be repeated with slight variations as the Alliance swept across the South and West in the next half-dozen years. The Alliance state president, Andrew Dunlap, denounced Lamb's boycott, declared it "null and void," and officially denied that the Alliance "had anything to do" with the spreading boycott. The editor of the young order's official newspaper warned against "busy bodies in other men's business."

Alliance organizers (referred to as "lecturers") were changed by their daily duties in building the cooperative movement. Day after day, the local lecturers traveled through the remote farmlands. The stories of personal tragedy they heard in their country meetings could be repeated at the next meeting a few miles down the road where, in an atmosphere of shared experience, they drew nods of instant understanding. If the Alliance was changing farmers by offering a new kind of tangible hope, the farmers were changing the lecturers who were, in effect, seeing too much and learning too much. The very duties of an Alliance lecturer, like the duties of its state purchasing agent, William Lamb, were driving home the need to "do something." Repeated often enough—and inside the Alliance cooperative lectures were routinely repeated again and again—these experiences had a powerful emotional effect: A nucleus of deeply committed activists were created from the daily experiences found in the cooperative movement.

The self-assured organizers were convinced that they grasped the grassroots temper of the movement better than their own high-ranking Alliance functionaries did. When Alliance President Dunlap denounced William Lamb's "unblushing impudence" and was supported by the journal editor who charged the boycott was "putting burdens on the farmers that they cannot bear," Lamb quietly outlined the specifics of monopolistic practices being "waged against us." A farmer-labor coalition was more than an idea: It was a way to act. With lofty confidence Lamb remarked, "I feel satisfied I know more about what is going on against us than the state president or our editor either."

THE COOPERATIVE MOVEMENT

After the Great Southwest Strike ended in a debilitating defeat for the Knights of Labor, the great gains in the organization's membership in 1885 disappeared and were fated never again to be approached. For its part, however, the Alliance underwent an internal revolution in which its lecturer-organizers moved into positions of leadership at every level of the organization, replacing, among others, the state president and its journal editor. The order's new flagship journal became the *Southern Mercury*, an aggressive advocate of farmer-labor coalitions as well as a proponent of a new, more democratic theory for organizing the monetary system.

In the summer of 1886, the Alliance issued a provocative manifesto titled the Cleburne Demands. In notable anticipation of the Populist platform of 1892, the Cleburne document called for the recognition of trade unions and co-ops and proclaimed the need to alter the basic rules of trade through the creation of a new federally administered national banking system based on the creation of a flexible currency. In the spring of 1887, the Texas Alliance launched a national organizing campaign by dispatching over 100 lecturers to organize in the South and West. The effort proved remarkably successful. Within two years, the National Farmers Alliance counted over a million members and cooperative experiments in both marketing and purchasing began to proliferate across the continent.

Taking stock, it is evident that the experience and lessons of the cooperative movement generated two levels of political meaning within the Alliance. From the western plains to the Carolina coast, local, county, and regional lecturers became transformed by their continuous association with the demeaning poverty they found as a pervasive feature of rural life. In short, their attention was directed inward in a new way. Secondly, the attention of the Alliance's marketing and purchasing agents was directed outward—as a function of their institutional contacts with the commercial world. As was the earlier case with William Lamb, the cooperative experience caused people to think more critically about the existing structure of the American economy and their own exploited condition within it.

Although these dynamics worked everywhere that the Alliance movement was able to put down sustaining roots, this awareness necessarily appeared first where the movement was most grounded in experience. In 1888, even as the cooperative movement was first getting organized in new states, the Texas Alliance started a bold venture in large-scale cooperation. The objective was nothing less than to market the entire cotton crop of the state through one centralized State Cooperative

Exchange. The plan of the Alliancemen was the most creative in the annals of American agricultural organizations and led directly to the one pathbreaking political concept of the agrarian revolt—a new democratic national banking system called the Sub-Treasury Land and Loan System. It also led to the formation of the People's party.

The marketing and purchasing plan, necessarily a bit complicated, turned on a simple discovery: The underlying problem hurting individual farmers—lack of access to low-interest credit—was also the problem haunting the Alliance cooperative itself. The attempted remedy was called the "joint-note plan." Landowning farmers were asked to place their individual holdings at the disposal of the group, including their tenants. Smallholding farmers and tenants alike would collectively purchase their supplies for the year—on credit—through the centralized State Exchange, the landowners signing the joint note. For collateral, they would put up their land and attempt to protect themselves against loss by taking mortgages on the crops of the tenants. Alliancemen would sink or swim together; the landless would begin the process of escaping the crop lien, too, or none of them would. As the joint notes flooded into the State Exchange in Dallas, the cooperative planners moved to sell the notes through bank loans. After exhaustive efforts, however, they were forced to report to the suballiances that "those who controlled the moneyed institutions of the state either did not choose to do business with us or feared the ill will of a certain class of businessmen who considered their interests antagonistic to those of our order. At any rate, be the causes what they may, the effort to borrow money in sufficient quantity failed."

The Exchange was suddenly in serious trouble. In response, the Alliance mobilized all of its collective resources and knowledge gained from five years of cooperation. In what was probably the most dramatic single day in the course of the entire agrarian revolt, county alliances met in some 200 Texas courthouses on June 9, 1888, in a desperate effort to raise additional funds to keep alive the cooperative dream.

Awed townspeople were astonished at the turnout: More than 200,000 farmers flooded the courthouses of the state. Observers were also startled by the passionate discussions that went on for hours in the summer heat. The Alliance had asked each farmer at the outset to contribute $2 to the joint-note undertaking, and this appeal was a centerpiece of the June 9 mobilization. A letter to the *Southern Mercury* had earlier portended the outcome of the effort: "We voted the $2.00 assessment for the exchange, and as soon as we are able, will pay it, but we are not able to do so at present." The dignity with which the admission was made, and the willingness of the *Mercury* to print it without comment, indicates that everyone recognized the prevailing poverty among many people participating in the Alliance movement. The implications for the movement were serious: The co-ops had precisely the credit problem that individual farmers did. Throughout the South and West where the Alliance movement had spread, farmers held their breath while the Texas Exchange collected funds, collected even more pledges, and, in so doing, fought for its life. For the moment, the Texans sent an ominous signal: The Exchange announced it was moving to a temporary cash-only relationship with its members.

The Alliance had a more promising outcome defending itself in the South against a bona fide national "trust." In 1888, a newly constructed combine of jute manufacturers announced that the price of jute bagging used for cotton bales would rise from seven cents a yard to twelve and even fourteen cents, levying "a tribute of some $2,000,000" that the nation's cotton farmers were forced to pay under duress. Alliance leaders from six cotton-producing states hurriedly met in Birmingham, Alabama, fashioned arrangements with a dozen cotton mills to manufacture cotton bagging, and, thus armed, announced a boycott of jute bagging. After a tense period, the combine, suddenly awash in its own jute, was forced to concede that the price-rigging scheme had failed.

Despite such encouraging defensive successes, broad-scale co-op plans continued to run headlong into concentrated corporate power.

An ambitious livestock marketing arrangement fashioned by Kansans and cooperatively extended to Missouri and Nebraska farmers, challenged corporations that dominated livestock marketing in the region. The farmers called their co-op the American Livestock Commission Company. Within a six-month period in 1889, the co-op had amassed over $40,000 in profits to distribute to members. But as the businessmen who operated the Chicago Livestock Commission, a commodities exchange, realized what the success of co-ops could mean, they abruptly terminated all marketing relations on the grounds that the farmer co-op "violated the anti-rebate rule" of the Chicago Commission. That proved to be the end of that early accomplishment for smallholding farmers.

Meanwhile, in Texas the State Alliance Exchange eventually was able to raise $80,000 to underwrite the expenses of the elaborate joint-note plan, but it was not enough to cover the credit crisis. In the summer of 1889, the Texas State Alliance Exchange went under, unable to market its joint notes in banking circles, and therefore unable to respond to insistent payment demands from its creditors. The tantalizing prospect of freeing everyone from the greedy Texas merchants in one dramatic season danced out of reach.

SUB-TREASURY SYSTEM

Into this situation stepped one of the most creative and enigmatic personalities brought forward by the agrarian revolt—Charles Macune. Born in Wisconsin and orphaned at ten, Macune roamed the West and arrived on the Texas frontier in 1870 at the age of 19. In the custom of the era, he "read" for the professions and in time came to practice both medicine and law. Macune, however, had untapped talents as a lucid writer, as a sonorous, authoritative public speaker, and as a movement diplomat. A strikingly handsome man, he also possessed a subtle eye for the strategic demands of organizing. He put all these gifts to good use during the tensions that surrounded the Cleburne Demands

of 1886 and succeeded Andrew Dunlap as state president prior to the great organizational expansion of the following year. Above all, Charles Macune was a creative monetary theorist. He participated actively in each evolving stage of the joint-note plan of 1887–88, pondered the implications of the cooperative crisis in 1888, and in 1889, conceived of an ingenious and sweeping new national monetary structure called the sub-treasury system.

Macune's proposal carried the agrarian agenda to a new level of advocacy. The federal government would underwrite the cooperatives by issuing greenbacks (paper money), to provide credit for the farmers' crops at the moment they were harvested and marketed. In the process, this influx of funds would create the basis of a flexible national currency. The necessary marketing and purchasing facilities would be achieved through government-owned warehouses, or "sub-treasuries," and through federal sub-treasury certificates paid to the farmer for his produce. In short, the sub-treasury system formed the instrument of credit that would remove furnishing merchants, commercial banks, and chattel mortgage companies from American agriculture. The sub-treasury certificates would be government-issued greenback money—"full legal tender for all debts, public and private," in the words of Alliance platforms in the years to come.

The structural implications of Macune's sub-treasury system were large: In the first instance, the plan financially backed the centralized Alliance marketing and purchasing co-op. In sustaining the co-ops, the sub-treasury sustained the popular movement. Beyond this critical democratic achievement, however, the greenback dollars that made possible America's annual agricultural harvest also formed the workable basis for a new and flexible national currency outside of the exclusive control of eastern commercial bankers. It also provided the U.S. Treasury with broad new options in giving private citizens access to reasonable credit. The line of nineteenth-century advocates of a flexible currency—one that included such businessmen as Edward Kellogg in the 1830s and such labor partisans as Andrew Cameron in the 1860s—culminated in the 1890s in the farmer advocate, Macune. As Macune foresaw, the agrarian-greenbackism underlying the sub-treasury system united southern and western farmers. As he did not foresee, it also provided political cohesion for a radical third party. Within three years of the appearance of Macune's sub-treasury plan, the People's party was to begin waging a frantic campaign to try to take over control of the American monetary system from the nation's commercial bankers and restore it, "in the name of the whole people," to the U.S. Treasury. It was a campaign that was never to be waged again.

ORGANIZING AND SPEECH-MAKING

Nineteenth-century Alliance populism is worth studying because of the marginal impact that speech-making, platform writing, and rhetorical display had upon popular social consciousness. The historical value of the agrarian revolt lies not in the rhetoric, but in the substantial alternative evidence of how social experiences of farmers participating in voluntary democratic organizations helped to shape the way they perceived their plight and framed new understandings.

For example, populism was viewed in Kansas as building on the foundation of so many early Kansas settlers' abolitionist ideas. Orators such as "Sockless Jerry" Simpson and Mary Elizabeth Lease testify to how quickly colorful language can find a prominent place in historical accounts and in later newspaper stories, but the egalitarian heritage that animated more important Kansas populists such as Henry and Cuthbert Vincent is obvious from their hands-on role in helping to introduce and energize the cooperative system in the farming regions of Kansas. Although Henry Vincent came to be one of the most articulate populist editors in the nation, he fully understood that it was the social experiences gained from working with the Alliance cooperative—far more than the driving language of his own deeply involved newspa-

per—that altered the politics of Kansas farmers between 1888 and 1892. Similarly, Evan Jones, the popular and modestly influential president of the National Alliance in 1889, could catch journalistic attention with his vivid critique of price-gouging railroad freight haulers: "These iron rails are binding us in iron chains." But he, like Vincent, knew that the social bonds of the movement came from the cooperative effort rather than in exciting and evocative language. Jones also knew that the long-term unity of populism depended upon finding some way to keep the co-ops going. That is why he, along with other informed agrarian radicals, became such an energetic defender of the sub-treasury system.

Although social experience was critical in shaping the populist movement, this is not to say that words and language are necessarily irrelevant to the evolution of insurgent democratic movements. Of course ideas dramatically spoken can be important—but only if an audience has previously been recruited to hear the ideas. Significant insurgent political movements happen when they are organized. They can happen no other way. Thus, the cooperative crusade of the Alliance was the cornerstone of American populism because it not only recruited people but also brought them together into shared activities for common goals in the future. Whether a given cooperative innovation succeeded or not—farmers learned from these experiences to understand the economic realities defining their relationship with commercial America. Indeed, it was precisely those economic and cultural insights that produced the language that would eventually become known as "populism."

The most important reform proposed by the populists was the fundamental redesign of the nation's monetary system. The goal was to change the way money was created, thus reducing the excessive power of creditors over debtors. Had it ever been enacted into law, a democratic system of money and credit would have created a substantial increase in economic growth as an enduring feature of a fundamentally reformed economy in America. As such, the populist sub-treasury system would have materially benefited working Americans in factories as well as farmers. (The reorganization of the monetary system would not have forestalled the need for industrial workers to organize collectively and form trade unions to improve their conditions.) These ideas, however, were not only heretical to the economic notions of the Gilded Age, they were crisply at odds with traditional assumptions among bankers that prevail to the present day. The so-called "sound money" theories prevailing in both major parties in the late nineteenth century significantly impeded economic growth in America. Not only working Americans but also the economy as a whole would—modern economists now concede—have been far better off in the twentieth century had the sub-treasury system been enacted.

Accordingly, when Macune appeared before the House Ways and Means Committee in 1890 to explain the sub-treasury system, the *New York Times* took it upon itself to offer the thought that Macune's plan was "one of the wildest and most fantastic projects ever seriously proposed by [a] sober man." So encouraged, Democratic and Republican congressmen on the committee responded to the Alliance spokesman with something less than devoted attention.

Although the economic rigidity of the two major parties might have been obvious on the national scene in 1890, it was not easy to see at the state level. Politically, the Alliance members viewed voting as a matter of electing good reformers to public office—or at least candidates who sounded like they were good reformers. As a result, people calling themselves "Alliance candidates" did very well throughout the South and West in 1890, but they accomplished little by way of reform. This unproductive result had been anticipated by monetary reformers, especially after it became starkly clear how hostile both parties were to the greenback principles in the sub-treasury plan. Although the needs of the farmers were great, and their intentions earnest, veteran Alliance greenbackers were frustrated by the sight of their comrades seeking serious economic reform through a corrupt party system. From Henry Vincent in Kansas and William Lamb in

Texas to the outgoing and incoming Alliance national presidents, Evan Jones of Texas and L.L. Polk of North Carolina, the movement's most fervent activists worked together through 1891 and into the spring of 1892 to create a political atmosphere that would allow for the birth of the third party. Stripped of pompous verbiage, the democratic dream of a national farmer-labor party was based in the practical task of organizing. Therefore, managing this task was the core challenge of the agrarian revolt.

PEOPLE'S PARTY

In terms of fashioning a national constituency, the first problem faced by third-party strategists was a cultural one. In post–Civil War America, the most searing cultural memory was the war itself and the long-lasting legacy of sectionalism it left embedded in the national party system. In late nineteenth-century politics, Kansas greenbackers looked out upon masses of Republican farmers who instinctively voted for the party of the Union; Texas greenbackers confronted masses of Democratic farmers, equally habituated to voting for the party of the Confederacy. So many Americans "voted as they shot." Routinely, northern officeseekers appealed to the wartime loyalties of their constituents by "waving the bloody shirt," while their southern counterparts achieved the same result through fervid oratory about the "lost cause." This explained why Alliancemen in many southern states instinctively sought "reform through the Democrats" in 1890 and why the movement in Kansas elected to field a less provocative "Alliance ticket" that year rather than a clearly labeled third-party slate. For a great many Americans, North as well as South, sectionalism still had a cultural dimension that transcended economics.

It was understandable, then, that one of the more emotional moments at the first nominating convention of the People's party in Omaha, Nebraska, in the summer of 1892 came when delegates who were former soldiers of the Union and Confederate armies came up to the

The People's (or Populist) party was met with routine hostility by most of the business-oriented press of the day. This 1891 cartoon depicts a kneeling symbol of the Democratic party either begging for support from a wild-eyed Populist or pleading with him not to destroy the Democratic party by running independent candidates. The image was originally captioned "A Pitiful Spectacle." *(Courtesy of the Library of Congress)*

podium to join hands under the banner of the new party. The gesture belied the cultural struggle that would continue in one form or another throughout the life of the People's party.

The populist platform was noteworthy because of the amount of exaggeration it included in its preamble: "The urban workmen are denied the right of organization for self-protection; imported pauperized labor beats down their wages; a hireling standing army, unrecognized by our laws, is established to shoot them down. . . . The fruits of the toil of millions are boldly stolen to build up colossal fortunes, unprecedented in the history of the world, while their possessors despise the republic and endanger liberty."

It is interesting to note that the platform itself was shorter than its preamble. It also was much more soberly written, being a simple codification of the alliance demands of 1890 and 1891 that emphasized the greenback doctrines featured in the sub-treasury system. The People's party also reproduced the Alliance concern about business centralization ("concentrated capital") as shown by a call for government ownership of the railroads. This reflected the organized farmers' declining confidence in the ability of the government to regulate railroads under the newly formed Interstate Commerce Commission. The old "freight-rate abuses" not only survived, they seemed to proliferate under the ICC. In retrospect, the agency seemed to be more effectively regulated by the railroads than the reverse. It was an insight that proved to be beyond the reach of subsequent Progressive Era politicians such as Woodrow Wilson and Teddy Roosevelt.

The public history of the People's party—restricted to the presidential elections of 1892 and 1896 and the off-year election of 1894—had its moments of moderate success, but as a body of historical evidence, the legacy it forms has less to teach later generations of democratic political movements than does the party's internal history.

As newcomers on the public stage of national politics, the first thing Populists discovered was that neither of the two major parties had the remotest interest in debating the relationships between farmers and bankers, debtors and creditors, or the systems of monetary exchange that connected the two. The rights of American workers to organize themselves—indeed, the growing need for them to do so—remained outside the political debate. Neither major party found it convenient to discuss in any detail the unequal distribution of income in American society. Rather, the political mainstream occupied itself with cultural issues. In the North, the southern origins of the agrarian movement were repeatedly focused upon as proof that western Populists were unwitting dupes of latter-day Confederates. The Topeka *Daily Capital* participated in this by informing Kansans to avoid an organization "officered by rebel brigadiers.'' For their part, southern metropolitan dailies focused on the fact that the Populists' 1892 presidential nominee, Iowa's James B. Weaver, had been a Union general in the Civil War. Southern Democrats charged that Populists, by ensuring that the white vote of the South would be ''split,'' were demonstrating their lack of loyalty to the ''lost cause,'' southern womanhood, and, above all, to the ''party of the fathers.'' The specter of Reconstruction was raised anew to make voters fear that southern populism was a forerunner to ''Negro domination'' and ''bayonet rule.''

These old scare tactics, used in North and South, drove monetary reformers to distraction, but they pointed to long-term barriers that historically have held back third parties in America. In many European systems a new party garnering 10 percent of the vote on its first effort would get 5 percent of the seats in the next parliament, which would provide immediate national visibility to the party's ideas as well as to its prominent representatives. This is not the case in America, however, where prompt invisibility is predictable for contenders who fail to get a majority of the votes.

Without such highly charged stimuli as revolution or civil war—events that can bring massive constituencies together overnight—any new institution such as the People's party faces the prospect of building itself out of the materials at hand. Third-party radicals dreamed of a North-South coalition of ''the plain people.'' Somewhat more specifically, they dreamed of a vast farmer-labor coalition to bring ''a new day to America.'' And finally, the abolitionist heritage of western populism, particularly in what had once been known as ''Bleeding Kansas,'' helped budding populists to understand that the ''plain people'' of the North and South were not only workers as well as farmers, they were black as well as white. Transparently, the Populist party brought an interesting part of the cultural heritage under review: The average white American could find a number of reasons not to be a Populist.

The People's party had organizational access to the rank and file of the National Farmers' Alliance. In addition, Terence Powderly, the Grand Master Workman of the Knights of Labor, had been swept along to the third party by his more activist executive board, but the Knights' own internal structure had been all but crippled. After the crushing defeat at the hands of Jay Gould in the Great Southwest Strike, the 700,000 national members of the Knights in 1886 had dwindled to less than 100,000 by 1892. The new American Federation of Labor that had emerged from the wreckage of the labor struggles of the 1880s was led by Samuel Gompers, a cautious craft unionist who intended to avoid distracting political adventures. To Populists, the most promising labor spokesman was an emerging railroad union leader named Eugene Debs, who believed that the People's party would come to power ''with a resistless rush.'' But while Debs had caught the attention of such Populist journals as the *American Nonconformist* and the *Southern Mercury*, he had scarcely placed himself in a position to lead large numbers of American workers into independent political action.

Few third-party strategists in 1892 looked at the Populist recruiting problem in what can be described as a ''constituency-based'' manner. To Alliance radicals, the People's party was a new political instrument constructed by popular forces for the transparent purpose of serving ''the people.'' The radicals felt that their party's principles were clear and strikingly evident in the Omaha platform. Without consciously thinking about their immediate task as a recruiting problem, they believed that the egalitarian basis of the Omaha platform might somehow recruit the American working class on its own! Veteran Alliance lecturers did not understand how detached they were from the world of urban labor. This distance caused them to misjudge the challenge they faced. The essential importance of recruiting to movement-building was not understood by Populist leaders in the Gilded Age in much the same way that modern political strategists do not value the concept. Thus, Populist strategists took solace in the hope that workers in American cities would somehow find their way to populism by reading the Omaha platform and deciding thereafter to join the third party! Such an outcome necessarily rested on the unexamined assumption that American workers had acquired a more intimate knowledge of greenback monetary principles than other Americans had managed to achieve. And, whether acknowledged or not, the hope rested on the further assumption that workers far removed from the world of the Alliance cooperative could somehow grasp the short- and long-term implications of the sub-treasury system that constituted the culminating logic of the Populist platform.

It was not to be. In the great urban commercial and industrial centers that lay east of Chicago, the People's party possessed nothing that resembled even the faint beginnings of an ongoing political presence. Alliance lecturers had a story to tell, but they did not know how to maneuver themselves into the same room with urban workers so they could tell it. This discovery—one of the central lessons of 1892—came as a great shock to the agrarian organizers who had constructed the People's party. On its inaugural venture into national politics, a general conclusion was strikingly evident: Over a six-year period between 1886–92, the Farmers' Alliance had recruited large constituencies and developed a further degree of internal cohesion through the cooperative struggle against commercial America. In those states of the South and West that had undergone these organizing experiences most intensely, the People's party emerged in 1892 with large followings. Everywhere else, the impediments to independent political action prevailed to a greater or lesser extent.

Be that as it may, the political achievement of the Farmers' Alliance in recruiting well over 1.5 million people into agrarian cooperatives and then persuading more than a million of them to identify themselves intimately with an egalitarian third party constitutes one of the more formidable democratic political feats of American history. To pass blithely over such an organizing achievement would be an impressive exercise in complacency.

Yet a central irony hovers over this accomplishment. Agrarian radicals went to extreme lengths in 1891–92 to mobilize their lecturing system so as to persuade their vast rural con-

stituency to journey from the Alliance to the People's party. This energetic effort extended to the editors of rural weeklies who had been politically activated by the Alliance and who had in 1890 organized themselves into the National Reform Press Association. The great majority of these journalists had become passionately engaged in the effort to recruit the citizenry to the People's party. Nevertheless, in the internal discussions between Alliance lecturers and reform editors, the challenge of recruiting urban labor did not materialize as a central strategic concern demanding sustained attention.

In evaluating the reasons why the agrarian movement did not form a viable third party, we must focus attention on the central failure of the People's party to recruit American workers into a farmer-labor coalition. An examination of this failing reveals both the radical essence of American populism and its democratic limitations.

In the 1890 campaign of "reform through the Democrats," Democrats attempted to capture the support of rural southern voters who had embraced the Alliance's message. Since the Democratic party (along with its Republican counterpart) had declared their opposition to the sub-treasury plan, the Alliance rank and file in the South needed to understand, quite simply, that "reform Democrats" did not exist. Toward this end, the task at hand for the Populists was to employ the sub-treasury issue to distinguish the Alliance and the Democratic "party of the fathers," therefore utilizing the Macune plan to overcome southern sectional loyalties once and for all. The same dynamic also applied in the West, of course, where the sub-treasury could be used to distinguish between the Alliance and both major parties.

This is precisely what third-party architects set out to do in the time preceding the 1892 election. The resulting campaign (which may be understood as "the politics of the sub-treasury") took place within local sub-alliances and therefore beyond the gaze of the metropolitan press. It was pushed most aggressively in Kansas and Texas. On a congressional district basis, schools for lecturers were established to rehearse in detail the fine points of the sub-treasury plan that would underwrite future cooperative efforts. Major-party opposition to financial reform would be driven home to all Alliancemen, together with the corresponding need for rank-and-file farmers everywhere to abandon major-party politics. In Kansas, an especially clear lecture on the sub-treasury was actually printed as a model for other lecturers and reproduced in booklet form for rank-and-file members. At first glance, the need for such special efforts might not have appeared necessary in Kansas where an independent "Alliance ticket" had been successfully fashioned in 1890 to oppose incumbent Republicans; however, as signs appeared in the presidential election year of 1892 that the Kansas GOP was dusting off time-honored "bloody-shirt" tactics (political strategy that hearkened back to the human cost sustained by the nation at the hand of southerners in the Civil War), the need for western Populists to demonstrate the cynical politics of "reform Republicans" seemed as necessary as the need for southern Populists to verify the impossibility of "reform through the Democrats."

To conceptualize popular politics in terms of the relevant organizing imperatives, two conclusions are immediately available here: A coordinated lecturing campaign on the sub-treasury was deemed to be necessary to complete the educational task of freeing rural Americans from inherited party loyalties (although more important than all the other cooperative feats that the Alliance had achieved in years of intense organizing, this was still one more effort), and a similar effort could not be mounted in the presence of urban workers because Alliance lecturers were never, in fact, in the presence of urban workers!

It is perhaps useful to make this distinction more vivid. The Knights of Labor had, a short time earlier, been "in the presence" of 700,000 workers; the American Federation of Labor would, a generation into the future, be "in the presence" of several million workers; and the Congress of Industrial Organizations (CIO) would place itself, two generations into the future, "in the presence" of even more millions of mass production workers. In the decisive months of party-building in 1891–92, however, Alliance radicals did not have a lecturing sys-

tem planted in the working-class districts of America's industrial heartland. The Alliance could form a coalition at the top with the leaders of the Knights of Labor, but the Alliance cooperative crusade never found a way to place itself in the presence of the nation's workers. The People's party was, therefore, the capstone of agrarian electoral insurgency. It was not a farmer-labor party.

DEMOCRATIC PARTY CO-OPTATION

In 1893 the country experienced what appeared at first to be a clear economic downturn but one that soon became acknowledged as a full-scale depression. The morale of many Democratic congressmen in the South was deeply shaken by the economic cataclysm. Most had managed to survive the first round of populism in 1892 principally through a combination of passionate appeals on behalf of white supremacy and even more earnest appeals for campaign financing from eastern business interests. The *New York Times* reported that commercial circles in New York City responded to urgent requests from Augusta, Georgia, by sending $40,000. The money was intended to save the republic from the "sworn enemies of capital"—as Populists were portrayed by Augusta businessmen.

Out West, meanwhile, other business interests had taken a different trajectory in their political lobbying. Silver mine-owners underwrote a well-financed and effectively coordinated agitation for "the free and unlimited coinage of silver." As the depression worsened, the effort began to strike a responsive chord among both western Democrats and their embattled southern counterparts. For Democratic politicians who were looking for an issue through which to survive in an era of reform agitation and hard times, silver coinage appeared ideal. The "free silver" issue seemed much easier to understand than greenback arguments about a flexible currency; indeed, the whole issue of banking and currency had been magically simplified in a cleverly written and profusely illustrated pamphlet financed by silver interests and titled "Coin's Financial School." The author was William H. "Coin" Harvey, a tract-writer employed by the Chicago office of the American Bimetallic League. Millions suffering from the maladies of depression and a declining value of the currency read Harvey's appealing, if wildly inaccurate, analysis of the monetary system and of various gold conspiracies by international bankers. The public campaign for silver, highlighted by the distribution of hundreds of thousands of Harvey's silver tracts, was so successful that a new political hybrid began to emerge in the land: Silver Democrats. One convert was a young Nebraska congressman who found the issue a godsend during his frighteningly close re-election campaign in 1892. His name was William Jennings Bryan.

As the depression deepened in the 1894–96 period, the Grover Cleveland–led "Gold Democrats" found themselves suddenly overwhelmed within their own party by a coalition of newly minted silverites. Concentrated in the southern and western states where populism had made financial reform a major subject of political debate, the silverites took over the Democratic party convention in 1896 and nominated Bryan as their presidential standard-bearer. This turn of events scarcely meant the country was headed for the kind of fundamental debate about money and credit that Populists had sought. Early on, Bryan had affably conceded that he "didn't know anything about free silver," adding the cheerful comment that "the people of Nebraska are for free silver and I am for free silver. I will look up the arguments later." In Washington, silver lobbyists assisted with the young congressman's education to the point that he was able to offer a fiery free silver speech on the floor of the House. The same admirers were able to help Bryan's name recognition by printing and distributing a million copies of the speech.

This story, however, fails to convey the dynamic nature of the relationship between the white metal (silver) and the Nebraska Democrat: In point of fact, silver money made Bryan's career. Western mine-owners played a decisive

role in shaping the 1896 presidential campaign, subsequently characterized by historians as the "Battle of the Standards." Exploring new means of influencing public opinion, silver lobbyists fashioned the American Bimetallic League as a vehicle to distribute Harvey's varied tracts as well as more topical news bulletins aimed at demonstrating the growing popular enthusiasm for the silver cause. Silver interests also purchased the Omaha *World-Herald* newspaper as their primary editorial outpost in the West and bought Edward Carmack's Memphis *Commercial-Appeal* newspaper as a companion silver flagship for the South. They even set up a regional front group, the Nebraska Free Coinage League, which appeared in time to "request" that Bryan run for senator in 1894 as a precursor to his bid for the Democratic nomination in 1896.

It might be argued that this analysis slights the Populist contribution to Bryan's career because it appears to pass too abruptly over the third party's causal contribution to the declining electoral strength of the Democratic party across the western granary and the southern cotton belt. It certainly is true that Populist gains in the South in the 1894 elections played an energizing role in wholesale conversions of old-line Gold Democrats into frantic enthusiasts for silver coinage. The mounting Populist presence could be understood as a necessary precondition enabling silver forces to muster enough Democratic convention votes in 1896 to wrest effective control of the party away from financially orthodox Cleveland forces. Unfortunately for this logic, however, while Populist strength was undermining the will of conservative southern Democrats, silver money was put to work undermining the Omaha platform of the People's party.

The motif employed was the presumed need to "unite the reform forces of the nation" behind the silver coinage issue. In the period between the 1894 elections and the 1896 nominating conventions, the Populist national chairman, Herman Taubeneck of Illinois, intermittently found himself bathed in a commodity normally in extremely short supply in Populist circles—fees for the political lecture circuit. The third-party chairman, it seemed, had accepted a post on a special silver committee organized to lobby in Washington on behalf of the white metal. Meanwhile, the 1892 party's standard-bearer, General Weaver, also appeared in a number of places where the paid publicists of the American Bimetallic League, led by Harvey himself, staged public rallies for free silver. Weaver began to characterize the Omaha platform as a barrier to "fusion" of the Democratic and Populist parties, which he dubbed "the reform forces" of American politics.

CONCLUSION

A detailed chronicle of the well-financed effort to "unite the reform forces of the nation" behind the silver crusade is well beyond the scope of this essay; suffice it to say that the nomination of Bryan by the Democrats in the summer of 1896 threw the People's party into disarray that ended in a tumultuous third-party convention presided over—disingenuously—by a Bryanite, Nebraska Senator William Allen. Bryan was also nominated by the Populist convention, which propelled the People's party into structural and ideological disarray, destroying the morale of its greenback organizers as well as of the reform editors who were its public spear-carriers. For a few months in the autumn of 1896, at least, the silver crusade was intact, but the agrarian revolt was over.

The election of 1896 nevertheless acquired a considerable historical reputation as "The Battle of the Standards" between gold and silver. Such fame was intellectually misplaced. As a serious political issue, the debate between the relative merits of "monometallism" or "bimetallism" was not directly related to the economic stakes at issue in how the way money is created determines interest rates prevailing throughout society. Such matters were quite beyond any economic horizons that Republican presidential candidate William McKinley and William

Jennings Bryan proved willing or capable of exploring.

The election did have long-term cultural meaning, however. Some students of the 1896 campaign have concluded that the enthusiasm for Bryan following his "Cross of Gold" speech was such that he would have swept to victory had the election been held in August. After that initial alarm, the massive campaign for "honest money" engineered by Republican campaign manager Mark Hanna—notably the sheer volume of money injected into the election process—not only dwarfed all expenditures by the silverites or any other group that had ever participated in politics, it became the enduring model for twentieth-century politics in America. Individual contributions for the McKinley campaign by some of the nation's leading capitalists exceeded the entire amount Democrats raised in their national subscription drive. Offerings by corporations were even larger as expenditures soared into the millions. Standard Oil contributed $250,000, a mammoth amount for that era, although an individual, financier J.P.Morgan, matched the figure. Mark Hanna and railroad king James J. Hill were seen in a carriage "day after day" going from Wall Street to the offices of the New York Central and Pennsylvania Railroads. By October the organizational apparatus assembled by Hanna had clearly swung the balance to the GOP.

Yet the election results appeared fairly close, McKinley receiving 7,035,000 votes to Bryan's 6,467,000. The Republicans had swept the North, and while their margin in the Midwest was not overwhelming, it was a region that Cleveland had carried for the Democrats four years before and that Bryan had been supremely confident of winning only a month before the election. Indeed, the results in the Midwest destroyed the party balance that had persisted since the Civil War, thus vastly changing national politics for the foreseeable future. In fact, a cataclysm had befallen the Northern Democratic party. Its progressive symbol in the Midwest, Governor John Peter Altgeld of Illinois, had suffered a surprising defeat, and state party tickets in the North had been thrashed.

Altgeld himself was utterly disconsolate. The political appeal supposedly implicit in the idea of "the people" had received a powerful defeat.

It took time for the full implications to become apparent. The cultural consolidation set in motion in 1896 did not prove in the ensuing century to be any more arbitrary than most other political systems that evolved in advanced industrial societies. The diffusion of power within the three branches of government established under the Constitution imposed certain limits on the triumphant corporate political culture that became the new American orthodoxy of the twentieth century. These safeguards were, perhaps, easily exaggerated, if for no other reason than that it was so reassuring for those who benefited from the progressive society to do so. In the immediate aftermath in 1896, however, those who extolled the doctrines of progress through business enterprise acquired a greater confidence while those who labored on behalf of "the people" suffered a profound shock. A number of the influential supporters of William McKinley, newly secure in their expanded powers after the election, advanced from confidence to arrogance; not only the nation, but the very forms of its economic folkways had become theirs to define. In contrast, a number of the followers of William Jennings Bryan, their idea of America rebuked by the electorate, became deferential, either consciously or unconsciously. The idea that serious structural reform of the democratic process was "inevitable" no longer seemed persuasive to reasonable reformers. Rather, it became evident that political innovations had to be advanced cautiously, if at all, and be directed toward narrower objectives that did not directly challenge the basic political interests of those who ruled. The thought became the inherited wisdom of the mainstream American reform tradition, passed from one generation to another. A consensus thus came to be silently ratified: Reform politics need not concern itself with structural alteration of the economic customs of the society. This conclusion, of course, had the effect of removing from mainstream poli-

tics the idea of people in an industrial society gaining significant degrees of autonomy in designing the structure of their own lives. The reform tradition of the twentieth century unconsciously redefined itself within the framework of inherited power relationships. The range of political possibility was decidedly narrowed—not by repression, or exile, or guns, but by the simple power of the reigning new culture itself.

Although it was not immediately noticed, the new and victorious Republican party of business had muted almost completely the egalitarian ideas that had fortified the party's early abolitionist impulses. As the party of "peace, progress, patriotism, and prosperity," the Republicans had become not only anti-Irish, but anti-Catholic and anti-foreigner generally. Its prior political abandonment of black Americans at the end of Reconstruction had quietly become internalized into a conscious white supremacy that was evident in the virtual disappearance of references to the antislavery crusade that had been part of the Republican service to the nation during the Civil War. The assertive party of business that consolidated itself in 1896 was in a cultural sense the most self-consciously exclusive party the nation had ever experienced. It was white, Protestant, and Yankee. It solicited the votes of all non-white, non-Protestant, or non-Yankee voters who willingly acquiesced in the new cultural norms that described gentility within the emerging progressive society. The word "patriotic" had come to suggest those things that white, Protestant Yankees possessed. The Democratic party, already tainted by its illicit "fusion" with Populists, was also repeatedly charged with being too friendly to foreigners, immigrants, and "anarchists."

For many of those who endeavored to speak for "the people," and for even greater numbers of the people themselves, no amount of fidelity to the new cultural values could provide entry to the new progressive society that was emerging. While black Americans were to learn this truth most profoundly, its dimensions extended to many other kinds of "ethnic" Americans as well as to a number of economic groups and to women generally. The bloody shirt could at last be put away: The party of business had created in the larger society the cultural values that were to sustain it on its own terms throughout the twentieth century.

LAWRENCE GOODWYN

See also: William Jennings Bryan; **Map 14:** People's (Populist) Party (1892); National Silver Party; Silver Republicans; Silver Party of Nevada.

Bibliography

Goodwyn, Lawrence. *Democratic Promise: The Populist Movement in America.* New York: Oxford University Press, 1976.

———. *The Populist Moment.* New York: Oxford University Press, 1989.

Nugent, Walter T.K. *The Tolerant Populists.* Chicago: University of Chicago Press, 1963.

Palmer, Bruce. *Men Over Money: The Southern Populist Critique of American Capitalism.* Chapel Hill: University of North Carolina Press, 1980.

★★★★★★★★★★★★★★★★★★★★★★★★★★★★★★★★

PROGRESSIVE (BULL MOOSE) PARTY

1912–1916

Charges of "Fraud!" and "Thief!" filled the air during the "steam-roller" nomination of the presidential incumbent William Howard Taft at the 1912 Republican convention in Chicago. Responding to this "theft," the followers of ex-president Theodore Roosevelt bolted from the GOP to create the Progressive—or Bull Moose—party. As the Progressive party's candidate for president that year, Roosevelt eventually lost to the liberal Democrat Woodrow Wilson, but trounced the conservative Republican Taft and the Socialist candidate, Eugene V. Debs. Faring badly in the 1914 local and congressional elections and fearing even worse in the next race, the Progressive party disbanded in 1916, with most of its leaders following Roosevelt back into the Republican party. While the Progressive party waged the most successful third-party presidential campaign in American history, they never achieved the electoral successes needed to directly implement their program of a "New Nationalism." Nonetheless, the Progressive party changed the terms of liberal debate on the role of the state in an increasingly complex, urban, and industrialized United States.

THEODORE ROOSEVELT

The beginning of the new century was a turbulent time in American politics. "A clear-eyed discontent is abroad in the land," wrote the Progressive Walter Weyl in 1912:

> We are in a period of clamor, of bewilderment, of an almost tremulous unrest. We are hastily revising all our social conceptions. We are hastily testing all our political ideals. . . . Men speak (with an exaggeration which is as symptomatic as are the evils it describes) of sensational inequalities of wealth, insane extravagances, strident ostentations; and in the same breath, of vast boss-ridden cities, with wretched slums peopled by all the world, with pauperism, vice, crime, insanity, and degeneration rampant. . . . According to some critics—among whom are conservative men with a statistical bent—American democracy is in a process of decay.

The rot of the Republican and Democratic parties contributed to this process of decay. Reporting from the Democratic convention in June 1912, an angry William Jennings Bryan wrote that both conventions were "controlled by predatory wealth. . . . Some of their bosses work under the name of Democrats and some bear the Republican label, but they all work for their masters." In a speech at the Progressive convention later that year, Roosevelt made much the same point: "No doubt the bosses of each party would prefer to keep absolute dominion all the time; but as they know that this is impossible, they are quite prepared to keep up their sham warfare with one another so that each set may preserve its dominion over the whole people for about half the time."

There were greater ideological divides within each party than between them, with both Republicans and Democrats split between business-as-usual conservatives and progressive reformers. In the Republican party this division had been bridged by the charismatic figure of Theodore Roosevelt. A war hero for his exploits with the Rough Riders during the war with Spain, a big game hunter whose adventures filled the papers, Roosevelt's tremendous personal popularity gave him the political prestige to "speak softly" and "carry a big stick." Even though Roosevelt became increasingly progressive during his presidency (1901–9), his personal friendships with prominent members of the conservative elite—such as Henry Cabot Lodge and Elihu Root—helped him forge compromises and hold his party together. Roosevelt's image as the great white hunter "Bwana Makuba," the rugged individualist, friend to cowboys and kings, allowed him to promote a progressive program, that, coming from almost any other elite intellectual, would have smacked of an effeminate "parlor" socialism. Roosevelt was, as one of his biographers has pointed out, "the best publicity man progressivism ever had," giving voice—if little action—to the ideas of Republican reformers such as Senators Robert La Follette of Wisconsin, Albert J. Beveridge of Indiana, Jonathan Dolliver and Albert B. Cummins of Iowa, William E. Borah of Idaho, Jonathan Bourne of Oregon, Moses Clapp of Minnesota, and Joseph Bristow of Kansas.

As president, Roosevelt managed to keep the battle within his party down to the level of a family squabble. His successor, William Howard Taft, could not. Presenting himself as a progressive while vice president, Taft drifted steadily to the Right in the oval office, and tensions between the conservatives and progressives escalated. One flash point for hostilities was the well-publicized political scandal known as the Ballinger-Pinchot controversy. Chief Forester Gifford Pinchot was a radical progressive, a staunch conservationist, and Roosevelt's personal friend. While in office, Pinchot offered up evidence that the Taft-appointed, pro-business Secretary of the Interior, Richard A. Ballinger, was almost giving away coal-rich public lands in Alaska to the powerful financial interests of Guggenheim and Morgan. The muckraking press quickly picked up the scandal: "Are the Guggenheims in charge of the Interior Department?" read a headline in *Collier's Weekly*. Taft defended Ballinger and fired the chief forester

for insubordination, demonstrating his loyalty to the pro-business wing of the party and further antagonizing the progressives.

REPUBLICAN DIVISIONS

As early as 1910, the Republican party had been coming apart at the seams. Disturbed by the electoral successes of progressive Republicans in that year's election cycle, conservative Republicans, with the aid of Taft, declared open war, denying the progressives seats on committees and spoils of patronage. The reformers fought back, drafting a manifesto in late December. On January 21, 1911, the insurgents met at the home of Senator Robert La Follette for the first time as the National Progressive Republican League. Ostensibly founded to advance progressive principles, the league's unstated purpose was to defeat Taft for the 1912 Republican nomination.

The principled choice for an insurgent Republican presidential candidate was the champion of progressivism, La Follette; the pragmatic choice was the wildly popular and politically savvy Roosevelt. Many progressives, wary of Roosevelt's uneven commitment to progressivism and his many conservative friends and advisors, preferred the unimpeachable credentials of La Follette. But as admitted even by Amos Pinchot, the ex–chief forester's brother and at the time a La Follette loyalist, the senator from Wisconsin had no chance of winning the nomination. The insurgents had to support the candidacy of Roosevelt; La Follette was too much of a reactionary. But Roosevelt was playing hard to get, ignoring an invitation to join the National Progressive Republican League sent by La Follette and refusing to state his intentions about seeking the nomination. La Follette was convinced that Roosevelt, the wily politician, was just biding his time, waiting for the progressive campaign to gather strength before stepping in and taking La Follette's place. Events would prove him correct.

On February 2, 1912, La Follette's hopes for the Republican nomination were dashed. During a late-night speech before the National Periodical Publishers Association dinner in Philadelphia, an exhausted and emotional La Follette, fortified with a shot of whiskey, humiliated himself with a rambling two-and-a-half-hour jeremiad during which he shuffled the pages of his speech, repeating whole paragraphs, and attacked the evil of commercialism in the modern press before an audience of unamused publishers, editors, and reporters. Some interpreted the confusion of a weary La Follette as a nervous breakdown. All but La Follette himself and a stalwart few of his loyal followers turned their eyes to Roosevelt.

Roosevelt, receiving regular reports while on safari in Africa and on tour in Europe, was certainly not against the idea of his nomination. Not only did he miss the political limelight, but he also felt personally betrayed by the conservative turn of Taft, his former friend and hand-picked successor. Ironically, one of the few progressive actions that Taft did initiate as president, the prosecution of the U.S. Steel Corporation under the Sherman Anti-Trust Act in October 1911, was the last straw. For it was President Roosevelt himself who had approved the corporate giant's acquisition of one of its major competitors, the insolvent Tennessee Coal and Iron Company, to prevent a financial panic in 1907. Roosevelt, while refraining from public criticism of Taft, interpreted the prosecution as a personal attack on his own reputation and began preparing for battle against Taft and the Republican old guard. In January 1912, Roosevelt wrote a letter to the progressive newspaper publisher Frank Munsey, stating that he wished to avoid "any action" that "should make it seem that [he] desire[d] the Presidency for [his] own sake." He wanted "tangible evidence" of "strong popular demand before speaking." The wily Roosevelt, however, quickly engineered "tangible evidence" in the form of a letter written by eight Republican governors asking him to seek the nomination. On Washington's birthday, in a railroad station in Cleveland, Roosevelt threw his "hat in the ring" as a candidate for the Republican nomination. He added "The fight is on and I am stripped to the buff."

Attacked by La Follette and his supporters from the Left, and on the Right by Taft and the old guard, Roosevelt was nevertheless optimistic about his chances. He was supported warily by some business leaders disappointed by Taft's recent anti-trust actions and Republican pragmatists convinced of the president's inevitable defeat. With more enthusiasm, many Republican progressives welcomed the man who they felt could lead them out of the political desert. And, most importantly, Roosevelt was embraced by the American public who genuinely loved the outspoken Rough Rider.

In the popular primaries, Roosevelt demonstrated the support of the people by outpolling—by large margins—both Taft and La Follette. Taft however, possessed something far more valuable at a time when few states held direct primaries: the party machinery. In most states, the delegates were not chosen directly by the voters. In a process that progressives planned to reform, delegates were chosen by party bosses in the proverbial smoke-filled rooms of state party conventions. Most of the Republican party bosses, often federal office-holders themselves, supported their patron William Howard Taft.

1912 CONVENTIONS

The 1912 Republican convention in Chicago was a bloody backroom brawl for control of the GOP and all its power and patronage. The podium at the front of the auditorium was covered in the patriotic trappings of a great convention, but the red, white, and blue bunting hid barbed wire wrapped tightly around the banisters. Even at night the empty podium was guarded by an additional detail of police requested by a Republican National Committee that feared a progressive putsch.

The press reported scenes of barely controlled chaos. The galleries were jammed with citizens who had come to see a good fight: "Spectators laugh uproariously at everything done or said, disturb the debaters and treat the national convention as a huge vaudeville show staged to please them," the *New York Herald* commented. If the scene on the floor was chaotic, the nomination was never really in doubt. Conservative party regulars under the leadership of Elihu Root controlled the National Committee and the convention itself using their powers to seat delegates who supported Taft and to refuse recognition for Roosevelt delegates. While Roosevelt may have played the heartstrings of the Republican rank and file, Taft drove the machine, a steam roller paving over popular will. This was clear to the delegates on the floor, as Kansas editor and Progressive party leader William Allen White reported: "Every time a motion was offered by the Taft people, a thousand toots and imitation whistles of the steam-roller engine pierced the air sharply, to be greeted with laughter that swept the galleries."

Realizing that a Roosevelt victory would mean that the control of the party organization would shift to the progressives, many conservatives, including it seems Taft himself, preferred a Republican loss to a Roosevelt victory. "I quite agree with you that the victory in November is by no means the most important purpose before us," Taft wrote in a letter to the New York Republican party boss William J. Barnes. The goal, he continued, "should be to retain the party and the principles of the party, so as to keep in a condition of activity and discipline a united force to strike when the blow will become effective for the retention of conservative government and conservative institutions."

Once it was clear that the party steam roller would not permit Roosevelt to be nominated, the progressive leaders began to call for a bolt. The blatant corruption of the proceedings offered an opening to the insurgents, and when Taft was renominated as the Republican party candidate for president the moment had arrived. Governor Hiram Johnson of California called for an immediate break with the party: "We are frittering away our time. We are frittering away our opportunity. And, what is worse, we are frittering away Theodore Roosevelt." The Progressive party was born.

"I'm feeling," Roosevelt told a reporter who inquired about his health and spirits, "like a bull moose." Taking on that name for their party, the Progressive party returned to Chicago for their first convention on August 5, 1912. Governor Johnson entered the hall marching at the head of the delegation from California bearing a banner that drew cheers and laughter from the crowd,

> I want to be a Bull Moose,
> And with the Bull Moose stand,
> With Antlers on my forehead,
> And a Big Stick in my hand.

The Progressives' spirits were slightly dampened by the Democratic nomination of the progressive (and therefore competitive) governor of New Jersey, Woodrow Wilson, and the abandonment of a few key progressive Republicans (including the defection of the spurned La Follette to Wilson), but the Bull Moosers still smoldered with the fires of righteousness. When in Chicago, Roosevelt had ended his speech with the words, "We stand at Armageddon, and we battle for the Lord." The faithful had returned ready to do battle for Roosevelt and their new party.

From its opening, the tenor of the convention was that of a religious revival. Scripture was freely quoted by those speaking, and Protestant hymns erupted spontaneously from the crowd. Like many reformers of the day, progressive activists infused their political work with their religious beliefs. Followers of a social gospel that emphasized good works and education over faith and ritual, they were Christian soldiers working to rebuild the ideal of the Christian community they believed was disappearing within America's factories and cities.

Their reverence for Christ was matched only by their love for Roosevelt. At times during the convention it seemed as if the lines between the two were blurred. At one point, the revival hymn "Follow, Follow, We Will Follow Jesus" became "Follow! Follow! We will follow Roosevelt, Anywhere! Everywhere! We will follow on." In the absence of a mature and coherent organization, Roosevelt provided a much-needed focal point for the convention goers. But

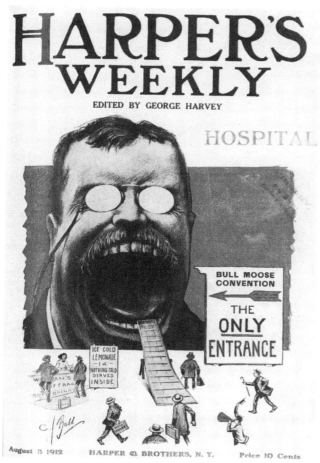

Among the most successful third-party efforts in American history, Theodore Roosevelt's "Bull Moose" Progressive party captured over four million popular and eighty-eight electoral votes in 1912, far outstripping the Republicans but swinging the election to Woodrow Wilson and the Democrats. (*Harper's Weekly,** 1912, Courtesy of the Library of Congress)*

the attention on the man also foreshadowed what was to be a real weakness—an identification of the Progressive party solely with Roosevelt. "An anxious correspondent wishes to know whether the plural for bull moose is 'bull mooses' or 'bull meese,'" the *Chicago Record-American* satirically commented. "There is no plural for bull moose. There is but one bull moose."

On the second day of the convention, after fifty-two minutes of cheering, bandanna waving, and hymn singing, the Bull Moose gave his "confession of faith." Roosevelt's speech laid out the principles of the Progressive party platform and touched upon the burning issue of the day: trusts and monopolies.

Between 1898 and 1904, 234 trusts were incorporated in the United States. Including giants such as U.S. Steel, Standard Oil, Consolidated Tobacco, and Amalgamated Copper, nearly three times as many trusts were formed in those six years than in all the years preceding. The investigations of the Pujo Committee of 1912 revealed that at their peak, Morgan interests held 341 directorships at 112 corporations with a total capitalization of $22,245,000,000—an amount three times greater than the assessed value of all real and personal property in New England. The growing dominance of, and public furor over, these gargantuan trusts and "interlocking directorates" demanded a response from all the parties. Taft and the conservative Republicans, whose base lay in big business, made polite noises but proposed nothing of substance. Reform-minded Democrats such as Wilson, as well as many in the Progressive party, argued the traditional liberal line of a limit to the size of business and increased competition through the more rigorous enforcement of the Sherman Anti-Trust Act and similar monopoly-busting legislation. The Socialists, meanwhile, had little problem with concentrated ownership of industry, they merely felt that it should be the public who owned and benefited from it. Roosevelt charted a tortured passage between the parties, calling for private ownership with public regulation—big business overseen and guided by the federal government. This path was called New Nationalism.

NEW NATIONALISM AND THE PARTY PLATFORM

The chief architect of New Nationalism was Herbert Croly, author of *The Promise of American Life* (1909) and, later, founder of the *New Republic*. Since the founding of the republic, Croly argued, a spirit of competitive individualism had guided the nation. The traditional threat to this sort of individualism had been tyrannical government, therefore, it was believed, the state that governed the best was the one that governed the least. But times had changed, and the freedoms that once ensured liberty from autocratic rule were now permitting the creation of huge organizations that threatened individual liberty as completely as monarchies once had. If personal liberty was to be retained in the coming century, the federal government had to abandon its laissez-faire philosophy and play a pro-active role in the control of corporate trusts, political machines, and labor unions. As historian George Mowry put it, Croly proposed using Hamiltonian means for Jeffersonian ends.

In itself, this was nothing new. For years, reformers had called for the breaking up of gargantuan trusts and the dismantling of monopolies, just as conservatives had used existing anti-trust legislation and federal troops to bust labor unions. Croly, however, challenged traditional liberal thinking by arguing against the dismantling of large organizations. "Huge corporations," he wrote, "have contributed to American economic efficiency. They constitute an important step in the direction of the better organization of industry and commerce. . . . It should be the effort of all civilized societies to substitute cooperative for competitive methods." The problem with large organizations is not that they are large, but that they are "free" to disregard the public interest. What is needed then is an *even larger* organization to oversee and regulate them in the public interest—that is, the national state.

Roosevelt had laid out this new politics of a strong national state in one of his most radical speeches (honoring the abolitionist martyr John Brown) at Osawatomie, Kansas, in 1910. "The American people are right in demanding the New Nationalism," Roosevelt said,

> without which we cannot hope to deal with new problems. The New Nationalism puts the national need before sectional or personal advantage. It is impatient of the utter confusion that results from local legislatures attempting to treat national issues as local issues. It is still more impatient of the impotence which springs from overdivision of governmental powers, the impotence which makes it possible for local selfishness or for legal cunning, hired by wealthy special interests, to bring national activities to a deadlock. This New Nationalism regards the executive power as the steward of public welfare.

In the Osawatomie speech, Roosevelt described the nation as still fighting, at least metaphorically, a civil war. Just as Lincoln had used the federal government and the army to defend the Union from sectional interests of "cotton and slavery," Roosevelt proposed to use the federal government to defend the Union from what he called "the great special business interests."

Roosevelt was a politician, not just a pontificator. His frustrating experiences as governor of New York had shown him that a reform-minded legislature could not battle injustice when a conservative state court could simply overturn progressive legislation as unconstitutional. For example, a workmen's compensation act passed by the New York State Legislature had been overturned by the Court of Appeals because it was an unconstitutional taking of property without due process of law. Thus, his program for a New Nationalism argued for the people's right to amend state constitutions in order to preserve free government. He also called for ballot initiatives and referendums to make representative government more responsive to the will of the people. And, most controversial of all, he demanded "judicial recall"— the popular recall of judicial opinions.

New Nationalism was fiercely attacked by the press and the competing parties. "[A] manifesto for revolution" that "proposes state socialism," the conservative *New York Sun* called Roosevelt's relatively conciliatory "confessions" speech. Roosevelt saw it differently, for in that speech he pointedly argued that "the propositions I make constitute neither anarchy nor socialism, but, on the contrary, a corrective to socialism and an antidote to anarchy." Both the progressive elite and the conservatives shared an upper-middle-class fear of a violent uprising of the lower orders. Roosevelt was as much afraid of revolution as the staunchest reactionary. The difference lay in their perceptions of economic reform. Roosevelt and most progressive intellectuals saw political and economic reform as a solution, a last chance to save their civilization from class conflict, while the reactionaries saw reform as the first step toward revolution and class war. In this sense, both the progressive and the conservative Republicans wished to preserve the foundations of the social order. "I do not know whether we will be able to succeed in the great movement for social and industrial reform," wrote Roosevelt to a friend in 1912, "but I do know that the alternative is a general smashup of our civilization."

The New Nationalist plan for a rationalized "efficient" economy held in private hands, and the "trustworthy" figure of Roosevelt, won the progressive cause the support of a few prominent business leaders. An early convert was George W. Perkins, former partner of the baron of trusts, J.P. Morgan, and board member of International Harvester and U.S. Steel. Perkins became the primary financial supporter of the Progressives and a firm ally of Roosevelt's. Over the strenuous objections of a number of prominent Progressive party leaders, Perkins was also elected national chairman of the party.

PROGRESSIVE PARTY PLATFORM

During the convention, the Progressive party platform was written by a committee and approved by Roosevelt, Perkins, and the other "dough moose," wealthy publisher Frank Munsey. When Perkins succeeded in convincing the others to pull an anti-trust plank from the platform, an acrimonious battle broke out. To the many anti-trusters in the party, removing the plank was confirmation that Perkins wanted to give the party and the country over to the monopolists. It also gave ammunition to the Democratic candidate Woodrow Wilson, who later

said that Roosevelt "got his ideas with regard to the regulation of monopoly from the gentlemen who control the United States Steel Corporation." To the New Nationalists, however, anti-trust legislation was at best romantic, and at worst it stood in the way of economic efficiency and progress. As usual, Roosevelt calmed the warring parties and forced a compromise. The anti-trust plank stayed out, but Roosevelt reaffirmed his support for enforcement of the Sherman Anti-Trust Act in his campaign speeches.

With the exception of the anti-trust quarrel, the adoption of the rest of the Progressive party platform was relatively conflict free. Their platform called for the end of boss rule and political corruption with a demand for direct primaries, popular elections of senators, registration of lobbyists, limits on campaign contributions, the short ballot, and initiative, referendum, and recall. Women's suffrage was claimed as well as the right of the people to vote on legislation found to be unconstitutional by the courts (i.e., judicial recall). The Progressives demanded educational programs to wipe out illiteracy and train youth in useful trades, public research laboratories to encourage more efficient national production, and implementation of methods to assimilate immigrants. They called for the construction of national highways and a parcel post, conservation of public lands and for natural resources to be utilized for the general welfare, the regulation of corporations, and a graduated income tax. They stood for the recognition of unions; a six-day work week and eight-hour day; minimum wage; an end to child and contract prisoner labor; accident, unemployment, and old age insurance; safety and health standards; and a cabinet-level department of labor. All these demands were to be enforced by a federal government that would be able to enact reforms in situations where individual states could not.

The platform of the Progressive party—with the notable exclusion of a call for "free silver"—resembled the demands of the Populist party of 1892. Both movements also arose out of the Midwest. But here the resemblance stopped. The Populists wanted to return the republic to the hands of what they called the "plain people"—the farmers and, to a lesser extent, mechanics who made up their base. The Progressives had a different notion of the proper relationship between the government and the plain people. Yes, the government should be responsive to the needs of the plain people, but these needs should be administered by urban, educated professionals. It was this professional class that filled the convention hall in Chicago that August. "Roosevelt's underdog was not proletarian. He was a middle-class, white-collar dog," William Allen White remembered in his memoirs. "Proletarian and plutocrat were absent," he continued:

> I had seen many a protest convention. As a boy I had watched the Greenbackers. As a young man I had reported many a Populist convention. Those agrarian movements too often appealed to the ne'er-do-wells, the misfits who couldn't make the grade, and neurotics full of hates and ebullient, evanescent enthusiasms. I knew that crowd well. But when the Progressive convention assembled at Chicago I looked down upon it from the reporters' stand and saw that here was another crowd. Here was the successful middle-class country-town citizens, the farmer whose barn was painted, the well paid railroad engineer, and the country editor.

The professionals—who resembled professors and social workers more than White's idyllic country-town farmers—came to Chicago looking for respect. Once the pillars of society, professionals, and the middle class in general, found their status eroding with the maturation of the Industrial Revolution. From above, they were eclipsed by the money power of captains of industry and titans of finance. From below, their position was threatened by the organization of the immigrant working classes into political machines and labor unions. With the Republicans courting business and the Democrats the working classes, professionals were left homeless. In addition, new advances in science, the daily triumphs of the engineer, and the birth of disciplines such as sociology and its practical offspring social work, convinced professionals

that solutions of age-old social problems were near—if only people would listen to their new gospel of planning, efficiency, and reform. The great inventor Thomas Edison was a convert to progressivism. In an interview in the *Progressive Bulletin*, he rationalized his support:

> You see, getting down to the bottom of things, this is a pretty raw, crude civilization of ours—pretty wasteful, pretty cruel, which often comes to the same thing, doesn't it? . . . Our production, our factory laws, our charities, our relations between capital and labor, our distribution—all wrong, out of gear. We've stumbled along for a while, trying to run a new civilization in old ways, and we've got to start to make this world over.

The Progressive platform called for studies, reports, and standards, as well as publicity and education. It was a professional's kind of party.

GENDER AND RACE ISSUES

It was also a women's party. When Roosevelt's name was called at the convention it was seconded by Jane Addams, the famed social worker and the first woman to speak from the platform at a national political convention. "A great party has pledged itself to the protection of children, to the care of the aged, to the relief of overworked girls, to the safeguarding of burdened men," Addams explained to the crowd:

> Committed to these human undertakings, it is inevitable that such a party should appeal to women, should seek to draw upon the great reservoir of their moral energy, so long undesired and unutilized in practical politics—one is the corollary of the other; a program of human welfare, the necessity for women's participation.

"When Miss Addams finished," an observer reported, "she seized a great banner bearing the words 'Votes for Women,'" and marched around the hall "while the whole convention . . . jumped on chairs and tables and cheered her amid a sea of waving flags and bandannas."

Not only did the Progressive party call for women's suffrage, but women played an important part in the party organization. The Progressive convention was the first major party to admit women delegates. Helen J. Scott was named a Progressive elector and became the first woman to cast a vote in the electoral college. Frances A. Kellor later headed the Progressive Service, the largest division of the Progressive party. The party's emphasis on education, social service, and community drew from female strongholds, and for many professional women, the Progressive party provided a relatively open platform for their ideas and ambitions.

For the men—not discounting some genuine desire for gender equality—women's suffrage had other uses as well. The Jacksonian era had enfranchised immigrant, working-class men who swelled the roles of the Democrats and brought "foreign" ideas of socialism and anarchism into the political arena. The entrance of women into the ring, it was thought, might tip the balance back in favor of the "responsible" voters. "We invited women delegates and had plenty of them," William Allen White wrote, describing the convention. "They were our kind too—women doctors, women lawyers, women teachers, college professors, middle-aged leaders of civic movements, or rich young girls who had gone in for settlement work." Progressive women were not just women, they were "our kind" of women: middle-class, educated, and of Northern European stock.

While the party embraced women, the "progressive" convention was a different experience through the eyes of a black man. "I sat in the gallery of the Coliseum at the birth of the new party," W.H. Lewis, an African-American assistant attorney general under Taft, recalled:

I saw men and women work themselves into a frenzy of enthusiasm. . . . I listened to the strains of the music of "John Brown's Body" and the "Battle Hymn of the Republic." My heart sank within me when I thought that there were men

outside clamoring for admission who were denied admission on account of their race and color. Since all men did not include Southern Negroes I could not feel that John Brown's soul was marching there.

While the Progressive parties of the northern states were integrated, with black delegates from thirteen states elected to the national convention, it was a different story in the South. Southern Progressives banned blacks from their state conventions, arguing that the presence of blacks within the Republican party had resulted in the Democratic control of the South. If the Progressive party was to win in Dixie, they reasoned, it had to be a whites-only party. Shut out of their state conventions, black Progressives from Alabama, Mississippi, and Florida elected their own contesting delegations and it was left up to the provisional Progressive National Committee and Roosevelt to decide who to seat at the national convention.

Roosevelt's record on African Americans was mixed. He was a paternalistic racist, believing in the superiority of the white race and of Western civilization. He agreed with Booker T. Washington's gradualist approach to racial uplift. As president, he made few moves to use federal power to stop lynchings or protect the voting rights of blacks. But he also was the first president to invite a prominent black leader—Booker T. Washington—to a White House luncheon, a social event that scandalized the white South. Desperate to win white votes away from the Democrats in the South, Roosevelt and the professional politicians decided that state parties had the right to constitute their parties in the manner they wished. Only on the issue of race did the New Nationalism yield to the defenders of "states' rights." In other words, they recognized the racist, lily-white state party organizations of the South.

The Progressives, so bold in other areas, side-stepped the issue of race in their platform as well. Before the convention, W.E.B. Du Bois had prepared a plank on Negro rights for the Progressive platform. But even a diluted version presented by white allies that gently called for a "gradual recognition by North and South of the principle that the colored man who has the same qualifications that are held to entitle the white man to political representation shall receive the same treatment" was rejected by the platform committee. In the end, the Progressive party platform took no stands on the Negro question. Disgusted "by the extraordinary attitude of the Progressive party under Mr. Roosevelt, which despite its vast enthusiasm of song and tears absolutely refused to even consider" the plank, Du Bois endorsed Wilson.

CANDIDATE ROOSEVELT

On the last day of the convention, all that was left to do was nominate Roosevelt as presidential candidate and the popular governor of California, Hiram Johnson, as his running mate and prepare for the few months of feverish activity until the election. The "Battle Hymn of the Republic" was sung for the umpteenth time.

Competing for the popular anti-trust vote, both Wilson and Roosevelt accused each other of being in the pocket of the trusts, while defining their own parties as the truly "progressive" one. According to Wilson, the Progressive party was not truly progressive because their program of regulating trusts through federal intervention accepted "the established monopolies as inevitable, their control as permanent." The fundamental difference between the Progressive party and the party of Jefferson, was that the Democrats fought to defend liberty by limiting government. As Wilson noted, "The history of liberty is a history of the limitation of government power, not the increase of it." Roosevelt responded to these charges by declaring that "every progressive measure means an extension, instead of a limitation, of government control." He also challenged Wilson to explain how he could support progressive goals and not increase government control: "We propose to limit the hours of working girls to eight hours a day; we propose to limit the hours of workingmen in continuous industries to eight hours a day, and to give them one day's rest a week. Both of these proposals represent an in-

crease in the exercise of governmental power. Does Mr. Wilson mean that he is against this extension?" Roosevelt argued that the "extreme individualism and the minimized government control" of Jeffersonian democracy "are in our day no longer serviceable." It is interesting to note that Wilson—the defender of limited government—during his first term, and especially during World War I, presided over the greatest extension of the powers of the federal government since the Civil War.

Eugene V. Debs, the Socialist party candidate, dismissed all of the other candidates as representing parties of capital. Debs believed that the Progressive party was controlled by the trusts because it did not challenge the ownership of the means of production. In a letter, Debs dismissed Roosevelt—as well as Alexander Hamilton—as a "rank individualist." The Republican party, meanwhile, wasted no time in attacking the Progressives as radical collectivists. The vice-presidential nominee, James S. Sherman, described a Progressive party convention where "red bandannas were preferred to the Stars and Stripes, where the scene was scarlet overmuch, like the flag of anarchy, not red, white, and blue, the symbol of patriotism." Taft, a man who would later—allegedly—shed tears at Roosevelt's grave in 1919, characterized Roosevelt and the Progressive party as dangerous rabble-rousers fanning the flames of class conflict. He stated: "We are living in an age which by exaggeration of the defects of our present condition, by false charges of responsibility for it against individuals and classes, by holding up to the feverish imagination of the less fortunate and the discontented the possibilities of a millennium, a condition of popular unrest has been produced." Taft claimed that the Republican party was defending the Constitution against a radical attack: "I fear the equal opportunity which those seek who proclaim the coming of a so-called equal justice involves a forced division of property, and that means socialism." He appealed to other Americans for a "defense of our constitutional system by those who share the same aversion that we Republicans do to the radical propositions of change in our form of government that are recklessly advanced to satisfy what is supposed to be popular clamor."

Less than a month before the election, on his way to give a speech in Milwaukee, Roosevelt was shot by a deranged New York saloon keeper. The bullet was slowed by the folded fifty-page manuscript of the speech in his breast pocket. Minutes after being hit, the old soldier—knowing that his life was in no danger because he was not spitting up blood—went ahead with his dramatic speech. Displaying a bloody handkerchief he stated, "I have just been shot; but it takes more than that to kill a Bull Moose." He spoke at length until his worried aides convinced him to stop.

1912 ELECTION RESULTS

The Progressives, with a nearly martyred Roosevelt at the helm, were hopeful, but the results of the 1912 election were sobering. Roosevelt was not elected president. Garnering 4,119,207 popular votes, he finished second to Wilson's total of 6,293,152. Roosevelt did, however, roundly beat his Republican rival William Taft, who received 3,486,333 votes. The Socialist candidate, Eugene V. Debs, finished impressively with a tally of 900,369, but also predictably in fourth place. Roosevelt carried Pennsylvania, Michigan, South Dakota, Washington, and eleven of California's thirteen electoral votes for a total of eighty-eight electoral votes. Taft carried only Utah and Vermont for a paltry eight. Wilson won the lion's share of electoral votes with 435. Roosevelt lost, but he lost impressively, receiving 27.4 percent of the tally, the largest proportion ever received by a third-party candidate.

The rest of the Progressive party candidates fared poorly. Even with the popular Beveridge running in Indiana and Oscar S. Straus in New York, no Progressive party candidates for governor won, nor did any Progressives capture senatorial seats. Thirteen Progressive congressmen and 260 state legislators were victorious, but this paled beside the three governors, five

senators, ten representatives, and hundreds of state legislators elected by the Populists of 1892.

Roosevelt and the Progressive party fared well in the cities and did poorly in rural areas. According to historian George Mowry, Roosevelt's "paternalistic philosophy of government," high tariffs, the regulation of monopoly and labor reform, "offered little to the farmer." Party candidates polled strongly among WASP professionals, but despite their progressive stance on labor and the work of such organizations as the National Progressive Italian American League and the American Progressive German Alliance, they did not attract the votes of working-class immigrants. Tied closely to urban machines, the immigrant working class voted Democratic or, if looking for reform, Socialist. The Protestant missionary fever that animated the Progressive faithful also alienated the urban working class, many of whom were Catholic or Jewish. Samuel Gompers and the American Federation of Labor supported Wilson.

Party supporter Walter Lippmann's postmortem of the Progressive failure to attract immigrant labor votes was biting and incisive:

> We rail a good deal against Tammany Hall. Reform tickets make periodic sallies against it, crying economy, efficiency, and a business administration. And we all pretend to be enormously surprised when the "ignorant foreign vote" prefers a corrupt political ring to a party of well-dressed, grammatical, and high-minded gentlemen. . . . [It] does things which have to be done. . . . The cry raised against these men by the average reformer is a piece of cold, unreal, preposterous idealism compared to the solid warm facts of kindness, clothes, food and fun.

Roosevelt also lost big in the "solid South," picking up less than 20 percent of the vote in five key states and less than 10 percent in three others. The Progressive party's cynical decision to support lily-white parties in the South backfired. Black southerners saw the party in the South as a whites-only party, while white southerners rejected the national organization as an integrated party. In brief, the showing of

The enormous appeal of Theodore Roosevelt's 1912 run for president on the "Bull Moose" Progressive party ticket is captured in this panoramic shot of the party's convention in Chicago. *(Courtesy of the Library of Congress)*

the Progressives reflected that of their base—white, well educated, urban, and professional—and this profile did not fit enough Americans to ensure victory.

The New Nationalism, the ideological cement that bound together the planks of the party platform, was a natural fit for the Progressive lawyers, engineers, and social workers who saw themselves as guiding the beneficent and paternalistic state. "We can no longer treat life as something that has trickled down to us," Lippmann wrote in *Drift and Mastery* in 1914. "We have to deal with it deliberately, devise its social organization, alter its tools, formulate its method, educate and control it." These were soothing words for many in the Progressive party, but they rubbed against the grain of many native-born citizens schooled in the

laissez-faire spirit of competitive individualism. They also did not sit well with the urban immigrant working class for whom the state, outside the familiar confines of the ward, was foreign and hostile, and all too given to "educate" and "control." As Croly acknowledged, "The American people could never adopt the accompanying program . . . without unsettling some of their most settled habits and transforming many of their most cherished ideas."

Woodrow Wilson, who had the good sense to later co-opt much of the Progressives' New Nationalism ideas about a pro-active and regulatory state, also had the good sense to campaign under the more traditional "New Freedom" banner. The Progressive positions on the tariff and trusts were too complex. The Democrats were simply and clearly anti-trust and anti-tariff, the Republicans for, but Roosevelt was proposing a "non-partisan scientific tariff commission" of experts to determine rationally the question of tariffs and a federal industrial commission to regulate the trusts because trusts were inevitable—if not always bad. Neither clearly for nor against, the complexity of Progressive policy was confusing and provided a broad target for opponents to shoot at.

Roosevelt's appeal to the public was himself, not his message or his party. His personal biography of rugged individualism balanced his message of the strong state and the benefit of large organizations. His much-publicized machismo assuaged the voters' fears of a feminized social worker state. But his celebrity status was also the party's weakness. The American people loved Teddy and would vote for him, but this affection did not translate into votes for his party and its policies.

What hindered the Progressives most, however, was their lack of party machinery. Roosevelt and the professional politicians of the party knew this and spent the months between the convention and the election feverishly building an organization and convincing state Republican machines to rally behind them. Though working with the machine bosses repulsed many of the party purists, from a pragmatic point of view it was time well spent; in those locales where the party had the support of the machine they fared well. But with less than half a year to organize, they were simply unable to assemble an electoral apparatus equal to that of the Democrats or Republicans.

The defeats of 1912, however, did not cool the fire of the Progressive party. With only four months to organize, they had put up an impressive showing. They had forced the Democrats to nominate a reformer and thrust the issues of women's suffrage, direct primaries, labor reforms, and the role of the federal government in managing the excesses of capitalism onto the national political stage. Most importantly they had beaten the Republicans. Few of the more experienced Progressive leaders thought they had a chance of actually winning in 1912, particularly after the nomination

of Woodrow Wilson. According to Progressive leader O.K. Davis, from the "moment" Wilson was nominated, headquarters knew that there was no "practical possibility" of electoral victory. In fact, Roosevelt himself did not believe it. The party leaders did believe, however, that they would deal the Republican party a blow so fatal that, as Herbert Knox Smith wrote, "There will remain by 1914 only two great national parties, Progressives and Democrats."

1912 ELECTION AFTERMATH

Over the next two years the Progressive party refashioned itself into a rational organization in place of the ad hoc assemblage of the 1912 election. The party was divided into four divisions: Finance, Organization, Publicity, and Progressive Service. The first three of these were run by professional politicians and were charged with politics-as-usual: raising money, assembling a machine, and getting word out about the party and its candidates. The Progressive Service, the largest of all the divisions, was an innovation, well suited to the proclivities of the Progressive troops. In addition to researching and writing legislation, the Progressive Service carried out the social education component of the party. From 1912–13 it produced twenty books, distributed 30,000 pieces of literature (ranging from the words of Roosevelt to informative pamphlets on sickness insurance), wrote six complete speeches (each with fifty accompanying stereopticon slides), and furnished countless speakers for local groups and meetings. Headed by author and social worker Frances A. Kellor, the Progressive Service was, in her own words "a party laboratory, manned by experts." In modern parlance, it was a think tank.

During this interim period, George Perkins continued to come under fire by the Progressive's left wing as a "monopolist" whose position as national chairman undermined the party's progressive image. Amos Pinchot, aligned with the social educators and more populist politicians, staged a coup to replace Perkins as chairman and backed off only after Roosevelt asserted that "when they read Perkins out they will have to read me out too." Labeling the idealistic radical Progressives the "lunatic fringe," Roosevelt complained in a letter to his son Quentin in 1913: "I am having my usual difficulties with the Progressive party, whose members sometime drive me mad. I have to remember, in order to keep myself fairly good tempered, that even though the wild-asses of the desert are mainly in our ranks, our opponents have a fairly exclusive monopoly on swine." In response to this attempted putsch by the idealists, Perkins and the professional politicians counter-attacked, calling the social reformers impractical and taking funds away from their Progressive Service, arguing that it was wasting valuable money needed for electing Progressive candidates. Looking back with the luxury of hindsight, it may have been the idealists, sowing ideological seeds of social reform in the hopes of future fruit, whose efforts were truly more pragmatic. The election was a disaster.

"The Progressive party has become a cropper [i.e., fails]," Roosevelt complained after the 1914 elections. In nearly every state its candidates were defeated. In most states Progressive party candidates came in third, behind Republicans and Democrats, and in a handful they ran fourth behind the Socialists. Worse, the big winners were the Republicans. They captured governorships in the key states of New York and Ohio and reduced the Democratic margin in the House from 147 to 129. Many of the old guard Republicans who had earlier been routed by reformers regained their seats. "As for the Republican party," Roosevelt wrote to White, "at the moment the dog has returned to its vomit." The election returns of 1914 dashed any Progressive hopes that the Republican party would wither away.

The national Progressive party conference following the 1914 election was a dispirited affair, with Roosevelt not even attending. "We went through all the motions," White later re-

ported to Roosevelt, "all the wonted motions of real crusading soldiers—but the whole thing was automatic. The spiritual well from which we dipped was physically low." Without victories, the moral fire of the social reformers banked and the professional politicians, looking after their future, began excusing themselves from the drawing room. Roosevelt still spoke out for progressive issues like women's suffrage and national flood control programs, but another issue captured his attention: national preparedness. Roosevelt's old militaristic obsession was reborn and he set his sights on new targets: the aggression of Germany and the "yellowness" [cowardice] of Wilson.

Roosevelt and many Progressives considered military readiness as a logical extension of a strong state and sense of national purpose, part of what Herbert Croly's *New Republic* called "Newer Nationalism." Progressives such as Jane Addams, however, saw the buildup of armaments and calls for mandatory service as the antithesis to the ideals of social justice and voluntary good citizenship that had defined the Progressive party. Militarism fractured an already weak Progressive party. "The worst crowd we have to deal with," Roosevelt wrote to Henry Cabot Lodge in 1916, "is the progressive senators and their followers." As his choice of correspondent demonstrates, Roosevelt's patriotism also moved him back into the company of his old conservative Republican friends. The issue of militarism—as well as the drubbing that the Progressive party received in the 1914 election—shifted the entire party in the direction of the conservative Republican party. The platform that came out of the 1916 Progressive party convention was far from the righteous reforming document of 1912. Indiana Progressive Albert Beveridge asked, "What has become of the wonderful platform, especially the economic features? Has it all been abandoned for what you say is now 'Americanism, preparedness, and a protective tariff?'" The few social reforms mentioned were reduced to a paragraph, with the rest of the platform given over to calls for national defense, patriotism, and the old Republican bugbear, the high tariff.

The similarity between the Progressive and Republican party platforms was not coincidental. Roosevelt and other party pragmatists, such as Frank Munsey, had been courting the Republicans for a proposed "amalgamation." Holding their 1916 nominating convention at the same time as the Republicans, Progressive leaders hinted that they would not be opposed if the Republicans and they selected the same standard-bearer—that is, Roosevelt. Nominating the progressive Supreme Court Justice Charles E. Hughes for president, the Republicans left the Progressives standing at the altar. Against his wishes, the Progressive party nominated Roosevelt anyway. Roosevelt declined, endorsed Hughes, and rejoined the Republicans. The Bull Moose had bolted and the Progressive party was finished. As Amos Pinchot remembered,

> The convention broke up in a sullen mood; a crowd without a leader, it filed slowly out of the Auditorium. Among those who had joined the movement for selfish interest, there was probably a deep feeling of disappointment. But for the many men and women who had followed Roosevelt for four years with great hopes and unselfish motives, there was the added grief of disillusionment.

A small group of Progressive party anti-fusionists immediately called for a new National Progressive Convention. In April 1917, they met in St. Louis, decided to join with the Prohibition party, and then promptly disappeared (though a later incarnation of the group joined with Robert La Follette's Progressive party in 1924). Other Progressive leaders—mainly those who had defected from the Democratic party in 1912—backed Woodrow Wilson, and the progressive vote gave Wilson the victory he needed in key states such as California. But most of the Progressive party troops followed Roosevelt back into the Republican party. After his presidential defeat in 1916, Roosevelt, the indefatigable politician, was making plans for his campaign to return to the White House as a progressive Republican president in 1920 when he died in 1919.

FALL OF BULL MOOSE PARTY

The demise of the Bull Moose party can be attributed to a variety of factors: The passage of progressive legislation during the first Wilson administration accomplished a number of progressive reforms and made a Progressive party seem less essential. In addition, World War I brought on an upswing in the economy, dampening enthusiasm for reform and quieting labor unrest. The American public grew tired of the sensationalism of the muckrakers and the constant harping of the reformers and shifted its attention to the troubles brewing in Europe. The conservative dominance of the print media was also an obstacle. According to Roosevelt, "One of our great troubles is that the representatives of privilege in finance and politics control most of the newspapers, so that the ordinary man finds the channels of information choked. I do not so much mind the editorial columns being against us; but it is a matter for real regret that the news columns are closed to us."

Internally, the lack of an extensive party organization at the local, state, and national levels, and the lack of money and patronage to build and reward such an organization was crucial. Historian John Gable believes that the Progressive campaign showed that it was impossible to run a successful, national third-party campaign without the money of wealthy backers. The cost of a modern media campaign could not be sustained by small individual donations alone. Most of the Progressive party money came either from the Roosevelt family, George Perkins, or Frank Munsey. Less than a third of the almost $600,000 spent by the Progressive National Committee came from small donations.

Dissension within the progressive movement also hurt. La Follette's bitter refusal to back Roosevelt's candidacy, the conflict over Perkins's leadership of the party, and the tension between the reformers and educators and the hard-nosed politicians of the party crippled the fledgling institution. The inability of progressives, both Republican and Democrat, to work across traditional party lines to further the progressive cause was another factor. Progressive Democrats saw the split in the GOP as a way of beating the Republicans instead of an opportunity for uniting progressives across party lines.

Finally, the radical mix of moral, economic, and political planks that made up the Progressive platform appealed only to a limited middle-class and elite public. To paraphrase William Allen White, the underdog to which the Progressive party appealed was a middle-class, white-collar dog. Proletarian and plutocrat were absent.

The most politically successful third party in United States history, the Bull Moose party never attained the political power necessary to implement their New Nationalism agenda. But the questions they raised and the ideas they put forth had a powerful impact. Ironically, it was the Democratic party that Roosevelt so vehemently detested that would follow the trail of the Bull Moose. Woodrow Wilson acted on many of the Progressive party's planks, creating the Federal Trade Commission, the Federal Reserve Act, and a Tariff Act. And it was not a large leap (navigated by several prominent progressives including Harold Ickes and Frank Knox) from Roosevelt's "square deal" New Nationalism to his cousin Franklin Delano Roosevelt's New Deal. The Progressive party's lasting significance was to signal the end of the nineteenth-century liberal identification with competitive individualism and bring forth the twentieth-century liberalism of the welfare state.

STEPHEN R. DUNCOMBE AND ANDREW MATTSON

See also: Jane Addams; Eugene Victor Debs; Hiram Warren Johnson; Robert M. La Follette, Sr.; **Map 17:** Progressive ("Bull Moose") Party (1912); Theodore Roosevelt.

Bibliography

Bowers, Claude G. *Beveridge and the Progressive Era.* New York: Literary Guild, 1932.

Broderick, Francis L. "Progressivism at Risk." In *Contributions in American History,* ed. Jon L. Wakelyn, No. 134. New York: Greenwood Press, 1989.

Bryan, William Jennings. *A Tale of Two Conventions.* New York: Funk and Wagnalls, 1912.

Croly, Herbert. *The Promise of American Life.* Boston: Northeastern Press, 1909.

Davis, Oskar K. *Released for Publication.* Boston: Houghton and Mifflin, 1925.

Debs, Eugene V. *The Letter of Eugene V. Debs,* ed. J. Robert Constantine. Urbana: University of Illinois Press, 1995.

Du Bois, W.E.B. *Writings by W.E.B. Du Bois in Periodicals Edited by Others,* Vol. 2, ed. Herbert Aptheker. Millwood, NY: Kraus-Thomson, 1986.

Duncan-Clark, Samuel J. *The Progressive Movement: Its Principles and Programme.* Boston: Small, Maynard, 1913.

Gable, John A. *The Bull Moose Years: Theodore Roosevelt and the Progressive Party.* Port Washington, NY: Kennikat Press, 1978.

Hofstadter, Richard. *The Age of Reform: From Bryan to F.D.R.* New York: Alfred A. Knopf, 1955.

Lewis, W.H. "Warning Against Theodore Roosevelt." 1912. Reprinted in *The Negro American,* ed. Leslie H. Fishel, Jr., and Benjamin Quarles. Glenview, IL: Scott Foresman, 1967.

Lippmann, Walter. *Drift and Mastery: An Attempt to Diagnose the Current Unrest.* Madison: University of Wisconsin Press, 1914.

———. *A Preface to Politics.* New York: Mitchell Kennerly, 1914.

Mowbray, Jay H. *Roosevelt: the People's Champion.* New York: Progressive National Service, 1912.

Mowry, George E. *Theodore Roosevelt and the Progressive Era.* Madison: University of Wisconsin Press, 1946.

Pinchot, Amos. *History of the Progressive Party, 1912–1916.* Westport, CT: Greenwood, 1978.

Roosevelt, Theodore. *New Nationalism.* New York: Outlook, 1910.

———. *Progressive Principles.* New York: Progressive National Service, 1913.

Schlesinger, Arthur M., Jr. *History of American Presidential Elections,* Vol. 3. New York: Chelsea House, 1971.

Sullivan, Mark. *Our Times,* Vol. 4. New York: Charles Scribner's Sons, 1932.

Weyl, Walter. *The New Democracy.* New York: Macmillan, 1912.

White, William Allen. *The Autobiography of William White.* New York: Macmillan, 1946.

Wilson, Woodrow. *Crossroads of Freedom,* ed. John Wells Davidson. New Haven: Yale University Press, 1956.

PROGRESSIVE LABOR PARTY

1960s–

The Progressive Labor party (PLP) was founded in the mid-1960s by members of the Students for a Democratic Society (SDS), as a pro-Maoist subgroup attempting to bridge the political gap between students and workers. Indeed, disputes between the leaders of the PLP and other members of the SDS—including the direct-action Weathermen—precipitated the breakup of the SDS at its national convention in June 1969.

The PLP was part of a broader trend within the New Left politics of the 1960s known as anti-revisionism. The term was borrowed from Chinese communists, who argued that the post-Stalinist Soviet leadership had deviated from and revised the true communist principles of Karl Marx and Vladimir Lenin. And because much of the 1930s-era American Left had established such tight allegiance with Moscow, they too were labeled revisionists.

At the same time, many within the PLP and other anti-revisionists groups such as the Revolutionary Communist party (RCP) were strong believers in Maoism. This strain of communism included several key components. First, it propounded the Leninist idea of the vanguard party, in which intellectuals and other leaders who had absorbed the principles of Marxism would lead the way for the masses of workers. In addition, anti-revisionists strongly believed in the idea of intellectuals reaching out and organizing workers, as had been the case in revolutionary China.

In contrast to the secretive manipulation of the old Left—which tried to infiltrate existing organizations at the top and then turn them to-

The Progressive Labor party—an offshoot of the Students for Democratic Society—was an attempt to create links between students and workers. In this 1971 flyer, the PLP ridicules conservative AFL-CIO president George Meany as out of touch with working-class issues. *(Courtesy of the Gary Yanker collection, Library of Congress)*

ward communism—the anti-revisionists believed in direct confrontation with capitalism and the overcoming of worker apathy and ignorance through the will power of and example set by the vanguard party members. Many former student radicals and SDS members were drawn to the PLP and anti-revisionist movement by the excitement of the third-world revolutions of the period, which ranged from Castro's rise to power in Cuba to the war in Vietnam. Thus, the PLP was known for its vociferous and militant support for striking workers; many members of the party also became involved in radical community politics and the welfare rights movement.

Ultimately, the PLP provided the critical institutional link between the SDS and other New Left groups of the 1960s and the overtly Maoist radicals of the 1970s, including the RCP. By the early 1970s, the PLP had declined with most of its members either gravitating to other radical parties such as the RCP or else leaving revolutionary politics and focusing on community activism or the social welfare rights movement.

JAMES CIMENT

See also: Revolutionary Communist Party; Socialist Workers Party; Workers World Party.

Bibliography

Costello, Paul. "A Critical History of the New Communist Movement, 1969–1979." *Theoretical Review* 13 (November–December 1979).

Ignatiev, Noel. "Anti-Revisionism." *Encyclopedia of the American Left,* ed. Mary Jo Buhle et al. Urbana: University of Illinois Press, 1992.

U.S. News & World Report. *Communism and the New Left.* London: Collier/Macmillan Books, 1970.

PROGRESSIVE MOVEMENT OF 1924

*I*n the summer of 1924, the Republican and Democratic parties nominated Calvin Coolidge and John W. Davis, respectively, for president. They were perhaps the most conservative pair of presidential candidates in the twentieth century. Partly in response to this conservative drift, a coalition of activists ran 69-year-old Senator Robert Marion La Follette of Wisconsin for president on the Progressive party ballot. On November 4, La Follette carried Wisconsin, ran second in eleven other states, and won nearly five million votes, one-sixth of the total. This was the third highest percentage a challenger to the major parties would receive in the twentieth century.

That a candidate running with the active support of the Socialist party at a time when redbaiting was in fashion, and against a popular incumbent in the seemingly prosperous 1920s, would carry as many votes as La Follette did is a tribute to the persistent appeal of progressive ideas, to La Follette's reputation for integrity, and to the coalition of liberals and radicals that campaigned for him. Nevertheless, historians have tended to view the Progressive party campaign of 1924 as a series of mishaps and lost opportunities. In the long run, however, the campaign not only scored an impressive total of popular votes, but was also a bridge for numerous voters who had been Republicans but would enroll in the New Deal coalition of the 1930s. In addition, the 1924 progressives would provide the New Deal with personnel and policies.

PROGRESSIVISM REINVENTED

As a movement, progressivism had taken many forms and been represented in both major parties in the first two decades of the century. To the Republican La Follette, it meant cleaning up politics, instituting political reforms to replace the power of special interests with majority rule, and using government to improve the lives of the common people. Its political apogee had been the election of 1912, when all four leading presidential nominees could claim at least part of the progressive heritage. That year, Theodore Roosevelt launched his Progressive party and came in second.

When Roosevelt dropped out of the race in 1916, he left his party high and dry, and its national treasurer, J.A.H. Hopkins, a wealthy New Jerseyan, soon established what became the Committee of Forty-Eight. This committee possessed the legal title to the Progressive label, and in a conference in 1919 in St. Louis, it laid plans to launch a new party. In 1920, it met again in Chicago and passed a platform calling for greater economic competition.

By the early 1920s, three other groups were searching for a new political home. The Socialist party, which had reached its zenith in 1912, had been battered by its opposition to World War I, the imprisonment of Eugene V. Debs and other leaders, and the red scare of the post-war period. The labor movement was damaged by the post-war depression, redbaiting, and anti-union legislation. Relatively strong supporters among labor were the Railroad Brotherhoods, but even they were on the defensive after their strike was broken in September 1922. Finally, agrarians were especially hard hit by the depression and the defeat of the McNary-Haugen farmers' aid bill by the House of Representatives in 1924. In the upper Midwest, the Nonpartisan League (NPL) had been running candidates since 1915, but its financial dependency on struggling farmers limited its effectiveness after the war. In 1920, the Farmer-Labor party convention had been taken over by radicals, which deprived moderate agrarians of a political vehicle.

On February 21, 1922, at the invitation of the Railroad Brotherhoods, 300 delegates met in Chicago to form the Conference for Progressive Political Action (CPPA). These delegates represented fifty international unions, the Committee of Forty-Eight, Socialists, moderate Farmer-Laborites, the NPL, and numerous civic and religious groups. The conference established a fifteen-member executive committee under the chairmanship of William H. Johnston, head of the machinists' union, and adopted a platform that attacked the "invisible government of plutocracy and privileges." They decided only to endorse other parties' candidates for the 1922 elections and wait until after those elections to decide where to go from there.

THE FUTURE LOOKS PROMISING

The 1922 elections turned out to be very good for progressives, as more than 100 of the CPPA endorsees, including La Follette, won. On December 2, the Wisconsin senator hosted an organizing dinner for the group in Washington for numerous members of Congress, labor leaders, and independent intellectuals and activists. They resolved to work to unite progressives and adopted several policy proposals. Nine days later, the CPPA held a second convention in Cleveland. In response to the Farmer-Labor experience, delegates voted almost unanimously to exclude Workers Party (Communist) members. Strategic issues, however, divided the

delegates, with Socialists and most leftists and intellectuals wanting to organize a new party immediately, with a specific program, while labor and farm organizations counseled caution and a brief platform. After a long debate, caution won out, on a vote of 64 to 52, and the delegates adopted a brief, six-point program. Despite this disappointment, the Socialist executive committee voted to affiliate with the CPPA the following May.

This strategic debate would continue through the life of the movement and reflected fundamental strains in the coalition. Most Socialists and intellectuals had a broad vision of social change and saw a new party as the way to achieve it. Most union and farm leaders had shorter-term economic goals and therefore wished to preserve their ties with allies in the major parties. Indeed, the Railroad Brotherhoods thought they had a candidate for 1924 in William G. McAdoo, a Democrat who as railroad administrator during the war had compiled a pro-labor record. However, in early 1924 it was revealed that McAdoo had received thousands of dollars from Edward L. Doheny, a wealthy oilman who had been implicated in the Teapot Dome scandal. McAdoo's chances for the Democratic nomination dimmed.

Otherwise, progressive hopes rose all through 1923 and early 1924. Among the encouraging developments were the successes of mass left-wing parties in Britain and Canada and the Teapot Dome scandal, which had damaged both major parties in the United States. State CPPA organizations grew, and La Follette's tour of Europe in late 1923 bolstered his foreign policy credentials. On February 11, 1924, more than thirty state CPPA organizations convened in St. Louis and decided to hold a nominating convention in Cleveland in July. By then, La Follette had decided to run, and in May he released a letter in which he repudiated Communist support. No doubt a shrewd move politically, the letter also reflected La Follette's genuine aversion to Communist opposition to civil liberties and majority rule. Unlike many anti-Communists of his and later days, however, the Wisconsin senator was careful to defend "their right, under the Constitution, to submit their issues to the people." That spring, La Follette received thousands of votes in Republican presidential primaries, despite suffering from pulmonary illness.

CREATING A CAMPAIGN

On July 4, 1924, about 1,000 people met in Cleveland to select a presidential nominee and platform. The usual labor, agrarian, and ideological groups were represented, and so were many college students. Very few women or African Americans attended, although a representative of the National Association for the Advancement of Colored People read a message to the delegates. As in the earlier Cleveland meeting, Communists were excluded. The major power blocs at the convention were the Railroad Brotherhoods, the Socialists, the La Follette supporters from Wisconsin, and the NPL forces from the upper Midwest. Again the question whether to establish a party arose, and again the answer was not yet. On the other hand, consensus did arise over the nominee once the party was established. Only La Follette could unite these disparate groups, and through his son, Bob Jr., the senator communicated that he did not wish to run on a full slate of candidates and jeopardize the re-election prospects of his congressional allies in the major parties. CPPA chair Johnston had earlier wired La Follette an invitation to run, and La Follette's telegram of acceptance arrived the day before he was formally nominated by acclamation. The delegates authorized the CPPA national committee to select a vice-presidential candidate after the convention.

The platform that the delegates adopted by voice vote began with the blunt statement, "The great issue before the American people today is the control of government and industry by private monopoly." After some discussion of this issue and the farm crisis, the platform presented a twelve-point "covenant with the people" and a fourteen-point "program of public service." Among the more controversial provisions were congressional power to override Supreme Court

decisions that declared federal laws unconstitutional, the election of federal judges for fixed terms, public ownership of railroads, water power, a steeply progressive tax code, the abolition of the use of injunctions in labor disputes, aid to farmers and veterans, a child labor amendment and federal protection of children, direct nomination and election of the president, the use of initiatives and referenda at the federal level, and referenda to be used in deciding whether to go to war. Also of note is what was omitted from the platform, such controversial issues, including advocacy of diplomatic recognition of the Soviet Union, denunciation of the Ku Klux Klan, and any reference to prohibition or the League of Nations. On the whole, the platform reflected the diverse interests of the political forces that wrote it, although the emphasis on monopoly was hardly the way that Socialists or the labor movement would have written the document.

Within a week of the Cleveland convention, the Democrats nominated Wall Street lawyer John W. Davis on the 103rd ballot. On July 15, progressive Democratic Senator Burton K. Wheeler of Montana announced that he could not support Davis. Four days later, Wheeler was designated the party's vice-presidential candidate. There is some speculation that La Follette had been turned down by Supreme Court Justice Louis D. Brandeis to be his running mate. Wheeler, an energetic 42-year-old freshman senator who had been a key investigator of the Teapot Dome scandal, balanced the ticket along the lines of age, party, and geography. Wheeler proved a vigorous campaigner and an asset to the ticket.

Now the Progressive party had to face the daunting task of capturing votes from the major parties. This is never easy in American politics, and it was especially difficult in the 1920s. Since the realignment of the 1890s, most of the North was firmly Republican territory, while the Democrats controlled the Solid South. The result was that all of the presidential elections since 1896 (except that of 1916) had been won with at least 60 percent of the electoral vote, usually by the Republican party. Except for the period between 1910 and 1918, the GOP had ruled Con-

Progressive party presidential candidate Robert La Follette, Sr., (on steps, right) speaks to some newly enfranchised women voters outside his home in Washington, D.C., in August 1924. (*Underwood and Underwood, August 13, 1924, courtesy of the Library of Congress*)

gress as well. Moreover, most sections of the country were governed by the dominant party's wealthy elites, and by the 1920s corporate policies, personified by Secretary of the Treasury Andrew Mellon, prevailed. Warren G. Harding's call for "normalcy" meant that progressivism was in retreat, and so the timing was inauspicious for the La Follette-Wheeler campaign of 1924.

Even more troubling were matters of organization, finances, and the usual electoral barriers to new political movements. A twelve-member Joint Executive Committee, chaired by Republican U.S. Representative John M. Nelson, was established to guide the progressives' campaign. Headquarters were set up in Chicago

and Washington to run the western and eastern campaigns, respectively. Hastily assembled, managed by largely inexperienced activists, and lacking coordination between the two headquarters, the campaign had more than its share of organizational problems. Only in Wisconsin and where the NPL was active was the campaign well managed. In addition, the frictions among elements of the coalition that had always existed were exacerbated during the stresses of the fall drive. Finally, the lack of other candidates on the ticket deprived La Follette and Wheeler of an infrastructure of local candidates who could help with the campaign. One consequence was that few prominent politicians endorsed the ticket. For example,

Idaho's Senator William E. Borah backed Coolidge, and Nebraska's Senator George W. Norris stayed neutral.

Not surprisingly, this insurgent campaign with an anti-monopoly theme had a great deal of trouble raising money from wealthy people. According to later congressional findings, in the 1924 presidential campaign the progressives spent about $222,000, compared with $900,000 for the Democrats and $4.4 million for the Republicans. Labor donated probably no more than $50,000, while beleaguered farmers could give little. The campaign had to resort to such devices as charging admission to rallies, passing the plate there, and selling campaign buttons and other paraphernalia. Nearly one-fourth of the budget came from ten people who each gave at least $1,000. Three were from Wisconsin, two from elsewhere in the Midwest, three from the Northeast, and two from the District of Columbia. Heading the list of supporters was the national treasurer, William T. Rawleigh, an Illinois patent-medicine mogul, who gave $28,000. Many years later, vice-presidential candidate Wheeler was to claim that the source of an anonymous $1,000 contribution was Joseph P. Kennedy.

The final major problem was getting on the ballot. This task used up much of the campaign's scarce resources. The Socialists, who endorsed La Follette promptly after the Cleveland convention, were on the ballot in all but four states, but many voters resisted the label. The progressives tried to put La Follette on the ballot under other designations, and in different states he appeared under different labels. In Louisiana, whose laws required that only independent voters sign La Follette's petitions, he was thrown off the ballot because many signers were Democrats. The ticket was on the ballot in only nineteen counties in North Carolina; deadlines were missed in Florida and West Virginia; and no La Follette workers were allowed to watch the polls in Ohio. However, few expected La Follette to win any of those states. Far more damaging was the situation in California, a major progressive state that Roosevelt had carried in 1912. Its laws did not permit petitioning one's way onto the ballot, and so La Follette appeared only on the Socialist line, which probably cost him votes.

Undeterred by these disadvantages, La Follette began to make waves in early August, when he denounced the Ku Klux Klan. His courage embarrassed Democratic nominee Davis and Republican vice-presidential nominee Charles G. Dawes, a Chicago lawyer and financier, into following suit. On Labor Day, La Follette delivered what may have been the first nationally broadcast radio speech.

However, he was not an effective user of the new medium, the gimmick was costly, and his natural constituents were too poor to own sets. On September 18, 14,000 people heard him speak at Madison Square Garden. However, financial constraints and rumors of health problems deferred a speaking tour until October 6. The tour lasted through October, including three days in the Northeast, fourteen in the Midwest, and eight back east. La Follette delivered no fewer than twenty major speeches in thirteen states. His tour of the eastern regions of the country was intended to demonstrate that La Follette intended to win the race for the presidency, but the time might have been more wisely spent in the midwestern heartland of progressivism.

Aside from being anathema to conservatives, La Follette may have alienated some other segments of public opinion. The Klan of course vehemently attacked him, but La Follette made little effort to woo black voters to compensate for Klan opposition. On prohibition, the platform was noncommittal, but La Follette's personal opposition to the Noble Experiment (a common term for prohibition) may have cost him votes. His opposition to entry into the world war helped him with German Americans, but probably hurt him in the Northeast, where international sentiment was widespread. The platform advocated Irish independence, but some Catholics feared the progressives' call for limits on the courts. In a number of states, Fundamentalist Protestants controlled the legislature and many Catholics saw the courts as a bulwark against legislative actions hostile to Catholics.

As the campaign wore on, the progressives became the target of attacks by the major parties. This may have been in part due to polls taken in mid-October by the Literary Digest and the Hearst papers, showing La Follette running second in the race. It also may have reflected the Republicans' concerns about losing part of their western base. Democratic nominee Davis, a pillar of the bar, defended courts against the progressives' attacks on the courts. As for Coolidge, he adopted a strategy of leaving the campaigning to running mate Dawes. (Wheeler had fun debating an empty chair, pretending that Coolidge was occupying it.) One of Dawes's favorite tactics against the progressives was redbaiting: "Where do you stand, with the President on the Constitution with the flag, or on the sinking sands of socialism?" Republicans also hinted that Soviet money was pouring into the progressive coffers, despite American Communists' bitter attacks on La Follette. Other Republican themes included La Follette's opposition to war in 1917 and his threats to the judiciary and to continued prosperity.

The most striking scare tactic was started by the *Saturday Evening Post* and picked up by Republicans. In an attempt to broaden Davis's base, the Democrats had selected as his running mate William Jennings Bryan's younger brother Charles, the governor of Nebraska. Opponents accused La Follette of running as a spoiler, who would deadlock the electoral college. If a deadlock occurred, and if the House of Representatives could not decide on a new president before Inauguration Day, it was charged, the new vice president could take over. In that case the Senate, which elects vice presidents when the electoral college is deadlocked, might select Democratic vice-presidential nominee Bryan. The prospect of poorly regarded Charles Bryan becoming president out of such a deadlock was presented as a reason to resist La Follette.

To make matters worse, some of the progressives' constituent groups provided little help or backed the opposition. Although the dying Samuel Gompers gave his reluctant consent, the executive committee of the American Federation of Labor broke with its longstanding policy of neutrality in presidential contests and endorsed La Follette. Many unions ended up withholding their backing, especially as it be-

came clear that the progressives would not come close to winning. The pressmen's union endorsed Democrat Davis, and the carpenters' union and mine workers' union backed Coolidge. Even worse, five days before the election, the Central Labor Council in New York City switched its endorsement from La Follette to Davis. Even the unions that remained supportive of La Follette provided little financial aid.

Farmers, too, went only part of the way for the ticket. A failure of the Canadian wheat crop temporarily drove up farm prices in the United States, and many farmers lost their desire for change. Wealthier farmers joined their urban counterparts in fearing the more radical aspects of the La Follette program, especially regarding the courts. La Follette's Socialist allies, the fear of a Charles Bryan presidency, and the decline of the NPL also hurt the progressives with agrarians.

Despite all these problems, La Follette and Wheeler claimed an illustrious group of Americans as supporters. They included Senators Smith Brookhart of Iowa and Hiram Johnson of California; Representative Fiorello La Guardia of New York; leading attorneys Louis Brandeis and Felix Frankfurter; prominent African Americans W.E.B. Du Bois and James Weldon Johnson; liberal intellectuals Herbert Croly and John Dewey; social reformers Jane Addams and Oswald Garrison Villard; scholars Thorstein Veblen and Franz Boas; social critics Helen Keller and Theodore Dreiser; activists Margaret Sanger and Norman Thomas; and political retainers Arthur Garfield Hays and Harold Ickes.

While most of the press was staunchly Republican, La Follette received the endorsements of the *Nation* and the *New Republic* magazines and Scripps newspapers. Local newspaper support in Cleveland, Toledo, and Sacramento helped his cause in those cities.

These distinguished Americans and publications were not alone in supporting La Follette. On election day, the Wisconsin senator won 4,814,050 votes, or 16.6 percent of the total. Republican Coolidge received a solid majority of 54.1 percent, and Davis polled 28.8 percent—the lowest percentage a Democratic presidential nominee has ever received. La Follette won in his own state of Wisconsin by a thumping majority and came in second to Coolidge in eleven other states: California, Idaho, Iowa, Minnesota, Montana, Nevada, North Dakota, Oregon, South Dakota, Washington, and Wyoming. On the local level, he carried Cleveland and Milwaukee, nearly won San Francisco, and in the East ran relatively well in large cities. While voter turnout across the nation was only around 50 percent, La Follette ran well in high-turnout states. His vote showed great regional variation: He received more than one-fourth of the vote in the Far West and trans-Mississippi Midwest, around one-tenth of the votes in the Northeast and Great Lakes regions (excluding Wisconsin), and about one-twentieth of the votes in the South. Seventy-nine percent of La Follette's votes came from the Progressive party line, 18 percent from the Socialist line, and 3.5 percent from the Farmer-Labor line. Kenneth Campbell MacKay, who wrote the standard work on the campaign, estimated that about half of La Follette's vote was cast by farmers, and one-fifth each came from Socialists, liberals, and protest groups.

ELECTION ANALYSIS

Behind the regional character to the La Follette vote is the role of political culture. The political scientist Daniel Elazar once posited the presence of three such cultures in the United States: individualistic, which underlies machine politics; moralistic, which is based on ideology and ideals; and traditionalistic, which is based on deference to elites. The predominantly traditionalistic states of the South and Southwest gave La Follette a mean vote of 6.3 percent; the individualistic states, mostly in the Northeast and lower Midwest, gave him a mean of 14.8 percent; and the moralistic states of the northern tier and Far West gave him 26.7 percent (25 percent without Wisconsin). This is in keeping with the interpretation of many historians that the appeal of progressivism was along cultural lines and greatest among certain ethnocultural groups such as Yankees from New England and

those of Scandinavian descent. However, without individual-level data it is difficult to compare ethnocultural effects with those of class.

In assessing which party was hurt more by the La Follette-Wheeler ticket, we are confronted by two striking facts: the abysmally low vote that Davis received, and the western concentration of the progressive vote. The first leads to the suspicion that La Follette hurt Davis more, the second to the hunch that he drew more votes from Coolidge. Examining how poorly the major parties' showings in 1924 fell from those of the presidential election of 1920, the historian MacKay concluded that nationally, La Follette hurt Coolidge slightly more than he hurt Davis; however, he hurt Coolidge far more in the Midwest, South, and New England and Davis far more in the Far West and mid-Atlantic states.

Another historian, David Burner, compared the parties' presidential showings in 1924 with their congressional vote that year and came to the opposite conclusion that, nationally, La Follette hurt the Democrats more than he hurt the Republicans. In Burner's view, this effect was particularly pronounced in the Rockies. A third historian, Paul Kleppner, used statistical techniques to conclude, implausibly, that all of La Follette's voters who had voted in 1920 for a major-party candidate had voted Republican. The only firm conclusion we can draw from the data is that Calvin Coolidge would have won a second term regardless of whether La Follette had run.

Coolidge won that term because the nation seemed firmly on the path of prosperity under a famously taciturn and sober-faced chief executive. The industrial and agrarian workers who could have provided the base for a protest party of the left were seduced by the same prosperity, which included a temporary boost in farm prices. More fundamentally, perhaps, they preferred to place their faith in American upward social mobility rather than in an ideologically driven assault on big business. "Violent political passions have but little hold on those who have devoted all their faculties to the pursuit of their well-being," political scientist de Tocqueville wrote. "The ardor that they display in small matters calms their zeal for momentous undertakings." For this reason, several historians have taken La Follette to task for emphasizing the old populist issue of monopoly, rather than tailoring his appeal to the concerns of the 1920s, such as immigration and regulation of the economy.

CONCLUSION

While La Follette received one of the highest vote totals of any third-party candidate in American history, that total was not enough to sustain the movement. Early in 1925 the American Federation of Labor returned to its earlier non-partisan stance and withdrew from the new movement. On February 21, 300 CPPA delegates met in Chicago, presided over by William Johnston of the machinists. Again, the Socialists pushed for a new party while most labor delegates opposed the idea. Soon it became clear that despite the pleadings of Socialist leaders Eugene Debs and Morris Hillquist, labor delegates would walk out rather than join a new party. Delegates unanimously adopted a motion to adjourn temporarily, so that the bolt by labor would occur quietly. When the remaining delegates reconvened, they unanimously passed Arthur Garfield Hays's call for a "new independent political party." Soon Socialists and agrarians began to fight over the apportionment of delegates for a convention to be held that fall, as well as over the name of the new party. The Socialists wanted functional representation at the convention to be on the basis of occupation and similar criteria, and the party to be called the American Labor party. The agrarians preferred representation by geographic area, and resisted use of the labor label. On a vote of 93 to 64, the agrarians won the battle over apportionment of delegates.

After all these deliberations, attempts to raise money for the new party were unsuccessful, which made the question of the next convention academic. The executive committee of the party met sporadically until late in 1927, occasionally publishing a bulletin, and this committee and the Railroad Brotherhoods paid off the CPPA's debt. On November 3, 1927, three members of the executive committee met in Washington and adjourned indefinitely.

Robert Marion La Follette, who planned to build a real party by 1926, did not live to see the poignant end of his movement. Expelled from the Republican Senate caucus for his apostasy and deprived of his seat on the Commerce Committee, La Follette's health rapidly declined despite a sojourn in Florida in early 1925. A severe bronchial attack on May 9 was followed by a heart attack nine days later. He died at the age of 70 at his home in Washington on June 18, 1925, less than six weeks before the death of that other progressive candidate, William Jennings Bryan.

Burton K. Wheeler, La Follette's vice-presidential candidate, served in the Senate until his defeat in the Democratic primary in 1946. Regarded as the model for the Jimmy Stewart character in the 1939 film *Mr. Smith Goes to Washington*, Wheeler was to lead the charge against Franklin D. Roosevelt's court-packing plan as well as to oppose Roosevelt's moves to aid the Allies before Pearl Harbor. Maverick to the end, Wheeler also opposed the attempts of Congress and the special prosecutor to obtain the Nixon tapes during the Watergate scandal, fearing erosion of presidential power. Wheeler died in Washington in 1975 at the age of 92.

Numerous scholars have suggested that the progressive movement of 1924 had historical significance far beyond demonstrating the limits of leftist political activity in the United States. In their view, in two respects the progressives were a forerunner of the New Deal. First, in shaping his policies, Democrat Franklin D. Roosevelt drew on some of the progressive ideas. For all his disagreements with Roosevelt, Burton Wheeler wrote in his memoirs that the progressive platform of 1924 "became the ideological basis for the New Deal" and that "much of it found its way to the statute books by 1935." Perhaps Wheeler was thinking of

Roosevelt's policies in the areas of antitrust, public water power, progressive taxation, the rights of organized labor, relief for farmers, banking regulation, and conservation.

Second, as Wheeler also wrote, the progressive campaign was "an opportunity to try to force a realignment in the old parties with all the conservative Democrats and Republicans on one side and on the other side an amalgamation of all progressive, forward-looking people of whatever political faith." Political scientists have long seen third-party movements as way stations for people moving from one party to the other. In this regard, perhaps the answer to the question as to which party was hurt more by La Follette is neither and both; he attracted Republicans who were moving toward the Democratic party. This seems to be true on the elite level: The La Follette family and many other veterans of the 1924 progressive campaign worked for Roosevelt in 1932 and several, most prominently Harold Ickes, were appointed to high office.

Many voters followed the same path. On a state-by-state comparison, there is a high correlation between La Follette's vote percentage and the improvement in the Democrats' showing between 1920 and 1932. Moreover, within four of the five states where La Follette ran best, there were statistically significant county-by-county correlations. The exception is Montana, which had a higher concentration of Catholic voters than the others. In addition, historian Paul Kleppner indicated that most La Follette voters voted Democratic in the 1928 presidential election. Over a time span of twelve years, the data suggests that La Follette may indeed have provided a way for dissident Republicans to avoid voting for Coolidge without taking the final step of supporting a Democrat, especially one as conservative as Davis. When a more attractive Democrat came by, in a period of economic crisis, the journey was completed.

Hindsight has not been kind to the progressive movement of 1924. Historians have called it naive, antiquated, disorganized, fractious, and unwilling to create a real party that might have improved its showing. However, in several respects it was one of the most successful of such campaigns, not only in achieving a relatively high total of votes—more than half that of the Democrats that year—but in providing ideas, personnel, and voters for the New Deal. Its candidates were two bold senators who kept true to their principles, rejected the support of Communists while defending their civil liberties, attacked the Ku Klux Klan, and pointed out some of the enduring problems of a democratic political system that coexists with great contradictions of private wealth. "The presidency," wrote the Wisconsin political scientist Frederic A. Ogg of La Follette, "is not for such as he. His role was that of an awakener of thought, a stimulator of action, a purifier of the public life." It is also the role of the best of our insurgent political movements.

HOWARD L. REITER

See also: American Labor Party; Communist Party; Robert M. La Follette, Sr.; **Map 18:** Progressive Party (1924); Minnesota Farmer-Labor Party; Socialist Party.

Bibliography

Burner, David. "Election of 1924." In *History of American Presidential Elections, 1789–1968,* vol. 3, ed. Arthur M. Schlesinger, Jr. New York: Chelsea House, 1971.

Elazar, Daniel J. *American Federalism: A View from the States.* 2d ed. New York: Thomas Y. Crowell, 1972.

Greenbaum, Fred. *Robert Marion La Follette.* Boston: Twayne Publishers, 1975.

Kleppner, Paul. *Continuity and Change in Electoral Politics, 1893–1928.* Westport, CT: Greenwood Press, 1987.

MacKay, Kenneth Campbell. *The Progressive Movement of 1924.* New York: Columbia University Press, 1947.

Maxwell, Robert S., ed. *La Follette.* Englewood Cliffs, NJ: Prentice-Hall, 1969.

Mowry, George E. "The Progressive Party 1912 and 1924." In *History of U.S. Political Parties,* vol. 3, ed.

Arthur M. Schlesinger, Jr. New York: Chelsea House, 1973.

Murray, Robert K. *The 103rd Ballot: Democrats and the Disaster in Madison Square Garden.* New York: Harper and Row, 1976.

Nye, Russel B. *Midwestern Progressive Politics: A Historical Study of Its Origins and Development,* *1870–1958.* East Lansing: Michigan State University Press, 1959.

Thelen, David P. *Robert M. La Follette and the Insurgent Spirit.* Boston: Little, Brown, 1976.

Wheeler, Burton K., with Paul F. Healy. *Yankee from the West.* Garden City, NY: Doubleday, 1962.

PROGRESSIVE PARTY
1948

WALLACE AND THE DEMOCRATS

Henry A. Wallace and the Progressive party campaign of 1948 remain inextricably linked. The Progressive party challenge of 1948 was born of frustration with the emerging bipartisan cold war foreign policy consensus and with the failure of President Harry S. Truman to follow through on domestic New Deal policy commitments. Although discontent with Truman produced substantial disaffection among staunch New Deal liberals, opposition to Truman and to the new direction of U.S. foreign and domestic policy coalesced around Wallace's powerful voice, and it seems doubtful that a progressive third-party attack on the growing conservatism in national politics would have taken off without him. Thus, the circumstances of Wallace's growing estrangement from the Democratic party is a key part of the story of that third-party effort.

Wallace's independent crusade was ignited when Franklin Roosevelt heeded the advice of conservative Democratic party regulars that Wallace should be replaced as his vice-presidential running mate for the 1944 campaign. Wallace himself came from a progressive Republican family, and while he served in Roosevelt's cabinet as secretary of agriculture since 1933, he did not register as a Democrat until 1936. Thus, Wallace's political independence was longstanding and, alongside his commitment to liberal reform, earned him the enmity of the conservative forces that controlled much of the Democratic party machinery.

While Wallace almost pulled off the nomination despite the scheming against him, Truman took his place on the ticket beside Roosevelt. Wallace was disheartened by the vote of no-confidence but was convinced nonetheless to campaign actively for the Democratic ticket that fall. The Democrats needed Wallace's voice and presence, given his popularity among the Democratic faithful, his campaigning prowess, and because of Truman's pronounced limitations in these same areas. In turn, Wallace's command performance campaigning for his fellow Democrats in 1944 earned him Roosevelt's gratitude and a greatly enhanced stature among liberals hoping for a continuation of New Deal reform efforts. Roosevelt responded by granting Wallace's request to replace his main adversary within the cabinet, Jesse Jones, conservative Texas businessman and commerce secretary.

Shortly after taking his new office, however, Franklin Roosevelt died and Harry Truman took his place. Wallace hoped to continue as a forceful advocate for postwar liberal reform and Truman encouraged this aspiration. However, Wallace and other liberals found much of Truman's rhetoric about postwar social and economic goals to be weak and empty, especially as Truman replaced many of Roosevelt's associates in the cabinet with Democrats of much less stature and with little commitment to reform. Wallace became an isolated voice within the cabinet, and his isolation became particularly pronounced as postwar foreign policy moved to the center of Truman's concerns. Truman, unsure of himself in domestic politics and even more unprepared for handling the massive international responsibilities handed to the

United States after the war, leaned heavily upon a conservative group of advisors who saw the Soviet Union as a great threat to postwar U.S. international hegemony. Wallace, seeking to promote a peaceful and cooperative relationship with Soviets, increasingly became the odd man out in the cabinet. And after a forceful speech that seemed to undercut the official hard-line U.S. attitude toward the Soviets, Wallace was asked to resign.

Wallace continued to maintain a high profile as a speaker and as editor of *New Republic,* and he continued to dissent from the conservative tenor of Truman's domestic policies and from hard-line administration policy toward the Soviets. At the same time, as New Deal liberals became increasingly alarmed by Truman's drift to the Right, they hurried to organize themselves in order to reinvigorate the liberal movement. Dashing hopes for a united front, however, they split over the issue of communism. The most prominent New Deal liberals formed themselves into the anti-communist Americans for Democratic Action (ADA). Wallace, however, concerned about the dangerous demagoguery and threat to civil liberties involved in propagating anti-communism, associated himself with an alternative group, the Progressive Citizens of America (PCA), which included many communists and fellow travelers. Wallace spoke at the PCA's founding meeting and became its symbolic leader.

TRUMAN'S ANTI-COMMUNISM

Because of Wallace's concerns about the growing hostility between the United States and the USSR, he leapt to dissent when Truman announced his "doctrine" for using military force to prevent the spread of communist influence abroad. Designed to support U.S. military aid to reactionary and repressive elements in both Greece and Turkey under the rationale of halting communist advances, the Truman Doctrine set the United States on a path of military con-

tainment of communism. Truman followed this up with a loyalty program for federal civil servants that greatly legitimized the charge that communists had infiltrated the national government and legitimized the power of the state to investigate U.S. citizens so tarred. Wallace's powerful dissent from these policies obviously struck a popular chord since, in a subsequent nationwide speaking tour, he was met by huge, enthusiastic crowds. Encouraged by this outpouring of support, Wallace considered his options for the 1948 election: Should he challenge Truman for the Democratic nomination in 1948 or lead a third-party protest against the Democrat's reborn conservatism?

With the Democratic party machinery safely in the hands of party conservatives, Wallace in late December 1947 finally announced his decision to embark on a third-party crusade. The new party would be named the Progressive party. Wallace, convinced that workers, blacks, and independent liberals would support his candidacy, expected four to five million votes. Yet, rabid redbaiting by the press almost immediately began to erode Wallace's support, especially as the leadership of the powerful Congress of Industrial Organizations (CIO) deserted and denounced Wallace, citing Communist sponsorship of his campaign, and even those congressional liberals critical of Truman returned to the fold to help strengthen a severely weakened Democratic party for a crucial election contest.

Truman, following a script written by his close advisor Clark Clifford, transformed himself for the election into one of the most populist presidents of the century as he proposed progressive domestic measures to lure the key Democratic constituencies of workers, blacks, and independent liberals that Wallace counted on back into the Democratic fold. In fact, Truman's rhetorical support for civil rights prodded many southern Democrats to support a third-party insurgency of their own, the States' Rights or Dixiecrat party with Strom Thurmond tapped as presidential candidate. Truman was also encouraged by Clifford to enlist prominent liberals in the ADA and CIO to lead a hue and cry calling their erstwhile colleague Wallace a communist dupe. Wallace, knowing full well that their presence would cost him substantial support, refused to dissociate himself from communists working in his campaign. Such action would undercut his very message of contempt for the growing anti-communist hysteria and would sanction the attack on civil liberties by the Truman administration. In the end, the redbaiting of Wallace by Truman and his allies effectively trumped any Republican attempt to paint the Democrats as Reds, and with official sanction, the press tore into Wallace in one of the more sensational campaigns of vilification and distortions in U.S. history. Wallace would thus ironically play the perfect foil for Truman's come-from-behind victory in 1948.

THE PROGRESSIVE PARTY INFRA-STRUCTURE

PCA local chapters provided the grassroots organizational apparatus for Wallace's campaign. While the ADA remained an elitist organization, the PCA made significant strides toward building a mass organization, growing from 17,000 dues-paying members in May 1947 to 47,000 by September. Of course, with so little time to build up their organization, the party remained strongly organized in states such as New York, California, Illinois, Massachusetts, and in big cities. The party's real strength lay in its National Wallace for President Committee that included many cultural, entertainment, and academic celebrities. C.B. "Beanie" Baldwin, a colleague of Wallace's from his days at the Department of Agriculture and later co-chair of the PCA, was the focal point for much of the pressure to get Wallace to run and he managed the campaign itself. The party's organizational structure, hammered out during the party convention, made it more democratic and representative than the major parties, but its decentralization meant that factional battles within the party continued to develop throughout the campaign. Volunteers worked tirelessly to gather the requisite number of signatures to qualify for a place on the ballot.

Former Agriculture Secretary Henry Wallace displays his farming roots in this official photo from his 1948 campaign for the presidency on the Progressive party ticket. (*Courtesy of the Library of Congress*)

And, despite archaic state election laws designed to keep third parties at bay, Wallace and the Progressives were able to get on the ballot in all states except for Nebraska, Oklahoma, and Illinois. In Ohio, electors committed to the Progressive party could appear on the ballot, but Wallace and his running mate, Idaho Senator Glen Taylor, could not. Still, scholars find it possible that Truman's narrow victories in Ohio and Illinois—and therefore his election—could have been overturned had Wallace been allowed to fully compete in these states.

Despite the tremendous amount of organizing work completed by the summer of 1948, the tide had already turned against Wallace. At the high point of Wallace's public support, during his 1947 summer tour in opposition to Truman's growing hostility to the Soviets, 13 percent of the electorate polled supported a Wallace candidacy. After six months of active campaigning, his support had ebbed to 7 percent, and fell even further by the time of the Progressive party convention in late July 1948. The problem was the foreign policy focus for the campaign. Wallace and the Progressive party campaigned on domestic issues, promising action on fighting postwar inflation, strengthening national labor laws recently weakened by the Taft-Hartley Act, enacting civil rights, and expanding national health, housing, minimum wage, and Social Security guarantees. Foreign policy and the peace theme, however, remained the paramount centerpiece for the campaign. Americans grew weary of foreign policy issues, and more aggressive Soviet actions, specifically the Czechoslovakian coup and the Berlin blockade, increased anti-Soviet sentiment, and further isolated Wallace and the new party. Of course, the tireless drumbeat of anti-communism also took its toll in this regard.

The CIO leadership used its organizational clout to discourage its member unions from supporting Wallace, and the ADA published distortions about Wallace's record on civil and labor rights to undercut his support among key Democratic constituencies. The postwar boom began to mute much of labor's anger at Truman's conservative domestic policies, and the large numbers of Roman Catholics in the CIO were especially susceptible to the anti-communist hand played by both the CIO and ADA. As a result, polls right before the election showed Wallace gaining the support of only 3.5 percent of CIO members, while gaining twice that among members of the more conservative American Federation of Labor. And, despite Wallace's heroic efforts to champion civil rights and voter rights for blacks in the South—going so far as to stand up to southern authorities and racists in refusing segregated meetings or facilities—Wallace gained less than 10 percent of the black vote. Strong Democratic organization in urban areas and Truman's timely conversion to support of some civil rights reforms brought home the black vote (over two-thirds) for the Democrats.

Wallace continued to draw substantial crowds and publicity throughout the summer of 1948, but by the autumn, the effort lost steam as the list of allies and supporters who turned against the candidate and party grew. As even the crowds and excitement of the campaign trail dimmed, the party turned to a series of radio addresses that failed to stem the tide of reversals in support. Thus, the election results were disastrous for the Progressive party and for Wallace. They gained a mere 1,157,057 votes (only 2.38 percent of the total vote) as against the four million that Wallace predicted. The vote total was even less than the Dixiecrat candidate Strom Thurmond received, although Wallace most likely cost Truman the electoral vote in New York, Maryland, and Michigan. In fact, the Progressive ticket gained almost half their national total in one state, New York, where they merged with an already strongly organized third party, the American Labor party, which had fielded candidates since 1936. Truman, of course, won the election.

Despite the dismal results, Wallace and others active in the Progressive campaign claimed success since Truman was forced to embrace their more populist domestic agenda; in this way, Truman effectively reconstructed New Deal political loyalties and reassembled the New Deal political coalition of the pre-war period. And by deflecting charges of communist sympathizer and other forms of radicalism from the Democratic party, Wallace enabled the Democrats and Truman to harvest the votes of those disaffected by some of the more adventurous policies of the New Deal. Wallace and the Progressives also claimed that they slowed the trend toward the new foreign policy consensus. Certainly, Wallace and the Progressives had stood up for civil liberties at a time when it was difficult to do so, and they raised a critique of the increasing influence of major corporations and the military over national policy. In fact, the issues and problems raised by Wallace—civil liberties, civil rights, the cold war, militarization, the inordinate power of U.S. corporations—represented the central questions of postwar U.S. politics. The Progressive party struggled after the election to remain an ongoing political entity, but sank into obscurity as many of its supporters and partisans, including Henry Wallace, abandoned it and embraced the cold war bipartisan consensus that enveloped the United States.

BRIAN WADDELL

See also: **Map 19:** Progressive Party (1948); States' Rights Democratic Party (Dixiecrats); Strom Thurmond; Henry Agard Wallace.

Bibliography

Blum, John Morton. *The Price of Vision: The Diary of Henry A. Wallace, 1942–46.* Boston: Houghton Mifflin, 1973.

MacDougall, Curtis D. *Gideon's Army.* 3 vols. New York: Marzani and Munsell, 1965.

Markowitz, Norman D. *The Rise and Fall of the People's Century: Henry A. Wallace and American Liberalism, 1941–1948.* New York: Free Press, 1973.

Schmidt, Karl M. *Henry A. Wallace: Quixotic Crusade, 1948.* Syracuse: Syracuse University Press, 1960.

Sirevag, Torbjorn. *The Eclipse of the New Deal and the Fall of Vice-President Wallace, 1944.* New York: Garland, 1985.

Walton, Richard. *Henry Wallace, Harry Truman, and the Cold War.* New York: Viking Press, 1976.

White, Graham, and John Maze. *Henry A. Wallace: His Search for a New World Order.* Chapel Hill: University of North Carolina Press, 1995.

PROGRESSIVE PARTY OF WISCONSIN

1934–1946

The Progressive Party of Wisconsin emerged in an era of Republican dominance of state politics that extended from 1855 until the 1950s. At times, the Democratic party was so weak that it seemed to be almost a minor party. For example, in 1926 its gubernatorial nominee received only 17 percent of the vote. Not only was the Democratic party electorally weak, it was also extremely conservative. One observer noted that the Wisconsin Democratic party in the 1930s was a "political shell manned by job conscious people" and another noted that the party was "about as progressive as Tammany Hall." In this context of one-party Republican dominance, the state's real electoral competition from the turn of the century until 1934 occurred within the Republican primaries in which the conservative stalwart faction was frequently aligned against the progressive faction led first by Robert M. La Follette, Sr., and later by his sons Robert, Jr., and Philip. The failure of the Democratic party to develop into a meaningful opposition party can be attributed in significant degree to the presence in Republican politics of the La Follettes and their progressive movement. The senior La Follette's capture of the governorship as a Republican in 1900 and his progressive faction's dominance of the party during much of the next quarter-century prevented the emergence of a liberal Democratic party until the 1940s. Liberals and progressives from the turn of the century until the post–World War II period were followers of the La Follettes, not the conservative Democratic party of Wisconsin.

The sons of the "Old Bob" La Follette took full advantage of the Democratic party's weakness by winning primary elections in the dominant Republican party. In 1925, Robert, Jr., ("Young Bob") won his father's U.S. Senate seat in a special election, while Philip captured the governorship in 1930. However, in the Democratic landslide of 1932, Franklin Roosevelt's coattails were so strong that the long dormant party elected a U.S. Senator and governor while also gaining a majority in the state assembly. That same year, progressives received a warning that even a La Follette could not be assured of winning the GOP nomination: Philip lost his bid for re-election by losing the Republican gubernatorial primary to a member of the stalwart faction, Walter J. Kohler, Sr.

As the 1934 elections approached, the La Follette brothers were confronted with a difficult electoral problem. Robert was up for re-election to the U.S. Senate and Philip wanted to regain the governorship. In the context of the Depression and Roosevelt's popularity, it was apparent that being on the Republican ticket was not the place to be for a family accustomed to winning elections. Nor was the Democratic party a promising alternative. The old-line Democrats were conservatives with antipathy toward progressives. In addition, many old-line Democrats, surprisingly, had won elective office in 1932 and they were not about to share spoils of office with their old rivals. Also, given the Democrats' past weakness, there was no assurance that the party's 1932 victories were more than a passing phenomenon.

Faced with a need to find a viable electoral vehicle for the 1934 elections, the La Follettes

Following the 1924 campaign and the death of their standard-bearer, Robert La Follette, the Progressive party disappeared from the national scene, increasingly confined to its Wisconsin base, as this cartoon from the late 1920s indicates. In the 1930s, many former Progressives would form the Wisconsin Progressive party. (*Courtesy of the Library of Congress*)

led most of their followers out of the Republican party and formed a separate progressive party organization. At a convention in May 1934, the new party nominated Robert, Jr., for the Senate and Philip for governor. The delegates also adopted a platform that called for guaranteed employment for every able-bodied person, a government-owned central bank, a fair profit for farmers, the right of labor to or-

ganize, and public ownership of electric power.

With President Roosevelt giving Robert, Jr., his informal endorsement and the national Democratic party maintaining a neutral stance in the gubernatorial election, the La Follette-led Progressive party won the Senate seat, the governorship, and control of the state assembly. Two years later in 1936, the Progressives re-elected Philip as governor and gained control of both chambers of the legislature.

The mid-1930s were the high point of the Progressive party's strength as the Democratic party was reduced to a third-party status. Thus, in 1938, the Democratic candidate for governor received only 8 percent of the vote. Meaningful electoral competition in state elections was between the Republicans and the Progressives, not as was nationally between the Republicans and Democrats.

Beginning in 1938, things began to unravel for the Progressives. The alliance with the Democratic administration in Washington collapsed amid Philip La Follette's abortive attempt to form a national third party and splits between the isolationist La Follettes and the internationalist Roosevelt. In addition, state Republicans and Democrats formed an alliance that defeated Philip in his bid for re-election as governor. In a three-way contest, Young Bob managed to win a narrow re-election (45.3 percent of the vote) victory to the Senate in 1940. In 1942, the Progressive party's successful gubernatorial candidate died before taking office and was replaced by a newly elected Republican lieutenant governor, Walter Goodland, a popular, progressive Republican. In 1944, with no La Follette on the ballot and Roosevelt winning a fourth term, the Progressives' share of the gubernatorial vote fell to just 6 percent.

With their electoral base narrowing, the Democratic National Committee on record that it would no longer support Progressive candidates (including Robert La Follette) in Wisconsin, and Republican prospects looking highly favorable as the 1946 election approached, the Progressive party voted to disband and Young Bob sought the Republican senatorial nomination in his quest for re-election. As a liberal seeking the nomination of a generally conservative party, La Follette was defeated in the primary by Joseph McCarthy, who went on to win the general election.

With La Follette's rejoining the Republican party and his subsequent defeat in the primary, Wisconsin's brief interlude of three-party politics ended and the state entered a period of competitive two-party politics between the Republicans and Democrats. The Progressive party had never had a strong organizational base. It was instead heavily dependent upon the La Follette family's personal following.

The demise of the Progressive party of Wisconsin demonstrated that it was not possible to maintain a state party system so totally out of line with national politics. Partisan loyalties tend to be forged in the fires of presidential politics and voters tend to vote for the same party in presidential and state elections. The national political alignment was simply too strong a force for the Progressives to counter. In Wisconsin this meant that organized labor and persons who identified with the policies of Roosevelt and Truman realigned themselves with the Democratic party and away from the Progressives.

With the demise of the Progressive party, its followers had to choose between the Republicans and Democrats if they wished to stay involved in politics. It appears that many older and rural Progressives moved back into the GOP, while younger, liberal, and urban Progressives migrated to the newly liberal Democratic party that was strongly backed by organized labor. The net effect of these transfers of party loyalties was to help the Republicans maintain their dominant electoral position for another decade by infusing the party with added followers, while at the same time providing the Democrats with liberal adherents who made the party a competitive force in state politics, one that was closely aligned with national Democratic policy positions.

JOHN BIBBY

See also: Robert M. La Follette, Jr.; Robert M. La Follette, Sr.; Progressive Movement of 1924.

Bibliography

Dykstra, Robert R., and David R. Reynolds. "In Search of Wisconsin Progressives, 1904–1952." In *The History of American Electoral Behavior*, ed. Joel H. Silbey, Allan G. Bogue, and William Flanigan, Chap. 8. Princeton: Princeton University Press, 1978.

Epstein, Leon, D. *Politics in Wisconsin.* Madison: University of Wisconsin Press, 1958.

Johnson, Roger T. *Robert M. La Follette, Jr., and the Decline of the Progressive Party in Wisconsin.* New York: Anchor, 1970.

Sundquist, James L. *Dynamics of the Party System: Alignment and Realignment of Political Parties in the United States.* Washington, DC: Brookings Institution, 1983, pp. 244–249.

Thompson, William F. *The History of Wisconsin.* Vol. 6. Madison: State Historical Society of Wisconsin, 1988.

PROHIBITION PARTY
1869–

AMERICA'S LONGEST-RUNNING THIRD PARTY

Even though the Prohibition party is the oldest third party in the United States, and even though it has nominated a candidate in every presidential election since 1872, it has never achieved more than a modicum of success. Its lack of success is partly due to the fact that prohibitionists, like women, have never united behind a single party. Historically, most prohibitionists chose to remain within either the Democratic or Republican party because they believed their chance of true reform was stronger within the mainstream of the political system. To leave a major party in a two-party system, one must reject existing political norms and learn a new set of political behaviors. Americans, however, are not inclined to do so. Americans are much more likely to cluster around the middle of the political spectrum—a point that is consistently represented by the Democrats and Republicans.

It is a given in American politics that third-party candidates rarely win in major elections. Therefore, it requires a commitment to a particular candidate and/or the cause represented by that individual to cast a vote that many consider to be a throwaway. The task of third parties in the United States is also made more difficult by the tendency of the two major parties to usurp reform movements and bring them under the umbrella of their own party platforms. This wide-range appeal of the Democratic and Republican parties has always made them more attractive than single-issue parties to voters.

While the Prohibition party has frequently developed an extensive party platform, it has generally been perceived and tends to be, in fact, a single-issue party.

The Prohibition party was made up of crusaders with a well-defined cause, not politicians who were out to win elections at all costs. The point that the major parties have changed in response to the changing political landscape while the Prohibition party has been consistent in their views is a good one.

Political scientist David Leigh Colvin maintains that the individual who started the temperance movement in the United States was Dr. Benjamin Rush, a signer of the Declaration of Independence from Pennsylvania, who published an essay, "Effects of Ardent Spirits upon the Human Mind and Body," in 1785. Colvin notes that both Washington and Jefferson spoke out against heavy drinking. Historian Sean Dennis Cashman suggests that there were four kinds of arguments that led people to support Prohibition: medical, industrial and economic, religious, and social and political. Whatever the reason, by 1829, state temperance societies could claim more than 100,000 members in 1,000 local societies. Before 1900, the efforts of the temperance movement had targeted the saloons, placing high license fees on proprietors and instituting a dispensary system and local options. By the nineteenth century, saloons had become ordinary sights in American cities and towns. The sight of these dramshops was loathsome to most middle-class Americans—particularly to those who were religious and who saw anything to do with hard drink as sinful. Most towns were also forced to deal with the aftermath when certain individuals began to frequent saloons to the detriment of those who were depending on them for livelihood.

In 1851, Maine became the first state to pass a temperance law. Within the next five years, Connecticut, Delaware, Indiana, Iowa, Michigan, Minnesota, Nebraska, New Hampshire, New York, Rhode Island, and Vermont had followed suit. However, as the opposition became more organized, many states either retracted their support or had their laws declared unconstitutional. Maine, which had, with remarkable foresight, instituted its law through a constitutional statute, remained steadfast to the temperance cause.

Support for temperance continued during the Civil War but was frequently pushed to the back burner. It was only after the United States Brewers' Association was established in 1862 in New York that the movement again became energized. The Brewers had successfully lobbied to reduce the price of beer from one dollar a barrel to only sixty cents a barrel. The Good Templar Lodge, a group that had maintained its membership throughout the war, became the guiding spirit of the Prohibition movement and were soon joined by other independent groups, swelling its membership to 400,000. Since neither the Democratic nor Republican party seemed inclined to support Prohibition, the time for a separate party devoted to the prohibition cause was ripe. Newspapers, such as *The Chicago Tribune*, quickly approved this action, maintaining that it would prove beneficial to both the new party and the existing ones.

The first political convention of the Prohibition party was held in Chicago, Illinois, in September 1869. They initially called themselves the Temperance party but became known as the Prohibition party in 1873. Five hundred delegates from twenty different states showed up to make political history. The name was again changed in 1980 to the National Statesmen in hopes that the party would attract a broader audience. The measure failed, so the name change was revoked before the next election in 1984. Many of the 500 delegates who attended that first convention were women, taking an equal part in the political process as never before. The

delegates pledged that they would thereafter run a candidate in every election. They have, indeed, run a candidate in every election since 1872, but they have never carried a single state. In 1869, the Prohibition party of Ohio became the first state party to offer a candidate for office. Even though the candidate in Cleveland's city elections won barely 1,000 votes, the Prohibition party had made its presence known. Some historians contend that the activism of the prohibition movement became more focused in 1869 because the success of the Brewers' Association had increased the availability of alcohol. In addition, the end of slavery—in which many prohibition reformers had once been involved—allowed for more time and attention to be paid to other kinds of political activism. Much of the credit for the revived enthusiasm for prohibition was due to the evangelical element of the party. Ministers frequently devoted Sunday morning services to the evils of alcohol, rousing their congregations to action. Among the noted revivalists who supported prohibition were: Billy Sunday, the Reverend R.A. Torrey, the Reverend J. Wilbur Chapman, W.J. Dawson, and Rodney (Gypsy) Smith.

Most people mistakenly believe that the Prohibition party was responsible for the passage of the Eighteenth Amendment in 1919, but credit for that goes to the Women's Christian Temperance Union (WCTU), created in 1874, and to the Anti-Saloon League (ASL), created in 1893. Women, in their designated roles as guardians of the nation's morals and as wives and mothers who were appalled by neglectful heavy drinkers, aroused a spirit of remorse in the American community that the ministers and intellectuals of the Prohibition party had failed to tap.

One of the women most closely associated with the Anti-Saloon League and the Prohibition party was Frances Elizabeth Willard (1839–1898), American educator and reformer who succeeded in aligning the WCTU with the Prohibition party. Growing up, Willard eschewed typical female behavior, wearing trousers until she was 16 and learning carpentry. She was the president of Evanston College for Ladies, the first female dean of Northwestern University, and secretary and second national president of the WCTU. Willard led the WCTU to pass a resolution that refused support to any party that did not support temperance. Only the Prohibition party agreed.

LEADERSHIP OF THE PARTY

Within the Prohibition party, the most well known leaders were James Black, Neal Dow, Edward Delevan, Gerrit Smith, and John Bidwell. James Black (1823–1893), the first Prohibition party candidate for president, was chief organizer of the National Temperance Society and Prohibition House, a publisher of temperance literature. A former Washingtonian, Black was also co-founder of his local division of the Sons of Temperance, a chapter of the Good Templar Lodge. Neal Dow (1804–1897), third presidential candidate for the Prohibition party, was a Quaker and a speculator whose legislative efforts succeeded in making Portland, Maine, America's first dry city. Edward Delevan (1793–1871), owner of the *Evening Journal* (Albany, New York), furthered the cause of the temperance movement through his exposé of local breweries, proving in court that they used polluted water to make beer. Additionally, Delevan served as chair of the American Temperance Union's Executive Committee. Gerrit Smith, eccentric prohibition supporter and advocate of women's dress reform, became involved in John Brown's revolt in Harper's Ferry, Virginia, by contributing money and land to his anti-slavery endeavors. Smith, a follower of Adventism, an evangelical form of Christianity, established his own temperance hotel and wanted to name the Prohibition party the Anti-Dramshop party. John Bidwell (1819–1900) was the most successful presidential candidate in Prohibition party history. In 1892, Bidwell carried 2.3 percent of the total popular vote. He had experienced distinguished careers in both politics and the military. After serving in Congress in the 1860s, he ran unsuccessfully

as the Prohibition gubernatorial candidate for the state of California in 1890.

Despite the fact that the Prohibition party has long been identified as a single-interest party, it developed well-defined party platforms. This was particularly true in the 1890s. The party was in favor of certain tariffs, believing that they should protect industry and raise revenue. Their interest in foreign policy was that it should protect the interests of the American public. The Prohibition party was visionary in its support of women's rights. The 1892 platform contained a progressive proposal for an equal rights amendment: "No citizen should be denied the right to vote on account of sex, and equal labor should receive equal wages without regard to sex." The Prohibition party platform favored restrictions on immigration, religious liberty, universal suffrage, and nationalization of certain public utilities. Despite their views on rights for women, the party has traditionally been against the right to choose an abortion.

The Prohibition party platform of 1892 (their most successful election) comes closest to explaining the party positions through the history of the Prohibition party. It contained the following planks:

1. Liquor trafficking is antithetical to civilization and popular government, as well as being a public nuisance.
2. Equal Rights Amendment.
3. The money of the country should consist of gold and silver, and should be issued by the general government only, and in sufficient quantity to meet the demands of business and give full opportunity for the employment of labor.
4. Tariffs should be levied only as defense against foreign governments that levy tariffs upon or bar our products from their markets.
5. Railroads, telegraphs, and other public corporations should be controlled by the government in the interest of the people.
6. Foreign immigration has become a burden upon the economy.
7. Non-resident aliens should not be allowed to acquire land in this country.

The continuing appeal of the Prohibition party, America's longest-lived third party, is the source of a contemporary joke in these 1920 photographs of presidential candidate Aaron Watkins. He is shown drying his laundry, a reference to the popular name for members of the anti-alcohol party: "dries." *(Courtesy of the Library of Congress)*

8. Years of inaction and treachery on the part of the Republican and Democratic parties have resulted in the present reign of mob law, and we demand that every citizen be protected in the right of trial by constitutional tribunals.

9. All men should be protected by law in their right to one day of rest in seven.

10. Arbitration is the wisest and most economical way to settle national differences.

11. Speculation in margins, the cornering of grain, money, and products, and the formation of pools, trusts, combinations for the arbitrary advancement of prices should be suppressed.

The Prohibition party is still active in 1999 and is already making plans to run a candidate in the year 2000. The six planks in the current platform are relatively consistent with earlier positions: anti-choice, religious freedom, right to self-defense, a sensible fiscal policy, American independence, and telling the truth about drugs and alcohol.

The most successful element in the history of the Prohibition party is its longevity. The party has survived devastating losses, splits within the party, ridicule, the repeal of Prohibition, and being ignored and misunderstood by the majority of the American public. Yet, they refuse to die. In the midst of Prohibition fever in the 1890s, it was even briefly known as the "Snowball party" because it doubled its votes in every election. Undaunted by its lack of success, party leaders claimed in an 1889 speech that they had demanded attention, made people think about their cause, brought their views into prominence, served as a thorn in the sides of other politicians, and forced the country to think about temperance.

Even though the Prohibition party cannot take total credit for the passage of the Eighteenth Amendment, the party can congratulate itself on some spectacular legislative successes spanning several decades. These successes included two anti-canteen laws; a ban on the sale of alcohol on certain Pacific Islands; a ban on alcohol at immigrant stations and in and around the Capitol Building; the Pure Food and Drug Act requiring accurate labeling of alcohol and drugs shipped across state lines; identification of whiskey as straight, rectified, or blended; and a ban on the shipment of liquor by mail.

In the early 1890s, the Prohibition party succeeded in electing the following state legislators: Wendell P. Stafford of Vermont; U.E. Mayhew of Connecticut (two terms); George L. Jones of Connecticut; W. P. Buffen and George F. Varney of Rhode Island; and W.A. Sager of Virginia. The following were elected as mayors: Jethro C. Brock of New Bedford, Massachusetts; C.W. McClair of Ogdensburg, New York; Henry Johnston of Washington, New Jersey; C.W. Pettit of Norfolk, Virginia; Samuel L. Jewett of Haverhill, Massachusetts; and William McCarthy of Nashville, Tennessee.

Successes of the Prohibition party contin-

ued into the twentieth century. In 1950, Indiana elected four township officials, and the party was represented by two town councilmen in 1959. Kansas produced a number of successful Prohibition party candidates: eleven township officials in 1948, nineteen township officials in 1950, and a sheriff in 1952. Still, the most significant victories of the Prohibition party took place in the late nineteenth century, including in Colorado where seven towns elected a straight Prohibition party ticket in 1894. There were also notable increases in support for the party in New York, New Jersey, and California during this period. In 1890, the Prohibition party even managed to get a representative in Congress: Kittel Halvorsen, an American of Scandinavian descent from Minnesota, won on the Prohibition ticket—partially because of an endorsement by the Farmer's Alliance.

PARTY MEMBERSHIP

The traditional interpretation of the membership of the Prohibition party is that it was made up of evangelicals and farmers. However, a 1976 re-examination of the make-up of the party revealed some surprising conclusions. Political scientist Jack S. Blocker maintains that support for the party was evident in fifteen separate states: New York, Pennsylvania, New Jersey, Michigan, Ohio, Indiana, Illinois, Wisconsin, Minnesota, Iowa, Missouri, Kansas, Nebraska, South Dakota, and North Dakota. Blocker also found that 37.8 percent of the party members came from areas of at least 100,000 people, and another 18.6 percent were from areas of at least 10,000. While four-fifths of the membership was, indeed, evangelical, only 37.2 percent were clergymen. Businessmen made up an additional 17.2 percent, and lawyers comprised another 15.9 percent. Most members of the Prohibition party were educated above the norm: 22.6 percent graduated seminary; 26.8 graduated college; and another 15.7 attended college. Blocker

ELECTION RECORD OF THE PROHIBITION PARTY

Year	Popular Vote	% Gains/Losses
1872	3,371	Not Applicable
1876	6,743	+70
1880	9,674	+8
1884	147,482	+1,359
1888	249,813	+67
1892	270,770	+6
1896	125,072	−50
1900	209,004	+58
1904	258,539	+24
1908	252,821	−2
1912	207,972	−2
1916	221,030	−1.7
1920	188,391	−10
1924	54,833	−69
1928	34,489	−66
1932	81,916	+31
1936	37,668	−56
1940	58,685	+53
1944	74,733	+29
1948	103,489	+37
1952	73,413	−29
1956	41,937	−42
1960	44,087	+10
1964	23,266	−53
1968	14,915	−35
1972	13,505	−3
1976	15,934	+14
1980	7,212	−56
1984	4,242	−57
1988	8,002	+67
1992	935	−80
1996	1,298	+44
2000	—	—

Note: It would serve little purpose to detail the percentage outcome of each year for the Prohibition party. Until 1884, they received less than 1 percent in three elections. In all elections, they rarely received more than 2 percent. When it would have been feasible to expect a large measure of support in light of the ratification of the Eighteenth Amendment, they actually lost votes. Therefore, it is more helpful to examine the gains and losses of the party than to focus on percentage points of the popular vote.

Source: Popular votes and gains/losses are courtesy of the Prohibition party, which maintains a presence on the Internet and at the University of Michigan.

concluded that the commonality among them was that they all believed in America's transcendent purpose to provide a model society for the world.

The success or failure of any third party in the United States is greatly dependent upon electoral factors beyond the control of the party. A study by political scientist Paul S. Hernnson revealed that only nine states have lenient ballot access, making it easier for third parties to get on the ballot. There are also thirteen states that require high filing fees for potential candidates. Since the major parties have more funds available, this puts all third parties at a disadvantage. Hernnson notes that no third parties have won victories in these thirteen states in the last fifty years. In addition to these obstacles, third-party candidates are pitted against the well-organized and professionally produced campaigns of the Democrats and Republicans. The winner-take-all system in place in forty-eight states dictates that third-party candidates do not win electoral votes. For example, Ross Perot earned 19 percent of the popular vote in 1992, but his electoral votes were non-existent. At the legislative level, single-member districts result in victories only for Democrats and Republicans. Finally, the fact that the major parties develop umbrella platforms aimed at pleasing the most people and their tendency to reconfigure themselves over time threaten the appeal of third parties, which are generally seen as more radical and with less chance of success.

It is unlikely that the Prohibition party will become more effective in the American political system as time goes by. Nonetheless, it serves a viable purpose in reminding all citizens that dissent is integral to democracy and that all viewpoints have a right to be heard. It is also important to recognize the contribution that the Prohibition party made to women's rights. The equal rights amendment never became part of the United States Constitution, and women still do not receive equal pay. Yet, women have broken down many barriers that were entrenched before the Prohibition party included an equal rights amendment in their party platform. Ultimately, much credit should be given to any third party that can surmount so many obstacles to earn its place in American history as the country's oldest third party.

ELIZABETH PURDY

See also: **Map 20:** Prohibition Party (1884); **Map 21:** Prohibition Party (1888); **Map 22:** Prohibition Party (1892); **Map 23:** Prohibition Party (1896); **Map 24:** Prohibition Party (1900); **Map 25:** Prohibition Party (1904); **Map 26:** Prohibition Party (1908); **Map 27:** Prohibition Party (1912); **Map 28:** Prohibition Party (1916).

Bibliography

Behr, Edward. *Prohibition: Thirteen Years that Changed America.* New York: Arcade, 1996.

Blocker, Jack S. *Retreat from Reform: The Prohibition Movement in the United States, 1890–1913.* Westport, CT: Greenwood, 1976.

Cashman, Sean Dennis. *Prohibition: The Lie of the Land.* New York: Free Press, 1981.

Cherrington, Ernest H. *The Evolution of Prohibition in the United States of America.* Westerville, OH: The American Issue Press, 1920.

Colvin, David Leigh. *Prohibition in the United States.* New York: George H. Doran, 1926.

Hernnson, Paul S., and John C. Greer, eds. *Multi-Party Politics in America.* Lanham, MD: Rowman and Littlefield, 1997.

Hesseltine, William B. *Third Party Movements in the United States.* Princeton: D. Van Nostrand, 1962.

Kobler, John. *Ardent Spirits: The Rise and Fall of Prohibition.* New York: G. P. Putnam's Sons, 1973.

Nash, Howard Pervear. *Third Parties in American Politics.* Washington, DC: Public Affairs Press, 1959.

Rosenstone, Steven J., et al. *Third Parties in America: Citizen Response to Major Party Failure,* 2d ed. Princeton: Princeton University Press, 1996.

READJUSTER PARTY OF VIRGINIA

1877–1883

The Readjuster Party of Virginia enjoyed a brief heyday from about 1877 to 1883 when they controlled the state legislature, elected members of the U.S. Congress, named two U.S. senators, and elected William E. Cameron as Virginia's governor. Originally a movement within the conservative Democratic party that dominated Virginia politics, most Readjusters were ultimately absorbed into the Republican party. Readjusters received strong support among whites in the south and west and in many of the eastern counties with large black populations. However, the Readjusters also united urban blacks, white ethnic minorities and middle-class voters in the urban areas. Most party leaders also came from urban areas, leading recent scholars to dismiss older works that characterized the Readjusters as an agrarian revolt.

Unlike the other "reconstructed" southern states, Virginia never elected a radical Republican government. As a result, when people began to blame the incumbent government for the economic troubles after the panic of 1873, their ire was directed at conservatives (the state's Democrats), not radical Republicans like elsewhere in the South. Nonetheless, the Republican party was so weak and divided that they did not even run a candidate in the 1877 gubernatorial election.

Without Republican opposition, there appeared to be little need to maintain white unanimity in the conservative party. As a result, more conservative candidates began to capitalize on discontent with the state economic policy. The contended economic policy was the payment terms of state debts from before the war (including notes owed by what was now West Virginia and interest that had compounded from the war years). To make payment on the debt, conservative leaders underfunded the newly established public schools. Those who opposed the policy were called "readjusters" since they wanted to renegotiate the payment schedule.

Five candidates sought the conservative nomination for governor, but only former railroad president and Confederate General William Mahone openly indicated that he supported the readjuster cause. Mahone controlled the most delegates at the party convention, but fell short of a majority. After determining that their cause was futile, Mahone's lieutenants released his delegates to William M.K. Holliday, who some allies thought to be sympathetic. Following his defeat, General Mahone organized a readjuster campaign within the party. Twenty-two independents sympathetic to the readjuster campaign won seats in the state legislature.

Realizing that he could use the debt issue to his advantage, Mahone and his allies in the state legislature called for a Readjuster State Convention in 1879. Most participants were disgruntled and disaffected conservatives, but there were also Republicans, Greenbacks, and other independents in attendance including black delegates from two counties. Harrison H. Riddleberger, a lawyer from the Shenandoah Valley, drafted an address that established the conditions under which the Readjusters would support any debt settlement. These included releasing Virginia from West Virginia's share of the debt, requiring that the payment schedule be compatible with the tax rate, and ensuring that the bondholders not receive tax receivable coupons or tax exemptions. Further, they argued that any settlement must be subject to ratification by referendum and modified by future legislators. In response, the Democratic party, firmly controlled by the Readjusters' opponents, declared that all conservatives must accept the debt-reconstructing McCulloch Act (the party's solution to the debt crisis).

This demand formally split the conservatives. Relying on separate campaign organizations, the two sides contested almost every district in the state. Public meetings were used extensively by the parties, and many featured speakers from each side. On election day, the Readjusters triumphed, winning 20 of the 40 state senate seats, and 42 of 100 state house seats. After agreeing to repeal the poll tax and other concessions to the blacks and other sympathetic Republicans, the Readjusters' plurality became a secure majority in both houses.

Once in office, the Readjusters used the spoils system to solidify the party's support and killed the conservatives' financial program. However, State Senator Riddleberger proposed a bill that included most of the Readjusters' original stipulations, but Governor Holliday vetoed the bill, and the Readjusters were unable to override the veto.

In the federal elections of 1880, the Republicans and Readjusters ran separate tickets after Mahone failed to unite both behind an independent electoral scheme. Ostracized by the national Democrats, the Readjusters' ticket finished a distant third in the presidential race, polling 31,507 votes to the National Democrats' 96,449 and the GOP's 84,020. The Readjusters won two congressional seats, as did the Republicans. The state legislature, though, named Mahone to the U.S. Senate, although he initially did not indicate which party caucus he would join. Refusing to join the Democrats after being snubbed during the campaign, he joined the GOP, breaking a tied Senate to give the Republicans a bare majority. In return for his support, Mahone solicited financial support from national Republicans and gained control of federal patronage from the white, anti-Readjuster "straight-out" Republicans in Virginia.

In 1881, the Readjusters nominated Mayor William E. Cameron of Petersburg as their gubernatorial candidate. Earlier that year, he had successfully helped lobby the Negro state convention to support the Readjusters. With the support of many black delegates and most "Mahonites," he defeated John E. Massey, a long-time advocate of readjustment popular with western farmers. Aided by drought conditions and out-of-state Republican contributions to pay poll taxes, Cameron won the general election with 53 percent of the vote, and the Readjusters rode his coattails in the legislature. Riddleberger was named to join Mahone in the Senate that same year.

No longer blocked by the governor's veto, the Readjusters passed the Riddleberger Act in February 1882. The final bill repudiated a third of the debt and authorized bondholders to exchange their securities for new bonds with only a lower interest rate. Readjusters also passed new school funding bills requiring the state to retain at the local level 90 percent of all taxes collected for schools. More money was allocated to colleges and mental hospitals. Farmers enjoyed a 20 percent cut in the property tax. To compensate, government expenses were cut and the tax-collection process was made more efficient. Cameron personally led a high-profile expedition against the "oyster pirates" who were illegally dredging the shores of the Chesapeake.

Once their initial legislative victories were realized, the Readjusters divided. Much of the dissent focused on Mahone's firm leadership style and his courtship of the Republicans. Massey left the party, joined by Congressman Abram Fulkerson and enough state senators to deadlock the upper chamber. Desperate to stem the losses and eliminate confusion over who was really a Readjuster candidate in districts with multiple Readjuster and Republican candidates, Mahone attempted to obtain pledges from Readjuster candidates that they would vote for all men and measures approved by the party caucus. The conservatives welcomed the defectors and used Mahone's autocratic image to their political advantage. Still, the Readjuster-Republican Coalition carried six of the ten congressional seats in 1882 including a statewide race that became a kind of referendum on Massey.

After the Supreme Court upheld part of the Riddleberger Act, the conservatives accepted the outcome, essentially healing the schism, and invited former conservatives back into the Democratic fold. As a result, many Readjusters such as Massey happily returned to the Democrats. Exploiting a race riot in Danville three days before the election, the Democrats resorted to racial demagoguery. Aided by a strong white turnout and a suppressed black turnout, the Democrats swept to a landslide victory. Once in control, they controlled patronage, gerrymandered the congressional districts, launched investigations into alleged graft and corruption by the Readjusters, and publicly called on Mahone to resign his Senate seat for being an instigator of strife between the races. In response, Mahone united the Readjusters with the Republicans in 1884, only to watch his party's patronage power destroyed by Grover Cleveland's presidential victory.

The Democrats won the gubernatorial race in 1885 and resumed their domination of Virginia politics except for pockets still controlled by the Republicans. The Readjuster legacy lived on through both parties. Much of the old "Bourbon," or reconstituted antebellum, Democratic leadership was replaced by younger, more liberal politicians who adopted Readjuster policies including increased support for public schools, colleges, and mental institutions. Some histori-ans credit the Readjusters with sowing the seeds for populism in Virginia a decade later.

RENAN LEVINE

See also: William E. Cameron; William Mahone.

Bibliography

Blake, Nelson M. *William Mahone of Virginia: Soldier and Political Insurgent.* Richmond: Garrett and Massie, 1935.

Calhoun, Walter T., and James Tice Moore. "William Evelyn Cameron: Restless Readjuster." In *The Governors of Virginia, 1860–1978,* ed. Edward Younger et al., pp. 95–110. Charlottesville: University Press of Virginia, 1982.

Lowe, Richard. *Republican and Reconstruction in Virginia, 1856–70.* Charlottesville: University Press of Virginia, 1991.

Maddex, Jack P., Jr. *The Virginia Conservatives 1867–1879: A Study in Reconstruction Politics.* Chapel Hill: University of North Carolina Press, 1970.

———. "Virginia: The Persistence of Centrist Hegemony." In *Reconstruction and Redemption in the South,* ed. Otto H. Olsen, pp. 113–155. Baton Rouge: Louisiana State University Press, 1980.

Moore, James Tice. *Two Paths to the New South: The Virginia Debt Controversy 1870–1883.* Lexington: University Press of Kentucky, 1974.

Pearson, Charles Chilton. *The Readjuster Movement in Virginia.* New Haven: Yale University Press, 1917.

Pulley, Raymond H. *Old Virginia Restored: An Interpretation of the Progressive Impulse, 1870–1930.* Charlottesville: University Press of Virginia, 1968.

REFORM PARTY

1995–

*T*he Reform party bears the unique distinction as the first major American political party born on television. To be exact, it came to the attention of the world on "Larry King Live," aired on September 25, 1995, on the CNN network. The guest was Texas billionaire, Ross Perot, who announced that he was starting a third party to satisfy the millions of Americans who wanted an alternative to the Democratic and Republican parties. Perot, whose presidential bid made him a force to be reckoned with on the national scene, predicted that his new party would either replace one of the two major political parties, or remain in business as an unpredictable swing bloc of voters siding with the party most sympathetic with the Reform party's centrist agenda.

HOW AND WHY THE PARTY AROSE

Perot's new party originated with United We Stand America (UWSA), the organization he created to support his first run for the White House in 1992. Although UWSA started as a political party, the group was quickly converted into a self-styled non-partisan grassroots citizen watchdog group, a form designed to counter the negative feelings many Americans held toward the two-party system and, in particular, the parties' aversion to issues. UWSA was used in 1992 to organize volunteers (many of whom were paid) to conduct campaigns to get Perot on the ballot in all fifty states. The party was initially called the Independence party—a name that was quickly discarded because it was already in use. The name Reform party was finally chosen. Perot would utilize the existing UWSA infrastructure for his new party.

So far, the Reform party has kept Perot's presidential aspirations alive; at the same time, the party has helped to keep many of Perot's favorite issues at the forefront of the American political agenda. Created at a time of profound disappointment with the two-party system, the organization has served as an outlet for the political frustrations of many voters, as well as a vehicle for issues (such as campaign finance reform) that most politicians in power would prefer to sweep under the rug. The 1980s and 1990s have witnessed increases in voter apathy as well as voter anger; indeed, the rancorous nature of political discourse has turned many voters off politics altogether. The 1996 presidential contest, for example, saw the lowest percentage of voters pull the lever for the leader of the world's only superpower since 1920. Another percentage point would have dropped the year to 1820. What political scientist Charles Jones calls "separated government" (the Democrats in the White House and, since 1994, Republican control of the House and the Senate) has raised the stakes between the two major political parties. As a result, politics has become more divisive, and bipolar. In the "new" political environment, issues have become paramount, while the old patterns of consensus and compromise have receded in political dialogue, reflecting the winner-take-all attitudes of the combatants.

Divided, or separated government, has also caused an increase in what is known as politics by other means, the strategy by which parties employ non-electoral means to bring down their opponents. The most familiar technique is known as RIP (Revelation, Investigation, and Prosecution). Most recently, the Clinton presidency suffers under the RIP of the Starr investigation and report, but RIP's bipartisan legacy reveals a recent history of several dozen special prosecutors and independent counsels, appointed to root out a wide range of abuses. The Reagan administration, for example, was thoroughly investigated for the Iran-Contra scandal; Democratic House Speaker Jim Wright of Texas was forced to resign under the prodding of then back-bencher Representative Newt Gingrich (Republican, Georgia); and in a striking turnabout several years later, Speaker Newt Gingrich found himself the target of ethics probes, although he managed to retain his office. The use of ethics probes and criminal investigations occupies center stage, in place of issue-related debates between the two parties.

In the context of the end of the cold war, politics has focused on the enemy from within as opposed to fighting the foes of cold and hot wars that have plagued the nation for the last 100 years. National unity is easier to perpetuate in the face of economic and political external threats; ironically, peace and relative prosperity brings out issues that have long festered beneath the surface.

American voters, increasingly frustrated by the incessant negative politics and scandal-mongering all around them, were ripe for a third-party movement in the 1990s. Ross Perot's 1992 run for the White House crystallized voter anger and scared many adherents of the two-party system. In 1992, Ross Perot captured 18.86 percent of the vote, a hefty number for a third-party candidate in any race. Significantly, later analyses showed that Perot took equal numbers of votes from both political parties, even though initial estimates concluded that the Republicans suffered more than the Democrats.

In contrast to other third parties, the Reform party appeared uniquely positioned to take advantage of voter anger and frustration. The Libertarian party, the Green party, and the Right-to-Life party, for example, seemed unable to surmount the organizational obstacles to become truly viable national parties. Ironically, along with ballot access, the major obstacle is still money, and thanks to Perot's financial resources, this obstacle was surmounted, at least initially. Perot hoped that voters would prove their commitment by contributing some of their own money to the party. The Reform party also had the advantage of retaining the infrastructure of volunteers and staffers (not to mention mailing lists, media contacts, etc.) from UWSA, as well as the party's proven ability to get their candidate on the ballot in all fifty states.

MAJOR PLAYERS, ORGANIZATION STRUCTURE, AND ACTIVITIES

Like the Bull Moose party and its standard-bearer, Theodore Roosevelt, the Reform party owed its initial success to the determination and charisma of one man, Ross Perot. Paradoxically, while other third-party movements dissipated with the abdication of their leaders, who typically returned to the warm embrace of their original parties, the fate of the Reform party hinges on Perot's willingness to stay with the party and continue to lend it his considerable financial support: When Perot announced the creation of the party on national television, he implied that he would not necessarily continue as the party's leader. Many of Perot's own advisors believed that the viability of the party in the long run depended on the group's ability to develop into something more than a Perot campaign organization. Those who argue, on the other hand, that the fate of the party rests with Perot's inclination to relinquish his leadership role are historically naïve.

Perot initially said that the party would not run candidates for Congress in 1996. Instead, he said, the party would concentrate on the presidential race in the year 2000 and continue to endorse candidates sympathetic to the Reform agenda. This strategy, he contended, would allow his followers to act as swing voters in congressional elections. Nevertheless, the thirty-two congressional candidates who ran for Congress in 1996 under the Reform label were all soundly defeated.

In 1996, Perot tried to take a backstage role in the presidential elections, reportedly attempting to court prominent politicians to run as the party's designated candidates. Perot's wish list included: former Senator David Boren (Democrat, Oklahoma), former Senator and Independent Governor of Connecticut Lowell Weicker (Republican, Connecticut), and then retiring Senator Sam Nunn (Democrat, Georgia). Only former Colorado Governor Richard Lamm—not Perot's choice by a long shot—announced that he would mount a challenge for the Reform party nomination. Shortly after Lamm's announcement, Perot decided that he would also seek the nomination. Governor from 1975 to 1987, Lamm's long and distinguished career included professional work as a lawyer, accountant, and law professor, as well as service in the Colorado State Legislature. He attempted a political comeback in a run for the U.S. Senate in 1992, but was defeated by Congressman Ben Nighthorse Campbell.

By the time he decided to run for president, Lamm had become a decidedly controversial figure, having already offended some leading interest groups. Known as Governor Gloom for his pessimistic view of America's problems, Lamm earned a reputation for frankness to the point of insensitivity. His most notorious stance involved the view that terminally ill patients had a duty to die and get out of the way. Similarly, he also argued that government money was wasted on teaching severely handicapped children to roll over.

Quickly dubbed the sacrificial lamb, the former governor fought an uphill battle to wrest the Reform party's nomination from Ross Perot without factoring in all the odds stacked against him. Perot's supporters had designed the nomination process to favor Perot's hold on the party: a complicated process, it consisted of a survey of Reform party members in which respondents were asked to identify the person they would like to see nominated. The survey, including only the names of Perot and Lamm, required respondents to write in the name of their choice and allowed them to choose someone other than Lamm or Perot. Anyone who received 10 percent or more of the votes would be invited to speak at a convention to be held in Long Beach, California, on August 11, 1996.

After the convention, Reform party members voted by e-mail, regular mail, and by phone for their chosen nominee. The winner would be announced at a second convention in Valley Forge, Pennsylvania, on August 18, 1996. The location of the second convention was intentional; it was chosen for its historical significance in the hope of identifying the Reform party's presidential candidate with America's most famous presidential icon, George Washington. Not surprisingly, Ross Perot beat Governor Lamm by a two-to-one margin.

The fight for the presidential nomination weakened the party. After the nomination, Lamm's allies complained bitterly that the Perot forces had rigged the election. Additionally, many Perot supporters were angered by Perot's announcement as he accepted the nomination that he intended to accept $30 million in federal matching funds; this was tantamount, they felt, to a betrayal of his previous position opposing public financing of election campaigns. For his part, Perot argued that he was entitled to these funds, fair and square; indeed he qualified for them, because of the number of votes he won in the 1992 presidential election.

REFORM PARTY DISSENSION AND UNEASE

Alas, Perot's about-face on campaign funding, coupled with Lamm's highly vocal opposition, cast a dark cloud on his second run for the White House. Many Perot supporters abandoned him at this point, claiming that in view of his acceptance of campaign funds and the Byzantine nomination process they blamed him for engineering, Perot had doomed the party. By accepting matching funds, Perot also restricted the amount that he could spend of his own money, a portent that to many supporters signaled a diminishing commitment on the part of the crusading billionaire. Another criticism revolved around the nomination process, with some advocates arguing that if Perot had allowed Lamm to win the nomination, the party would gain legitimacy as a broad-based organization, and thus escape the criticism that it existed only as a vehicle for one man's ego.

Bruised from the nomination battle, and saddled with low poll ratings, Perot decided to give his campaign a boost by choosing a highly visible running mate as vice-presidential candidate. In 1992, his choice was retired Admiral and former prisoner of war James Stockdale. Stockdale's lack of experience emerged quite vividly in the vice-presidential debate, embarrassing the campaign during the broadcast with his widely lampooned query, "Why Am I Here?" In 1996, Representative Marcy Kaptur (Democrat, Ohio) and David Boren (former Democratic Oklahoma senator and then president of the University of Oklahoma) reportedly turned down Ross Perot's requests to run as vice president on his ticket. He then turned to distinguished economist Pat Choate, with whom he had co-authored *Save Our Country: Why NAFTA Must Be Stopped Now*, a book opposing the North American Free Trade Agreement. The 55-year-old Choate grew up in Maypearl, Texas, and earned a Ph.D. in economics from the University of Oklahoma. He served as an economic advisor for two governors and later as Tennessee's Commissioner of Economic and Community Development, where he was responsible for organizing and administering the state's programs for industrial development, community development, tourism promotion, and worker training. He also held senior positions in the Commerce Department and the Office of Management and Budget in the Ford and Carter administrations, before becoming vice president for policy with TRW, a diversified multinational corporation. His six

books and many articles have been widely cited for their originality and substance. In his book *High-Flex Society*, for example, he introduced the concept of competitiveness to the professional literature, and *America in Ruins* explored the decay of U.S. infrastructure; today, these ideas have become very important additions to the language of politics and industry. Choate's most recent book, *Agents of Influence*, traced the flow of Japanese money in American politics and presaged the current debate over the role of foreign money in presidential elections.

Choate added considerable vigor to the national campaign, especially with his skills as a brilliant debater and platform speaker. His presence was not enough, however, to offset the major political obstacles strewn in the path of the Reform party. For openers, Perot and Choate were denied access to the series of presidential and vice-presidential debates aired in the weeks before the election. A bipartisan national commission (including the two former chairmen of the Democratic and Republican National Committees) handed down their decision that even though Perot and the Reform party qualified for federal funds, they had virtually no chance of winning; therefore, they would not be entitled to occupy a place on the debate platform. A very controversial decision on its face, legal efforts on the part of Perot and Choate failed to convince the courts, the Federal Elections Commission, and the Federal Communications Commission to invalidate this decision. It was too bad: The debates without the lively additions of Perot and Choate were lackluster and had very little impact on the election. In 1992, even though Perot did not win, he forced two issues on the agenda—international trade and the budget deficit—which enlivened the debates and changed the face of American politics in the 1990s. Challenged by the popularity of Perot and the budget issue, the Clinton administration and the Republican Congress worked hard for the following three years to bring down the deficit by several hundred million dollars, a task that had eluded both parties for well over a decade. Thanks to Perot and Choate, the international trade issue continues to occupy a larger role than it had before; even

The only Reform party candidate to win major office, Jesse Ventura was elected governor of Minnesota in 1998, winning 37 percent of the popular vote in a three-way race against Republican Norm Coleman and Democrat Hubert Humphrey III. *(Courtesy of the Office of Governor, State of Minnesota)*

though NAFTA was passed, legislation giving the president fast-track authority on trade several years later failed to muster the necessary votes.

ELECTORAL RESULTS

Perot and Choate emerged from the 1996 election with less than 8 percent of the vote, thanks in part to the lowered visibility they suffered by not being included in the debates. But the Reform party continues to exist, albeit with a lowered profile. Perot, Choate, and Lamm remain vocal on issues involving international trade, budget reform, and campaign finance; Choate

now hosts a national radio call-in show and writes books and columns on these issues. In the absence of inclusion in the debates, Perot was forced to rely on infomercials, thirty-minute specials geared toward explaining the nation's economic problems to the public. These worked very well in 1992, but in 1996 many of the networks refused to give Perot air time, even though he was willing to pay for it.

Reform party National Chairman Russell Verney also speaks out on behalf of the party on budget issues. Verney, the former executive director of UWSA, took over the new party. A 52-year-old decorated Vietnam veteran and former air traffic controller, Verney remains the most prominent "non-candidate" in the newly constituted political party. He served as a staff member in the New Hampshire State Legislature, then as an appointed member of the New Hampshire Public Employees Labor Relations Board. Before joining UWSA, Verney was the executive director of the New Hampshire Democratic party.

The Reform party emerged as a potential player in the 1998 elections with the surprise victory of Jesse "The Body" Ventura, a retired professional wrestler, who won the race for governor of Minnesota on the Reform ticket. With 61 percent of the eligible voters turning out on election day—almost double the national average—no one could detract from Ventura's victory by arguing that the electorate was apathetic! Ventura, who now insists on being called Jesse "The Mind" Ventura, ran away with 37 percent of the vote; the highest number of votes came from 18- to 29-year-old males.

Ventura spoke to mainstream Minnesotans, with the Reform party's message of fiscal conservatism and social liberalism. He swept aside such political pros as Norm Coleman, the Republican mayor of St. Paul, and Hubert "Skip" Humphrey III, the son of former vice president Hubert Humphrey. Most analysts expected Humphrey to win the governorship: As the state's attorney general, he had earned a reputation throughout the state as the hero of a $6 billion settlement with the tobacco industry; he had also emerged victorious from a scathing Democratic primary—dubbed

"My Three Sons"—from a field that included two other political scions.

Ventura injected spice and eccentricity into a lackluster campaign season. Indeed, who would not pay attention to the six-foot four-inch, 250-pound candidate with the shaved head and unconventional opinions, among them vetoing all tax hikes and rejecting contributions over $50? He also showed that a candidate with great name recognition—in addition to his wrestling career, he was also a radio talk show host, a former Navy SEAL, and a TV actor—could run and win office without a stash of big money supporting him. He traveled the state quoting Jerry Garcia (late guitarist for the Grateful Dead) and attracted considerable press attention, which more than compensated for the paucity of television advertising in his campaign.

In the aftermath of the lackluster 1996 congressional elections, the Reform party's national committee has become relatively inactive—at least compared with 1992 and 1996. They have endorsed a full slate of candidates running on the Reform party ticket but have not provided them with any financial assistance, a condition that may cancel out the party's effectiveness. In addition, the party was forced to deal with a Federal Elections Commission decision, handed down in March 1998, which elevated the party to national committee status for the purposes of federal election law. That means abiding by a stricter set of regulations, at the same time the party suffers from uncertain fundraising potential and very little money. The party's biggest asset remains Ross Perot, and at this writing, the uncertainty of his candidacy in 2000 leaves the party in political limbo.

PARTY PLATFORMS, ISSUES, AND POLICY PROPOSALS

The Reform party platform reflects its label—Reform—and has nine reform principles: high ethical standards for the White House and Congress; balancing the budget; campaign reform; term limits; creating a new tax system; Medicare, Medicaid, and Social Security reform; lobbying restrictions; foreign lobbying reform; and domestic lobbying restrictions.

In the face of the tremendous progress in reducing the budget deficit, the Reform party has seized on the issue of the projected budget surplus. Russell Verney argues, for example, that there is no surplus; on the contrary, the escalating national debt puts the very idea of U.S. budget surpluses in the realm of pure fiction. The Reform party strongly advocates using every penny of surplus to pay off the trillions of dollars that add up to the nation's domestic and foreign debts.

To achieve higher ethical standards on Capitol Hill and in the White House, the Reform party platform calls for a ban on gifts to elected officials, elimination of trips and junkets paid for by special interests, elimination of free meals for elected officials, and the passage of ethics laws with significant penalties. Finally, the Reform party proposes to reduce the comprehensive retirement and health plans of Congress and the president to that of the average citizen! The last proposals resonate with the latest polls, which reflect most Americans' anger at their nation's health care insurance system, with special focus on health maintenance organizations.

Like their counterparts in the Democratic and Republican parties, the Reform party platform has been criticized for offering scant details on how to accomplish its goals either politically or organizationally but, of course, platforms are not intended to do that. The budget plank, for example, recommends the development of a "detailed blueprint to balance the budget" and the passage of a balanced budget amendment. It also calls for eliminating the practice of keeping some programs off-budget, as well as creating a budget plan that all Americans could understand.

The Reform plank's suggestion for reforming the campaign process reflects the British view that electoral campaigns should have time limits. The party calls for the reduction of the campaign season to four months and for election day to be held on weekends, so that working people would be able to get to the polls more easily. Hearkening back to the Carter-Mondale election, when Carter conceded his presidency before the West Coast had reported in, the Reform party would also prohibit announcing exit poll results until all the ballots were in and voting had been completed all over the country. To avoid the problem of political "carpetbagging," the party also calls for a requirement that U.S. Representatives raise all their campaign money in their own districts; similarly, senators would be required to raise all of their money within their own states. Most important, the Reform party seeks to eliminate the electoral college, allowing the results of the popular vote to determine the winner in presidential elections.

On term limits, the platform would simply limit members of the House to serving three terms and senators to two terms. The tax system plank calls for a new system that is fair, paperless, and capable of raising enough revenue to pay the nation's bills. All future tax increases, the plank continues, should be approved "by the people at the next federal election."

As far as reforming Medicare, Medicaid, and Social Security, the Reform party seeks clear, consensual plans to fix these programs, as well as the pilot testing of any new plans that are eventually approved. In addition, the plans should be sufficiently flexible to change with the times.

The remaining three planks deal with limiting the power of lobbyists, particularly lobbyists who have previously worked for the government. The platform seeks new laws to restrict the ability of former government officials from becoming lobbyists for domestic as well as foreign corporations and to prohibit foreign contributions or gifts from foreign sources.

The Reform party faces major constitutional hurdles in reaching closure on its wish list. Term limits and the balanced budget amendment both clearly call for a constitutional amendment. On campaign finance, the party faces the *Buckley* v. *Valeo* decision, which equated soft money (contributions by the major parties to major candidates) in campaigns to the

free speech provisions of the Constitution. Advocates for the continuation of unrestricted foreign and domestic lobbying also cite constitutional protections for their issue.

Another problem facing the Reform party's issue reforms is historical. Third parties have never taken root in the United States because of the adaptability of the two majority parties; as soon as an issue seems attractive to voters—attractive enough, that is, to garner votes—one or both parties embrace its principles until there is no longer a need for the third party. Absorption, therefore, is the problem: The appealing, vote-getting issues are absorbed into the major parties until there is no longer a need for voters to express their feelings through a third party. Indeed, the 104th Congress adopted many of the Reform party's proposals on ethics reform. For example: gifts are banned to a large extent in both the White House and in Congress, where members cannot accept even a lunch if it costs more than $9.99! Term limits have already been adopted in over twenty states, while many members of Congress campaign on the promise that they will only serve two or three terms, lest they become a "professional politician." While many of these developments may signal the influence of the Reform party, they may also reduce its long-term impact and encourage its demise.

SOCIAL, CLASS, IDEOLOGICAL, OR REGIONAL BASE OF THE PARTY

Unlike many third-party movements of the past, the Reform party (or its predecessor, the UWSA) is not based in any particular region. Its adherents are drawn from all over the country. The common denominator among Reform members is disgust with the two major political parties and with politics-as-usual. They are people who were attracted to the 1992 Perot campaign and viewed joining the party as the next logical step. Not radicals of either the Right or the Left, most came from what commentator Kevin Phillips called the "radical center," or more realistically, the forgotten center.

Surprisingly, Ross Perot drew 20 percent (or higher) in thirty-one states, with the poorest showing in the South. Except for Texas and Florida, Perot's campaign received less than 20 percent of the vote in every southern state, the result, primarily, of his poor showing with minority voters. In 1992, the lion's share of Perot voters were white, were under forty-five years old, had college degrees, and enjoyed incomes well above average. They tended to dislike both major parties and harbored visible distrust of mainstream politicians. Although analysts initially thought Perot drew more votes from the Republican than the Democratic party, later data indicated definitively that the Perot/Stockdale ticket attracted votes equally from both political parties.

The election of 1996 revealed an electorate characterized by its lack of distinguishing characteristics. The Perot/Choate ticket attracted slightly more male than female voters; there were no appreciable differences among income categories within the general population among those voting for Perot; and the ticket suffered a drop (especially in contrast to 1992) among wealthier voters. No apparent regional bias appeared, although the Reform ticket's best showing occurred in the Midwest. Likewise, no ideological patterns emerged: Perot/Choate voters were drawn almost equally from self-described liberals, moderates, and conservatives.

Race continued to be one area that remained consistent: Reform party voters were overwhelmingly white in 1996, as they were in 1992. Issue areas were similarly congruent: Perot/Choate voters were more concerned with the federal deficit than their counterparts. Reform party voters in 1996 also held a generally pessimistic view of the economy and tended to believe that the nation was on the "wrong track."

Reform party members felt alienated by Democrats, who catered to liberals, and Republicans, who leaned too far toward the Christian right. Their problem was that they could not find their political identity in either camp.

Perot's 1992 campaign energized millions of these disaffected centrists, many of whom became Reform party members in 1995 and 1996.

Even though Reform party members come from many different ethnic, racial, and social backgrounds, it is still accurate to characterize the movement as essentially middle class, especially in terms of the values espoused by its leaders. Squarely in the middle of the ideological spectrum, party members also claim the middle ground in socioeconomic terms, with many adherents coming from the middle and upper middle classes. While party members remain united by their anger, they are also united by an affirmative agenda, with most of their positions—except for lobbying, abortion, and campaign finance reform—falling along conservative lines. These include strong positions on immigration, opposition to affirmative action programs, and support for term limits, welfare reform, and reduced spending.

A recent study of public attitudes about parties and major issues by Ronald B. Rapoport and Walter J. Stone suggests that the Reform party's most important niche falls in the area of economic nationalism. Many of these voters were fearful of the job losses entailed by America's entry into the global economy and distrusted the nation's abdication to international organizations to solve its own economic dislocations. They were energized by Perot and Choate's early opposition to NAFTA, and later to the World Trade Organization (WTO) and fast-track legislation, and looked to them as leaders who supported trade policies that were not as laissez-faire as past experience had dictated.

SUCCESSES AND SHORTCOMINGS

Judging the success or failure of a third political party is difficult. If one uses electoral success as one of the major criteria—namely, the number of public officials elected to office—then the Reform party is clearly a failure, having elected not one congressional or presidential candidate. In 1996, Perot won 8,085,402 votes, or 8.4 percent of the total number of votes cast. Of the thirty-three candidates running on the Reform ticket, none received more than 6 percent of the vote.

But despite its electoral deficiencies, the Reform party can boast a number of successes in other quarters, particularly if the party is linked with its predecessor, UWSA, and with its founder, Ross Perot. Clearly, the party has accomplished a great deal of what it set out to do in terms of elevating issues such as international trade, the budget deficit, political ethics, and term limits to the national agenda. Without the impetus of the Reform party, its leaders, and enthusiastic constituents, it is doubtful whether the budget deficit would have been reduced, ethics laws would have been strengthened, campaign finance would have been discussed seriously, and greater care in passing trade legislation would have ever occurred.

The problem is whether the Reform party has built a sufficiently strong organizational structure for the future. The party has very little money and a lot of internal factionalism. Perot's autocratic style of leadership has turned many away from the party, leaving splinter groups and disaffected voters in the wake of battles. One such splinter group, the American Reform party, held its convention at the same time as the Reform party in the fall of 1997, apparently in an unsuccessful attempt to steer the mantle of reform away from the original owners.

Thanks to Perot's showing in the 1996 race, the Reform party will qualify for approximately $12.5 million in federal funds for the general presidential election in 2000, and the party's national committee will receive an additional $2.5 million to conduct its nominating convention. But party experts conclude that the cash-strapped Reform party will have a difficult time competing with the two major parties in 2000, unless Ross Perot runs again or, if not, in the unlikely event that party leaders can recruit another self-financing candidate to carry the party's banner. Undeterred, the Reform party is endorsing, and in some cases, supporting 120

candidates for federal, state, and local offices throughout the nation in 1998.

Ross Perot continues at this point to lead the Reform party, which is both an advantage as well as a disadvantage. Until the party can exist without Perot at the top of the ticket, critics charge that it will not be taken seriously by a wider segment of the American public. At the same time, the party without Perot risks eventual disintegration, a dilemma that was illustrated by its experience in the 1996 election. In that case, if Perot had decided not to run, the party would not have benefited from federal matching funds; in addition, because of election laws, Perot would not have been able to finance another candidate for federal office—were he inclined to do so. With the clarity of twenty-twenty hindsight, perhaps if Perot had decided to run earlier, both he and the party would have done better in the general election.

IMPACT OF THE REFORM PARTY ON MAJOR PARTIES OF THE AMERICAN POLITICAL SYSTEM

Although the Reform party has not elected any major policy-makers, its impact has been felt by the two major parties. In the 1996 presidential elections, for example, the Clinton and Dole campaigns were very much aware of Perot and his Reform party followers, and both parties openly courted Perot voters. Even after the 1996 election, politicians from both parties continued to speak at Reform party conventions, court voters, and flirt with the party's issues.

On balance, the impact of the Reform party and Perot on American politics has been profound, particularly in terms of forcing both political parties to confront the issues that concerned so many voters. Perot was often ridiculed by the media for making extensive use of charts and graphs, but when he spoke up on the budget deficit, the national debt, or trade policy, it was evident that many people listened closely to what he said and understood what he was talking about, thanks to his willingness to spend whatever time it took and use whatever visuals he needed to explain these complex issues. Voters also respected the fact that he was sufficiently committed to the promulgation of these issues to invest his own financial resources to guarantee that his views reached the largest possible audience.

The laughter stopped when Perot and the UWSA drew 18.86 percent of the votes in 1992, ample evidence for the media and the political elites to take notice. Reform party officials count the public's "raised awareness" as their greatest contribution. Their Herculean efforts to get their own candidates on state ballots also highlighted an entirely new issue: restrictive ballot access laws across the country. The two major parties have always spent a great deal of money and political resources to maintain their electoral monopoly, throwing up an imaginative array of roadblocks designed to keep "maverick" candidates and parties off the ticket. These included requiring an arbitrary number of signatures on petitions to get candidates' (or parties') names on the ballot, and then invalidating some of those names in the state capital (usually accomplished by a cooperative patronage appointee of either party). All of these roadblocks forced third parties to hire expensive lawyers and lobbyists to fight for reinstatement; the price was often a sufficient deterrent to challengers. Prior to Perot's candidacy, most Americans were completely unaware of the institutional hurdles set up by the system to prevent the success of third-party candidates and parties.

The Reform party has continued to press for fiscal responsibility, promoting the unpopular argument that instead of more tax reductions, budget surpluses ought to be used to reduce the national debt. The party has also maintained its interest in ethics reform and campaign finance reform.

In the last analysis, there is no doubt that the Reform party and its standard-bearer, Ross Perot, have made their most significant impact on the issues of debt, trade, and fiscal policy.

They were also responsible, many argue, for playing a role in the election of the Republican Congress of 1994, thanks to Perot's endorsement of many Republican candidates, as well as his seal of approval on vital points of their agenda—the Contract With America.

As with so many third parties in past experience, the Reform party will probably continue to exert influence on issues—as long as the major parties persist in ignoring trade, campaign finance, and the debt for as long as they can.

SUSAN J. TOLCHIN AND JEROLD J. DUQUETTE

See also: H. Ross Perot; Jesse Ventura.

Bibliography

Barrett, Laurence I. "Aw Shucks, Y'all Want Me." *Time* (March 18, 1996).

Choate, Pat. *Agents of Influence.* New York: Alfred A. Knopf, 1990.

Cook, Rhodes. "Third Parties Push to Present a Respectable Alternative." *Congressional Quarterly Weekly Report,* July 13, 1996.

"Final Choice: Economist Pat Choate Is Perot's Running Mate." *Time* (September 23, 1996).

Fleming, Heather. "Debate Lockout Compounds Third-Party Efforts: Limits on TV Access Limits Campaign Effectiveness." *Broadcast & Cable* (October 14, 1996).

Greenblatt, Alan. "Reform Party's Chief Rivals: David and Goliath." *Congressional Quarterly Weekly Report,* July 17, 1996.

Jones, Charles. *The Presidency in a Separated System.* Washington, DC: Brookings Institution, 1994.

Judis, John B. "The Third Rail—Ross Perot: America's Charles de Gaulle?" *The New Republic,* May 20, 1996.

Kalb, Deborah. "Perot Gets Reform Party Nod, Will Take Matching Funds." *Congressional Quarterly Weekly Report,* August 24, 1996.

Lowi, Theodore, and Benjamin Ginsberg. *The American Government: Freedom and Power.* 5th ed. New York: W.W. Norton, 1998.

Pattison, Kermit, and Ron Stodghill II. "Body Slam." *Time* (November 16, 1998).

Pisano, Mark. "Leading Minnesota Race, 'The Body' Surprises Political Pros." *Washington Post*, November 4, 1998.

Rapoport, Ronald B., and Walter J. Stone. "1996 Party Leadership and Presidential Selection Survey Results." Manuscript, Department of Government, College of William and Mary, Williamsburg, Virginia, 1997.

Tolchin, Susan J. *The Angry American—How Voter Rage Is Changing the Nation.* Boulder, CO: Westview Press, 1998.

Walsh, Kenneth T. "Will This Man Be the Perot Nominee?" *U.S. News & World Report,* July 15, 1996.

———. "It's My Party and I'll Run if I Want To." *U.S. News & World Report,* July 28, 1996.

RESTORATION PARTY

1976

The Restoration party was less a party and more the 1976 presidential campaign of Ernest L. Miller. Miller was born in Virginia in 1898. He was a teacher, school principal, and minister before becoming the owner and operator of a health food store in Harrisonburg, Virginia. He also published a bimonthly Christian health magazine called *The Truth Crusader*, which circulated in all fifty states.

In 1974, Miller announced in the pages of *The Truth Crusader* that he had been directly called upon by God to run for president. At that time, he said he would be "God's independent, non-denominational, non-party candidate." He later called himself the Restoration party candidate, whose aim was the "restoration of national sovereignty and constitutional government" and the "restoration of the Constitutional right to unmolestedly worship and exercise faith in the supreme, sovereign creator, preserver, and ruler of all things."

Miller was convinced of the existence of a satanic conspiracy that aimed to abolish Christianity, private property, marriage, and the sovereignty of all nations, consolidating them under a one-world government. In an argument familiar in far-right circles, Miller traced this conspiracy to "an evil secret order known as the 'illuminati,'" organized in 1776 by Adam Weishaupt. This secret order is said to have taken various forms over 200 years, including "International Communism." Miller argued that this conspiracy had successfully infiltrated the U.S. educational system, news media, major political parties, and all the branches of government. Henry Kissinger, Nelson Rockefeller, and Ger-

ald Ford were said to be part of the conspiracy. Miller's platform claimed that "the survival of the United States and Christian civilization is dependent upon the exposing and complete eradication of this evil secret conspiracy." His long platform pledged some of the following: repeal the Federal Reserve Act; repeal the Twenty-fifth Amendment, which allowed the appointment of a new vice president in case of death or resignation, which Miller believed was designed to impose a communist dictator on the United States; repeal of the Sixteenth Amendment, which allows for a federal income tax; outlaw the Communist party; abolish the Department of Health, Education, and Welfare; adopt strict anti-abortion laws; "bring the Bible, prayer, patriotism, honesty, chastity, personal integrity, and a free economic system" back into public schools and remove "the devil, sensitivity training, sex education, one-worldism, socialism, Marxism, witchcraft, and brainwashing"; end federal aid to education and abolish compulsory attendance laws; impose rigid immigration controls and deport illegal immigrants and subversives; end weather modification and cloud seeding and "turn the weather completely over to Almighty God where it belongs."

Miller also pledged to have around-the-clock shifts of men praying in the White House. Miller was joined in his campaign by a vice-presidential running mate, Roy N. Eddy. Eddy, a former military officer and Florida police officer, contributed articles on survival supplies and strategies to *The Truth Crusader*. He resigned from the campaign just prior to the 1976 election for undisclosed personal reasons.

In its filings with the Federal Election Commission, Miller's national campaign committee listed officers and members from Virginia, Maryland, Pennsylvania, Tennessee, and Illinois. Some of these officers had been associated with George Wallace's presidential campaign in 1972. The campaign mounted efforts to qualify for the ballot in many states but succeeded only in Tennessee. Federal Election Commission records indicate that the campaign spent just over $50,000. The campaign raised money from subscribers to *The Truth Crusader*, purchasers of Miller's health food products, and from collection baskets passed at his campaign events.

Miller and Eddy received 361 votes in the 1976 general election, mostly in Tennessee, but with a handful of write-in votes in California, Colorado, Maryland, Georgia, and Florida. Miller campaigned in many states, speaking before various church groups and at colleges and high schools. He is said to have been a powerful and flamboyant speaker.

Miller never ran for office after 1976. He died in 1984, at the age of 85. His prolific writings and presidential campaign mark Miller as part of what historian Richard Hofstadter described as the "paranoid style in American politics." His arguments were consistent with many of the political themes of contemporary far-right activists such as fellow Virginian Pat Robertson and conspiracy-minded groups such as the Christian Patriot movement and the militia movement.

RAYMOND B. WRABLEY, JR.

See also: Ernest L. Miller; George C. Wallace.

Bibliography

Miller for President Committee, "Platform of Ernest L. Miller," 1976. P.O. Drawer 959, Harrisonburg, VA.

Obituary for Ernest L. Miller. *Daily News-Record* (Harrisonburg, Virginia), March 12, 1984.

REVOLUTIONARY COMMUNIST PARTY

1975–

The Revolutionary Communist party (RCP), a small Maoist-oriented political party, was founded in 1975, as a merger of several revolutionary movements, including the Black Workers Congress, the Puerto Rican Revolutionary Workers Organization, the Revolutionary Union, and the August 29th Movement of the American Southwest. The party has continued through the present and has spun off a significant youth organization known as Refuse and Resist.

The antecedents of the RCP go back to the Chinese revolution of 1949 and the split between the Chinese and Soviet Communist parties that emerged in the Nikita Khrushchev era of the late 1950s and early 1960s. Supporters of the Chinese revolutionary model were known as "anti-revisionists" because of their belief—initiated by Mao Zedong—that the Soviet bureaucratic socialist model represented a dangerous and destructive revision of the original communist ideas of Karl Marx and Vladimir Lenin.

Anti-revisionism received an impetus in the mid- to late 1960s by a number of political developments in the United States and abroad. At home, anti-revisionism won important and widespread support among the more radical New Leftists in the Students for a Democratic Society and the Progressive Labor party. From abroad came the inspiration of third-world revolutionaries from countries such as Algeria, Cuba, and Vietnam. The anti-revisionists—many of whom were students and intellectuals—were also inspired by the Chinese model, in which academics lent their hand to the rev-

The 1979 arrest of Maoist Revolutionary Communist party leader Bob Avakian at a protest against Chinese Premier Deng Xiaoping's visit to Washington sparked a nationwide protest campaign by the party (as shown in poster) and a three-and-a-half year legal battle. (*Courtesy of the Gary Yanker collection, Library of Congress*)

olutionary cause by going into the countryside to work with and organize peasants.

The first overtly Maoist, anti-revisionist organization in the United States was the Bay Area Revolutionary Union (BARU), founded in San Francisco in 1968. Attempting to bridge the divide between workers, students, and blacks, BARU organized among oil workers in Richmond, California, and established links with the Black Panther party in Oakland. A year later, BARU's main spokesperson, Bob Avakian, was elected to the board that headed the Students for a Democratic Society; 1969 represented the last year of the SDS's existence and the election of the working-class-oriented Avakian marked the student movement's growing awareness that links to workers were necessary to promote revolutionary politics in America. To overcome the obvious regional limitations in its name, BARU relabeled itself the Revolutionary Union in 1975 and became the core of the RCP when the latter was formed later that year.

With the overthrow of the pro-Maoist "gang of four" in China and the turn to the right among that nation's communist leadership, the RCP—which never boasted more than several hundred members—split in two. One half formed the Communist Party–Maoist-Leninist, which became more pro-Chinese than pro-Maoist. The Avakian wing kept the RCP name and became the only Maoist party in the United States by the 1980s. Throughout that decade and into the 1990s, the party supported the Maoist "shining path" revolutionaries in Peru and organized Refuse and Resist, to reach out to young people—and particularly young people of color—in the United States.

JAMES CIMENT

See also: Communist Party.

Bibliography

Ciment, James. Interview with Connie Julian, May 1, 1999.

Ignatiev, Noel. " 'Antirevisionism' (Maoism)." In *Encyclopedia of the American Left,* ed. Mary Jo Buhle et al. Urbana: University of Illinois Press, 1992.

☆☆☆☆☆☆☆☆☆☆☆☆☆☆☆☆☆☆☆☆☆☆☆☆☆☆☆

RIGHT-TO-LIFE PARTY

1970–

ORIGINS OF THE PARTY

The New York State–based Right-to-Life party (RTLP) is a single-issue minor party devoted to the abolition of abortion; it considers itself "the political voice of the unborn in the Empire State." The party's antecedents trace back to a book study group of Merrick, Long Island, housewives. During the New York State Legislature's consideration of a more liberal abortion law in 1968 and 1969, the formerly apolitical study group became involved in an unsuccessful effort to defeat the law. Subsequent enactment of a liberalized abortion law in New York in 1970, coupled with the Supreme Court's ruling in *Roe* v. *Wade* (1973), removing most state restrictions on abortion, accelerated their interest in the abortion issue.

FORMATION OF THE PARTY

Party leaders date the formation of their party to 1970, when they attempted to run two candidates for office. Right-to-life activist Jane Gilroy ran for governor, but she was disqualified when her nominating petitions were ruled invalid. Congressional candidate Vincent Carey won a ballot spot as a candidate for Congress from New York's fifth congressional district, running against incumbent Democrat Allard Lowenstein and Republican Norman Lent. Lent won a slim victory and, according to party leader Ellen McCormack, began to adopt anti-

abortion positions after the election in response to Carey's ballot showing. In 1976 the activists worked for the state Conservative party nominee for the U.S. Senate, Barbara Keating, who campaigned largely on opposition to abortion. Her 16 percent showing encouraged right-to-life activists.

In 1976, McCormack ran a single-issue campaign as a candidate in the Democratic party's presidential primaries in order to bring attention to the abortion issue. McCormack garnered 238,000 votes in eighteen primary states and acquired twenty-two convention delegates. In the process, she qualified for federal matching funds by raising the minimum of $5,000 in each of twenty states, as required by the Federal Elections Commission. In all, her campaign raised about $285,000, which was matched by $247,000 in federal funds. More than half of this was spent on television advertisements.

Despite what some considered a promising showing by a political unknown, this right-to-life group opted out of major-party channels, and in 1978 succeeded in placing Mary Jane Tobin, a party founder, on the ballot as a gubernatorial candidate in New York (McCormack ran as lieutenant governor). The leaders had decided that working within the major parties was fruitless, since neither party was considered adequately sympathetic to the right-to-life concern. In the election, Tobin received 130,193 votes (2.6 percent)— more than the New York State Liberal party's candidate. The significance of her showing extended far beyond the seemingly small vote total. According to New York law, a political party obtains official ballot status by running a candidate for governor who receives at least 50,000 votes. Parties reaching this threshold have an automatic line on the ballot for the next gubernatorial election (parties are rank-ordered on the ballot according to gubernatorial vote total). For the RTLP, winning a ballot line represented a major victory. First, it meant that the party's anti-abortion position would be an automatic part of the ballot landscape in New York. Second, it meant that the party could engage in important bargaining with candidates for office through a unique feature of state law, the cross-endorsement rule. According to this provision, parties may nominate candidates already endorsed by other parties. The votes for a candidate from all lines are then added together. Natural political insecurity combines with competitive politics in the state to produce a situation where most office-seekers are anxious to appear on as many ballot lines as possible. The importance of the cross-endorsement rule is underscored by the fact that the RTLP has survived for several decades in one of the most strongly pro-choice states in the United States. Like other minor parties in New York, the RTLP has used its ballot line to bargain with candidates by offering the line in exchange for support for the anti-abortion position, and by threatening to run its own candidates with the hope of siphoning votes away from opponents. In 1979, the party claimed to have endorsed over 600 candidates running for office throughout the state. In 1980, the party endorsed McCormack for president, despite some sentiment within the party that it should have endorsed Republican presidential nominee Ronald Reagan, who took an anti-abortion stand in the 1980 presidential campaign (as California governor in the 1960s, Reagan had signed a liberalized abortion law, which cast some doubt on his anti-abortion credentials). In the eyes of some RTLP people, Reagan's campaign made what was considered a half-hearted effort to win the RTLP endorsement, and this helped tip the endorsement to McCormack. She appeared on the ballot in three states (New York, New Jersey, and Kentucky; McCormack ran as an independent in the latter two states), receiving 32,327 votes (24,159 in New York). The endorsement of McCormack precipitated a

major split with the National Right-to-Life Committee, then the nation's largest anti-abortion group, because it had endorsed Reagan. In 1984, after an intense intraparty struggle, the RTLP decided not to endorse anyone for president. Reagan was rejected because of the feeling that his opposition to abortion was weak. This position illustrated the single-mindedness and what many considered inflexibility of the party on abortion, as Reagan was indeed an opponent of abortion. The RTLP has feuded with other right-to-life groups that the RTLP perceived to be too willing to engage in bargaining and compromise.

In 1988, the RTLP endorsed William A. Marra for president. Appearing only on the New York ballot, he garnered 20,497 votes. The party made no presidential endorsement in 1992. Four years later, it endorsed Howard Phillips, who ran in forty-five states on the Taxpayers party line. In New York, he received 23,580 votes on the RTLP line.

NEW YORK STATE POLITICS

The RTLP devotes most of its energies to New York State politics. Although the stated preference of its leaders has been to endorse major-party candidates for Congress, the state legislature, and local races, it has not hesitated to run its own candidates. In fact, many of the candidates it endorses run solely on the RTLP line. The RTLP's zenith year was 1980, when it endorsed candidates in more than three-fourths of all races for Congress, state senate, and state assembly—a total of 200 elections alone. The average vote on the RTLP line for major-party candidates for these races was about 3.5 percent; the average vote for RTLP candidates running without a major-party endorsement was about 2.4 percent. In addition, the party made numerous other endorsements for county and local races around the state. The party's most visible symbolic victory was its endorsement of successful Republican U.S. Senate nominee Alphonse D'Amato. His vote total on the RTLP line exceeded his narrow margin of victory, thereby fostering the RTLP claim that it had elected D'Amato. Since the early 1980s, however, the number of RTLP candidates and endorsements has declined, as has their vote percent.

Specifically, the number of RTLP endorsements is dwarfed by those of other state minor parties. In 1990, for example, the state Conservative party endorsed 59 percent of all candidates running for the state legislature (covering a total of 211 state legislative seats— 150 in the state assembly, 61 in the state senate), and the state Liberal party endorsed 35 percent of all state legislature candidates. The RTLP endorsed 9 percent of state legislature candidates. This small endorsement rate might be interpreted as meaning that few New York office-seekers are anti-abortion, but this is not so. Far more officeholders and office-seekers share antipathy to abortion, but many with pro-life sympathies have rejected the RTLP endorsement because of the party's reputation for inflexibility and extremism. In 1996, according to the party, it endorsed a total of 107 candidates. Of those, 16 won election. This small number of endorsements underscores the party's diminished reach as compared with the early 1980s. Voter enrollment in the RTLP has increased gradually. In 1980, it stood as 8,031. By 1986, it was 21,606. In 1991, it was 25,066. In 1997, it was 48,855. Most of these enrollees are found in suburban and Upstate areas, as only 14,118 of the 1997 enrollees live in New York City (the city makes up nearly half of the state's population).

DECLINE OF THE PARTY

The importance of the gubernatorial race to formal party recognition has made quadrennial gubernatorial elections pivotal for the party. Its gubernatorial fortunes rise when it nominates more prominent public figures in years when the state's other conservative parties fare less well, and fall when its nominees are less well known and are opposed by stronger conserva-

tive candidates. After Tobin's strong showing in 1978, the 1982 RTLP gubernatorial candidate, lawyer Robert Bohner, received 52,356 votes, dropping the party's ballot position from fourth to fifth for the 1983–86 period. This dip prompted the party to seek a more well known candidate in 1986, when it turned to an anti-abortion Democrat, Nassau County District Attorney Denis Dillon. His vigorous campaign netted the party 130,802 votes. In 1990, the party nominated a Staten Island consultant and Republican, Louis Wein, who won 137,000 votes. In the 1994 gubernatorial race, candidate Robert Walsh received 67,750 votes.

The relative decline of RTLP fortunes after the early 1980s is attributable to several factors: 1) their emphasis on single-issue purity over conventional political norms of bargaining and compromise; 2) consequent alienation of many right-to-life sympathizers, including candidates for office who began to view the RTLP endorsement as a stigma more than a benefit; 3) the relative political liberality of state politics; and 4) the absence of any concrete political victories for the party in New York.

One example of the ostracization of the RTLP is seen in Nassau County, a strongly Republican and conservative suburban county on Long Island. From 1981 to 1997, the county Republican party formally barred any Republican nominee from accepting the RTLP endorsement, regardless of the candidate's views on abortion. Such a move is unheard-of in a state where multiple party endorsements are the norm. The ban was lifted in 1997 only because an RTLP endorsement of a Democrat helped that candidate upset a Republican to win a local election.

A study of the leaders and members of the RTLP in the 1980s revealed that many party leaders and activists were formerly uninvolved in politics but were activated by their strong feelings against abortion. Even among those whose only involvement with the party is by virtue of their enrollment, 75 percent reported engaging in abortion-related political acts beyond voting, such as attending protest meetings or contributing money. The study also found among identifiers high levels of political awareness and efficacy yet also high levels of cynicism toward government. The vast majority are either Catholic or fundamentalist Protestant. In general, the social and attitudinal characteristics of RTLP identifiers and leaders conform closely to studies of other New Right groups motivated by social-issue concerns. Party leaders in particular revealed devotion to the anti-abortion cause that eclipsed the desire to win more votes or elections. Thus, they rated education of the public on the issue to be a more important goal than winning elections. The leaders' inner-directed behavior, focused on issue purity over compromise and coalition-building, underscores their devotion to the anti-abortion cause, and their narrow electoral base.

These goals are reflected in contemporary party documents. According to its 1998 statement of purposes, the RTLP seeks to encourage passage of a constitutional amendment to reverse *Roe* v. *Wade*. Lacking that, it supports any and all legislative efforts to restrict abortions, and similarly opposes any effort to promote euthanasia (mercy killing). Their nine-point program includes ending Medicaid-funded abortions, support for educational efforts to inform women about the consequences of abortion, support for parental notification for minors seeking abortions, an end to so-called "partial-birth" abortions, opposition to restrictions imposed on those who picket at abortion clinics, opposition to physician-assisted suicide, opposition to granting legal protections to surrogates for sick persons who may be able to make life or death decisions over the ill, increased funding for groups that support women with troubled pregnancies, and ending public funding for groups that support abortion rights. The party's chair in 1998 was Lena Harknett. Despite the agenda focus on euthanasia, abortion continues to be the party's primary focus.

PROSPECTS FOR THE FUTURE

The future of the RTLP suggests no dramatic change in its fortunes. The dominance of the concern for issue purity over expanding the party's base has sharply limited its growth potential. Its survival in the 1980s and 1990s is attributable in large measure to New York's electoral rules, which have the effect of giving minor parties some basis for bargaining despite the continued dominance of the major parties. As long as the party continues to field or endorse gubernatorial candidates who win 50,000 votes, the party will continue to serve as an electoral voice against abortion.

ROBERT J. SPITZER

See also: Ellen McCormack; Howard Phillips; Mary Jane Tobin.

Bibliography

Herrnson, Paul S., and John C. Green, eds. *Multiparty Politics in America.* Lanham, MD: Rowman and Littlefield, 1997.

Scarrow, Howard A. *Parties, Elections, and Representation in the State of New York.* NY: New York University Press, 1983.

Smallwood, Frank. *The Other Candidates: Third Parties in Presidential Elections.* Hanover, NH: University Press of New England, 1983.

Spitzer, Robert J. *The Right-to-Life Movement and Third Party Politics.* Westport, CT: Greenwood Press, 1987.

Stonecash, Jeffrey; John Kenneth White; and Peter W. Colby, eds. *Governing New York State.* 4th ed. Albany: State University of New York Press, 1999.

☆☆☆☆☆☆☆☆☆☆☆☆☆☆☆☆☆☆☆☆☆☆☆☆☆☆☆☆☆

SHARE OUR WEALTH MOVEMENT

1934–1935

The Share Our Wealth movement in the 1930s was a challenge to the Democratic party and the presidency of Franklin Delano Roosevelt. Huey Long's Share Our Wealth movement was populist. As Louisiana governor and U.S. senator, Long was arrogant and even dictatorial. Long was willing to fight powerful economic elites in Louisiana to pass his program of progressive taxation, infrastructure projects, and social programs. His Share Our Wealth movement helped push the New Deal in a more progressive direction. But Long's assassination and the movement's meteoric rise through the power of the radio without a strong national organization led to the movement's quick demise.

HUEY LONG AND THE POPULIST TRADITION

Huey Long and his Share Our Wealth movement emerged from the radical populist tradition of the late nineteenth century. Long's slogan "Every Man a King" comes directly from Populist-Democratic presidential candidate William Jennings Bryan, who stated "Every man a king, but no man wears a crown."

Huey P. Long was born on August 30, 1893, in the town of Winnfield, Louisiana. In the midst of an economic crisis, Winn Parish had a strong radical populist and socialist tradition. As late as 1908 half the elected parish officers were socialists. Long's politics were cultivated in this atmosphere. Louisiana was underdeveloped, almost a third world enclave. Farmers

and workers in Louisiana were disgruntled, and Long ultimately became a vehicle for their concerns.

When Long burst onto the national scene it was during the Great Depression. The economy was in shambles. The Dow Jones Industrial Average dropped from a high of 381.17 in 1929 to a low of 41.22 in 1932. In 1933 unemployment reached an annual average of 25.2 percent overall and 37.6 percent for non-farm workers. Millions were destitute. These were fertile times for Long's brand of politics.

LONG'S RISE TO POWER AND PROMINENCE

Huey Long first ran for public office in a race for Railroad Commissioner of Louisiana in 1918 at the age of twenty-five. He won. As Railroad Commissioner he attacked Standard Oil and the railroad interests and built a reputation as a shrewd populist politician. In 1924, still only thirty years old, the legal minimum age to run for governor in Louisiana, he entered the Democratic primary and finished a strong third in a three-way race, garnering 30.9 percent of the vote. By 1928 Long won the Democratic gubernatorial primary with 43.9 percent of the vote in a three-way race. He swept the general election with 96.1 percent of the vote. The Kingfish had arrived. According to Harry Williams, Long got his nickname, the Kingfish, after he jokingly referred to one of his aides as "Brother Crawford," a character in the lodge on the popular "Amos n' Andy" radio show. This aide then started referring to Long as the "Kingfish," the leader of the lodge. Long loved it and would often call people on the phone and say, "This is the Kingfish."

As governor, Long was despised by corporate interests in Louisiana. After attempting to impose a 5-cents-a-barrel "manufacturers' tax" on the oil companies, Standard Oil and his enemies organized a campaign to impeach him. Long was accused of everything from bribery to plotting murder. There was an impeachment trial in 1929 but the move backfired. Long remained as governor and became more powerful and ruthless than ever.

Long moved forward with his plans for the state. Before Long became governor, Louisiana had only 331 miles of paved roads and three bridges. In 1928 a fifty-mile drive from Opelousas to Baton Rouge took six hours. By 1931, 10 percent of all the people working on roads and bridges in the United States were in Louisiana. During his tenure as governor he built 111 bridges, 1,583 miles of concrete roads, 718 miles of asphalt roads, and 2,816 miles of gravel roads. He also created a variety of social programs and construction projects: night schools for illiterate adults, free textbooks for school children, new hospital constructions, and the pumping of natural gas into New Orleans.

While building the state's infrastructure he was also building his political machine. The Long organization withheld part of the salaries of state employees. These monies—held in the infamous "deduct box"—were used to finance Long's operations. Few people who paid into the deduct box complained, at least publicly. For contractors, who paid up to 20 percent, it was just part of the cost of doing business. Manual laborers, who paid between 2 percent and 5 percent, were happy to just have jobs during the Depression. When the U.S. Senate investigated these practices, the head of Long's organization said with a straight face, "All the people employed have to pay or had to pay that 10 percent voluntarily."

In 1930, Long ran for the U.S. Senate and defeated incumbent Senator Joseph E. Ransdell with 57.3 percent in the Democratic senatorial primary. Long remained in office as governor and took his seat in the U.S. Senate after his governor's term expired in 1932.

In his short time in Washington, D.C., Long gained national prominence. He was colorful. He wore loud ties, drank heavily, and often presented the image of a playboy. He even got himself involved in a brawl that gave him a large cut over one eye. Even after Long had changed some of his bad habits, he was still arrogant, often giving lectures to other politicians and journalists on their own unhealthy practices. It was after these changes in his behavior that Long decided to start the Share Our Wealth Society.

THE SHARE OUR WEALTH MOVEMENT

President Franklin Delano Roosevelt's use of the media in his "fireside chats" has become legendary, but Huey Long was also a master of the airwaves. On February 23, 1934, Long announced on the radio the formation of the Share Our Wealth Society. The response to his message was tremendous. By April 1935 he received an average of 60,000 letters after each broadcast reaching a high of over 30,000 letters a day for more than twenty-four days in a row. He employed thirty-two full-time typists to answer his mail and needed extra office space in the Senate.

People were responding to the Share Our Wealth's bold economic proposal for progressive taxation and increased welfare state spending. Long wanted a tax that would limit family wealth to $5 million, which was about 300 times the fortune of a typical American family. He would also limit yearly income to $1 million, which was also around 300 times the average American income. This money would provide a "homestead" of $5,000 for each American family. The federal government would then guarantee a $2,000–3,000 income to all families, approximately one-third of average income, provide an "adequate" monthly pension, finance the college education of qualified students, and pay bonuses to veterans. The plan also called for limiting work to thirty hours a week and eleven months a year to create more jobs for the unemployed.

Long's plan was the most extensive of the wealth redistribution proposals that were being advocated by others such as Dr. Francis Townsend, Father Charles Coughlin, and novelist Upton Sinclair (who ran for governor in California in 1934 on the End Poverty in California campaign). All of them, including Long, called for inflationary or redistribution plans designed to help the poor. The actual numbers of Long's plan did not add up, but he believed in the general idea of wealth redistribution.

Long's history as Louisiana governor clearly showed that he was willing to take on powerful business interests in order to redistribute wealth. Extreme unequal distribution of wealth in the midst of widespread poverty was a central, if not *the* central, moral and economic issue of the Depression era. Although Long in all likelihood knew that the numbers did not add up, particularly after they were argued about and debated nationally, in his simple way he clarified the issue for millions.

Within a year and a half there were, according to Long's secretary, Earle Christenberry, 27,431 Share Our Wealth clubs with 4,684,000 members. Share Our Wealth also claimed nearly three million more supporters because they had 7,682,768 names and addresses. Long's enemies never disputed these figures.

These numbers do not tell the whole story. The Share Our Wealth clubs were primarily a southern, even a Louisiana regional, phenomena. One-quarter of the clubs were in Louisiana followed closely behind by Arkansas and Mississippi, but there is mixed evidence about the nature and extent of Long's potential support.

It is hard to gauge where Long's support would have been the strongest had he entered the presidential race in 1936. Louisiana and the surrounding southern states would have formed his organizational core. There is some reason to believe, however, that Long perhaps would have been able to make inroads beyond the South. A 1935 poll commissioned by the Democratic National Committee showed that

Long's support for a presidential bid was highest in the South at 14.5 percent, but not far behind in the Mountain States at 13.6 percent, the Great Lakes at 12.5 percent and the Pacific Coast at 12.1 percent. Nationwide, his support was 10.9 percent, and in the cities his support only dropped off to 9.8 percent. Some cities, such as Cleveland, showed a 16.3 percent preference for Long. Sectionalism was part of Long's appeal, but class seems to have played a large role as well. Among those who had received some form of government relief, his popularity rose to 16.7 percent nationwide and was actually higher in the Mountain States at 21.6 percent than in the South at 20 percent among these recipients.

A comparison of the Populist era of the late nineteenth century and the Depression era of the late 1920s and 1930s is instructive in ascertaining the likelihood of the Share Our Wealth movement having national success if Long had not been assassinated in September 1935.

The biggest obstacle to a possible alliance between southerners, western farmers, and northern industrial workers in the late nineteenth century was sectionalism. This was also a barrier for the Share Our Wealth movement. But there were significant differences between the populist and the Depression eras that might have helped Long develop a base beyond the South.

The populist movement appealed to southern and western farmers against corporate power within the era of the decisive shift of workers from agricultural to industrial labor. Between 1870 and 1900 the work of the nation changed. In 1870, 85.3 percent of the paid workforce was male and over half of these men (52 percent) still worked in agriculture. By 1900 the paid workforce was 64.3 percent industrial workers. By 1930 the country's work was even more industrial; 78.6 percent of the paid workforce was involved in industrial production.

This further shift to industrial work, the economic hardship of the Depression, and the fading memories of the Civil War all blunted sectionalism, providing Long with an opportunity for his class politics to succeed. In 1896 northern business interests were able to successfully "wave the bloody flag" of sectional hatred against Populist-Democratic presidential candidate William Jennings Bryan. By 1934, it is not likely that a similar appeal against the South would have worked.

Another crucial difference between America in the populist era and the Depression was the advent of radio, and its impact on organizing mass movements. Before the mass medium of radio the populists had traveling organizers (or "lecturers" as they were called) throughout the South and the West. Before the Populist party was even formed every local farmers' cooperative had a "lecturer" who organized educational activities, such as study groups. By 1890 traveling "lecturers" had organized over a million members. By 1892 the Populist party had elected five U.S. Senators, ten members to the U.S. House of Representatives, three governors and over 1,500 state legislators. Share Our Wealth had a grassroots organization in Louisiana, but nationwide Long was a voice of dissent on the radio. Long had hoped that an organizational vitality would emerge. He hired the Reverend Gerald L.K. Smith as the national organizer for Share Our Wealth. Smith traveled around the nation speaking to all who would listen. A minister with the Disciples of Christ, Smith had moved from Wisconsin to Shreveport, Louisiana, at the age of thirty-one. Long called him, "Next to me the greatest rabble-rouser in the country." Smith was a spellbinding speaker, and his sermons were broadcast on the local Shreveport radio.

Ironically, Share Our Wealth's organizing problems came from its source of vitality: the powerful oratory on the radio. While Long would stir people who listened to his weekly addresses, there was little for them to actually do. Organizing often consisted of gathering to listen to Long's radio address. While the nineteenth-century populists organized farmer cooperatives to work around the power of the landowners, corporations, and trusts, Huey Long urged people to write letters and listen to him. If he had run in 1936 and challenged the Democratic party, or had created a dissident group within the party, he may have been able to work out some of these organizing difficul-

ties. The radio spread his message far and wide on the air, but did not provide much support on the ground to unite the organization.

After Long's assassination in September 1935 there was nothing to sustain the movement. In the South, most of the Share Our Wealth clubs were not run by local radicals or dissenters but by local ministers and other establishment figures. Most of the Share Our Wealth clubs outside of the South were run by local organizers with their own local concerns. The movement had spread so quickly because of the radio that Long was not able to create enough of an organization in a short period of time to control the inevitable problems that were to arise. Often local infighting overshadowed Long's national agenda.

Dissident faction leaders of existing groups often emerged as the local Share Our Wealth club organizers. In California, Share Our Wealth leader Robert Noble, who had been an organizer for Upton Sinclair's End Poverty in California campaign for governor, broke off with Sinclair and used Share Our Wealth to attack him. In St. Louis, a local businessman, Arthur Mullen, used Share Our Wealth to create a local ticket of candidates under his own control as well as making money for himself. In Hoboken, New Jersey, and Philadelphia, local veteran's organizations took control of the Share Our Wealth clubs and singularly promoted Long's proposal for a veterans' bonus bill.

The Share Our Wealth movement had a similar impact on the party system that third parties often do in the United States. They move the major parties to address some of the issues and problems that the third parties are calling attention to. Huey Long had threatened to make a third-party run in 1936, but had not made any announcement before his assassination in Baton Rouge, Louisiana, September 1935. From 1928 to 1936 the Democrats had amassed a huge majority in Congress. The Republicans had lost 182 seats in the House of Representatives and 39 in the Senate. By 1936 the Democrats controlled the House by 333 to 89 (with thirteen from third parties or independents) and the Senate by 75 to 17 (with four from third parties or independents). In this political atmosphere, criticisms of President Franklin Delano Roosevelt from the Left had greater impact. A "second" New Deal emerged in which Social Security, the Wagner Act, and jobs creation programs became central to the New Deal's legacy. The Share the Wealth movement helped push Roosevelt to the left during and after the election of 1934.

HUEY LONG, SHARE OUR WEALTH, AND THE FASCIST QUESTION

There are those who argue that Long and his Share Our Wealth movement were not progressive, but instead represented some form of American fascism. There is little agreement among scholars on exactly what fascism is or was. Several characteristics, such as demagogic rhetoric appealing to mass sentiment, a dictatorial style, and scapegoat politics tinged with nativism, anti-Semitism, and/or racism, appear to be central to fascism.

Does Long fit this model? Long never openly identified with fascism but he had some of these traits. He certainly used demagogic rhetoric that appealed to mass sentiment attacking international financiers. This could be construed as nativist, but he attacked the American wealthy as well. His style of rule in Louisiana was increasingly vindictive if not dictatorial. He helped his friends, was ruthless with his enemies, and could be corrupt. But these are qualities that were also displayed by other political leaders who were never accused of fascism.

On the charge of anti-Semitism there is little support for this accusation. Long is often linked with the anti-Semitic radio preacher Father Charles Coughlin. He did work with Coughlin, but before Coughlin lurched into scapegoat politics. Long was assassinated in 1935, and Coughlin did not turn openly anti-Semitic until 1938. Long was shot by Dr. Carl Weiss, who people mistakenly thought was a Jew, which falsely created the impression that Long must have been anti-Semitic. Long's chief Share Our Wealth or-

ganizer, the Reverend Gerald L.K. Smith, was anti-Semitic before he became associated with Long. Smith attempted to contact Hitler in 1933 to help create a pro-Nazi American organization. He was also connected with the Silver Shirts, a pro-fascist organization in North Carolina. But there is no evidence that Smith ever talked to Long about this. After Long's death Smith complained that there were too many Jews in the Share Our Wealth organization.

Was Long prejudiced against African Americans? In the southern politics of this era, Long was a progressive on race, which meant that his rhetoric focused on class rather than race. He would make the obligatory genuflection to white supremacy when the situation called for it. His nickname, "the Kingfish," clearly played into the racial stereotypes of the era. But on key controversial issues while he was Louisiana governor, Long refused racist efforts to deny African Americans inclusion in his free textbook program. He understood that African Americans would gain the most from his redistribution program, and it did not bother him. Long was involved in organizing African Americans around the nation, including Louisiana, into his Share Our Wealth clubs. This was clearly not done to court black votes in Louisiana since African Americans made up less than 0.5 percent of the state's voting population. Long was attacked by Ku Klux Klan leader Hiram Evans, who pledged to campaign against him for an "un-American" attitude toward "authority." Long responded, "Quote me as saying that that imperial bastard will never set foot in Louisiana and that when I call him a son of a bitch, I am not using profanity, but am referring to the circumstances of his birth."

Although Long was demagogic and could be dictatorial, he did not use anti-Semitism or racism as a part of his appeal. The term fascist does not fit.

CONCLUSION

Huey Long and the Share Our Wealth movement grew in the fertile soil of economic catastrophe. Its program had its roots in the populism of the late nineteenth century. Long's appeal combined a progressive populist message with a flair for strong oratory that was sent to millions by the radio. The movement catapulted spectacularly onto the national scene, but Long died before there was a possibility of building a lasting movement. Share Our Wealth, although plagued with organizational deficiencies, did help push the Democratic party further to the Left during and after the election of 1934.

While Long's style of leadership in Louisiana became increasingly demagogic, arrogant, and dictatorial, accusations of fascism seem to miss his main message. His populism focused on class, not scapegoat politics.

TIMOTHY J. KILLIKELLY

See also: Huey Long; Upton B. Sinclair; Gerald L.K. Smith; Francis Everett Townsend.

Bibliography

"Agrarian Response, 1870–1900." I.(c) (2)(3) available from Marshall University, Web site (http://www.marshall.edu/history/mccarthy/hst331/lecture/agrarian.2). See also "Populist History" (class outlines and notes) (http://incolor.inetnebr.com/dennis/populist.shtml).

Brinkley, Alan. *Voices of Protest: Huey Long, Father Coughlin and the Great Depression.* New York: Alfred A. Knopf, 1982.

Burns, Ken. "Huey Long" Ken Burns's America series. Atlanta: PBS Video, 1986.

Congressional Quarterly's Guide to United States' Elections. 3d ed. Washington, DC: Library of Congress, 1994.

Dow Jones averages for 1920–29 and 1930–39 available from Dow Jones Web sites (http://www.dowjones.com and http://averages.dowjones.com/home.html).

Goodwyn, Lawrence. *The Populist Moment: A Short History of the Agrarian Revolt in America.* New York: Oxford University Press, 1978.

Hair, William Ivy. *The Kingfish and His Realm: The Life and Times of Huey P. Long.* Baton Rouge: Louisiana State University Press, 1991.

Hicks, John D. *The Populist Revolt: A History of the Farmers' Alliance and the People's Party.* Minneapolis: University of Minnesota Press, 1931.

Historical Statistics of the United States: Colonial Times to 1970. Washington, DC: United States Bureau of the Census, 1975.

Jeansonne, Glen. *Gerald L.K. Smith: Minister of Hate.* New Haven: Yale University Press, 1988.

Schlesinger, Arthur, Jr. *The Politics of Upheaval.* Boston: Houghton Mifflin, 1960.

Williams, T. Harry. *Huey Long.* New York: Alfred A. Knopf, 1969.

SILVER PARTY
OF NEVADA

1893–1900s

The struggle over slavery and the Civil War tended to obscure many of the nation's problems at mid-century—problems that regained the public's attention once emancipation had been achieved and the guns of war had fallen silent. Many of these problems were economic ones: the rapid expansion of the railroads and their growing influence over the nation's farmers, the diverse and serious financial inequities facing the working class during the industrial revolution, and the question of money or, more specifically, what kind of money—silver or gold—the nation would use.

A seemingly obscure question to modern readers, the form money would take was perhaps the most controversial economic question of late-nineteenth-century America. On one side were those supporting the use of gold: the major financial interests of the eastern cities including bankers, insurance companies, and financiers. They supported gold because it kept the value of money strong. Since there was a limited supply of the precious metal—with few major discoveries of new mines until the 1880s and 1890s (in South Africa and the Yukon)—allowing gold as the only backing for money kept the supply of money limited. This kept the value of the currency strong, preventing inflation and even producing deflation. This was good news for bankers who lent money because the loans would be paid back in ever more valuable currency.

Deflation was disastrous, however, for debtors. Prime among this latter group were farmers. Farmers who plant commercial crops—whether they own their own land or share-crop—are perpetually in debt, financing their operations by borrowing against the next crop. Because the value of the money supply goes up with gold, the price of their produce goes down. That is to say, a dollar buys more wheat with each passing year. That makes it more and more difficult to pay back loans. Utilizing plentiful silver as a way to back currency would ensure an expansion of the money supply, which, in turn, would lead to inflation and an easier means to pay back loans. For that reason, farmers and other debtors backed bimetallism—that is, the use of both silver and gold (at a sixteen to one ratio) to back the nation's money supply. In this political goal, they were supported by many westerners who lived in states where silver was mined. Utilizing the metal as a way to back the nation's currency would surely enhance the price of silver and boost the economy of the West.

In 1893, the Silver party was formed. While its agenda was primarily focused on the money question, it also advocated a host of issues that had been raised by its political ally—the Populist party. Among these were economic and political reforms, including a shorter working day, a progressive income tax, referenda, secret balloting, direct election of U.S. senators, and the subtreasury plan. This latter element concerned the establishment of government purchasing agencies, whereby the federal government would lend money to farmers and buy their crops at consistent prices. While the Populist party gained advocates throughout the country—particularly among farmers in the Midwest and South—the Silver party was strongest in the West, and most especially in the "silver state" of Nevada.

For the most part, silverites—as supporters of the metal were called—were defectors from the two main parties, although most had been Democrats, as the Republicans were increasingly associated with big business, finance, and gold as the nineteenth century ended. Not surprisingly, given their former membership in the Democratic party, silverites pursued fusion politics, cross-endorsing Democratic candidates or trying to persuade the Democrats to back Silver party candidates. Indeed, with the nomination of pro-silver William Jennings Bryan in 1896, the silverites would capture the Democratic party completely.

In the meantime, however, they worked in their western strongholds to get candidates elected under the Silver party banner, and they had some success at this. They elected silverites John E. Jones and Reinhold Sadler as governors of Nevada in 1894 and 1898 respectively, the former winning with 49.9 percent of the vote and the latter, running in a multicandidate race, winning with 35.7 percent of the vote.

The Silver party's moment in the sun was brief. With the Democratic party having adopted its central plank—a fate typical of many third parties in American history—the Silver party's membership and leadership was largely absorbed into the more mainstream organization. In addition, bimetallism had largely faded as a political issue by 1900. The vast new discoveries of gold in South Africa and the Yukon expanded the supply of the metal and, by implication, the supply of money generally, thereby creating the inflation silverites hoped to trigger by the introduction of their preferred metal.

ANITA CHADHA

See also: William Jennings Bryan; National Silver Party; Populist Movement/People's Party; Silver Republicans.

Bibliography

Durden, Robert. *The Climax of Populism.* Lexington: Kentucky Publishers, 1966.

Gillespie, J. David. *Parties at the Periphery: Third Parties in Two-party America.* Columbia: University of South Carolina Press, 1992.

Reichley, A. James. *The Life of the Parties: A History of American Political Parties.* New York: Free Press, 1992.

SILVER REPUBLICANS

1891–1900

The Silver Republicans were a western faction of the Republican party which supported the 1892 party platform committing the party to a bimetallic standard and the free coinage of silver. Drawn largely from the newly admitted western states, the Silver Republican party, founded in 1891 by Fred Dubois of Idaho, nominated its own candidate for the U.S. presidency, staged a series of Senate revolts against the gold supporters of the eastern party, and on several occasions joined with Silver Democrats and Populists to support measures remonetizing silver.

The recognition of silver as a legal tender was very important to western Americans for three reasons. First, there were more silver mines in the West than there were gold mines, and these silver mines were controlled by westerners. Second, with silver demonetized in 1873, the price of silver relative to gold had declined. Since many western farmers and miners had invested heavily in silver, they faced financial ruin. Finally, the issue of the gold standard represented a battle for power between eastern industrialists and western miners and farmers. The West, with its sparse population, could only exercise influence over national policies in the Senate. Such an opportunity presented itself in the election of 1894 with the election of six silverite Republicans to the U.S. Senate: Henry Moore Teller (Colorado), Richard F. Pettigrew (South Dakota), Lee Mantle (Montana), Frank J. Cannon (Utah), and William Stewart and John P. Jones (both of Nevada).

The election of six strong silver advocates was a blow to the Republican party, because during the 1880s and 1890s, the party leader-

ship's strategy had been to control Congress rather than the presidency. As the power of the Senate increased during the 1880s, the election of these six Silver Republicans meant that a substantial faction of Democratic, Republican, and Populist senators supported the silver standard and were in a position to stall legislation and potentially force concessions on the silver issue. In two years, Republican fears of a silver revolt would materialize.

The presidential contest of 1896 centered on the debate over a monetary standard for the United States. Western Republicans, openly campaigning as Silver Republicans, fought hard for a bimetallic plank in the Republican party platform. Eastern Republicans, fearing a bimetallic standard would create inflation, opposed this position. The Republican convention met in St. Louis in June to build its platform and nominate its candidate for the presidency. By all accounts, most delegates expected a heated debate over the gold standard, but expected the gold standard plank to remain. Henry Moore Teller offered the silver or bimetallic alternative, but his motion was soundly defeated. When the convention nominated and approved William McKinley as the Republican standard-bearer, many western silverites left the convention in disgust.

During the late summer of 1896, Silver Republicans debated several strategies, including joining the National Silver party and pressuring the Democratic party to nominate Teller. Silver supporters then made a critical error. They had expected the Democratic party to adopt a gold standard plank as well and decided to hold their nominating convention after the Democratic convention to capitalize on the silver is-sue. When the Democrats and William Jennings Bryan supported the silver standard, many sup-porters of silver monetization went with Bryan. Thus, the silverites lost their best opportunity to capture an issue that reflected a shifting power base in the United States and a potential reorganizing force in electoral politics. Silverites rallied to Bryan, but lost in the general election to McKinley.

The loss of the presidency was a blow to sil-ver supporters, but many silver senators gained re-election. Early in 1897, Silver Republicans, Silver Democrats, and Populists staged a revolt against the Republican leadership of the Senate and attempted to reorganize the Senate by the silver issue. The move was short-lived, how-ever. Except for each group's support for a sil-ver standard, they had little in common. More-over, the economic upturn of 1898 essentially undercut the salience of the monetary issue. The Silver Republican party's last official cam-paign occurred in the 1900 election, for which the party held its own convention and nomi-nated Teller again for the presidency.

The Silver Republicans were largely progres-sive Republicans, as can be seen from their 1900 party platform. This platform addressed the party's position on economic and political re-form, international policy, and western devel-opment. Economically, the party supported the restoration of a gold and silver standard, at a sixteen to one ratio, a graduated income tax, control of monopolies, and public ownership of utilities. Politically, the party supported direct election of senators and the merit system in public service. Internationally, the party sup-ported development of what would later be-come the Panama Canal, limited immigration and strictly regulated foreign ownership of U.S. lands and companies, an expanded pension program for U.S. veterans, and support for Phil-ippine and Cuban independence. Regionally, the party pushed for public transportation and irrigation of western lands for farming. In many ways, the Silver Republicans of 1900 had more in common with the Populist, Rooseveltian fac-tion of the Republican party than the conser-

The importance of the monetary issue to late nineteenth-century politics is captured in this July 4, 1896, cartoon. The pro-inflation and pro-farmer faction of the Republicans—the Silver Re-publicans—advocated the coinage of silver, or "free silver." This faction seriously divided the Republicans and destroyed the political career of Democratic President Grover Cleveland (on left, with fingers in ears). Their presidential candidate, William McKinley (depicted at right as Napo-leon) went on to win a decisive victory over pro-silver Democratic candidate William Jennings Bryan (closest to dynamite). *(Courtesy of the Li-brary of Congress)*

vative Taft wing, aside from its opposition to what would be called U.S. imperialism.

Although successful in winning elections in western states, the Silver Republicans were in-effective in shaping Republican policies. By 1904, most Republican historians had written the epitaph of the Silver Republicans. Reflecting that sentiment was George Seilhamer: "[The Sil-verites] threatened the allegiance to the Repub-lican party of many Republicans in the mining states, but it was not a serious menace even in these, because the more important principle of Protection served to modify and thwart it."

The Silver Republican party is today a nearly forgotten footnote in U.S. history. Yet, it should be noted that for these men and women, the battle for a bimetallic currency was more than a battle for silver or gold; it was a fight over the center of power in the United States. Silver advocates believed that eastern economic interests were using monetary policy to control western development and to control the growth of the West. In the thirty years after 1900, many of the policies and programs the Silver Republicans advocated would come to pass; however, few of the founders would live to see that success.

MICHAEL P. BOBIC

See also: Frank J. Cannon; John Percival Jones; Lee Mantle; National Silver Party; Richard Franklin Pettigrew; Populist Movement/People's Party; Silver Party of Nevada; William Morris Stewart; Henry Moore Teller.

Bibliography

Argersinger, Peter H. *Populism and Politics: William Alfred Peffer and the People's Party.* Lexington: University Press of Kentucky, 1974.

Durden, Robert F. *The Climax of Populism: The Election of 1896.* Lexington: University Press of Kentucky, 1965.

Ellis, Elmer. *Henry Moore Teller: Defender of the West.* Caldwell, ID: Caxton, 1941.

Faulkner, Ronnie W. "North Carolina Democrats and Silver Fusion Politics, 1892–1896." *North Carolina Historical Review* 59, no. 3 (1982): 230–251.

Hicks, John D. *The Populist Revolt: A History of the Farmer's Alliance and the People's Party.* Lincoln: University of Nebraska Press, 1961.

Hunt, Robert V., Jr. "The Heyday of the Denver APA, 1892–1894." *Journal of the West* 35, no. 4 (1996): 74–81.

Johnson, Donald Bruce. *National Party Platforms*, Vol. 1. Urbana: University of Illinois Press, 1978.

Merrill, Horace Samuel, and Marion Galbraith Samuel. *The Republican Command: 1897–1913.* Lexington: University Press of Kentucky, 1971.

Rutland, Robert Allen. *The Republicans: From Lincoln to Bush.* Columbia: University of Missouri Press, 1996.

Schlesinger, Arthur M. *History of U.S. Political Parties.* New York: Chelsea House, 1973.

Seilhamer, George O. *History of the Republican Party: Narrative and Critical History, 1856–1898.* New York: Judge, 1904(?).

www.potifos.com/tpg/bio. "The Political Graveyard" web page.

Young, Bradley J. "Silver, Discontent, and the Conspiracy: The Ideology of the Western Republican Revolt of 1890–1901." *Pacific Historical Review* 64, no. 2 (1995): 243–265.

SOCIAL DEMOCRATIC PARTY

1898–1901

Looking for a vehicle to provide an alternative to William Jennings Bryan's defeated populism, and a viable ideological framework that specifically addressed the needs of American urban workers, socialists experimented with a series of political organizations in the late nineteenth century. After failing to unite socialists under the umbrella of the Social Democracy of America (SDA), reformist socialist activists led by Victor Berger and Eugene Debs formed the Social Democratic party (SDP) in 1898. The SDP's role was transitional and its three-year lifetime notably brief, but the party did advance the first socialist presidential candidate, Debs (a leader of the Pullman strike of 1894), in the 1900 election. The death of the party the next year also served as the birth of the longer-lasting Socialist Party of America (SPA), as the SDP merged with a group of dissidents from the Socialist Labor party (SLP) and other socialist rivals.

The SDP leadership was galvanized initially by the abortive Pullman strike and the defeat of populist William Jennings Bryan in the presidential election of 1896. Debs had supported Bryan during the campaign, as he provided workers and middle-class Americans with an alternative to traditional, capitalistic candidates. Debs also believed that a failure to support Bryan's candidacy could split what he believed was a growing anti-establishment sentiment. Disappointed by the failure of the third-party candidate, Debs concluded that the conditions were ripe for the formation of a party that could focus on the interests and gain the support of the working class.

The January 1897 national convention of the American Railway Union (ARU)—of which Debs was president—provided the attentive audience he needed. Debs utilized the winter meeting to give voice to his specifically socialist agenda. Then he set off on a speaking tour to gain support for his program, which included explicit calls for a colony of laborers to form in a western state, where an egalitarian utopia could be established. Eschewing the strict class analysis of Marx and Engels, Debs's colonization idea was a substitute for the Marxist notion that the proletariat would arise as victors from an inevitable society-wide struggle. Debs sought to create an egalitarian society, free from the burdens of class consciousness. There would be no "dictatorship of the proletariat" through a party apparatus. Once the colonists had created their western communities, Debs said, they would seek wider political power via the electoral process and call for other American laborers to join them.

Debs hoped next to use a June 1897 convention of the ARU to bring together the ARU trade unionists with explicitly socialist activists, providing a widening forum for his economic and political agendas, inserting ideology into a more pragmatic existing labor movement. At that convention, Debs turned an ideological theory into political action: He and fellow activist Victor Berger formed the SDA. The formation of the SDA created a noteworthy split in socialist forces, especially those led by SLP leader Daniel DeLeon. Supporters were forced to choose between divergent ideological frameworks and strong-willed leaders. More orthodox socialists—initially joined by Berger—had been openly critical of Debs's colonization plan. Although Berger himself had sought to adapt socialist theory to fit American conditions, he was wed to the broad theory that capitalism should and inevitably would be replaced by an overall system of collective ownership. For Berger, the problems of the working class were not to be solved by what he saw as a passive retreat from capitalist society into colonies, but rather by a fundamental transformation of the American economic system. He insisted that the fundamental Marxist notions of powerful, irreconcilable class conflict remain, but, like Debs, he believed that the path of the conflict need not be a shattering, physical war, but could incorporate the American notions of political democracy. Berger believed that the inevitable revolution would take shape in the framework of the American electoral system and that the war could be won by non-violent, democratic means.

The differences of opinion came to a stormy climax at the June 1898 SDA convention. Colonization, the rigidity of class analysis, and the proper form of political action—all were contentious issues. Despite having joined together only a year earlier in order to advocate working-class rights, ideological factions maneuvered to control debate. Berger even attempted to prevent the seating of delegates who sponsored a colonization platform, still hoping to promote his more global approach to socialism.

Debs, on the other hand, avoided all controversies for the first two days of the June meeting. His grand entrance into both the convention and the debate over the SDA platform came in a speech featuring a scathing rebuke of the use of strict class analysis by his SDA comrades. The speech both energized convention-goers and alarmed Berger, who feared that Debs's electric energy could reduce his own influence. With this in mind, Berger chose what he thought was a politically viable course of action—bringing Debs into his camp, despite their differences as to the colonies.

Berger met with Debs following Debs's speech. The result of the meeting was unexpected. Debs initially decided to forgo directly involving himself in the debate, merely moderating the presentation of the "minority" report (advocating the powerful clash of classes) and "majority" report (advocating incremental electoral struggle). However, once the assembly gathered to undertake the final platform vote, Debs threw his weight behind the Berger majority draft. Nonetheless, the majority forces lost the vote, but they believed that Debs's endorsement, coupled with his mass appeal outside the convention, would pave the way for future success.

Not surprisingly, the unification (and defeat) of the Debs and Berger forces in the midst of sharp ideological divisions at the convention did not bode well for the unity of the SDA. Sparked by their failure to shape the SDA platform, Debs, Berger, and their supporters—thirty-three in all—left the convention with the intention of establishing a new party. The SDP was thus created, another attempt by Berger and Debs to control the shape of the socialist movement.

The new party members officially adopted Berger's majority report only hours after leaving the SDA convention, but waited until the next morning to convene the first organizational meeting of the SDP, which took place in Chicago's Hull House. Recovering from illness, Debs was absent from the June 11, 1898, meeting, but was elected to the party's executive committee. Frederick Heath, Victor Berger, Jesse Cox, and Seymour Stedman joined Debs on the leadership panel of the fledgling party, and Debs's brother Theodore was installed as the party's first secretary. Chicago would continue to serve as the base of operations.

Well aware of the ideological—if not political—gulfs that separated them, Berger realized the benefits of Debs's absence from the meeting. It gave Berger the opportunity to shape the party's platform to match his own ideological model: Utilizing the theories of class analysis that Debs found repugnant and divisive, the SDP platform called for the gradual dismantling of the capitalist system and the economic trusts rampant within it, which, it said, served only to funnel benefits to a wealthy few. This system of oppressive capitalism would be replaced with a democratically distributive socialist system, the products of which would therefore benefit *all* economic segments of American society. The working class, the SDP argued, would lead this struggle for economic egalitarianism.

In order to achieve these results, SDP leaders proposed two fundamental elements: The first element involved their declaration of the importance of political action, particularly in the electoral process. The nature of the class struggle, they argued, was inherently political. Reminded of the 1896 presidential election and the capitalist base of the Republican and Democratic parties, the SDP reasoned that the working class was in need of its own political party. They declared that the SDP would serve that role and emphasized the necessity of electoral gains in order to further their program. Further theorizing that the working class would fail to see the importance of the electoral victory, they advocated the strengthening of trade unions and were particularly supportive of the American Federation of Labor (AFL). They did, however, make a sharp distinction between the work of the trade unions and that of the SDP: Union activity existed to provide solidarity and education to workers, in which socialists would participate, whereas the political arena was the sole territory of the new party.

The SDP thus starkly distinguished itself from the SLP, which opposed Samuel Gompers's AFL. The SDP's distinction between politics and trade union activity allowed its labor plank to endorse in full the role and status of the American Federation of Labor. Although the SDP sought to establish a close relation with the AFL, it hoped to teach Gompers and the federation the lessons of socialism. Berger favored (unsuccessfully as it turned out) the process of "boring from within" the AFL; that is, joining the AFL in order to gain control of its leadership and change its politics.

The second element, which the SDP leadership hoped would lead to the egalitarian society that they sought, involved the development of cooperatives and the establishment of a cooperative commonwealth. As socialist candidates solidified their position in the electoral system, they would, argued the SDP, begin to use their gains to obtain control of the means of produc-

tion. Nationalization of trusts and large corporations, and the municipal ownership of public utilities, would be their primary means to gain control of the American economic system. These worker-friendly institutions would reduce the hours of work and improve working conditions, it was said. Unlike the cataclysmic Marxist model, this incremental approach would be accomplished one trust and company and utility at a time, as the workers' increasing electoral strength allowed. SDP organizers argued that the ultimate result would be a system of economic production that would ensure that the output of the laborers was equitably distributed.

As a special appeal for farmers' support, the SDP's platform included in its cooperative plan a program of government land grants, government-operated grain elevators, standard rates for the transportation of farm products, public credit for community projects, and the nationalization of railroads, telegraphs, and the telephone.

Finally, and in addition to the two-pronged political and economic reforms, the SDP called for the end of the social evils produced, it said, by capitalism. Liberty, temperance, and equality for women were advocated, as were the restriction of divorce and the elimination of crime, insanity, corruption, and prostitution. The vices it opposed were not human vices, but the result of an economic regime, whereas a national system of cooperatives would return morality to middle-class America.

The SDP was plagued by some often-virulent disagreements, including the central issue of the role of labor unions. Debs in particular harbored much hostility toward AFL President Gompers, whose openly anti-socialist views did not hold out much promise for the success of the Berger platform. Similarly, the SDP was divided over its relationship to farmers, who some leaders suggested were merely small-scale capitalists. Nonetheless, the SDP was able to utilize its platform to field local slates of candidates and achieve some success as a political party, electing twenty individuals to office. By early 1900, the organization could claim the membership of 4,636 dues-paying individuals organized into 226 branches in thirty-two states. The SDP could boast the support of twenty-five socialist newspapers. The party was particularly successful in Massachusetts, where a socialist mayoral candidate, John Chase, was elected in Haverhill. Milwaukee and St. Louis were home to fairly strong SDP chapters. The organization's newsletter, the *Social Democratic Herald,* and the omnipresent charismatic Eugene Debs, spread the party's message rapidly at first.

Debs maintained the political alliance between himself and Berger by offering his public support to the planks of the new SDP platform, despite fundamental ideological disagreements. He was no doubt fully aware of the political costs of another split in the movement. In the background, the SLP and the remaining members of the SDA denounced Debs as a traitor and a threat to any socialist organization. Try as he might to hide his discontent with the SDP platform, Debs did allow some of his critique of the program to come to light, particularly the platform's emphasis on the role of the trade unions. Debs continued speaking to audiences around the nation, quietly questioning the role of the unions within the socialist movement, but never fully attacking the platform of the SDP. While the SDP had organized support only in pockets of socialist activity, Debs gradually strengthened his national constituency. Accordingly, Debs was chosen by the delegates to the convention as the candidate of the socialist movement in the 1900 presidential election.

A faction of rebellious SLP members, the "Kangaroos," led by Morris Hillquit, bolted in winter 1899 from the SLP and offered their support for Debs and the SDP, hoping to lead the way toward the unification of the parties. At and after the March 1900 SDP convention, many SDP and Kangaroo rank-and-file members wanted unity, but the factional leaders remained intense rivals. Delegates to a joint unity meeting went so far as to begin debate on the name of the future unified organization, but this debate was scrapped as political warfare broke out among the national leadership of both groups. By May 1900, despite their

initial support for the SDP, the Kangaroos refused to join the Chicago-based organization and split into their own independent SDP wing, headquartering their organization in Springfield, Massachusetts. Although Hillquit's departure left the shrunken SLP more ideologically homogeneous, the Social Democrats were now divided into two separate organizations, with two independent headquarters and leadership corps.

The only helpful result of the unity talks was the nomination of Eugene Debs. Having survived a tumultuous nomination process, Debs set off on an exhausting six-week tour of the United States to promote his candidacy. Ignoring his poor health and the factional spirit that remained within the socialist movement, he and his running mate (and fellow Indianan) Job Harriman campaigned vigorously for the presidency in the South, Midwest, and Southwest, where pockets of Debs sympathizers (although not necessarily registered SDP members) provided enthusiastic audiences for the candidates. In spite of this flurry of activity, however, Debs's showing in the general election was poor. Debs and Harriman came in fourth of seven slates, garnering 86,935 popular votes, less than 1 percent of the total. They were beaten by Prohibitionist, Democratic, and Republican candidates. New York gave over 10,000 votes to the slate, the greatest individual state total. Massachusetts (where half of the SDP members lived), Illinois, California, Wisconsin, and Missouri contributed modestly more votes than most other states, and no southern state except Texas gave Debs more than 1,000 votes. Debs, however, was not disappointed by the loss, believing that the education of the masses, especially in the form of voter education efforts initiated by the movement, would lead voters inevitably to the socialist cause.

Following the election, the SDP was forced to face up to its factional struggles, which could be blamed for its apparent lack of political viability. There no longer existed a national presidential campaign that could mask the organization's internal problems. The Berger-led faction of the SDP had lost nearly one-third of its membership, and the *Herald* was in the midst of a financial crisis. At the January 1901 SDP convention, Berger's supporters intended to refocus the party's agenda, but control of the convention was wrestled from their hands by the more grassroots-oriented Springfield faction. Finally cognizant that without the unification of the SDP wings the Berger faction would disintegrate, the Berger forces agreed to another meeting in July 1901 in Indianapolis, Indiana, where the Berger and Hillquit forces finally brought together their respective camps, forming the SPA. Socialist newcomer Leon Greenbaum was selected to act as the party's first national secretary.

Although the name and headquarters (now St. Louis, Missouri) of the new organization changed, and the rigidity of factional doctrine was softened, the formal platform remained quite similar to that initially proposed at the 1898 SDP convention. The SPA maintained its support of the AFL and trade unionism in general and continued to draw a clear distinction between the role of the union and the political party. Incremental political change was still advocated, though the rhetoric of eventual if peaceful revolution was re-emphasized at the 1901 convention in response to rank-and-file demands. Thus, the SDP gave shape to the program of the SPA. Equally important, the SPA kept the SDP's presidential standard-bearer, Eugene Debs. The candidate's (and the party's) electoral successes improved over time, either because of the decrease in open factionalism or the increased appeal of the party's

doctrine or both. Debs ran in the 1904, 1908, 1912, and 1920 presidential races. His vote totals increased exponentially during these years, reaching over 900,000 votes in 1920. Victor Berger served four terms in the U.S. House of Representatives, under the banner of the SPA. The defining struggles of the three-year SDP, inconclusive and unsuccessful as they were, provided the ideological and operational basis for the SPA's larger and somewhat greater achievements.

PENNY M. MILLER

See also: Victor Luitpold Berger; Eugene Victor Debs; Morris Hillquit; Socialist Labor Party; Socialist Party.

Bibliography

Critchlow, Donald T., ed. *Socialism in the Heartland.* Notre Dame, IN: University of Notre Dame Press, 1986.

Green, James R. *Grass-Roots Socialism: Radical Movements in the Southwest, 1895–1943.* Baton Rouge: Louisiana State University Press, 1978.

Kipnis, Ira. *The American Socialist Movement, 1897–1912.* New York: Columbia University Press, 1952.

Miller, Sally M. *Victor Berger and the Promise of Constructive Socialism, 1910–20.* Westport, CT: Greenwood Press, 1973.

Salvatore, Nick. *Eugene V. Debs: Citizen and Socialist.* Urbana: University of Illinois Press, 1982.

Shannon, David A. *The Socialist Party of America.* New York: Macmillan, 1955.

SOCIAL DEMOCRATS OF THE UNITED STATES OF AMERICA

1972–

Although small in size, the Social Democrats of the United States of America (SDUSA) have wielded significant influence within the AFL-CIO hierarchy, the foreign policy establishment, and several presidential administrations since their founding in 1972. Not exactly a political party, since they do not run their own candidates for office, SDUSA operates as a faction within the higher circles of the Democratic and Republican parties. SDUSA defies the traditional liberal/conservative dichotomy; liberal on domestic issues, they are conservative anti-communists on foreign policy. Pro-labor domestically, they have opposed Left-influenced unions in other countries. They routinely endorse Democrats for president, but their greatest influence was with the administrations of Republican presidents Ronald Reagan and George Bush. With headquarters in Washington, D.C., SDUSA is governed by a president, a national vice chairman, and an executive director, who work with a national committee. In addition, there is a national advisory committee, whose members need not belong to SDUSA, and it holds a semi-annual convention. Although they have all but rejected socialism, SDUSA is still a member of the Socialist International, the league of Socialist parties worldwide.

In 1972, two important political events played key roles in the foundation of the SDUSA and the crystallization of its political philosophy. First, SDUSA was formed when the Socialist party split into three camps over the Vietnam War. One faction, which opposed U.S. involvement in the war and favored working within the left wing of the Democratic party, went on to form the Democratic Socialist Or-

ganizing Committee under the leadership of Michael Harrington (now the Democratic Socialists of America). A small group of party stalwarts, which also opposed the war in Vietnam, continued under the Socialist party name. The largest of the three groups, which favored continued support for the war effort, became the SDUSA.

Second, most Social Democrats attributed the Democratic party's landslide loss to Richard Nixon in 1972 to George McGovern's liberal domestic policy and dovish foreign policy. Consequently, they began to work within the newly formed Coalition for a Democratic Majority to counteract the Democratic party's move to the Left. The Center-Right faction led by senators Daniel Patrick Moynihan (New York) and Henry M. "Scoop" Jackson (Washington) generally favored moderate domestic policies, but more conservative, anti-communist positions on foreign policy. Many SDUSA members supported Jackson's failed Democratic presidential bids; others favored Hubert H. Humphrey. A hawkish foreign policy has been the overriding concern of SDUSA through the years, and by 1980, they had more in common with Ronald Reagan than President Carter. On paper, SDUSA's strategy of working within the Democratic party had not changed, but in practice it identified more closely with President Reagan's Central American policy supporting the Contras and the government in El Salvador, and his African policy backing the Union for the Total Liberation of Angola's (UNITA) war against the Angolan government. They also favored Reagan's massive increase in the military budget, his willingness to take a tough line on the Soviet Union, and his opposition to the nuclear freeze movement.

SDUSA's category-defying mix of Left and Right positions can be explained by the rightward political path traveled by its intellectual godfather Max Shachtman. A founding member of the American Communist party, he was expelled in 1928 on the charge of Trotskyism. Shachtman then became a leader in the American Trotskyist movement. More critical of the Soviet Union than Trotsky, Shachtman split from his mentor in 1939 to form a small "third camp" socialist sect. The Shachtmanites joined the Socialist party in 1958 and continued their move to the Right. Although the Shachtmanites supported the civil rights movement during the 1960s, they grew critical of the insurgent New Left, feminist, and black power movements. Increasingly, they embraced the AFL-CIO leadership as the voice of the working class and supported U.S. involvement in the Vietnam War as an effort to stop Soviet aggression.

Since its inception, the SDUSA has made common cause with neoconservatives such as Jeane J. Kirkpatrick, Nathan Glazer, Sidney Hook, Irving Kristol, Norman Podhoretz, and Midge Dector, among others, and has been involved with publications such as *Commentary, The Public Interest,* and *The American Spectator,* and conservative think tanks such as the American Enterprise Institute, Freedom House, and the Heritage Foundation. Like Kirkpatrick, many Social Democrats became Democrats for Reagan. Appointed by President Reagan to be ambassador to the United Nations, Kirkpatrick hired SDUSA's executive director Carl Gershman to be her aide. Gershman later worked for the Kissinger Commission on Central America and then became the president of the Reagan-inspired National Endowment for Democracy (NED), which funds many anti-communist groups around the world. Recipient groups included Prodemca, headed by SDUSA member Penn Kemble, which received NED funds to organize support for Reagan's anti-Sandinista policy in Central America. Kemble was later made the deputy director of the U.S. Information Agency. The A. Philip Randolph Institute received NED support in its effort to nurture South African groups that were more conservative than the African National Congress; it was headed by Bayard Rustin, SDUSA's national chairman.

Unlike the Reaganites, SDUSA supports national health insurance and economic justice. It favors labor's right to organize and bargain collectively and increasing the minimum wage, and opposes the use of permanent replacement workers and the North American Free Trade Agreement. SDUSA has had a close relationship with the AFL-CIO, primarily under former presidents George Meany and Lane Kirkland. Many of its members have held important positions within the AFL-CIO hierarchy, especially in its State Department–funded International Affairs Department and Free Trade Union Institute. Under SDUSA member Tom Kahn's direction, the federation's "foreign policy" mobilized support for Solidarity in Poland and dissident workers in the Soviet Union and Eastern Europe. But critics charged that it opposed labor unions in South Africa, Latin America, and Western Europe that were on the left of the political spectrum. SDUSA also maintains close ties with labor's leadership through its national advisory committee. The presidents of the American Federation of Teachers, the Bricklayers and Allied Craftsman Union, the International Federation of Metal Workers Union, and the Union of Needletrades, Industrial, and Textile Employees (UNITE) sit on its national advisory council. SDUSA has also had close relations with the United Steel Workers of America through former presidents I.W. Abel and Lynn Williams. SDUSA's influence has somewhat diminished under John Sweeney's tenure.

The SDUSA thrived in the cold war environment of geopolitics, but the absence of a communist threat abroad, and declining interest in global affairs at home, have done much to lessen its influence in U.S. foreign policy-making circles in the 1990s. Never strong at the grassroots level, SDUSA's membership has fallen from an estimated 5,000 in the mid-1970s to well under 1,000 today.

VERNON MOGENSEN

See also: Michael Harrington; Max Shachtman; Socialist Party.

Bibliography

Isserman, Maurice. *If I Had a Hammer . . . : The Death of the Old Left and the Birth of the New Left.* New York: Basic Books, 1987.

Hitchens, Christopher. "Minority Report: Politics in America." *The Nation,* July 6, 1985.

Massing, Michael. "Trotsky's Orphans: From Bolshevism to Reaganism: Social Democrats, USA." *The New Republic,* June 22, 1987.

Puddington, Arch. "A Hero of the Cold War." *The American Spectator* (July 1992).

Samuels, David. "At Play in the Fields of Oppression: A Government-funded Agency Pretends to Export Democracy." *Harper's* (May 1995): 47.

✰✰✰✰✰✰✰✰✰✰✰✰✰✰✰✰✰✰✰✰✰✰✰✰✰✰✰✰✰✰✰✰
SOCIALIST LABOR PARTY
1876–

The Socialist Labor party (SLP) is the first significant socialist party in America and the country's second-oldest "third" party. Organized as the Workingmen's Party of the United States (WMPUS) in 1876, the party renamed itself at its first national convention in December 1877. As the only nationally organized party of socialism before 1901, the SLP attracted socialists of all tendencies to its ranks. By 1891, however, the SLP had emerged as an explicitly Marxist party. Marxists believed that labor unions were the arenas through which workers could be most easily educated about capitalism and socialism and then organized around their own interests to pursue the socialist goal rather than improvements under capitalism. Marxists believed that labor unions would eventually create their own political party.

Despite its minor-party status, the SLP has played a prominent role in the economic and political life of the country. It ran the first socialist presidential campaign in 1892 and received 21,173 votes from the five states where its presidential ticket of Simon Wing for president and Charles Matchett for vice president appeared on the ballot. The SLP continued to nominate presidential candidates until 1976. It received its highest presidential vote in 1972, when its ticket of Louis Fisher for president and Genevieve Gunderson for vice president received 53,831 votes from twelve states. The party has participated in thousands of state and local elections since the 1870s, winning a scattering of local offices mostly before 1890. The SLP also played a decisive role in the development of the labor movement by its insistence that labor unions accept the principle of the class struggle and socialism as their goal. The party considers the class struggle to be a conflict over the division of labor's product between wages and profits. This struggle manifests itself at the workplace through strikes and the organization of labor unions. Socialism would end this struggle by ending the division of wealth between those who produce it and those who appropriate it. There is no connection between the SLP and the Socialist or Communist parties. The former was set up in 1901 before a group of former SLP members absorbed the Social Democratic party of Eugene V. Debs and Victor Berger. The Communists emerged following the Russian Revolution.

ORIGINS OF THE PARTY

During its early years, the SLP membership was made up mainly of immigrant workers from Germany, which contributed more to American immigration during the second half of the nineteenth century than any other European country. Nearly one-quarter of all Europeans who crossed the Atlantic to settle in the United States between 1861 and 1900 came from Prussia and other German states. Like other immigrants, Germans brought their political ideas with them. Many were socialists whose decision to leave the "fatherland" was prompted, at least in part, by the anti-socialist campaign of persecution then being waged by the Prussian government of Chancellor Otto von Bismarck.

The post–Civil War era was a tumultuous period in which a massive change took place in American society—a change that did much to explain why so many millions of immigrants were welcomed into the country, almost without restriction. It was a period in which small individual producers and farmers—despite their skills—were thrown together with millions of others into huge, newly built factories equipped with huge new machines, where they worked cooperatively in the production of enormous quantities of commodities. The era was marked by the unbridled growth of industrial capitalism, vicious competition, the concentration of capitalist wealth, and, above all, the malicious and unrestrained exploitation of a largely immigrant working class. It was, in fact, a period in which a new nation was established and divided, not between North and South as before, but between a class of propertyless, wage-earning "operatives" and a class of industrial and financial capitalists.

It is not surprising, then, that it was additionally a period marked by the growth of working-class organizations—the National Labor Union (founded in 1866), the Knights of Labor (founded in 1869), and the American Federation of Labor (AFL) (founded in 1886). Socialist organizations also appeared in Chicago, New York, and other cities where German and other immigrant workers and socialists settled. The immigrant socialist organizations that sprang into existence during the 1870s reflected a division of opinion that existed within the European movement at the time. Some followed the teachings of Ferdinand Lassalle (1825–1864), who, among other things, had stressed the importance of working-class political organization and action in a country (Germany) where workers could not vote and dismissed as insignificant—even as detrimental to the establishment of socialism—their economic organization into trade unions. Lassalleans felt that the SLP should appeal directly to all workers—which could only be done politically because the vast majority of workers were not in unions. Others were influenced by the views of the International Workingmen's Association, established in London in 1864, largely under the influence of Karl Marx, which emphasized the primacy of the economic organization of workers as the essential foundation for any political party of the working class.

The difference over tactics that divided the socialist movement in Germany in the 1870s was overridden by the need to combat the policy of persecution pursued by Bismarck, and, in 1875, the two branches merged into a single party, which, in spite of strenuous objections voiced by Marx, adopted what was essentially a Lassallean platform dangling a long list of reform demands on the newly consolidated single state of the German Empire.

It was against this background of burgeoning industrial capitalism, continental expansionism, immigration, and exploitation that the uneasy union of Marxist and Lassallean wings of the socialist movement in Germany found its expression in America at a Union Congress held at Philadelphia in July 1876. That congress resulted in the formation of the aforementioned WMPUS—the first nationally organized party of socialism in America—while simultaneously laying the foundation for recurrent waves of internal disputes and schisms that would hamper the development of an assimilated party of socialism in the United States for more than a decade. Less than two years after its formation, the party changed its name to the Socialistic Labor party in 1878, and it was out of this Socialistic Labor party that the modern SLP eventually emerged.

POLITICAL ACTIVITIES

In spite of its Lassallean views on tactics, the pre-1890 SLP never entered a national election campaign in its own right. The 1880 national convention nominated three men as potential presidential candidates, but party members voted instead to support the Greenback party ticket. The SLP did manage to attract a few workers from the trade unions of the time, but most tended to be anarchists. Some of these formed armed "defense clubs" in preference to running candidates in local elections in the 1880s and soon brought chaos and disruption into the party. In 1883, Phillip Van Patten, the party's national corresponding secretary since 1877, abandoned his post in despair.

By 1885, the dissolution brought by the anarchists served to shift the balance of power in the SLP from Chicago to New York. The seat of the executive committee was transferred to the latter, and a new secretary was elected. He was William L. Rosenberg, who also continued as editor of the SLP's new official newspaper, *Der Sozialist.*

Rosenberg and a majority of the executive committee were Lassalleans of a sort. They also distrusted trade unionism in principle and eventually urged that the SLP take "independent political action" on its own. Before the seat of the executive committee had been transferred, however, socialists in New York City had played a critical role in bringing local trade unions together into a Central Labor Union (CLU). Unions across the country began to agitate forcefully for the eight-hour day and other measures that would benefit workers.

Trade unionism was still in its formative period. The official corruption and class-collaborationist policies that would eventually come to dominate the unions had not yet taken a firm hold. Many unionists understood the class struggle, and some of their organizations called for the abolition of the wage system and even for socialism. They welcomed the socialists and began to listen as the SLP members urged the CLU to take independent political action in the New York City mayoral election campaign of 1886.

This led directly to the formation of a United Labor party (ULP) and the search for a candidate. The ULP settled on Henry George, author of *Progress and Poverty,* a book in which he claimed that poverty could be eliminated by placing a "single tax" on land. The socialists did not accept George's theory, and he was reluctant to accept the ULP's nomination. By all accounts, he was politically ambitious. He would not run unless the ULP could guarantee him a large vote. The CLU and SLP went to work circulating petitions and gathering 30,000

signatures from workers pledging to vote for George.

The ULP and its candidate placed second, with 68,000 votes, far more than anyone had expected. The results had an electrifying effect, not only among workers, but also within the major parties. George understood the implications as "labor demands" suddenly began to appear in the platforms of the Democratic and Republican parties in response to the 1886 elections. When, in preparation for the 1887 state elections, he succeeded in having the ULP adopt a "tax reform" platform devoid of all labor demands, the socialists objected. The fight that followed resulted in the SLP being expelled from the ULP.

Some SLP and CLU members immediately organized the Progressive Labor party with a "radical platform," which nominated its own candidates. But, the party did not attract a large vote. These developments were carefully observed from two quarters that took no direct part in the events themselves. They were closely observed by the AFL and its president, Samuel Gompers, and by the executive committee of the SLP. By 1887, the SLP had acquired a newspaper published in the English language—the *Workmen's Advocate.* This paper had formerly acted as the official voice of the New Haven Trades Council in Connecticut and was edited by J. F. Busche.

The membership of the SLP was overwhelmingly German, and the party had never succeeded before in establishing a permanent newspaper in English. The most important socialist paper of the time was a German daily, the *New Yorker Volkszeitung.* Unlike *Der Sozialist* and the *Workmen's Advocate,* however, it was not party owned. It was operated as a private business and depended heavily on advertising for its financial support. Its advertisers included unions and "friend-of-labor" politicians, who sprang up in abundance after the 1886 campaign. In those days, local SLP organizations (sections) used the language spoken by their membership. New York had three sections— German, "American," and Jewish. The German section was the largest by far, and it was strongly influenced by the *Volkszeitung* and its editor, Alexander Jonas.

Early in 1888, Rosenberg and Busche began to agitate for "independent political action" by the SLP, with or without CLU support. By summer they had prevailed and the sections nominated Jonas for mayor. But the SLP ticket received only 2,000 votes. A dispute quickly broke out within the SLP. Rosenberg and Busche discounted the small vote and continued to agitate for independent political action. But they were tactless, and allowed their contempt of the unions to color their articles and editorials. This led to trouble for socialists within the CLU, where the influence of the major parties was starting to be felt. The *Volkszeitung* also felt the pressure in terms of lost revenue. The conflict within the SLP was waged during the first half of 1889. In September, the German section voted to remove Rosenberg, Busche, and a majority of the executive committee. They physically occupied the editorial offices of *Der Sozialist* and the *Workmen's Advocate,* locking the officers out. This "coup," as it was later called, was sanctioned by the SLP's Eighth National convention in October 1889. A new executive committee, with Benjamin J. Gretsch as secretary, was installed, and Lucian Sanial was made editor of the *Workmen's Advocate.* The convention also adopted a new national platform, which would be the model for subsequent SLP platforms for decades to come.

The split of 1889 was not over "independent action," but over who should take it—the SLP or the unions. A similar dispute soon broke out inside the CLU, where the Democrats, frightened by the ULP campaign, sought to defuse the "spirit of 1886." The rupture came in June 1890, when a number of unions withdrew from the CLU and established the Central Labor Federation (CLF). The newly reorganized SLP was instrumental in that decision and simultaneously issued a call inviting all labor organizations to a conference to decide on entering the 1890 state elections.

In the meantime, a new movement had arisen around another book—*Looking Backward,* by Edward Bellamy. Bellamy envisioned a new society organized on a cooperative basis with-

out class conflict or poverty. The movement attracted many liberals and academics, some of whom had left the George movement in disgust. A number of these sympathized with the socialists and workers. As the 1890 state election campaign approached, the Nationalist Clubs (inspired by Bellamy) in New York divided into two groups. Those who feared and rejected socialism formed the Commonwealth party. Those who sympathized with the socialists withdrew and invited unions and other labor organizations to attend a conference for the purpose of nominating a labor ticket for the 1890 elections. The date for the conference was deliberately set to coincide with the SLP conference. The SLP conference, supported by the CLF, decided to nominate a ticket and proceeded to adopt a platform. This platform was virtually identical to that adopted by the SLP's 1889 convention.

These conferences were held separately but simultaneously over several weeks' time. In the meantime, socialist and Nationalist Club speakers worked together staging campaign meetings throughout New York City. On September 25, the Nationalist Club conference merged into the SLP conference. The conference proceeded to nominate candidates, and a vigorous campaign in which the SLP received over 13,000 votes followed. New struggles and conflicts lay ahead, but for now the SLP was united and had finally and irrevocably "come out" as an independent political party based on a sound Marxist platform. However, it entered the new period having acquired a new member—Daniel De-Leon—whose name would soon become synonymous with the socialist movement in America. DeLeon was an instructor of international law at Columbia University in 1886 when his sympathies were aroused by the labor movement. In 1890 DeLeon became an active member of the SLP and ran for governor of New York as a member of the party in 1891. In 1892 he became editor-in-chief of the SLP's weekly newspaper, an influential post he held until his death in 1914. He was a prominent advocate of revolutionary socialism that opposed compromise and reform.

THE SLP AND THE UNIONS

From 1880 to 1894, two union organizations dominated the field—the AFL, which was just gaining a foothold in the labor movement, and the Knights of Labor, whose strength was ebbing at this time. The 1893 AFL convention, for instance, endorsed the principle of "collective ownership by the people of all means of production and distribution." When the demand was dropped at the 1894 convention, socialists in the union were strong enough to retaliate by defeating Samuel Gompers for the AFL presidency. But the re-election of Gompers as president of the union in 1895 led the SLP to conclude that the conversion of the AFL to socialist principles was not possible.

During this era, SLP members had also become involved with the Knights of Labor. In 1893 the New York District Assembly of the Knights sent DeLeon and a few other SLP members to the General Assembly. Though few in number, they held the balance of votes in a power struggle between James R. Sovereign and Terence Powderly, the Grand Master Workman of the Knights. The SLP delegates agreed to help Sovereign replace Powderly in the office of Grand Master Workman. In exchange, Sovereign promised he would make SLP member Lucian Sanial editor of the *Journal of the Knights of Labor*. When Powderly was out, Sovereign reneged on his promise. The final blow came at the 1895 General Assembly, where DeLeon was refused his convention seat.

In view of these developments, the SLP concluded that the time had arrived to launch a new union, one based upon the interests of the workers as a class. Accordingly, it initiated the Socialist Trade and Labor Alliance (ST&LA) and formally endorsed it at the 1896 SLP national convention. The ST&LA recognized that social revolution was still a long way off. It therefore aimed at fighting the workers' daily battles in order to wrest from the capitalists whatever it could in the way of higher wages and improved conditions—a fight that it believed it could conduct more effectively than the AFL and kindred unions.

At the same time, in its declaration of principles, the ST&LA pledged to "constantly keep in view its great object, namely: The summary ending of that barbarous [class] struggle at the earliest possible time by the abolition of classes, the restoration of the land and of all the means of production, transportation and distribution to the people as a collective body, and the substitution of the Cooperative Commonwealth for the present state of planless production, industrial war and social disorder; a commonwealth in which every worker shall have the free exercise and full benefit of his faculties, multiplied by all the modern factors of civilization."

With the launching of the ST&LA, the tactic of "boring from within" the pro-capitalist unions was given different emphasis. In the effort to build the ST&LA, the tactical weaknesses of this strategy were frequently emphasized. But this policy was not so rigid that it rejected taking advantage of every opportunity to agitate for working-class union principles within the existing craft unions.

While the majority of workers were first being organized into the conservative, industry-based, AFL-type unions, there was a real mass of workers who were prepared for organization on a class basis. The socialist unions that arose in opposition to the AFL and kindred unions were not simply the artificial creations of "socialist agitators." They were concrete products of the class struggle. While union leaders cast charges of "dual unionism" and "splitters" at the workers trying to organize on a class-based level, socialists recognized this class-conscious trend as one to be cultivated and expanded.

The independent existence of the ST&LA ended with its absorption into the Industrial Workers of the World (IWW) in 1905. Significantly, the overwhelming majority of those who joined forces to form the IWW did not come from among the unorganized workers of the day. They came from already organized unions whose members wanted to break away from the class collaboration policies of compromise and reform of the AFL hierarchy. In fact, the call for a convention to establish "an economic organization of the working class" emanated from a conference held in Chicago in January 1905, attended by representatives of such existing organizations as the United Brewery Workers, the United Brotherhood of Railway Employees, the American Labor Union, the United Metal Workers, the Western Federation of Miners, and, of course, the ST&LA. These organizations were among forty-six that were represented at the first convention of the IWW, which convened on June 27, 1905. At the time, at least thirteen of the forty-six were still affiliated with the AFL.

The ST&LA, too, had been organized almost ten years earlier, not from among the unorganized, but from a merger of existing labor organizations. According to John R. Commons and his associates in their book *History of Labour in the United States,* "The socialistic Central Labor Federation of New York, Brooklyn and Newark, the United Hebrew Trades and District Assembly 49, with an aggregate membership of about 15,000, merged into the new [ST&LA] organization." Similarly, after the anarchists forced a split in the IWW in 1908, the new, SLP-endorsed, Detroit IWW consisted not of new elements recruited from the unorganized majority of workers but of elements that had seceded from the original IWW as a result of the conflict over political action. (The Detroit IWW was renamed the Workers International Industrial Union in 1915 and was thereafter known as the WIIU.)

From 1910 to 1920—the decade during which DeLeon died, World War I was fought, and the Russian Revolution took place—SLP activities with regard to economic organizations were not nearly as great as in the preceding decades. The one exception was the great silk strike of 1911–12 led by the Detroit IWW. By the end of that decade, however, the influence and membership of the WIIU had dwindled almost to the point of extinction.

With the decline of this last independent socialist union organization, the SLP once again confronted the question of how to reach the working class and create a new movement toward organizing industrial unions. Inevitably, it returned to the question of "boring from within." At the 1916 national convention of the party, the report by the editor of the *Weekly People* (newspaper) suggested "making greater efforts along the lines of 'locking horns' with the labor faker right upon his own domain—inside the union." SLP members "inside the AFL unions," it declared, "should not be 'asleep at the switch.' . . . They should be 'boring from within.' "

In response to that report, the convention passed a motion concurring "with the general ideas expressed in the report of the editor of the *Weekly People,* wherein he urges the SLP members, who are compelled to belong to craft unions, make use of every possible opportunity to oppose not only outside of craft unions, but also inside of the same, the nefarious work of corrupt union leaders and their policies, and to agitate for constructive principles of socialism and industrial unionism."

In another action the convention rejected a resolution proposed by the party's Hungarian Federation that would have prohibited SLP members from accepting salaried offices in the AFL, despite the obvious fact that the prevailing sentiment was that "boring from within" was not to be a quest for union office. No one challenged the expressed view that it was not the office but "the men and the organization" that the SLP was after. Nevertheless, the convention saw no reason to put restrictions on those members engaged in union work within the AFL.

Another reflection of the party's approach to the union question is the following, quoted from the SLP's "irreducible minimum of conditions for unity" with the Socialist party set forth by the 1916 convention: "As to Economic Action: . . . it is the duty of the party of socialism to teach essential principles of industrial unionism in order to enable the membership to advocate these principles both inside of the existing craft unions—to the extent as it may still be possible—and outside of the same."

Still another debate on union activity arose after World War I. In 1919 the SLP launched an intensive agitational campaign in the Illinois coal fields. As the party's official statement in the *American Labor Year Book* for 1919–20 (Volume III) explained: "Since the signing of the armistice, the party decided that besides the broad general agitation always carried on, the time had come to concentrate upon a given field so as to pull in shape, more rapidly, the industrial forces of the working class. The mining industry was selected and invaded and the propaganda of the SLP carried to the workers in the mines." At the time, the coal miners were 100 percent organized in the United Mine Workers (UMW). To that limited extent the UMW was industrial "in form" in contrast to the craft-oriented AFL. It also meant that coal miners in the SLP had to work within the UMW or leave the mines completely. Craft unions typically organized on the basis of skill (tool), while industrial unions organized industry wide (product).

The SLP urged the miners not to seek to organize a new and correct organization. "The miners," the SLP declared, "cannot and should not start another organization. They must take possession of the one they have." It called for a "fight against faker control" of the UMW— "a fight without let up and without intermission until the day is won."

The SLP made this appeal to the miners and sent agitators and speakers to urge it upon them. The post–World War I effort among the Illinois miners was the last organized effort by the SLP directly on the economic field. After some initial success, it tapered off and for want of financial resources was halted sometime in 1921. About the same time, relations between the party and the WIIU were approaching the breaking point. The size of the WIIU had dwindled sharply since its membership had reached a reported peak of about 12,000 members in the early 1910s.

The party, too, was having problems. At its 1923 session, the National Executive Committee of the party adopted a Resolution on Concentration of Effort. Noting the "low state and steady decline of finances, membership, activity, [and so on]," it urged upon the membership

of the SLP "that it concentrate all efforts, to the exclusion of everything else and all other activities, upon the party for the purpose of building a strong and effective educational and propaganda organization, until such time as the working class of this country has become sufficiently revolutionary and has absorbed the idea of industrial unionism sufficiently to precipitate a real industrial union."

The resolution engendered a heated debate between the WIIU and some party members and subdivisions on the one hand and the party's national office and executive bodies on the other. The matter finally came before the 1924 National Convention where the resolution of the National Executive Committee was endorsed. As a consequence, without the official support of the SLP, the WIIU soon disappeared. The final disappearance of this last independent socialist union organization, plus the continuing problems confronting the party in its struggle for survival inevitably had an effect upon its daily activities, particularly with regard to the tactics and strategy it applied on the economic field. Its union activity generally was reduced to a minimum as the party administration and membership concentrated on organizational and internal problems.

In addition, the absence of any independent socialist union to which workers could be directed or which could be held up as an example limited the field for union activity. In the circumstances prevailing in the party, no official effort was made to stimulate activity by party members who belonged to the existing pro-capitalist unions.

There were, of course, individual party members in those unions who did seek to exploit opportunities for socialist agitation, but they were limited individual efforts. For the most part, the party's efforts with regard to the economic field were limited to attacking and exposing the existing unions and their "labor faker" hierarchies and making generalized appeals to the workers to reject both in favor of socialist industrial unions that did not exist, and which the party lacked the physical and material resources to create.

THE RUSSIAN REVOLUTION

Still another development affected the course of the party's work. The Russian Revolution and the events flowing from it rendered a profound change in the socialist movement throughout the world. Gradually the focus of the socialist movement grew beyond a fight for working-class organization on the union field, beyond the labor movement itself. It became a political struggle between various groups claiming to speak for Marxism and socialism.

In addition to the Communist party, a host of socialist and communist groupings emerged, all vying for the attention of the working class. It became clear to the SLP that the fight against many of these groups, who distorted the meaning of socialism or upheld the Bolshevik revolution as the one universal path to socialism, was as crucial as the fight against the "labor fakers" in the unions. The party poured considerable resources into this area, which was fought out in the political arena essentially removed from union activity.

In short, the reduced resources and strength of the party, the collapse of the independent socialist union movement, the increased tasks confronting the SLP on the political field, all contributed to a restriction of organized party efforts within the unions. While it continued to keep alive the concept of socialist industrial unionism, and while individual members remained active within the unions, the SLP pursued no formal, concerted union strategy. The SLP's break with the WIIU in the early 1920s marked a distinct turning point in the SLP's strategy and activity.

During the 1890s and early 1900s, the SLP had been continuously, directly, and deeply involved in activity on the economic field. It was an active force in building and shaping the union movement. And it did so despite its early and strong commitment to independent socialist politics and the conduct of electoral campaigns on the local, state and national levels.

The SLP considered union activity and political action essential and complementary elements of the proper tactical approach to building a Marxian socialist movement in America. Accordingly, SLP members took part in the movement on the economic field as full-fledged trade unionists during the first quarter-century of the party's existence. The adoption of the Resolution on Concentration of Effort by the party's National Executive Committee in 1923 signaled a major change in the party's overall strategy and day-to-day activities. Specifically, the resolution was aimed at ending the WIIU's drain on the SLP's limited physical and financial resources. Inevitably, however, the call for the membership to "concentrate all efforts, to the exclusion of everything else and all other activities" on building the party was bound to deter SLP members from union activity generally.

THE DEPRESSION ERA

The mid-1930s were also marked by a number of major strikes that reflected an intensification of the class struggle that rivaled that of the late 1880s and early 1900s. These strikes were largely the result of initiating action by militant workers and they attracted widespread attention. As far as SLP involvement was concerned, however, there was a marked difference from earlier periods of widespread labor unrest. There were no SLP speakers on the podium during strike meetings. There were no SLP members on the strike or negotiating committees.

This is not to say that the party did not make a genuine effort to bring its socialist message to the workers and influence the direction of their militant actions. It published and distributed millions of leaflets supporting the strikes, explaining socialist principles and socialist industrial unionism, and so on. It conducted hundreds of meetings, organized study classes, and toured organizers through the areas where strikes were in progress. But the SLP was working on the fringe. The decade of concentration of effort on the political movement had isolated it from the mainstream of activity in the industrial field. It no longer had a ''base'' within the unions. Consequently, it failed to command the attention it had been able to command before the 1930s. Moreover, the tasks and problems confronting the SLP led it to continue to concentrate its efforts on the political field.

THE SLP TODAY

To this day, the SLP has concentrated on building the political party of socialism, attracting as many workers as possible to its socialist industrial union program. But with the latest profound crisis of capitalism, the stagnation and exposure of the AFL-CIO and its bureaucracies, and the growing militancy of workers both in and out of the unions, the SLP may once again confront new organizing tasks in the economic field.

ROBERT BILLS

See also: Communist Party; Daniel DeLeon; Socialist Party.

Bibliography

Bellamy, Edward. *Looking Backward.* New York: NAL Penguin, 1960.

Brissenden, Paul F. *The IWW: A Study of American Syndicalism.* New York: Columbia University, 1919.

Commons, John R., and Associates. *History of Labour in the United States.* 2 vols. New York: Macmillan, 1936.

Ebert, Justus. *American Industrial Evolution: From the Frontier to the Factory; Its Social and Political Effects.* New York: New York Labor News Co., 1907.

Ely, Richard T. *The Labor Movement in America.* New York: Thomas Y. Crowell & Co., 1886.

Fine, Nathan. *Labor and Farmer Parties in the United States, 1828–1928.* New York: Rand School of Social Science, 1928.

George, Henry. *Progress and Poverty.* New York: Schalkenbach Foundation, 1991.

Herreshoff, David. *American Disciples of Marx.* Detroit: Wayne State University Press, 1967.

Karp, Nathan. *The SLP and the Unions.* Palo Alto, CA: Socialist Labor Party, 1982.

Kuhn, Henry, and Olive M. Johnson. *The Socialist Labor Party During Four Decades, 1890–1930.* Brooklyn, NY: New York Labor News, 1969.

Petersen, Arnold. *Daniel DeLeon: Social Architect.* 2 vols. New York: New York Labor News Co., 1941–1953.

Quint, Howard H. *The Forging of American Socialism.* Indianapolis: Bobbs-Merrill Co., 1964.

Speek, Peter A. *The Single Tax and the Labor Movement.* (A thesis submitted for the degree of Doctor of Philosophy, the University of Wisconsin, 1915.) Bulletin of the University of Wisconsin, Vol. 8 (Oct. 1917), 247–426.

Trachtenberg, Alexander. *The American Labor Year Book, 1919–1920.* Vol. 3. New York: Rand School of Social Science, 1920.

Weekly People. Newspaper of the Socialist Labor Party, 1914–present.

SOCIALIST PARTY
1901–

*T*he Socialist party, more than any other left-wing third party, impressed its ideas upon the mainstream and propounded a credible, popular vision of socialism. Founded in 1901 and reaching its apex during the 1910s, it mirrored in its weaknesses, above all its susceptibility to political repression, the fundamental limitations of the American Left.

SOCIALISM IN AMERICA

The origins of the Socialist party lay in the radical movements of the previous era, and a majority of party members before 1910 almost certainly began their political activity here. The Socialist Labor party (SLP), founded in 1877, never enrolled more than several thousand. But its mostly German-born members had taken part in the creation of many unions (especially in beer-brewing, carpentry, cigarmaking, and assorted wood crafts) and vigorously participated in the creation of an expansive fraternal and cultural network including schools, theaters, choruses, and sickness-and-death benefit associations. Conflicts within the SLP over trade union policies in particular had precipitated a split in 1899 and propelled former members toward fusion with the Social Democracy of America, a quasi-political party led by erstwhile railroad unionist Eugene Victor Debs. As negotiations proceeded between the two groups, Debs ran on a joint presidential ticket in 1900, sealing the arrangement.

In a deeper sense, the tradition of utopian and agrarian movements of the later nineteenth century had also converted American socialism from an immigrant model to a far more native expression. Edward Bellamy's 1888 utopian socialistic novel, *Looking Backward*, became the third best-selling work of American fiction of the century, after *Uncle Tom's Cabin* and *Ben-Hur*. The utopian socialistic romance promised a peaceful way out of the seemingly inevitable industrial conflict of impoverished workers and haughty monopolists. Utopian colonies sprang up by the dozens—and failed quickly. Debs himself had sought to create such a colony after the 1894 Pullman strike, which he led, had been crushed by federal authorities. Debs had also refused a vice-presidential nomination on the People's party ticket in 1896, at the moment when that great interracial movement crashed as a third-party alternative. Thousands of veterans of the populist movement, many of them ardent supporters of William Jennings Bryan in 1896, moved over to the Socialist party thereafter, many of whom had been converted by the homespun socialist weekly, *The Coming Nation*.

Popular agitation and education offered the best means to reach the masses, with the press as the central mechanism. By 1910 or so, more than 300 periodicals, mostly weeklies but with many dailies and monthlies, were in circulation. The *Appeal to Reason* (successor to *The Coming Nation*), peaking at three quarters of a million, was for a time the most widely circulated weekly political publication in the world. The *Jewish Daily Forward*, reaching 200,000 by the close of the 1910s, was the most popular Yiddish-language publication anywhere. The *National Rip-Saw* from St. Louis reached 150,000 readers in the South and Southwest. Arkansas, Iowa, Kansas, Missouri, Texas, Pennsylvania, and Oklahoma each boasted more than a dozen local papers with circulations of less than 1,000; and among the non-English-language publications (more dominant after 1910), dozens of papers had a circulation of 10,000 or more. If no absolute estimate can be made, a combined circulation figure would run to several million.

Meanwhile, public and especially streetcorner ("soapbox") socialist speakers combined education and entertainment. Hundreds of such itinerant lecturers stayed on the road, often subsisting through sales of pamphlets, adjusting rhetorical styles to assorted potential constituencies. Southwestern socialists specialized in the tent meeting, borrowed from religious revivals and populist spectaculars, consisting of several days of speeches, music, and amateur athletic events.

The Socialist party, rising to 80,000 members by 1908, did best among older union men and experienced women political activists (often carried over from suffrage or temperance movements), tenant farmers of certain regions, hard rock or coal miners, and the middle class as well as workers of certain ethnic groups (especially Germans, Jews, and Finns, but also rising numbers of Slovenes, Hungarians, and Lithuanians). The party did not especially attract the numerous Irish-American workers, nor more than a small proportion of Poles and Italians, nor scarcely anyone within the old Confederacy (save parts of Louisiana), nor racial minorities of any kind. For that matter, and largely thanks to the vigorous antisocialist propaganda of the Catholic church, the socialist movement had peaked within New England (including a few victories in municipal elections) during the 1890s and never rose again.

But socialists attracted a wide following beyond party membership through the popularity of their dedicated literary masters. Before the turn of the century, Yiddish writers had already perfected the one-column short story—often a didactic tale of ghetto misery—in the *Jewish Daily Forward*. Upton Sinclair's *The Jungle* (1906), originally serialized in the *Appeal to Reason*, gave the author best-seller status for a suc-

cession of muckraking novels. Jack London, one of the most popular authors of the age, dealt with poverty and oppression, rising to his socialist apex in *The Iron Heel* (1911), a science fiction classic rivaled in contemporary circulation (if not skill) by fellow socialist George Allen England's *Darkness and Dawn* (1916), a fictional treatment of impending catastrophe serialized in *Munsey's Magazine*. A scattering of novels about free love found audiences of different generations concerned with the "sex question" and socialist solutions. Radical poetry, both didactic and modernist, found readers in virtually every socialist publication but especially those of immigrants for whom the revolutionary poet was a bard and a soothsayer.

FACTIONALISM EMERGES

Eager for success on the scale of European parties, socialists often failed to appreciate the real richness of their movement. Disputes on the failure to enroll larger numbers of the "real American worker" (defined usually as a native-born skilled worker) often framed political disagreements among socialists. On the "right," members and local officials of the American Federation of Labor (AFL) stressed the creation of a sturdy political machine such as the one operating in Milwaukee and the importance of maintaining "respectability." For these socialists, the AFL program of immigration restriction and even the racism voiced in the Milwaukee press constituted solidarity with skilled workers against the riffraff of the unemployable. On the "left," a variety of intellectuals and militants insisted that the goal could be reached only by consistent and thoroughgoing egalitarianism, including a militant anti-racism and internationalism.

The formation of the Industrial Workers of the World (IWW) in 1905 galvanized both sides. Those on the left saw in the IWW a potential way around the persistently low vote of the disinherited, unskilled, or foreign-born worker. As miners' leader William D. Haywood (future member of the Socialist party's National Executive Committee) framed the issue, the industrial union already potentially offered the framework for a post-capitalist industrial society with the disappearance of the coercive political state. Socialists would do best to help build the all-encompassing union while devoting political propaganda to its support. For socialists on the right, this proposal was worse than heresy. Their greatest or at least most prestigious success lay in winning over the middle classes and skilled workers in the cities, by dint of a municipal reform platform; they viewed themselves as the vanguard of the progressive intelligentsia with election results their proud barometer of success.

Both sides suffered deep disappointment in 1912, the banner year in which more than 100 socialists gained elected office and Debs won nearly a million votes. Behind the excitement, Theodore Roosevelt's Progressive party had stolen the thunder of socialist reformers, and dozens of municipal clean-government candidates (often merging Democratic and Republican tickets to undo previous socialist victories) offered overwhelming competition to underfunded socialist campaigns. With socialist factions at each other's throats and some supporters of the IWW actually expelled from the party, membership fell sharply, from 100,000 to barely half that figure within two years.

SOCIALISM'S RISE

In one other way, scarcely crucial to major political parties but essential to left-wing organizations, the Socialist party had also disappointed early aspirations. Its intellectual life was vitally strong at the bottom, with several non-degree socialist "colleges" and local study clubs numbering in the hundreds (including many small-town types such as the schoolteacher and the minister's wife), self-education and self-improvement through the socialist press and oratorical lessons, and a general spirit of eclectic learning, from evolutionary theory to sociology. The Rand School, founded in 1906, energetically educated working people in

courses on a variety of topics and hosted resident or guest luminaries including Charles Beard, Bertrand Russell, and John Dewey.

Socialist activity, however, created no significant milieu for Marxist theory proper, especially in the English language, where intellectually weighty publications failed and distinguished authors were privately advised to "lighten" their forthcoming volumes. After the *International Socialist Review* became a pictorial agitational magazine, only the Yiddish-language *Zukunft* (with a circulation a bit over 10,000) had the kind of depth and wide-ranging rumination of the German socialists' famed *Neue Zeit.* As in the nineteenth century, the supplements of newspapers, mostly in non-English languages, offered the most space for wide-ranging discussion, often on current books. The *New Review* (1913–17), endorsed by leading academics and boasting contributors including W.E.B. Du Bois, Walter Lippmann, and Mary White Ovington, was an early casualty to war, proof for many that the cerebral life of American socialism was doomed.

Ironically, on the morrow of heavy setbacks, the party's left wing was about to receive its greatest boosts: the emergence of a dynamic radicalized labor movement, the brief but brilliant flourishing of a cultural avant-garde, and the steady enrollment of newer immigrant workers and family members. Full of rich potential, each of these developments also had distinct contradictions and none was especially helpful to the Socialist party as it had existed hitherto. The effect of world war and the Russian Revolution made the contradictions explosive and, for party loyalists, catastrophic.

The IWW briefly attained its apex with the famed "Bread and Roses" textile strike in Lawrence, Massachusetts, in 1912. As socialist women aided the transport of workers' children from the strike scene, Wobblies, as members of the IWW were popularly called, led unskilled and foreign-born workers in resisting pressure from police, millowners, and the AFL to return to work. Tragically, the IWW could not maintain the initiative. The following year, textile operatives in Paterson, New Jersey, failed in their strike, sending the IWW westward (where

Delegates to the Socialist party convention in Chicago in May 1904 pose for a group photo. Presidential candidate Eugene Debs is front and center in inset at bottom. (*Courtesy of the Library of Congress*)

it successfully organized agricultural and lumber workers, until wartime repression struck).

Soon, the economic boom precipitated by the war in Europe created unprecedented opportunities for unionization of the unorganized, skilled or unskilled. The wartime cessation of immigration meanwhile tightened the labor market. From 1915 to 1919, each year saw unprecedented levels of strikes. New unions formed in many trades, often under socialist leadership, and many older unions took on new life with radicals of various kinds at the helm.

Socialists once dedicated to propaganda found themselves up to their necks in labor agitation and administration. With the U.S. entry into war, many felt uneasy about political discussions that might jeopardize organizing and even bring political persecution. As socialists gained influence, the specific role of the Socialist party grew more and more uncertain.

The same could be said for the Greenwich Village avant-garde and its many imitators across the United States. Publicized by the "Armory Show" of 1912, glamorized by the purported omnipresence of "free love," and realized in the gorgeous pages of the political arts magazine *The Masses*, the socialistic bohemians punctured bourgeois pretensions but had little time for organized socialist activities. The simultaneous race of woman suffragists (often led by socialist women) toward the vote and the publicizing of birth control methods (still illegal) by brave radicals such as Emma Goldman and Margaret Sanger surely brought socialism into the twentieth century. But what would it do, now that it had entered modernity?

The immigrant coming of age as an American carried yet more contradictions in its wake. Only in 1912 did the Socialist party resolve an old organizational uncertainty by granting "Language Federation" status to a half-dozen groups that spoke and published socialist propaganda in their own tongues (often legally, for the first time, in the United States). By 1915, as the party began to revive, members of what now constituted a dozen language federations (immigrant members who spoke a common tongue) equaled the native-born membership. By 1919, just before the Socialist party divided fatefully, immigrants constituted well over half.

New immigrants mostly from Eastern and Southern Europe (but also in significant numbers from Finland, the Scandinavian countries, and elsewhere) organized quickly as their communities swung into labor activities, but also as their homelands fell into the extremities of war. Some, supporting or even exceeding the official Socialist opposition to war, urged a cessation of conflict (or better, a war of each working class against its masters). Others (including South Slavs and Jewish anarchist leaders, if not their followers) supported the war as a means to achieve independence and smite the Kaiser. Still other groups broke into bitterly divided factions, foreshadowing the worse factionalism to come. Nevertheless and despite the turn of their attention to the respective homelands, immigrant groups were at the heart of the new labor mobilization; their ethnic cultural and fraternal societies provided crucial support (as they would a generation later) for strikes and organizing campaigns. Potentially, they bridged

the gap between the Socialist party and the industrial working class.

Nowhere was this so evidently clear as in the Yiddish-speaking streets of Greater New York, Philadelphia, Chicago, New Haven, and some other urban areas. The generation of "1905ers," those who had emigrated following the first Russian revolution and the widespread pogroms against Jews, were both more self-consciously Jewish than their predecessors and at the same time more frequently engaged with politics. Trained in the circles of the Jewish Bund of the Pale, a kind of trade union/political association, they rushed into trade union and Socialist party circles, but also into the educational centers of unions and the large fraternal wing of the Socialist party, the Arbeiter Ring (Workmen's Circle). By wartime, proliferating Yiddish day schools preached the socialist doctrine.

Socialists also reached out to English-speaking youth. The "Socialist Sunday schools" movement, organized in some sixty-four cities and towns in twenty states, drew thousands each year into weekly lessons on class struggle and the hopes for change. Recitations, songs, game-playing, and pageants punctuated weekly lessons. Teenagers joined the Young People's Socialist League (YPSL), 5,000 strong by 1915, mainly in a supportive capacity for the adult movement. The Intercollegiate Socialist Society, not officially socialist but dominated by Socialist party members and studded with luminary speakers such as Jack London and Charlotte Perkins Gilman, had branches on fifty campuses, conducting forums and raising consciousness among those going into professions (especially dentistry, popular among Jewish immigrants, who were commonly denied entrance to medical schools).

AMERICAN SOCIALISTS AND WORLD WAR I

The U.S. entry into war tested the character of the evolving party severely. At the St. Louis convention of 1917, the party opposed involvement and vindicated internationalism, acting bravely in the face of certain persecution and the example of European socialists capitulating to national defense programs. Socialist Anglophiles, mainly a scattering of intellectuals, defected and formed (with covert government support) a pro-war socialistic association. Far more serious, the Post Office department began a far-ranging campaign to wipe out the socialist press, banning an issue or two and then denying second-class mailing permits to dailies or weeklies that had missed an issue. Rural and small-town (i.e., native-born) socialists were worst hit by these and similar measures, such as banning socialist (or anti-war) meetings on the basis of a purported "threat to public health." Repression escalated, with dozens of orators including Eugene Debs arrested on a variety of charges, tied up in court cases, and often sent to prison. Desperate with frustration, hundreds of Oklahoma sharecroppers rose in armed rebellion and were immediately crushed, virtually extinguishing one of the strongest centers of socialist activism.

Yet the Socialist party fought back successfully, for a time, with aggressive anti-war propaganda. In New York, Pennsylvania, and large sections of the Midwest, from industrial Ohio towns to Chicago and rural Wisconsin, they won over Germanic voters, scored victories in local elections, or ran strong seconds. The People's Council for Peace and Democracy, a "front" organization for socialists and pacifists, garnered large crowds and carried the endorsement of union leaders opposed to AFL president Samuel Gompers's ardent support of war. For the first time, the African-American participation in the socialist movement (previously largely confined to Christian socialist circles) gained real substance and influence, especially in Harlem where they shared some outstanding intellectuals with black nationalism.

The widespread public disillusionment with the war, the continuation of strikes and the prominence of socialist-minded labor activists (notwithstanding the ferocious government persecution of the IWW) seemed to augur for a bright future for the Socialist party. But the Rus-sian Revolution pointed in other directions. The leaders of the new Comintern insisted that new revolutionary parties be formed out of the socialist movement, and most socialists were unwilling to buck orders from the only existing in-power Communist party in the world. Although American socialists had overwhelmingly remained loyal to their anti-war standards and just as overwhelmingly welcomed the Russian events, they could not escape the Comintern edict.

During 1918 and early 1919, proto-communist factions proliferated, attacking first the Socialist party leadership, and then each other, with seemingly wild enthusiasm. Set into action by Woodrow Wilson's administration, the new Bureau of Investigation (headed by a young J. Edgar Hoover) added to the confusion, with thousands of informers on Bureau payrolls, often doubling as the most extreme factionalists. Seizing control of a weak Massachusetts state socialist organization, a "Socialist Propaganda League" (funded by Latvian Americans, scarcely present outside the Roxbury neighborhood in Boston but tied closely, through homeland politics, to the Russian Bolsheviks) issued a manifesto and an irregular factional tabloid, the *Internationalist.*

Its editor, Louis C. Fraina, was typical of the socialist political intellectual who had outgrown the Socialist party. Beginning his radical career as a street-speaker for the tiny Socialist Labor party and an editor of the party's *Daily People* (which ended its publication in 1914), Fraina had moved on to *New Review* and the avant-gardist *Modern Dance* magazine, before enlisting with the *Internationalist* and its better-circulated successor, *Revolutionary Age,* as well as a new quarterly journal, *Class Struggle.* In 1917, Fraina rejoined a Socialist party that he had abandoned in 1909; by 1919, he received the highest vote for membership in the ruling National Executive Committee. His two precocious volumes, *The Proletarian Revolution in Russia* (1917) and *Revolutionary Socialism* (1918), both documented the importance of events abroad and sought to make them the model for the revolutionary crisis thought soon destined to reach the United States.

The psychological impact of the Russian events, the hopes for an all-European revolution (turned back, at last, in Hungary, where a Communist government was quickly overthrown), made the imperative for a new party and new leaders seem especially urgent to younger and foreign-born socialists. Older and native-born socialists who had borne in some ways the brunt of past repression (although the threat of deportation hung over the heads of new immigrants and their rights could be violated with greater impunity) looked on more cautiously. For them, too, the model of the Socialist party as an educational mechanism had fallen short, and the constant prediction of capitalism's decline had failed to anticipate the wartime boom. They could recall the destructive factional troubles of the 1890s or had simply reached an age (a survey of the *Appeal to Reason* "army" of subscription-gatherers found them, on average, well into mid-life) when they were skeptical of new adventures.

Experienced socialist leaders therefore rationalized the expulsion of large numbers of party members—including the entire state body in Michigan—as a proper pre-emptory strike against a threatened left-wing takeover. A bloc of language federations had already seceded to form the Communist party, while a rump group (including John Reed among other native-born radicals) fought one last battle at the 1919 Socialist convention before forming a Communist Labor party.

As these two new entities (and several warring factions within them) furiously quarreled over the next three years before settling into a single communist organization, propaganda and educational activities on all sides severely dwindled. A few socialist foreign language groups such as the Italians gamely regrouped, and several others (notably the South Slavs, mainly Slovenians) rejoined the Socialist party after the war ended. If active membership of the proscribed communists was no more than 10,000 or 20,000, the Socialist party following was even less—except for the presence of old-timers, mainly inactive sentimentalists and bureaucratic-minded labor functionaries.

Ironically, in 1920, a jailed Eugene Debs re-

ceived his highest vote total ever, nearly one million, despite the competition of a Farmer-Labor party ticket (including former Cleveland socialist leader Max Hayes), which polled a quarter-million in six states. Moreover, the YPSL successfully reorganized after the organization had almost as a body defected to the communist movement in 1919, establishing a new presence in communities and campuses. The recession of the early 1920s and growing disillusionment with war also opened fresh avenues for propaganda. Christian socialists, pacifists who had remained true to the party, had a new pronounced presence with charismatic former Methodist minister Norman Thomas and a circle around the new popular religious-political magazine launched in 1921, *The World Tomorrow*. Another new magazine, *Labor Age*, reflected socialist educators at work in the burgeoning labor schools, especially Brookwood Labor College (in Katonah, New York) headed by the Reverend A.J. Muste. The weekly *New Leader*, funded by the officialdom of the garment unions, also remained reliably socialist. The Rand School, finally, reached new success by branching out beyond the usual socialistic training to a broader curriculum of psychology, peace education, social work, and so on.

Unfortunately, Socialist party officials were unable, as they would prove to be repeatedly in the decade afterward, to take much advantage of the seemingly rich prospects. Even in Milwaukee, where socialists continued to hold municipal offices and successful struggles for re-election offered a live issue, actual party membership and party-building seemed to be mainly of interest to older socialists. Young radicals directly joined the Communist party or (like Albert Weisbord, the leader of YPSL during the early 1920s) defected after a trial with the Socialists. State branches that had been notably strong with native-born members, from Indiana to the Dakotas, simply faded away. Young and more vigorous cultural activists in the fraternal bodies formed their own summer camps, choruses, and theaters with a communist slant.

Worse in a way, the main function of Socialist-party membership and prestige within the garment trades was to provide a rationale for the self-serving labor bureaucracy. In a sometimes violent factional war with Communists, socialists such as David Dubinsky of the International Ladies' Garment Workers' Union and Max Zaritsky of the capmakers regularly denied opponents democratic rights, gerrymandered union districts to assure unpopular officials' re-election, even called upon gangsters (with whom they had a tolerant relationship), the police, the press, and manufacturers to help them defeat the newer and more virulent Left. These machinations by socialists threw such labor leaders into the arms of labor's extreme anti-socialist conservatives, such as the phlegmatic AFL president Matthew Woll, discrediting moderate socialism and union office-holding as sources for idealistic expression.

SOCIALISTS AND PROGRESSIVES

The campaign of Robert La Follette for president in 1924 on the Progressive party ticket gave socialists an opportunity to practice what they knew best, electoral politics. The withdrawal of the AFL from the campaign and La Follette's death soon afterward closed off electoral experiments until socialists found a new champion in Norman Thomas. Running perennially for public office in New York State, and regularly for president from 1932 onward, Thomas had the capacity to excite older and younger voters, draw college youth into campaigns, and revive to a degree the machinery of the Socialist party. Along with a return of municipal socialist victories in Wisconsin, and new ones in Pennsylvania and Connecticut, it seemed to give the Socialist party a raison d'être.

The failures of the Communist party had a still greater effect in the same fashion, especially with the outbreak of the Depression. So sectarian (and Russian-sounding) were Communist slogans, so overwrought their calls for mass demonstrations at the approaching end of cap-

italism, that the wave of younger and reinvigorated idealists turned in many places toward the Socialist party—with about 20,000 members in 1932 compared to the Communists' 18,000. The socialist-led League for Industrial Democracy (a successor to the Intercollegiate Socialist Society) mobilized pro-government job Unemployed Leagues with great success in Illinois, Michigan, Ohio, and Maryland. In 1935, these leagues gathered in the Workers Alliance of America under socialist David Lasser. Less inclined toward confrontations and public disruptions than Communists, the unemployed activists of the Socialist party often interceded with authorities rather than leading disruptive demonstrations and gained a reputation for practical success over propaganda. On campuses meanwhile, the Student League for Industrial Democracy helped lead "peace strikes" on dozens of campuses pledging non-participation in any future war.

The New Deal and the shift of the Communists to the popular front largely removed the unemployed as a source for party renewal. Socialists had worked effectively with local unionists for a national labor party in 1933–35, convincing many local AFL leaders and central trades councils that the day had finally come. Franklin Roosevelt's 1936 election campaign, building upon the popularity of the "Second New Deal" (with the Wagner Act, Social Security, and a series of other relief measures), swept these hopes away. Prominent Socialist party labor officials even resigned to take part in Roosevelt's campaign. The Communists, practically abandoning their own electoral campaigns for work within the Democratic party, further isolated the socialists. Only the American Labor party, created in 1936 to siphon socialist votes to Roosevelt, offered an alternative with significant socialist involvement. Ironically, however, the ALP encouraged New York unionists to devote energy to it, rather than the Democrats. At that, the uneasy relationship of socialists and communists (mirroring the uneasy relationship of communist ally Amalgamated Clothing Workers leader Sidney Hillman, with the more conservative David Dubinsky) pointed toward another unhappy ending. By 1940, Norman Thomas's electoral campaign became almost nominal, punctuated only by Thomas's opposition of U.S. involvement in impending world war, a socialist policy strongly backed by pacifists but bitterly resisted by older Jewish socialists.

Every major initiative brought further disappointment. The conflict between older and younger socialists during the early 1930s culminated in the 1936 withdrawal of the garment union bureaucracy and its following of several thousand, as the Social Democratic Federation, taking along the Rand School and the *New Leader*. Smaller but more determinedly radical, socialists welcomed the several hundred followers of Leon Trotsky, who began a furious propaganda campaign on the Spanish Civil War and other issues precipitating their own expulsion from the Communist party (along with most of the current YPSL) in 1937. Meanwhile, the formation of the Congress of Industrial Organizations, which offered the Communist party previously unimaginable influence in working-class America, nearly bypassed the socialists, who were rooted by this time among the older socialist generation within the AFL rather than in the mass production factories where the CIO was growing in strength. Only in Michigan, where socialist leaders became part of the braintrust of Walter Reuther's faction of the United Auto Workers, did their labor influence offer significant promise.

The Socialist party limped through World War II with less than 10,000 members, while the Communist party reached the apex of its respectability and size (at some 85,000 enrolled and a following of perhaps one million). Communist popularity could not survive the cold war and its persecutions, but the noncommunist Left experienced only a mild and temporary revival thereafter. Following Roosevelt's death, socialists looked once again to the promise of a third party. The electoral disaster of the Progressive party peace candidacy of former vice president Henry Wallace, supported by the Communists, ended these socialist hopes and placed them squarely if a bit uncomfortably in the anti-communist camp. Norman Thomas, the "Conscience of America," was by this time

a respected voice but with only a minimal organized following.

The Socialist party seemed hereafter mainly to serve the interests of those who sought institutional cover for the advancement of factional interests. By the early 1950s, the youth wing of a section of Trotskyists under veteran political leader Max Shachtman merged with a reorganized YPSL, followed by a merger of the adult faction of the Socialists in 1957 (with the Social Democratic Federation completing the socialist reorganization). Ironically, however, the entry of a Trotskyist grouping this time pulled the organization toward the center rather than providing a new meeting-point for the Left. The unified Socialist Party/Social Democratic Federation (SP/SDF) gained one key intellectual figure, Michael Harrington, but few other young members. Its leaders had also by now largely given up on independent political action, hoping instead to move the Democratic party into a European-style, social democratic direction.

The aging SP/SDF was unsuited, however, for the fresh energies of the civil rights movement and New Left. As newer peace movements grew up in the later 1950s and early 1960s opposing nuclear testing, YPSL briefly played a key role via the Student Peace Union. By the middle and later 1960s, however, when the Student League for Industrial Democracy had reorganized as the Students for a Democratic Society and became a central force in the campus anti-war movement, YPSL swung wildly rightward, denouncing demands for withdrawal of U.S. troops from Vietnam and defending the AFL-CIO bureaucracy around conservative president George Meany from criticism of its racial behavior and its international policies. After 1970, the AFL-CIO support for the Vietnam War and hostility toward student peace movements proved too much for socialists around Michael Harrington, who led a group to support presidential candidate George McGovern in 1972 and to form the breakaway Democratic Socialist Organizing Committee (DSOC). The Social Democrats USA (SDUSA) and a small Socialist party (best known for former Milwaukee mayor Frank Zeidler, who ran on the "new" Socialist party ticket for president in 1972) struggled for their own positions.

Only a few thousand in number but blessed with some union support and Harrington's reputation as intellectual father of John F. Kennedy's War on Poverty, DSOC entered the 1970s hopefully. Within a few years it had merged with a New Left offshoot, the New American Movement, forming the Democratic Socialists of America (DSA). Firmly united in supporting liberal Democratic candidates but determined to pull them further leftward into a coalition of labor, feminists, minorities, and environmentalists, the new DSA reached its highest point of prestige in the post-Watergate atmosphere of 1978. Thereafter, the rightward turn of Democrats, the resurgence of the distant Right, and the sullen conservatism of AFL-CIO leaders all eclipsed DSA expectations.

The Reagan years nevertheless saw socialists (or "social democrats" as they now styled themselves) in surprisingly high places. The SDUSA, which had supported Henry Jackson's candidacy in the 1972 race for Democratic nomination and thereafter refused to endorse George McGovern, had during the course of the 1970s and early 1980s become an influential factor in cold war operations, especially those involving intelligence agencies. The Reagan administration placed several former youth leaders of SDUSA in Jeane Kirkpatrick's United Nations office and the new National Endowment for Democracy. As a practical matter, other social democrats effectively ran the political operations of certain AFL-CIO unions (such as the Bricklayers Union and American Federation of Teachers) on a day-to-day basis. Hardline anti-communism and equally hardline support of Israeli policies provided the ideological ballast, while prestige appointments and the rise of neoconservative think tanks offered well-paying jobs for this curious rogue-socialist development.

Within the higher reaches of the AFL-CIO meanwhile, the stagnation of the domestic labor movement was offset—at least in expectations— by the social-democratic prospects of world labor leadership. Expecting to inherit a world

movement as communism failed, former socialists directed AFL-CIO international agencies, wrote position papers for leaders (especially Lane Kirkland, who took over from retiring George Meany in 1979), and fortified bodies such as Freedom House, which set anti-communism at the forefront of its own "human rights" agenda. By the early 1990s, these policies had indeed played important roles in providing a rationale for U.S. labor policies, especially in the third world, where guerrilla warfare or Communist governments were succeeded by elected neoliberal regimes. But American-directed labor organizations themselves had badly stagnated, unwanted by corporations ungrateful for labor officials' assistance, and unable to position themselves as democratic opposition to the new regimes. Most of all, social-democratic policies had failed at home. The AFL-CIO lost members at a staggering rate by the early 1990s, sometimes a half-million per year. SDUSA, whose leaders had for two decades rubbed shoulders with the powerful and distributed extremely large sums of money, had meanwhile slipped to several hundred elderly members. Critics quipped that it was the most conservative socialist party in the world.

In 1995, frustrated labor leaders joined by a cadre of vigorous socialist activists (some of them enrolled in DSA; most not) overthrew the existing labor leadership. In its place, a team headed by Service Employees Union International president and registered DSA member John Sweeney came to power. DSA, with a nominal membership of nearly 10,000, seemed poised to take advantage of this development. But as the century closed, it could not yet turn the interest of campus activists toward organizational affiliation. While labor conservatives maneuvered to return hardliners—some of them former socialists—to power in the AFL-CIO, the tiny Socialist party continued to elect a scattering of officials to local offices in Iowa City, Iowa, Salem, Oregon, and other college towns. No strategies had succeeded, and many had brought only disappointment and disillusionment. But the crises of capitalism had not ceased, least of all in a global sense, and the possibility of socialist reorganization remained.

PAUL BUHLE

See also: American Labor Party; Communist Party; Eugene Victor Debs; **Map 29:** Socialist Party (1900); **Map 30:** Socialist Party (1904); **Map 31:** Socialist Party (1908); **Map 32:** Socialist Party (1912); **Map 33:** Socialist Party (1916); **Map 34:** Socialist Party (1920); **Map 35:** Socialist Party (1928); **Map 36:** Socialist Party (1932); **Map 37:** Socialist Party (1936); Populist Movement/People's Party; Progressive (Bull Moose) Party; Progressive Movement of 1924; Upton B. Sinclair; Social Democratic Party; Socialist Labor Party; Norman M. Thomas; Henry Agard Wallace.

Bibliography

Bell, Daniel. *Marxian Socialism in the United States.* Princeton: Princeton University Press, 1967.

Buhle, Mari Jo. *Women and American Socialism, 1870–1920.* Urbana: University of Illinois Press, 1981.

Buhle, Mari Jo; Paul Buhle; and Dan Georgakas, eds. *Encyclopedia of the American Left.* 2d ed. New York: Oxford University Press, 1998.

Buhle, Paul. *Marxism in the United States.* 2d ed. London: Verso, 1991.

Buhle, Paul, and Dan Georgakas, eds. *The Immigrant Left in the United States.* Albany: State University of New York Press, 1996.

Draper, Theodore. *Roots of American Communism.* New York: Viking Press, 1957.

Johnpohl, Bernard K., and Harvey Klehr, eds. *Biographical Dictionary of the American Left.* Westport, CT: Greenwood, 1986.

Judd, Richard W. *Socialist Cities: Explorations into the Grass Roots of American Socialism.* Albany: State University of New York Press, 1990.

Salvatore, Nick. *Eugene V. Debs: Citizen and Socialist.* Urbana: University of Illinois Press, 1982.

Stave, Bruce, ed. *Socialism and the Cities.* Port Washington, NY: Kennikate Press, 1975.

Swanberg, W.A. *Norman Thomas: The Last Idealist.* New York: Scribner's, 1976.

Vogel, Virgil. *Bibliography of the History of Socialism in America.* Milwaukee: Socialist Party, 1977.

SOCIALIST WORKERS PARTY

1938–

The origins of the Socialist Workers party (SWP) go back to the late 1920s, when several Communist party officials—including James Cannon and Max Shachtman—broke away to form the Communist League of America (CLA). Disenchanted by the growing regimentation, authoritarianism, and conservatism of the Stalin government in Moscow, the CLA insisted that the true principles of communism could be found in the ideas and actions of Leon Trotsky, who was exiled from the Soviet Union.

With their popular left-wing magazine, *The Militant,* the party—although never possessing more than 2,000 members—had an influence beyond its size. In the 1930s, it became involved with the unemployed movement and industrial unionism. In 1934, CLA officials helped lead a militant Teamsters' strike in Minneapolis, which quickly turned into a city-wide general strike.

In 1934, the CLA merged with the American Workers party to form the Workers Party of the United States. Two years later, the new party folded itself into the Socialist party. That lasted but two years, before the Trotskyites were thrown out of the party for challenging the moderate leadership of Norman Thomas. Upon their expulsion in 1938—the same year that the Trotsky-led Fourth International communist movement was established—the former CLA members refashioned themselves as the Socialist Workers party.

Although a leading organization within the Fourth International, the SWP was under harsh government attack at home. Under the Voorhis Act, the party was forced to disaffiliate from the

The Socialist Workers party—one of the few radical parties of the 1930s to make the transition to the New Left of the 1960s—supported a host of progressive causes, including—as this 1976 campaign poster depicts—the controversial policy of busing children to desegregate schools. *(Courtesy of the Gary Yanker collection, Library of Congress)*

international organization. With America's entry into World War II, the SWP's insistence that the war was imperialist and that no worker should fight got the party into trouble. With the pro-Soviet Communist Party USA in support, the U.S. government imprisoned eighteen SWP leaders. Still, the party survived and became critical to the wave of strikes that immediately followed World War II. By 1960, however, the anti-communist hysteria and economic prosperity of the 1950s reduced the party to a shadow of its former self, with just 400 aging members—despite the fact that its standing was bolstered by Nikita Khrushchev's 1956 revelations of Stalinist crimes.

At the same time, the wave of anti-colonialism and third-world revolutions sweeping the globe in the 1950s and 1960s made many leftists in the United States take a second look at Trotsky's ideas about world revolution. In particular, the SWP gravitated toward Fidel Castro's revolution in Cuba. The party even formed a pro-Havana organization called the Fair Play for Cuba Committee. In addition, both the black liberation and anti-war movements in the United States drew inspiration from Trotsky's thinking, and the SWP played significant roles in the National Mobilization Committee to End the War in Vietnam (or "the Mobe"). Dur-

ing the 1970s, the SWP also became well known among the left for its vigorous and reasonably well-publicized electoral campaigns for state and federal office. By the 1980s, a series of internal feuds had broken the back of the party and driven hundreds to leave, although the party continued to survive and run candidates with little chance of winning through the 1990s.

JAMES CIMENT

See also: Communist Party; Revolutionary Communist Party; Socialist Labor Party; Socialist Party; Workers World Party.

Bibliography

Breitman, George, ed. *The Founding of the Socialist Workers Party.* New York: Monad Press, 1982.

Le Blanc, Paul. *Trotskyism in America: The First Fifty Years.* New York: Fourth Internationalist Tendency, 1987.

Wald, Alan. *The New York Intellectuals: The Rise and Decline of the Anti-Stalinist Left, From the 1930s to the 1980s.* Chapel Hill: University of North Carolina Press, 1987.

SOUTH CAROLINA PROGRESSIVE DEMOCRATIC PARTY

1944–1956

The South Carolina Progressive Democratic party evolved out of a search for a political strategy that would permit the African-American electorate to overcome the burdensome consequences of disenfranchisement and the accompanying political ideology of white supremacy. By the mid-1930s leaders in the state had begun to coalesce around the Negro Citizens Committee, a statewide organization with two tasks. The first was helping blacks register to vote; the second was to overturn South Carolina's whites-only primary system. To achieve this latter aim, it had to raise money, which it did through a number of local affiliates. Starting in 1940, the Citizens Committee began the arduous task of registering African Americans to vote in the state capitol in Columbia. But such a bold move simply would not be tolerated by the white Democratic officials and party elites. They put into place a counter-strategy. At the courthouse in Columbia, the registrar would let the committee register its people. Several days later, the registered individual would receive a letter in the mail stating that their name had been purged from the rolls because state law prohibited African Americans from voting. This effectively destroyed the committee's registration drives.

And before the committee could react, state party leaders started discussing the possibility that President Roosevelt's name should be left off the state ballot in the upcoming 1944 election. Now the leaders of the committee had a twofold problem: They were unable to register and, even if registered, were not able to vote for President Roosevelt in the 1944 election.

NEED FOR ORGANIZATION

Faced with this dual reality, leaders of the committee felt that they needed an organization that could hold its own primaries and put its own candidates on the state ballot. The first indication that the leaders of the committee had a different strategy for this dilemma appeared in the editorial column of the *Lighthouse and Informer*, an African-American newspaper published by John H. McCray, a member of the committee and community activist. The editorial that appeared in the March 18, 1944, issue declared that the "plan called for 'the formation of Fourth-Term-for-Roosevelt Clubs' throughout the state incorporated under the 'South Carolina Colored Democratic party.'" In addition, McCray told his readership that the party would hold its own convention, nominate its own leadership, and be completely controlled by African Americans.

Pursuant to the editorial, the city editor of the white *Columbia Record*, Brim Rykard, obtained permission to reprint the editorial in his paper so that whites could see what the African-American community was planning and thus could possibly adopt a reactive strategy. However, the Associated Press wire service picked up the editorial and made it available nationally. Responses came pouring in from around the country. Overnight, McCray found himself being pressured to launch the proposed South Carolina Colored Democratic party. Eight days later, McCray and members of the Negro Citizens Committee met in his office to discuss what to do about the innumerable responses to his proposal. The consensus of the meeting was that the party be launched. McCray was elected acting chairman, and his associate editor, Osceola McKaine, was elected acting secretary. J.C. Artemius was elected acting treasurer. A rudimentary organization was now in place and a date for the founding convention was set for May 24, 1944.

However, between the March 26 organizing session and the May 24 convention people continued to come to his office and to offer advice, support, and volunteer their time. One visitor, an elderly white lady, suggested to McCray that the party should be "progressive" and not only limited to blacks. Then she donated to McCray her five-dollar old-age pension check and indicated how delighted she was that her money could be used against a state government that expected her to live on such a monthly pittance. At the very next meeting, the name of the party was changed to South Carolina Progressive Democratic party (SCPDP).

FOUNDING CONVENTION

At the founding convention in Columbia on May 24, 172 delegates came from thirty-nine of the state's forty-six counties and visitors and observers came from Alabama, Arkansas, Florida, Georgia, Mississippi, North Carolina, and Virginia. Clearly, the AP wire service had spread the news about this rising state party. The keynote address to the convention delegates and observers was given by McKaine.

"It is to correct these unfair conditions, to give the disinherited men and women of both races in South Carolina some voice in their government, some control over their destinies, and some hope for reasonable security and happiness in the future that the Progressive Democratic party has been founded." With this charge in mind, the delegates elected permanent officers for the new party, named a state and national delegation, wrote and adopted a constitution and temporary rules, and created a three-tiered committee structure for the party. And as Professor Alexander Heard shows in his book, *A Two-Party South,* the new party was quite effective at fundraising. The budget for the organization appears in that book in detail. Before the convention ended, the new party adopted an anthem, to be sung at all party meetings and particularly at the close of each party function. The song was an old Negro spiritual called "Climbing Jacob's Ladder." With this device, the African-American members had now fused elements of their culture with the organization's goals and objectives.

Immediately upon leaving the convention, the SCPDP dispatched a delegation to meet with the chairman of the Democratic National Committee, Robert Hannagan. To this meeting with the group, Hannagan brought the new Democratic congressman, William L. Dawson from Chicago. The meeting ended with a pledge from Hannagan and Dawson that discriminatory practices such as those in the South Carolina state party would be eliminated. Exactly how this was to be done was not spelled out to the delegation.

Upon returning to the state, the SCPDP held another convention and nominated McKaine as its candidate to run against Governor Olin D. Johnston for the U.S. Senate in 1944. Before the election, the SCPDP sent a delegation to the Democratic National Convention to contest the seats of the regular state delegation. However, the group was quietly turned away, and the Credentials Committee never heard their challenge.

In the 1944 November election, the SCPDP candidate received less than 5,000 votes and this made the SCPDP leaders understand the need to shift its focus to voter registration drives and the mobilization of the African-American electorate at election time. However, before its annual 1946 convention, NAACP attorney Thurgood Marshall, U.S. District Judge J. Waites Waring, and the Reverend James Hinton, head of the state NAACP, urged McCray and the SCPDP to disband as a political party and reconstitute itself as a caucus group in the state, which would deal with issues and problems peculiar to black Democrats. The reasoning behind the appeal was that the SCPDP could not hope to defeat the regular party nor get it unseated at the national convention. Moreover, the action of the SCPDP was an embarrassment to the national Democratic party, which did not want to effectively deal with the problem. Hence, the party urged the small group to stand down.

At the 1946 SCPDP convention, it disbanded and reconfigured itself as a "Negro Democratic caucus" group in South Carolina. But it did not give up its mission. In 1948, it sent another challenge delegation to the National Convention. And even though the regular state delegation was now pledged to J. Strom Thurmond, who was running as the presidential candidate of the Dixiecrat party, the Credentials Committee voted to seat the regular delegation and issued a minority report expressing concern for the plight of the progressive-minded Democrats. When the minority report was made public, the all-white South Carolina delegation walked out.

The progressive Democrats waited an election cycle before sending yet another challenge delegation to the 1956 Democratic National Convention. It received yet another pledge that the party would revise its rules and prevent any future seating of all-white delegations from the South. As the action of the Mississippi Freedom Democrats showed in 1964 and the National Democratic party of Alabama showed in 1968, such revision of the rules did not take place.

After the 1956 convention, several of the leaders of the progressive Democrats were slowly absorbed into the regular South Carolina Democratic party at the lowest party levels available. For instance, John McCray was elected vice chairman of ward eighteen in Columbia. But once the media spotlight shifted to other matters, McCray's newspaper office was set afire and he was charged with burning down his own paper. Once in jail, he was quietly told that if he left the state and never came back, the charges against him would be dropped. He left the state and took the public relations job at Talladega College in Alabama. Once he left, others in the progressive Democrats were absorbed in local and county organ-

izations and the group, without its leaders, became invisible.

There is one ironic final note. John McCray told a Senate subcommittee public hearing on constitutional rights in April 1959 "that blacks in South Carolina had to form a *satellite* political party [in the state] because they were barred from participation in the regular state Democratic party." Then Senator Olin D. Johnston, a member of the subcommittee conducting the hearing and one of the individuals against whom the SCPDP had run in 1944, pretended he knew nothing of the party. Responding to McCray, Senator Johnston noted he had a statement from the chair of the regular Democratic party in South Carolina, Thomas H. Pope, which said "that the organization [which] claims to be represented by John H. McCray as the South Carolina Progressive Democrats, or South Carolina Progressive Democratic party or South Carolina Democratic Organization, whatever he may call it, is not a part of the South Carolina Democratic party and is not even recognized by the South Carolina Democratic party in South Carolina."

John McCray simply responded to these incredible charges by saying that the "National Democratic Party in 1956 'recommended' the SCPDP to the state party for inclusion." The very party which the senator had beaten to win his seat was politely forgotten about in the public glare of the Senate hearing. Moreover, the senator, a mere three years after the party had been absorbed, was still defending the regular party's racism and discriminatory exclusion of African Americans from the party and the electoral process. To have acknowledged the mere existence of the party would have forced him to have to apologize for his state's antidemocratic practices. He would not do this, particularly to an African American. In his mind, there was nothing wrong in his state, and no one's constitutional rights had been violated.

Overall, the chief impact of the SCPDP was to increase African-American voter registration in the state, run African-American candidates for office, and become the first such southern party to challenge the national Democrats to reform their state party in terms of racial discrimination. If the national party organization had acted on the requests of the Progressive Democrats instead of papering over them, the storm that came with the Mississippi Freedom Democrats and its national television coverage would have never happened. And the racial ruptures that occurred in the other state party units need not have splintered the organization so badly at some of its national conventions in the 1960s and 1970s.

Clearly, the SCPDP was a pioneer and forerunner in the effort to reform the Democratic party. Yet, given the times and the political context of the nation, the reform could not have occurred. Nor did the SCPDP have the political muscle to force the reforms. Eventually, its own reform efforts destroyed its leadership and thus the spirit of the party.

HANES WALTON, JR.

See also: National Democratic Party of Alabama; States' Rights Democratic Party (Dixiecrats).

Bibliography

Heard, Alexander. *A Two Party South.* Chapel Hill: University of North Carolina Press, 1952.

Hoffman, E. "The Genesis of the Modern Movement for Equal Rights in South Carolina, 1930–1939." *Journal of Negro History* (October 1959): 363–369.

Jackson, Luther P. "Race and Suffrage in the South Since 1940." *New South* (June-July 1948): 4–5.

McCray, John. Letter to Hanes Walton, Jr., 1971. In author's files.

Robinson, W.P., Sr. "Democracy's Frontiers." *Journal of Human Relations* 2 (Spring 1954): 63–71.

U.S. Senate. *Hearing Before the Subcommittee on Constitutional Rights of the Committee on the Judiciary,* Part I. Washington, DC: Government Printing Office, 1959, p. 561.

Walton, Hanes, Jr. *Black Political Parties: An Historical and Political Analysis.* New York: Free Press, 1972.

———. *Invisible Politics: Black Political Behavior.* Albany: State University of New York Press, 1985.

SOUTHERN DEMOCRAT PARTY

1860

*T*hird parties tended to be rather non-durable in the nineteenth century, usually persisting in one form or another for no more than two elections. This was especially true for the 1860 Southern Democrat party, which was formed during the 1860 Democrat conventions. The party only lasted through the presidential election that same year.

The late 1850s and early 1860s were a period of turmoil in U.S. history promoting sectional conflict between the North and the South. A series of rifts developed between the northern and southern Democrats and were in large part reflections of these sectional divisions. There was much rivalry between them, which resulted from differences in economic activities. For instance, the economy of the North was based on the dynamic forces of industrialization and modern technology. In the South, the economy was oriented toward agricultural activity such as farming cotton and tobacco. Slavery was also an important issue that created tensions between the North and the South. The southern commitment to the use of slave labor inhibited economic diversification and industrialization. Slavery was also important because it was deeply ingrained into key elements of southern life—the social and political ascendancy of the planter class and the authoritarian system of social control.

The rift that developed between the northern and the southern Democrats was reflective of these sectional divisions. It was not just a division in an economic or cultural context, but a division that was expressed in the realignment of political power. The sectional battles fought in Congress, in conventions, and in the legislatures were political. The objectives of the North and the South were political and included the organization of territories and the admission of states as free or slave states. The slave issue, which was the most divisive, solidified the internal split between the northern and southern Democrats. The defense of slavery became the primary goal and platform of the Southern Democrat party during the 1860 presidential election.

The Southern Democrats were very different from the other parties forming during this period. It was the first party to begin life in formal secession from a major party, the National Democrats. The National Democratic party had sensed the issue of slavery as being divisive within the party and had vigorously resisted its introduction into politics. However, the Southern Democrats felt that the National Democratic party had betrayed them because they believed that their slaveholder interests were not being adequately represented by the national party. The formation of the Southern Democrat party then became the only nationally significant American party ever to advocate unequivocally the defense of slavery. Under its leader, John C. Breckinridge, the Southern Democrat party even considered the withdrawal of slave states from the Union. Despite their staunch support of the pro-slavery issue, the Southern Democrat party represented not just the Solid South, but attracted far more national attention and support in its outreach than had other contemporary parties.

The 1860 Democratic conventions were pivotal for the Southern Democrats. At Charleston, during the first of the two Democratic conventions held that year, Southern Democrats demanded that the National Democratic platform include some measures for the defense of slave interests. Until then, the Southern Democrats had tried unsuccessfully to repeal the prohibition against the African slave trade or to promote a slave code that would protect slavery in territories that were under federal jurisdiction. When the convention refused and resolved that the Supreme Court would settle the issue of slavery (as they had done with the 1857 *Dred Scott* v. *Sandford* decision), delegates from the Deep South and others from Arkansas and Delaware withdrew in protest. Due to the failure to nominate a presidential candidate in Charleston, the National Democrats reconvened in Baltimore later that year. In Baltimore, the Democratic forces supporting Stephen Douglas as the Democratic presidential candidate nominated him and denied reinstatement to those delegates who had walked out in Charleston. Outraged, the delegates from the Deep South met in Richmond and endorsed a presidential candidate of their own, John C. Breckinridge. The split between the northern Democrats, led by Stephen Douglas, and the southern Democrats, led by John C. Breckinridge, were the beginnings of the Southern Democrat party.

During the 1860 presidential election a unique four-party contest for the presidency arose: In addition to Douglas and Breckinridge, the Republican ticket was led by Abraham Lincoln, and the Constitutional Union party was led by John Bell. As the results of the election depict, sectionalism did triumph. Lincoln, with 39.82 percent of the popular vote won the presidential election carrying seventeen free states and no slave states. Breckinridge finished second after Lincoln, collecting seventy-two electoral votes (18.09 percent of the vote), winning eleven southern slave states and no free states. Breckinridge did well in some states outside of the Solid South. He was just 254 votes short of victory in Oregon and finished a close third in California, where he took 28.4 percent of the popular votes cast. John Bell, placing third, won three slave states and no free states, and Stephen Douglas finished last with only nine electoral votes in Missouri and three in New Jersey.

Support for the Southern Democrat party was concentrated in the rural South, and it did

With the Democratic party torn apart by the slavery issue in the 1860 campaign, southerners bolted to form the Southern Democrats, with Kentucky Senator John Breckinridge—depicted in this 1850s portrait—as their candidate. Breckinridge captured seventy-two electoral votes, largely in the Deep South. (*Courtesy of the Library of Congress*)

best in counties with the fewest slaves. Commercial interests in larger cites, uncomfortable with talk of secession, were less supportive as were landowners who retained their historic ties to the Whigs (now represented under the Constitutional Union party). By 1864, there was no need for the Southern Democrat party. The Civil War had settled the slavery question once and for all. (It is interesting to note that during the Civil War, Breckinridge served as the Confederate Secretary of War). The Southern Democrat party, owing its existence to the pro-slavery issue, vanished.

There are several reasons why the Southern

Democrat party did not last. The party was not deeply rooted in political soil. It had organized around a temporary issue or as a protest against the National Democratic party. The Southern Democrats also spent little time trying to unite the party nationally. In addition, they did not have much of an ideological vision other than one concerned with slavery. Thus, the Southern Democrat party had little influence or longevity in the American political arena.

ANITA CHADHA

See also: Constitutional Union Party.

Bibliography

Collins, Charles Wallace. *Whither the Solid South? A Study in Politics and Race Relations.* New Orleans: Pelican, 1947.

Gillespie, J. David. *Politics at the Periphery: Third Parties in Two-Party America.* Columbia: University of South Carolina Press, 1993.

Holt, Michael F. *Political Parties and American Political Development, from the Age of Jackson to the Age of Lincoln.* Baton Rouge: Louisiana State University Press, 1992.

Maisel, L. Sandy, ed. *The Parties Respond: Changes in the American Party System.* San Francisco: Westview Press, 1990.

Polakoff, Keith Ian. *Political Parties in American History.* New York: John Wiley and Sons, 1981.

Potter, David M. *The Impending Crisis: 1848–1861.* New York: Harper and Row, 1976.

Rosenstone, Steven J.; Roy L. Behr; and Edward H. Lazarus. *Third Parties in America: Citizen Response to Major Party Failure.* Princeton: Princeton University Press, 1996.